Law for Professionals

The *Law for Professionals* book series contains publications in all fields of the law aimed at professionals and practitioners. The book series is dedicated to publish high quality books that provide in-depth insights into the workings and the practical functioning of the law, international organizations or regional legal frameworks.

The authors contributing to the book series are experienced legal professionals and practitioners whose expertise combines theory and practice.

Kai Jacob • Dierk Schindler
Roger Strathausen • Bernhard Waltl
Editors

Liquid Legal – Sustaining the Rule of Law

Artificial Intelligence, E-Justice, and the Cloud

Springer

liquid
legal
institute

Editors
Kai Jacob
Liquid Legal Institute e.V.
Wiesloch, Germany

Dierk Schindler
Liquid Legal Institute e.V.
Ottobrunn, Germany

Roger Strathausen
Liquid Legal Institute e.V.
Offenbach am Main, Germany

Bernhard Waltl
Liquid Legal Institute e.V.
Munich, Germany

ISSN 2662-141X ISSN 2662-1428 (electronic)
Law for Professionals
ISBN 978-3-031-78595-5 ISBN 978-3-031-78596-2 (eBook)
https://doi.org/10.1007/978-3-031-78596-2

This Springer imprint is published by the registered company Springer Nature Switzerland AG
The registered company address is: Gewerbestrasse 11, 6330 Cham, Switzerland

I dedicate this book to everyone striving to establish a stable and reliable legal system for the betterment of society.
Bernhard Waltl

To those who nourish my roots and fuel my desire to fly—professionally, my friends at the Liquid Legal institute—personally, my once-in-a-lifetime-companion Christina, and my beloved pilot into the future, Emily—I love you!
Dierk Schindler August 2024

I dedicate this book to a person close to me. After seven years, he is still involved in an unresolved court case due to life-threatening circumstances. It is my hope that this book will serve as a reminder of the need for a fair and timely trial to alleviate the suffering and bitterness caused by such protracted and unresolved situations. Too often: "Justice delayed is justice denied."
Kai Jacob

This book is dedicated to my twin brother Carsten who is even more an intellectual than I am.
Roger Strathausen

Foreword

The State, the Digital Transformation and AI

In recent decades, the digital transformation has revolutionized our world as profoundly as the invention of the printing press more than five centuries ago. Once regarded as little more than a niche trend, the digital transformation has risen to the top of the political agenda as an indispensable tool with which to tackle the many challenges of our time. Only a digitally agile state can be future-proof, efficient, and citizen-centered. Only a digital state can be sustainable.

This book explores the potential applications of AI in a state governed by the rule of law and examines key aspects of the digital transformation from a legal perspective in general.

The progress a state has made in the digital transformation manifests itself in various ways: its accessibility to citizens, the speed and efficiency of its processes—and its paper consumption. More digitalization means less paper used. This is an area in which Germany must do better: in 2022, the Federal Government and its subordinate federal administration agencies were still using nearly 740 million sheets of A4 paper annually. The ongoing rollout of an electronic file system (the "E-Akte") across the federal administration—to be completed by early 2026—will significantly reduce paper consumption. The Federal Ministry of Justice's file management system and workflows are already fully digital, and we advise other ministries on introducing and effectively leveraging the electronic file system.

The shift from paper to digital technologies can also open up new ways to access public services and information. For example, the Federal Law Gazette has been digital-only since 2023. This means that citizens can now consult official documents such as laws and statutory instruments online; previously, they had to either purchase the printed version, or look it up in the library.

Replacing paper with digital alternatives helps streamline processes and procedures. In this sense, the digital transformation is also a sustainable response to demographic change. Germany's skills shortage is already affecting businesses and public administration alike and is only expected to intensify in the coming years. The State will therefore have to become more productive—but with a smaller workforce. This is a problem that can be tackled by recourse to digitalization and artificial intelligence. Many law and legal tech firms already work with highly automated structures. With the help of AI, they can generate 150-page submissions in the space of minutes, while courts are hampered at every turn by the challenge of reconciling hard-copy and electronic formats.

While the courts are already testing AI applications to process files in mass claims—for example relating to air passenger compensation or the German "Dieselgate" scandal—in order to widen the use of AI, we need more training data. And right now, not enough judicial data are available in digital form. We need to address this issue, starting with judgments.

In the everyday work of the courts, numerous processes now take place digitally, and the use of video-conferencing has been expanded. We are making access to justice even easier with the establishment of digital filing offices. Even constitutional complaints can now be submitted electronically. We have come a long way: a look at the 2023 EU Justice Scoreboard shows that Germany can compete with the best when it comes to the digitalization of justice in Europe.

Our aim is to implement fully digital workflows wherever this is feasible and reasonable. Legislation on reducing bureaucracy is another way in which we are opening the door to digital processes. It will, for example, in future be possible to conclude employment contracts electronically. Wherever possible, we are relaxing the rules around paper documents and signatures. Any requirement for manually signed hard-copy documents has a highly disruptive effect on workflows.

By digitalizing public-sector processes, we are reinforcing acceptance for and strengthening the sustainability of our liberal democracy as a whole. Citizens perceive the digital transformation as part and parcel of their everyday lives. They expect politicians and the State to pave the way for it. A robust democracy relies on digitalization in the long run: the State must be in a position to act rapidly and efficiently, to offer its citizens easy access to justice, and to accelerate judicial processes.

At the same time, we must also ensure transparency on the use of AI, a vital condition for public acceptance of the digital State—particularly in the justice sector. As a result of the AI Act, uniform and binding standards are now in place throughout the European Union. And there will be no "robot-judges." Judicial powers under Article 92 of the German Basic Law are vested in human judges and in them alone. The justice sector does not have the freedom to exhaust every avenue that technology has to offer. It can harness technology's potential within the bounds of the law, but it must exercise moderation and ensure that citizens understand and accept the route being followed. This is the exciting and challenging environment in which we find ourselves.

Former Federal Minister of Justice
Berlin, Germany

Marco Buschmann

Foreword

Ensuring Technological Transformation is Secure by Design

In an era of digital transformation, law enforcement faces a multitude of new opportunities and challenges. As technology rapidly advances and the criminal landscape evolves, the scope and responsibilities of law enforcement simultaneously expand. Integrating emerging technologies such as artificial intelligence (AI) and data analytics enables law enforcement agencies to boost their capabilities for crime prevention, investigation, and prosecution, streamline administrative processes, and build trust with the communities they serve.

Sustaining the Rule of Law raises pertinent questions regarding the intersection of legal issues with new and emerging technologies. It delves into the pressing challenges and opportunities that arise from integrating these technologies in the field, allowing us to better explore how sustainable digital transformation can be achieved in law and law enforcement.

At the same time, there is a growing international consensus among law enforcement agencies about the need to balance the benefits of emerging technologies with the potential risks and challenges. The stakes are particularly high in the law enforcement context due to the unique responsibilities and competencies of these agencies. Any misuse or controversial application of emerging technologies could severely impact human rights, harm society at large, and undermine public trust in law enforcement.

For this reason, INTERPOL issues our own guidance on how law enforcement can leverage emerging technologies responsibly, bringing together global experts from different sectors. In this spirit, INTERPOL published *The Toolkit for Responsible AI Innovation in Law Enforcement* in 2023 and convened an expert group that provides an in-depth analysis of the Metaverse from a law enforcement perspective.

Addressing these challenges head-on is crucial as the risks of not fully engaging with digital transformation are equally concerning. Failing to adapt could leave law enforcement agencies ill-equipped to support their communities effectively, thus falling short on delivering their mandate.

To evolve from reactive approaches to proactive policing strategies, it is essential for law enforcement to conduct continuous scanning of various drivers and how they interplay. This includes considering such drivers from social, technological, economic, environmental, and political domains, and to understand the implications of emerging trends and patterns for crime and policing. INTERPOL helps its 196 member countries with their preparedness, conducting Global Horizon Scans that break down topics such as the impact of climate change on law enforcement, forecasting the future of crime.

Recognizing these issues is fundamental in adapting to new challenges, anticipating future threats, and enhancing the overall effectiveness of law enforcement efforts. Indeed, this book rightfully highlights the importance of continuous scanning and analysis exercises with the aim of identifying emerging trends and patterns that have implications for crime and policing.

From a technological standpoint, ensuring a sustainable digital transformation requires a robust and secure IT infrastructure, capable of providing scalability, high performance, and integration. Moreover, digital transformation strategies would need to adhere to the law while also considering the need for new rules and regulations. Within the social context, it is important to acknowledge concerns regarding privacy, fairness, and the appropriate use of emerging technologies as this may affect human lives and individual liberties.

This book aptly complements these efforts by providing a comprehensive exploration of the challenges and opportunities that digital transformation presents in the legal and law enforcement sectors. Moving forward, law enforcement agencies need to remain agile in adapting to these changes and actively shape the better future of law enforcement, fostering closer cooperation and engagement beyond our conventional stakeholders.

Former Secretary General of INTERPOL Jürgen Stock
Wetzlar, Germany

Foreword

Sustaining the Rule of Law Via Regulation of AI?

The legal market is undergoing unprecedented disruption, not least since generative language models such as ChatGPT took the stage. Digitalization is revolutionizing our world. The public authorities are increasingly being affected by this development. In Germany, the use of AI by state authorities is currently still limited to specific projects. However, their number has more than doubled in the last year (federal ministries and subordinate authorities: BT-Drs. 20/11648). AI innovations promise improvements in almost all areas of life, from fighting crime to medical care. Yet we see, on the other hand, a growing risk for democracy and the rule of law. Digital disruption should not become a disruption of democracy and the rule of law.

In order to safeguard democratic values and the rule of law, a regulatory race has started on a worldwide level. With the AI Act, the EU has recently created a comprehensive legal framework to regulate artificial intelligence. It remains to be seen whether these regulations, which are accompanied by tremendous of bureaucracy, will have the intended effect.

"The End of Justice"?—Access to Justice and E-Justice

As a judge, I would like to focus on the judiciary. "The End of Lawyers" was the provocative-sounding title of a publication by Richard Süßkind (2008). Of course, lawyers will not disappear in a digital world, but it is already clear that their job profile will change fundamentally and rapidly. The process of digital innovation of the legal market affects not only the lawyers but also the judiciary. Moreover, it also affects the law itself.

The judiciary has been under enormous pressure to innovate for years. The report commissioned by the Federal Ministry of Justice on the decrease in civil lawsuits emphasizes this impressively ("Erforschung der Ursachen des Rückgangs der Eingangszahlen bei den Zivilgerichten," https://www.bmj.de/SharedDocs/Downloads/DE/Fachinformationen/Abschlussbericht_Eingangszahlen_Zivilgerichte.pdf?__blob=publicationFile&v=2). And other areas of the judiciary are also experiencing a reduced demand. The times in which the courts were experiencing a real flood of lawsuits are over. Of course, the digitalization of the legal market is neither the only cause nor the only solution. But we should take it as an opportunity to scrutinize how the judiciary sees itself, to facilitate access to justice and strengthen trust in the judiciary.

In Germany, a first important step is, finally, about to be taken: With the statute for the development and practical testing of an online procedure, the basis for new digital forms of communication in civil proceedings will be created. The online procedure improves access to justice. However, the procedure is initially only being tested in some courts and will only concern payment claims with a low value in dispute.

As far as the use of generative AI in the justice system is concerned, the AI-Act seems to speak a clear language: „An AI system shall not be considered to be high-risk where any of the following conditions is fulfilled: the AI system is intended to perform a narrow procedural task; the AI system is intended to improve the result of a previously completed human activity; the AI system is intended to detect decision-making patterns or deviations from prior decision-making patterns and is not meant to replace or influence the previously completed human assessment, without proper human review; or the AI system is intended to perform a preparatory task to an assessment relevant for the purposes of the use cases listed in Annex III."

This provision (Article 6 para. 3), which was literally only included in the AI-Act at the last minute, is intended to clearly capture the status quo of software use in the justice system. But: what exactly is meant by "preparatory task"? And what is meant by "influence the previously completed human assessment"? What constitutes a human decision? And what relevance does the problem of automation bias have in this context? And does the question also depend on the extent to which the (growing) efficiency and time advantages of using AI outweigh the (shrinking) disadvantages or errors of hallucinating LLM?

Transparency and explainability are important parameters for the use of AI in the justice system. However, the demand for transparency can only be met to a limited extent, particularly with regard to the LLM.

Preventing discrimination is a key legal and ethical challenge when using AI. Training data should be as unbiased as possible. The decisive factor will be who has control over the data and its use. For this reason, the judiciary will not be able to readily agree to this task being taken over by the ministries of justice and thus by the executive.

Of course, those seeking legal protection have a right to a (human) judge, even in a digital justice system. This is constitutionally indispensable. In addition, the role of the judiciary, with the demands of individualization and scope for interpretation, reaches beyond the mere literal application of the law. AI will not be able to take over the innovative "updating" of the law—just think of the development of the understanding of Article 6 of the Basic Law or the climate decision of the Federal Constitutional Court.

E-justice, to take up the title of this book, is more than just the implementation of technical and digital support in the traditional system. The potential for change offered by digitalization and generative AI in particular goes much further.

Provisional decisions that are issued fully automatically are also conceivable (e.g., Weth/Krüger/Vogelgesang, Der Zivilprozess der Zukunft (Teil 1), jM 2024, 165–170). However, the litigants must have the right to have these provisional decisions reviewed by (human) judges in all cases and without any further obstacles. A justice system that is open to fundamental change can also manage to significantly improve access to justice. This involves more than simply making courts (digitally) accessible. A court ruling is only attractive if court proceedings are conducted swiftly and if the risk of legal costs is proportionate to the amount in dispute. Digitalization could be one way to achieve this goal.

Conclusion

The digital transformation of the justice system is a complex process that may, in the end, lead to a different justice system than the traditional one. Perhaps, this is precisely the way to secure and strengthen the rule of law in the digital age. This book addresses a wide range of vital questions concerning the transformation process. It offers multidisciplinary expert knowledge badly needed to get a clearer picture of the present-day challenges to the legal system.

Chairwoman of the EDVGT - Forum für digitale Innovation im Recht
Saarbrücken, Germany

Anke Morsch

Sustaining the Rule of Law: Artificial Intelligence, E-Justice, and the Cloud

This fourth book of the Liquid Legal series investigates how automated legal operations through Artificial Intelligence, electronic legal services through E-Justice, and shared legal infrastructures through the Cloud can sustain the rule of law.

Digital laws; *Agile* and *Design Thinking* as legal methodologies; Business and IT in legal education; Organizational, procedural, semantic, and technical interoperability of legal matters across disciplines and jurisdictions; Online-collaboration-platforms and private-public-buddyships in legal eco-systems; Sharing of legal knowledge and resources in the Cloud; Analysis of anonymized legal data for standardization and AI training; Transparency and accessibility as defining elements of justice—these are just some of the legal industry trends surrounding AI, E-Justice, and the Cloud.

Together, these trends help change the aggregation state of legal from *fossil* to *liquid*, fueling the fundamental belief of legal professionals in the rule of law as guarantee for freedom, prosperity, and security.

"The rule of law is better than that of any individual." (Aristotle)

Magna Charta, Bill of Rights, *Grundgesetz*—the struggle against tyranny and the search for the *common good* characterize the history of the rule of law. In the course of millennia, humanity has learned to govern interactions by principles of *right* and *wrong*, to install the judiciary as independent state power, and to establish state-certified lawyers as mediators of conflict.

Yet while the rule of law rests on it being the *same* at any given time, it also needs to *change* over time. In its never-ending search for justice, the law must reflect cultural and natural developments—lest it itself turns into a tyrant. As life evolves, society advances, and ethics transform, each legal case remains unique and causes us to reflect on and even alter the whole system.

The law-making process and democracy as a whole rest on a measured approach. Promoting societal discourse, hearing all voices, funneling insights into rules—all this needs time and increasingly collides with the speed and depth of technological disruption.

Will early regulation impede progress? Will late regulation erode our values and expose vulnerable groups in need of protection? Can we balance the speed of new developments with social interests? And how can we know in advance?

Sameness and change; equality and difference; society and individual are the poles we must keep in mind when exploring the pros and cons of technological innovations—innovations which, on the one hand, seem to threaten, yet on the other hand also hold the potential to sustain the rule of law in times of disruption.

"As artificial intelligence, I can provide general legal knowledge and information." (ChatGPT)

"In recent years, advancements in technology, specifically AI, have significantly impacted various sectors of society, including the legal field. AI, with its ability to analyze vast amounts of data and perform complex tasks, has the potential to revolutionize legal processes, ranging from document review and legal research to predicting case outcomes and supporting decision-making.

However, the integration of AI in the legal domain raises crucial questions concerning the rule of law. While technological advancements promise improved access to justice, greater efficiency, and enhanced outcomes, they also pose challenges related to transparency, accountability, bias, privacy, and ethical considerations.

Potential topics of interest include:

1. *Legal implications of AI adoption in the justice system*
2. *Ethical considerations and challenges of AI in legal decision-making*
3. *Transparency, explainability, and accountability in AI-powered legal processes*
4. *Bias and fairness issues in algorithmic justice*
5. *Access to justice and AI: Opportunities and challenges*
6. *The role of AI in legal research, analysis, and prediction*
7. *Cybersecurity, data protection, and privacy in E-Justice*
8. *Human rights and the rule of law in the digital era*
9. *AI-enabled dispute resolution mechanisms*
10. *The impact of AI on legal professions and legal education"*

(written by ChatGPT)

"LegalTech was yesterday. – E-Justice is Today!" (Liquid Legal Institute)

LegalTech was about the efficiency of legal transactions. Software tools were developed, processes streamlined, tasks simplified. In some legal departments, law firms, and public institutions, these LegalTech projects improved productivity and reduced costs; in other institutions, they added to the knowledge of what does *not* work.

E-Justice is about the effectiveness of the law. Surveys (e.g. forsa_2021.pdf (dbb.de)) show that citizens are losing confidence in courts. Especially in Germany, civil and criminal proceedings are too opaque, too expensive, and take far too long.

The Liquid Legal Institute believes that, by providing access to legal services anytime anywhere, E-Justice is likely to restore people's belief in the rule of law.

"With Cloud Computing, it is no longer a question of If, but rather When and How." (Ludmila Morozova-Bussva)

Especially in Europe, many legal professionals continue to be weary of the Cloud. Access to justice, data security, and judicial independence seem too important for simply processing legal cases in a nebulous myriad of interconnected machines that could be located anywhere and be controlled by non-democratic powers.

Yet the Cloud also holds the promise of end-to-end legal services for citizens and companies across communal, state, and national jurisdictions. Standardized IT architectures lay the foundation for a common understanding of legal matters; interoperable software systems and data save processing time and effort; and sharing computing resources via the Internet reduce operating costs.

When and how could the Cloud be detrimental to the rule of law, and under which circumstances will it increase legal sustainability?

Liquid Legal Institute e.V.
Offenbach am Main, Germany

Roger Strathausen

Contents

About the Editors and Contributors

About the Editors

Bernhard Waltl is co-founder and co-CEO of the Liquid Legal Institute. He is also Head of Legal Operations at the BMW Group. Bernhard holds a doctorate in computer science and works at the interface between law and computer science, specializing in artificial intelligence and the digital transformation of law.

Dierk Schindler is the co-founder of the Liquid Legal Institute and serves as Co-CEO, together with Kai Jacob and Bernhard Waltl. He is author and editor of numerous publications on innovation and transformation in the legal profession, most notably the three previous volumes of the book-series "Liquid Legal" in 2017, 2020, and 2022. In 2019, Dierk joined Robert BOSCH GmbH as their Vice President Corporate Legal Services, Mobility, Supply Chain, and Logistics. He drives the adoption of Agile practices and the digital transformation of the legal team at large. Prior to BOSCH, Dierk has spent 14 years with NetApp Inc., where he built the EMEA Legal Team, established the Deal Management function, and implemented the Global Legal Shared Services Team. He speaks and teaches on Innovation and Digital Business Law. Dierk is a certified lawyer, took his doctorate degree from Augsburg University, Germany, and his Master of International Law from Lund University, Sweden.

Kai Jacob is the founder and co-chair of the Liquid Legal Institute. Together with colleagues, he established the Legal Data Analytics firm in Munich. The company's objective is to combine human and artificial intelligence to scale the impact of legal work. He previously held partner positions at KPMG Law and Deloitte Legal and spent many years at SAP SE and Lufthansa. Kai is engaged in multiple projects and initiatives pertaining to the digital transformation of legal departments and law firms, the well-being of the legal profession, and the future of legal operations. He regularly contributes to professional journals, publications, and podcasts on these and other topics. Kai Jacob was admitted to the bar in 2004 and studied law in Marburg, Göttingen, and Osnabrück.

Roger Strathausen is co-founder of the Liquid Legal Institute. Roger accompanies digital transformation of the legal industry. As a digital leadership expert, Roger specializes in helping companies capitalize on the value of digitalization, bringing to bear decades of experience in the high-tech and software industry. Digitalization is not the answer to all problems, but its potential for disrupting traditional business models certainly warrants a closer look at the status quo.

Contributors

Thomas D. Barton California Western School of Law, San Diego, CA, USA

Tatiana Caldas-Löttiger Universidad El Rosario, Bogotá, Colombia, USA
International Business & Trade Law, University of Illinois Chicago School of Law, Chicago, USA
European Law, Stockholm University, Stockholm, Sweden

Barbara Chomika Turner & Townsend, New York, NY, USA

Mark A. Cohen Palm Beach Gardens, FL, USA

Robert Dilworth New Rochelle, NY, USA

Marcel Hajd LexRatio | MARIFARM d.o.o., Maribor, Slovenia

Alexander Holz ISiCO GmbH, Berlin, Germany

Anita Lamprecht DiploFoundation, Geneva, Switzerland

Ulf Marhenke Trustwork Consulting, Hamburg, Germany

Bruno Mascello Executive School of Management, Technology and Law, St. Gallen University, St. Gallen, Switzerland

Shân M. Millie Bright Blue Hare, Cambridge, UK

Robert Müller CureVac N.V., Tübingen, Germany

Philipp Müller-Peltzer Schürmann Rosenthal Dreyer Rechtsanwälte, Berlin, Germany

Erion Murati Berlin School of Law and Economics, Berlin, Germany

Marco Rau CureVac N.V., Tübingen, Germany

Sharon Naomi Reichl Rittershaus Rechtsanwälte PartmbB, Mannheim, Germany

Dierk Schindler Ottobrunn, Germany

Valentin Tanczik Schürmann Rosenthal Dreyer Rechtsanwälte, Berlin, Germany

Bernhard Waltl Liquid Legal Institute e.V., Ottobrunn, Germany

Stuart Weinstein Aston University, School of Law and Social Sciences, Birmingham, UK

The Reset Moment

A Discussion Between Mark A. Cohen & Dierk Schindler

Mark A. Cohen and Dierk Schindler

Contents

Abstract

Artificial Intelligence (AI)—especially *generative* AI—has an enormous potential to revolutionize the legal ecosystem. It will change how lawyers work, yet also challenges traditional legal roles and practices. It has the potential to democratize legal services by making them more accessible and efficient, but it might also just create a new avenue to generate revenue in a highly commercialized private legal sector. It creates the opportunity for much faster transactions, but it bears the immediate risk for the judicial system to fall ever more behind.

As we add digital 'steroids' (aka generative AI) to the legal ecosystem, we must ...

Many of Mark's comments derive from the extensive collection of his Forbes articles. They can be accessed at https://www.forbes.com/sites/markcohen1/?sh=2c58d38b28f7 or in the "Articles" section of the Legal Mosaic website at https://www.legalmosaic.com/.

M. A. Cohen (✉)
Palm Beach Gardens, FL, USA
e-mail: markacohen@legalmosaic.com

D. Schindler
Ottobrunn, Germany
e-mail: d.schindler@liquid-legal-institute.org

K. Jacob et al. (eds.), *Liquid Legal – Sustaining the Rule of Law*, Law for Professionals, https://doi.org/10.1007/978-3-031-78596-2_1

(i) ... be aware what the actual current dynamics in the legal system are—because unless we understand the paradigmatic shift that comes about with generative AI, we run the risk of scaling and intensifying exactly those;
(ii) ... refocus on what the societal role of the legal ecosystem is, i.e. what 'the people' can expect from it; and
(iii) ... reflect thoroughly and critically on what gaps exist between aspiration and reality, what the root causes are, and the potential counter measures.

The legal profession has already struggled for a long time to adapt to societal needs, to address issues like access to justice gap (an estimated 5 billion people have unmet justice needs globally, including people who cannot obtain justice for everyday problems, people who are excluded from the opportunity the law provides, and people who live in extreme conditions of injustice; for more details see the worldjusticeproject website) , ethical breaches, and to confront the byproduct of such shortfalls: the erosion of public trust in law. It has been too resistant to listen to the calls for a reevaluation of its role in society.

Based on that analysis, we must take stock and realize, that we do not face yet another phase of organic evolution in the legal ecosystem, but rather a 'reset moment'. The crucial question we inevitably must answer is: Do we let the commercial legal market own the programming of the new setup risking that the commercialization, the 'pay-to-play' in the legal ecosystem gets scaled—or do we find both, the self-reflection, the willingness and the appropriate means to reset with a clear vision of rebuilding and sustaining the Rule of Law, using the commercial levers in a positive way?

For the analysis, the discourse and ultimately the plan of action we have to reconsider what the Rule of Law requires. In principle we, the ever more diverse community in Law, needs to have ...

(i) ... a holistic perspective on the functioning of justice,
(ii) ... a shared commitment to the common responsibility for sustaining the Rule of Law,
(iii) ... the readiness to balance economic interests with societal responsibility.

How do we seize the Reset Moment?

- By breaking the trend of polarization in legal services and by promoting, anchoring, and incentivizing shared accountability for the Rule of Law.
- By creating robust and attractive venues to foster collaboration, to facilitate a diverse debate, and to ignite the reflection on common values.
- By rethinking the controls required to sustain the Rule of Law in an era of disruption and ambidexter.

1 Scaling: What?

Dierk Looking at digitization and generative AI, we—today's active players in the legal ecosystem—see mainly a huge *efficiency* play, i.e. massive potential to save time and cost, and consequently the opportunity to improve ROI and margin.[1] Raising *effectiveness* is already only a secondary thought, a by-product, somewhat like: *'Hey, applying the AI-powered legal co-pilots and agents that appear on the horizon is cheap, so why not also capture some effectiveness.'*

However, I think we are running an immediate risk of missing a major point here. We are scaling a legal ecosystem that is losing sight of its fundamental joint purpose of sustaining the Rule of Law. We are fueling a fire that might burn down the house, if you allow me to kick us off with a drastic metaphor.

Mark Well, then let's start this discussion with agreement on your initial observations. Law has operated as a professional cult; it is insular, homogeneous, lives by its own standards and rules, controls admission, and has resisted influence of the 'outside' world ('non-lawyers'). Lawyers have been ingrained they are uniquely qualified to determine what is a 'legal' problem, how it should be managed, valued, and billed. They have used self-regulation to thwart competition, proscribe ownership, and retain control over not only the practice of law, but also the business of delivering legal services.

Law's future has been fiercely resisted by the legal profession, not by the absence of tools, resources, and a digital transformation roadmap! What other trillion-dollar industry shares law's dearth of performance metrics and standards, transparency, lack of data agility, collaboration, multidisciplinary workforces, innovation fragmentation, and customer-centricity?

Dierk Well, it sounds like we agree on the finding, but maybe disagree in answering the question if we can expect the legal ecosystem to break free from its traditional limitations. You seem pessimistic, while I see a silver lining created by the following three major forces:

- First, in the awakening of generative AI, Law cannot hide anymore from the massive facilitation that comes with it for the clients—for ALL clients. Regarding the business clients, the sheer insurmountable 'billable hour'-model suddenly will

[1] See on law firms e.g. *Law firms embrace the efficiencies of artificial intelligence*, by Christina Criddle, Financial Times, May 4th 2023, https://www.ft.com/content/9b1b1c5d-f382-484f-961a-b45ae0526675 and, on inhouse legal, e.g. Stephanie Pacheco, *ANALYSIS: AI to Help In-House Counsel Manage Spend, Fees in 2024*, Bloomberg Law 2024, https://news.bloomberglaw.com/bloomberg-law-analysis/analysis-ai-to-help-in-house-counsel-manage-spend-fees-in-2024—more differentiated e.g. in a presentation Mike Abbot, Thomson Reuters Institute leader, February 4th 2024, as summarized at https://legal.thomsonreuters.com/blog/in-house-legal-teams-lead-the-way-on-ai/.

bite back, because obviously many hours are becoming 'unbillable' if legal co-pilots take over tasks and simply eliminate time and effort (e.g. basic research, summarizing, drafting memos, emails, letters, contracts ...). And for private clients, access to legal advice is bound to become a lot cheaper, given the ease of providing initial guidance at very little effort, time, and cost, using legal co-pilots.
- Second, computer scientists, operations experts etc.—i.e. 'non lawyers'—will take the co-lead in Law, if we like it or not! To thrive in a digitized legal ecosystem, professional legal entities (inhouse or law firms) must be able to leverage digital means. This needs 'non-legal' talent.[2] If we continue to not-integrate or even alienate those legal engineers, legal data scientists, legal operations colleagues, we will be conquered by alternative legal service providers that, already today, embrace that talent.
- Third, as Carville would say it *"It's the economy, stupid"*.[3] While traditional thinking in Law has been to go after winning a bigger share of the given, modestly growing "cake", digitization and GenAI have just started to take a big bite out of the existing legal market—while opening a whole new auxiliary market, right next to it. This means: A smaller "cake" for traditional lawyers—and a big 'buffet' for a diverse legal ecosystem that works multi-disciplinarily and at eye-level with other professions.[4]

Mark That all sounds good but let me share my deeply rooted concern before we focus on the opportunity side of things. After all, change is about challenge, opportunity, and the construction of guardrails to ensure they are not tipped to far in one direction.

Law remains an analog function in a digital world. So, why is the legal industry clutching the short end of the future stick? After all, lawyers are highly educated, trained to think critically, and high- achievers. They have well above-average IQ's, are focused, and have a strong work ethic. Most are aware of the convergence of macroeconomic changes that are transforming lives, business, and the planet. Can the myth of legal exceptionalism, hubris, and other denial mechanisms convince lawyers that what they do is somehow immune to these seismic changes? For some it

[2]As KPMG's Stuart Fuller already predicted in 2020 that by 2025 only 50% of the staff of an inhouse department will be lawyers, *10 Predictions: The Legal Function in 2025*, https://kpmg.com/xx/en/home/insights/2020/12/future-of-legal-article-series.html.

[3]Attributed to James Carville, strategist of Bill Clinton in his presidential campaign 1992, https://en.wikipedia.org/wiki/It%27s_the_economy,_stupid.

[4]On the overall growth of the legal services market and it being boosted by AI and predicting a 4.6% CAGR during the period 2022 to 2032, see future Markets Insight Inc., *Legal Services Market*, at https://www.futuremarketinsights.com/reports/legal-services-market#:~:text=The%20legal%20services%20market%20is%20estimated%20to%20garner,consumer%20spending%2Fmore%20disposable%20income%2C%20and%20legal%20sector%20deregulation.

can. Others, notably many legal 'leaders', are either 'too busy to change' and/or unclear about how.

To your point, this might finally change. Yet, stopping here would once again fail to focus on the drastic effect of such behavior—and on what we ultimately must cure for a better (digital) future: The past behavior of lawyers adds to undermining the citizens' trust in the Rule of Law! Derek Bok, a lawyer and former President of Harvard University and Dean of Harvard Law School nailed law's failings back in the 1980's. He famously noted *"There is far too much law for those that can afford it and far too little for those that cannot."*[5] Sadly, that is even truer today.

Lawyers may not be the proximate cause of record-law public distrust in government and institutions that has been playing out for decades and is nearing rock bottom. The profession has, however, contributed to it by an internal focus and self-regulation that has widened its gap with society. Anachronistic legal institutions, viewed by many as elitist and detached from society (except for big business and the wealthy), have contributed to social fragmentation and a search for something different. This has fomented populism, 'alternative facts', and 'bespoke realities', and other anti- establishment trends that challenge—and sometimes shatter—behavioral norms.

Dierk I hear you and agree that massive latency in transforming the legal ecosystem endangers the functioning of the Rule of Law. Yet, you seem to point to a more deeply rooted problem and a more immediate threat. Can you illustrate that a little more?

Mark Deborah Pearlstein wrote a stinging Op- Ed in The New York Times, rhetorically asking (then answering) why so many of Trump's alleged co-conspirators are lawyers. She cogently analyzed the profession's polarization, politicization, and ethical elasticity. She conceded the multi- layered challenge of changing this: *"Changing the increasingly polarized nature of the legal profession is a more complex enterprise—one centrally bound up in how we learn, teach, reward and punish what lawyers do. It is a long-term project. With little time to lose."*[6]

While the court of public opinion, turbocharged by social media, is rapidly challenging courts of law as arbiters of social fault lines, courts move at a glacial pace. Additionally, 'Lawfare', the weaponization of national judicial systems by political parties to delegitimize political opponents has become all too common. Its impact hinges on the willingness of lawyers to aid and abet it.

---

[5] Derek Bok, Harvard Magazine, May-June 1983, "A Flawed System".

[6] Deborah Pearlstein, *Why Are So Many of Trump's Alleged Co-Conspirators Lawyers?*, August 14th 2023, https://www.nytimes.com/2023/08/14/opinion/trump-indictment-lawyers.html.

A Presidential candidate charged with 91 counts of federal crimes in multiple proceedings[7] is the odds-on favorite in the presidential race. The snail's pace of legal proceedings is colliding with the Presidential election cycle. It is reasonably foreseeable that only one, perhaps none, of the criminal cases emanating from the 2020 election and its aftermath will be tried before the 2024 election. This could significantly influence the election's outcome and further marginalize, if not effectively render moot, those cases. What does that say about public regard for the rule of law and faith in the legal system?

Delay can no longer be a tactic (if not a strategy) in resolving any kind of dispute, much less the cases in question. The legal profession must coalesce around streamlining the judicial process. Failure to do so will marginalize the impact of judicial proceedings on the public's perception of their significance and legitimacy.

There is a long list of once unthinkable, now all-too-reasonably foreseeable scenarios that will further test the legal profession and the rule of law during the coming year. Will we witness a replay of January 6, 2020, perhaps even worse? Will lawyers involved in the election process uphold the Constitution and the rule of law, notwithstanding tremendous pressure and/or short-term personal gain not to? Will death threats and other forms of intimidation to lawyers, judges, court personnel, witnesses, election workers, and their families involved in the judicial and election processes have a chilling effect and, perhaps, change the outcome? The specter of raising all this speaks to how dire things are and how much worse they could become. This is America's crucible. Why is the legal profession collectively silent?

Dierk As democratic systems get under pressure in ever more countries, the legal profession—or as I prefer to refer to it: the legal ecosystem—must remind itself of its part in being a conduit for sustaining the Rule of Law. But you just pointed out that consciousness is not even enough: it is also about formulating and communicating that aspiration, and it is about stepping up when threats to democracy and the Rule of Law emerge!

And finally, this obligation includes all stakeholders of the legal ecosystems:

- *lawyers* in all their professional roles, in public or private office, in law firms or inhouse;
- *new profiles* like legal operations, legal engineers, legal designers etc.;
- *new service providers* in law, be it managed legal services, legal tech applications and/or AI-based solutions.

If there was a Hippocratic oath for the law[8], it would have to be sworn by and binding for *ALL* professionals in law, the lawyers and the 'non-lawyers'!

---

[7] As summarized by CNN on September 6th 2023, see https://edition.cnn.com/politics/live-news/trump-fulton-county-case-09-06-23#h_638d46bc3510712c1d9e435ef86e34e7.

[8] See the initiative of the Liquid Legal Institute in 2022 to this end and the winning proposal at https://www.liquid-legal-institute.com/wp-content/uploads/2021/07/The-Sentinels-Oath.pdf.

Mark What we are witnessing is a paradigmatic shift in business. It began with digital transformation and is now being turbocharged by AI and especially Generative AI. The speed of change is accelerating and so too are the opportunities expanding. A digital core—a workforce that uses powerful new tools responsibly and imaginatively—is essential to capturing the potential of data mastery and Gen AI. So too is a mindset that works collaboratively, cross-functionally, and agilely to solve complex problems and capture opportunities. Legal must play an integral part of that process. It is an enterprise junction—like technology—that touches all facets of business *and society*.

The legal function is principally focused on the corporate market segment; that's where the big money is. It must equally honor its social compact to honor the rule of law and to defend democracy. That is largely missing as reflected by the large segments of democracies where most individuals and small businesses cannot afford legal services as they are presently structured.[9] Your Hippocratic oath should include a social component.

2 Disruption: For the Better?

Dierk Based on our analysis above, we must take stock and realize that we do not just face yet another phase of organic evolution in the legal ecosystem, but rather a *'reset moment'*. The commercial forces in the legal ecosystem might well overcome the skepticism, if not resistance, of our profession to digitize and embrace the upside of fundamental technologies like generative AI.

However, this might simultaneously simply scale the shortcomings, or even negative effects, that we have discussed earlier, e.g. the issues around access to justice, driven by monetary, digital, or other barriers.[10] The digital revolution will optimize the operating system on which today's legal ecosystem runs—but it will not change it!

Mark I agree! Here is a partial list of those unmet challenges and I don't think that either the business dimension or digitization alone will fix any of them:

- 'The court of public opinion' is undermining courts of law, as they slow down, being handcuffed by an analogue modus operandi.

[9] See Artificial Intelligence and the Law, December 5, 2023, by Tomas Weber, Stanford Lawyer, Fall 2023 – Issue 109 https://law.stanford.edu/stanford-lawyer/articles/artificial-intelligence-and-the-law/.

[10] Interesting perspectives on this aspect in the interview of Harvard Law School's David Wilkins (by Jeff Neal), February 14th 2024, Harvard Law Today, https://hls.harvard.edu/today/harvard-law-expert-explains-how-ai-may-transform-the-legal-profession-in-2024/, who also points to the inglorious history of this problem as laid out by Galanter (1974), pp. 95–160 (66 pages).

- Backlogs of civil and criminal cases, an alarming rise in pro se litigants and default judgments, and the slow, costly, opaque and anachronistic judicial process is no longer responsive to societal needs.
- A worsening access to justice crisis further erodes the Rule of Law.
- Law schools fail to produce 'market ready' grads and create a fiscal sink hole from which many newly-minted lawyers cannot escape from. Law schools should morph from diploma mills to learning centers for life. This would be good for the profession, law schools, clients, society, and the rule of law.
- The legal profession's opposition to re-regulation designed to open up markets to competition, capital, and multidisciplinary practice that would benefit legal consumers and society evidences its protectionist stance.
- The opacity of legal language and procedure, high cost and unpredictability of legal services, dearth of data agility, and lack of empathy and humanity have further distanced law from the society it purports to serve.

These challenges are no longer law's headaches; they are incapacitating societal migraines! That is one of many reasons why business is taking the reins and will lead the legal function into the future in the corporate market segment. Business, government, and legal professionals can and must do more to ensure that fit-for-purpose services are accessible to individuals and small and mid-sized business.

Dierk What I am worried about is that leaving the lead to the business will inevitably overemphasize (further) the economic aspects of the law and of legal services. While an even more digitized world of legal (business) services might address the very real issue of cumbersome and excessively costly legal proceedings generating a barrier and potentially even an existential threat to SMEs, we must not expect it to fix all those other aspects you just raised.

The big question is, *can* we—and *how* can we make this a more fundamental disruption for the better? How do we, as professionals in law, find the self-reflection, the willingness, and the appropriate means to 'hit reset' with a clear vision of resolidifying and sustaining the Rule of Law?

Initially you would think that our own associations, be it the bar associations, the various inhouse lawyer associations, augmented by the many other networks and think tanks, saw this as one of their primary tasks. Yet, it seems that they are caught in a vicious circle: the legal ecosystem becomes both, multi-facetted, and multidisciplinary. This generates more role or sector-specific associations which, naturally, emphasize their respective needs and agendas. All in all, however, this complicates an effective debate about, and tangible work on the all-encompassing and fundamental topics.

Discussing the strengthening of each legal professional's role and, at the same time, how it affects sustaining of the Rule of Law, has no natural organizational home anymore.

Mark Indeed, let's just look at the United States: There are 1.3 million lawyers.[11] Most are competent, hard-working, ethical, professionals. Few have the luxury to analyze the profession at a macro level; they are engaged in practice, pro bono and community activities, and trying to adapt to the Warp-speed of an increasingly complex, uncertain world and to find their place in it.

Law has a leadership void. There is no harmonized forum to discuss and ultimately speak with one voice. In the US, the American Bar Association (ABA) was once that voice and wielded considerable influence within the profession and beyond. Forty years ago, 50% of all American lawyers were members. That figure has dwindled to 20% now.[12] Its key stakeholders are balkanized and rarely gather to discuss issues that affect the entire profession and the society it covenants to serve. Those conversations are essential to achieving a better integrated, more cohesive, less compartmentalized and polarized profession.

We must restore that holistic debate and a good starting point for the discussion is an action plan to restore the profession's commitment to furthering the common good.

3 What Does the Rule of Law Require in the Awakening of AI?

Dierk OK, so what do we need? In all fairness, so far, we have only talked about the new market entrants, the practitioners and their associations. As we are facing a moment of digital disruption, of fundamental questions around the role of lawyers, evolving new roles in the legal ecosystem, and the destabilization of the Rule of Law, isn't that the moment when legal scholars must enter the stage to lead a broad and deep debate?

And here we might look at the same challenge, just from a different angle. Law schools and legal scholars typically work in environments that are geared around (i) lawyers and (ii) the traditional profile of legal services. Fields like 'Legal Operations' or roles like 'Legal Engineers' do not exist in the vast majority of law school curricula. Taking care of designing, implementing, and applying digital legal services is left to learning-by-doing in practice or—if at all—to business schools or computer science.

However, generating, leading and maintaining the fundamental debate on sustaining the Rule of Law in the modern, rapidly evolving legal ecosystem, urgently requires a multidisciplinary debate also on a scholarly level. Cross-domain

[11] According to a survey of the American Bar Association (ABA) in 2022, as published on June 20th 2022 at https://www.americanbar.org/news/abanews/aba-news-archives/2022/06/aba-lawyers-survey/.

[12] For details and further thoughts on this see Mark A. Cohens forbes article, *Is the American Bar Association Passé?*, August 2nd 2018, at https://www.forbes.com/sites/markcohen1/2018/08/01/is-the-american-bar-association-passe/?sh=7058e25e59bd.

collaboration, research, and education must be institutionalized at universities[13]—and, of course, should include that voice of the practitioners, given that this is where the evolution takes place as we speak and at breathtaking speed.

Mark In the end, it's about human behavior and, more specifically, an adaptive mindset: To achieve the elevated expectations of business, the legal function must undergo a mindset change. Legal must function as an integrated team internally and with its supply chain. Then, it must integrate with other business units that have already begun their digital journey. That transition requires the legal function to replace its insular lawyer-dominated, narrow 'legal' role with a far broader, *business* and *customer*-oriented, multi-disciplinary, cross-functional one. Legal professionals—and that means not just lawyers—must work collaboratively, cross-functionally, and creatively to drive business value. Technology is a potent tool in their kit, but it by no means a panacea.

Such a transition requires a holistic, end-to-end re-imagination of the legal function from the enterprise, end-user, and societal perspectives. That means asking bold and fundamental questions such as:

- *"What do customers/ clients and society expect from the legal function and what differentiated role can we play?"*
- *"What kind of talent do we need to meet and exceed those expectations?"*
- *"What kind of culture and workplace must we create to attract the talent we need?"*
- *"What is our purpose and how do we create a culture that will attract, retain, and up-skill a digital workforce, supply chain, and strategic partnerships necessary to drive positive business impact and experience for our customers – and for society at large?"*

Driving impact to business and its customers is one part of law's future. The other is the reclamation of its purpose to better serve clients, those in need of its products and services, society, and the rule of law. Paradoxically, law's genuine transformation will take it back to its service and 'higher purpose' roots.

Dierk Allow me a provocative question: Are you saying that transformation will inevitably 'fix things', i.e. let's trust the process?

Mark No—not at all!—Law's impact on its clients and society will be driven by *human* behavior and adaptation. It will be enabled and scaled by technology, data, process, agility, integration of law with other functions, multidisciplinary

[13]The LLI has launched and supports several initiatives in that regard. One of the most recent ones is a project with the Technical University Munich (TUM) and the Law School of Ludwig-Maximilian-University in Munich (LMU) to establish the Munich Center for Legal Innovation as a tripartite engagement between those two renowned academic bodies plus the LLI.

collaboration, customer-centricity, and a commitment to constant improvement for the benefit of clients and society. These change components are inter-connected and interdependent. Law's future is a mosaic, not a disparate collection of isolated elements.

Dierk I hear you—and this requires a clear, holistic vision of legal professionals about the Law in the digital age. And it requires strategies towards that end and the willingness to not only serve the legal market, but also the Rule of Law in its entirety.

Mark The legal maxim 'Justice delayed is justice denied' is apropos. To further delay law's future is to deny society a reimagined legal function that will better serve us all—and the democracy so many take for granted.

Dierk To make the reimagination of the legal function happen—and robust—I believe that we need to build both, the *belief* and the *controls*. We—and with that I mean all stakeholders, especially those economically benefitting from the transformation—need to tirelessly promote, anchor and incentivize the shared accountability for the Rule of Law across the newly forming legal ecosystem.

But, at the same time, we also need to think hard about the controls required to make it happen. And that will be tough, given that we face disruption and ambidexterity: While we only find out about the new reality as we embrace it, we must maintain safeguards. While we want to sustain the Rule of Law, we might have to give up the rule of lawyers. But how could such safeguards and controls be established? And by whom?

Mark In a complex world that is moving at Warp-speed, the legal function must adapt and move at the speed of society. We are already witnessing the effects of its failure to do so: court backlogs, an alarming rise of pro se litigants, delay as a tactic to frustrate resolution (thereby denying decision making on the merits), etc. Law is more than lawyers now—it requires different expertise, perspectives, and *modus operandi* to compete with public opinion, a widely held view that "law is for the rich," and a growing lack of trust in legal institutions. The tools, human resources, and urgency exist to change things for the better. Lawyers have consistently been on the front lines of resistance. This is a problem the profession—and industry—must face up to. The failure to do so will result in the continued erosion of the rule of law and the death of democracy.

4 How Do We Seize the Reset Moment?

Dierk OK—let's get real and do a little experiment: Let's assume our debate has led us down the right path and we find acceptance with our perspectives.

So, let's now be bold and outline concrete ideas on how to leverage the disruption we are facing—on how to 'seize the Reset Moment'! Let's be specific—and a little uncomfortable and answer two questions:

1) What are the *three top priorities* the legal ecosystem should focus on in the next three to five years?
2) What are the *three personal commitments*, i.e. what do we personally commit to do, in the next 24 months to walk our talk?

Mark Deal!—Here we go with my top three—OK four—priorities:

1. *Focus on the purpose of law in the digital age and reimagine how it can fulfill that mission* for the betterment of society, a vastly expanded client base, the workforce, society, and the planet. Law is not intended to focus on the needs of lawyers; rather, lawyers and other allied professionals, together with a growing arsenal of powerful tools, carry out the important role of promoting law's purpose.
2. *Coalesce behind a paradigmatic shift of the legal profession and industry to serve the needs of existing clients, society, and the environment.* Legal services must be delivered at scale, not—as is presently the case--for a small segment of the population. Legal services must be faster, more accessible and affordable, transparent, data-backed, tech-enabled, and multidisciplinary. This is essential to maintain the rule of law and democracy as well as to streamline commerce, stimulate the economy, and geopolitics.
3. *If law is the glue that binds society, it must be accessible to the entire society.* The transition of medical practice the healthcare system provides a roadmap for scalable, more democratized access. Legal services are no longer the exclusive province of lawyers. Law schools are not the only way to acquire a legal education. The administration of justice need not be rendered exclusively in a courthouse. To be effective in supporting the rule of law and democracy, the legal ecosystem must align with other disciplines to leverage existing human and technological resources to democratize legal access and promote its transparency.
4. *One other critical element is humanity.* The legal community would benefit from diversity—cognitive, experiential, geographic, etc. It must be more compassionate, collaborative, and curious. Empathy is an undervalued, yet essential component of the workforce and its relationship with colleagues, clients, and others in need.

Dierk Big stuff—and right on! Here is what I would put as the top three priorities:

1. *Rethink the curriculum for lawyers—and make it one for professionals in law.* While lawyers will certainly remain at the core of the rule of law, it needs the full multi-disciplinary diversity to secure the functioning of the law.
2. *Focus on the judicial system.* If the judicative power falls behind in terms of digitization, the power of digital transformation in the private legal sector will inevitably turn into a destructive force for the rule of law.
3. *Foster and prioritize the scholarly debate about the rule of law in the digital age.* Deep and independent thinking, broad and bold ideas, multidisciplinary and diverse participants will show us the way.

Dierk And against that background—this is what I am committing to for the next 24 months:

1) *I will double down on my work at the Liquid Legal Institute e.V. (LLI).* It is multi-disciplinary by nature (and by the bylaws of the association), not for profit, invites bold and innovative thinking, and is all about creating results. I believe the LLI can serve perfectly as one of those bridges that re-connects the new, much more diverse and highly dynamic legal ecosystem.
2) *I will focus on our project for a center of legal innovation with two leading faculties in Munich—the law school and the technical university.* The goal is to start a curriculum and research projects at the intersection of the law and computer science. This is where cross-domain insights and education could find a home!
3) *I will start at home, with my team and our team's internal and external network to have the debate about 'the Reset Moment'.* We—like all stakeholders in law—must develop answers for our specific area of work and influence, and we must make that extra effort to consider what our contribution will be to maintain—or restore—the Rule of Law in the digital future.

Mark Not easy to be next in line looking at that list. Here are my three commitments for the next 24 months:

1) At this stage of my life and career, I am buying ripe bananas. I am focused on initiatives involving collaboration with other like-minded professionals across disciplines, geographies, and industries to capture the latent impact of the legal function to restore respect for the rule of law, democracy, and to better serve existing customers/clients. As well, I see opportunities to greatly expand access to legal services. This is fundamental to law's purpose.
2) To achieve the first commitment requires a reimagination of training—and not just "legal" training in the traditional sense. We need more than lawyers to capture the potential of the legal function in a digital, AI-backed world. I commit to working to refine what "talent" means to legal in a digital world and why its narrow construction by the legal establishment must be replaced by a far broader, more agile and diverse filter.
3) I pledge to spend even more time working with young people. I'd like to think we have quite a bit to teach each other. The new generations keep me fresh and open to new ways of thinking about and doing things. Hopefully, more experiences—as a human being and as a professional—can be helpful to them and enable them to help bring about a brighter future.

Dierk Mark—this has been fun, as discussing with you always is! At the same time, the transformation of the legal ecosystem is not only a mosaic, but it also appears to be a wicked problem which seems to be unsolvable, at times. So, allow me to close with a personal question: In five years from now—will we be debating the opportunities of a renewed, diverse, strong legal profession, or the ruins of the Rule of Law?

Mark I suspect it will relate to the interplay between humanity and machines. There will also profound socioeconomic and psychological changes resulting from the astonishing advances in technology and the acceleration of change. The debate will likely center around the role and purpose of human beings going forward—how will all but a handful of people be able to keep up and what will the vast majority that cannot do?

Dierk This concludes our short discussion, and we thank you, dear reader, to 'listen' to us until the end.

If we could ask one collegial favor from you, it would be that you chime in with our little experiment and take a moment to decide for yourself: *What are your top three priorities and what are your top three commitments to sustaining the rule of law in the digital age?*

> It is better to debate a question without settling it than to settle a question without debating it.—Joseph Joubert[14]

Liquid-Legal-Waves to Other Chapters, Written by the Editors

Dierk and *Mark* keep us honest as they point out how far off the current legal ecosystem has drifted from its mandate to sustain the rule of law. As lawyers we must rethink longstanding cultural patterns in our remit. *Robert* takes this call to action to a very personal level when he shares his authentic story on *"The remaking of a modern lawyer – an inhouse counsel's reinvention journey"*.

How deep we need to go about changing the cultural norms in our legal industry? And is this 'only' to sustain the Rule of Law—or even more fundamental to create a sustainable environment for the humans in Law? This is explored by *Ulf* who applies a system-psychodynamic lens to tackle the question: *"AI is here. But is the legal profession ready for it?"*

Building on the analysis by *Dierk* and *Mark* that the legal industry has hit a *"Reset Moment"*, read in the following chapter how *Thomas* addresses the widening gap between contemporary culture and the traditional legal principles and institutional values to answer the question: *"Can AI Save the Rule of Law?"*

[14] *The Notebooks of Joseph Joubert*, New York 2005, translated by Paul Auster.

Reference

Galanter M (1974) Why the "Haves" come out ahead: speculations on the limits of legal change. Litigation and Dispute Processing: Part One (Autumn), vol 9, no 1, pp 95–160 (66 pages). Cambridge University Press. https://www.jstor.org/stable/3053023

Mark A. Cohen is a global thought leader and innovator in the legal business industry. He is the CEO of Legal Mosaic (www.legalmosaic.com), a legal business consultancy; regular contributor to Forbes on the intersection of law, business, and technology (and more recently, Leadership Strategy); Moderator/Speaker at Economist Impact events; and frequent keynote speaker at international business, legal, and technology events. He has addressed the global legal leadership teams of approximately 60 Fortune 500 companies as well as leading global law firms and foreign sovereign Bar Associations.

Mark is the co-Founder and Executive Chairman of the Digital Legal Exchange, a global nonprofit community of leading multinational enterprises. The Exchange's mission is to elevate the impact of the legal function on the enterprise and its customers by aligning it with other business units.

Mark was appointed by the Singapore Academy of Law (SAL) to serve as its inaugural LIFTED Distinguished Scholar. He has been a Distinguished Fellow at Georgetown University Law Center and Distinguished Lecturer at Northwestern University Pritzker College of law. He has also taught at Bucerius (Germany), IE (Spain), and the College of Law (Australia). Mark has lectured frequently at leading global law and business schools including: Harvard, Stanford, Oxford, University College London, Kings College, and National University of Singapore. Mark was appointed an innaugural ALM Intelligence Fellow.

Mark was a co-Founder of Clearspire, a globally acclaimed pioneer law firm/legal services company that reimagined the delivery of legal services from the customer perspective. Clearspire's revolutionary use of technology; "two-company model," and hybrid workforce remain cutting-edge nearly 20 years after the company's launch.

Mark has focused on "the business of law" for the past 15 years. Prior to that, he was an internationally recognized "bet the company" civil trial lawyer. He served stints as a decorated Assistant United States Attorney (Civil Division), BigLaw partner, national boutique founder and managing partner, outside General Counsel (3 excess and surplus lines insurance companies), and Federally-Appointed Receiver of an international aviation parts business.

Dierk Schindler M.I.L. (Lund), is co-founder and co-CEO of the Liquid Legal Institute e.V. (www.liquid-legal-institute.com). He is co-author and co-editor of numerous publications on innovation and transformation in the legal profession, most notably the three previous volumes of the book-series "Liquid Legal" (Springer) in 2017, 2020 and 2022.

Following leadership roles in private practice and the IT-industry, in 2019, Dierk joined Robert BOSCH GmbH as their Vice President Corporate Legal Services, Mobility, Supply Chain and Logistics. In his role he drives the adoption of Agile practices and, jointly with the leadership team, the digital transformation.

Dierk is also the co-founder of Legal Data Analytics GmbH, a startup that builds co-pilots based on generative AI for the legal ecosystem.

Dierk teaches at the Management Center Innsbruck on Innovation Management and Digital Business Law. He is a certified lawyer, took his phD from Augsburg University, and his Master of International Law from Lund University.

Can Artificial Intelligence Save the Rule of Law?

Thomas D. Barton

Contents

Abstract

"Can Artificial Intelligence Save the Rule of Law?" explores the intersection of law and culture. It argues that Western legal systems are structured to advance a consistent and ongoing vision of individualism and detached rationality dating from the Enlightenment of the eighteenth and nineteenth centuries. In contrast, modern culture has slowly detached from these Enlightenment views to embrace a stronger sense of diverse identity coupled with more horizontal and participatory approaches to truth-seeking and authority.

The slow divergence of legal thinking and methods from contemporary culture threatens popular support for the Rule of Law. Law and culture must, urgently, find stronger common ground. Basic elements of the legal system and litigation, however, constrain its openness toward emerging cultural values. Left on its own, it is difficult to imagine the adoption of internal reforms that would enable more agile judicial decision making or the generation of stronger popular support.

The chapter therefore suggests that Western judiciaries augment their traditional methods by creating two advisory artificial intelligence tools. One would be public facing, a generative AI system that responds to inquiries about legal

T. D. Barton (✉)
California Western School of Law, San Diego, CA, USA
e-mail: tdb@cwsl.edu

K. Jacob et al. (eds.), *Liquid Legal – Sustaining the Rule of Law*, Law for Professionals, https://doi.org/10.1007/978-3-031-78596-2_2

matters using accessible vocabulary wherever possible. The second, for use by judges and other legal professionals, would be an advisory judicial assistant designed to spark the imaginations and creativity of judges and lawyers toward building a more socially organic "constitutive rationality" without compromising vital Enlightenment values of formal equality and due process of law.

Preventive Law pioneer Edward A. Dauer once wrote: "in a contest between law and culture, culture always wins."[1] I have always thought him right, and it now worries me. Traditional legal principles and the institutional values that we shorthand as the "Rule of Law" seem locked in ominous and escalating disagreements with a variety of aspects of contemporary culture. In addressing basic human questions of "Who am I? Where do I belong? Who listens and is responsive to me? How do I make sense of, and make my way in the world? What choices do I have and how can I act effectively in my life?", the answers supplied from deeply within the structures of Western legal systems increasingly reflect a different, older era than those of contemporary life.

This divergence of legal operations and values from contemporary culture deeply imperils the Rule of Law's historic preeminence as a formal default for securing order and resolving social problems. This chapter seeks to spell out the terrain of this conflict and explore the possibility of law and culture reconciling—at least partially—through use of Artificial Intelligence (AI) as an advisory assistant specifically within the judiciary, and more generally in legal systems and their public messaging.

The chapter proceeds by first identifying the parameters and severity of the challenges posed by the growing rift between law and culture. Section 1, entitled "The Dilemma," responds to the questions "what is the Rule of Law;" "how is it in jeopardy;" and "why should we care?"

Section 2 traces the origins of the law/culture divide to eighteenth and nineteenth centuries Enlightenment philosophy, economic structures, and limiting technologies. These shaped more than two centuries of outlook on human beings and social relationships and were institutionalized in the methods and decisional style of Western legal systems. Dubbed "How did Law and Culture Divide?" this second section probes the questions "how did we arrive at this law/culture dissonance;" "what conditions seem to have locked us into the downward spiral;" and "why can't legal systems keep pace with evolving cultural understandings?"

Finally, Sect. 3, "What Can We Do? Seeking a 'Constitutive Rationality' Through AI," outlines how non-binding generative and pattern-recognition AI tools might help to reintegrate law and culture through bringing people more easily to the law, and bringing law more empathically and expansively to its surrounding culture. This final section asks, "what can we do to resolve the dilemma;" and "what

[1] Dauer (2006), p. 98.

risks may an AI/Legal System alliance pose for fundamental Rule of Law values;" and "how can the AI tool best be publicly presented to instill trust in its findings and accountability in its use?" At its most ambitious, Sect. 3 depicts a shift from prevailing Western transactional, instrumental rationality to the unrealized "constitutive rationality" first suggested half a century ago by legal visionary Lawrence Tribe. He advocates legal decision making as embedded in a larger interconnected landscape of social, economic, and technological relationships. AI offers a vehicle not available when Tribe wrote: the possibility of opening out self-enclosed, binary, universalist legal norms to stronger cultural contexts for assessing liability; and supplying greater predictive and managerial powers to expand the range and competence of legal problem solving.

1 The Dilemma

The need is urgent. The Rule of Law, as a set of institutions and aspirational ideals, is clearly struggling. Across the globe many question the efficacy—and some even the legitimacy—of its claimed methods of non-biased application of transcendent, secular norms. Nationalist rhetoric, religious edict, defiant vigilantism, and raw personal ambition tacitly combine to threaten dilution of judicial authority and the idea of stable, independent legal constraints.

Many, like me, despair of this erosion but are also dumbfounded. Even given its evident incompleteness and imperfections, what can people imagine as plausible structures to replace a deliberative, professional, justice-oriented rule system? Are whole nations willing to let the Rule of Law slide into authoritarian control or be hijacked piecemeal for transitory political goals, weaponized to advance ideology or simple vindictiveness? What are people thinking?

The realistic answer may be "not much, at least not yet." Concerns about the decline of the sense of legal legitimacy or effectiveness do not figure prominently in public discourse. That may seem less overtly threatening than vocalized rejection of legal processes, but it remains disturbing. The lack of direct conversation on what for many lawyers seems so pressingly central to orderly public life may stem from two sources. First, Rule of Law issues may seem detached from everyday life—and thus not cause for immediate alarm. Most people have lived apart from formal aspects of the law and are likely happy for that. Encounters with the law are often perplexing, expensive, or maddeningly impersonal. Hence few are likely to have reflected on the seeming decline of the Rule of Law. If they have, ironically they may experience a sense of relief from perceived burdens of legal authority, rather than a sense of sadness or apprehension of what the world really might look like without its stabilizing continuity.

The second possible reason for the relative invisibility of diverging law and culture is that the causes of the schism are very deep, multi-pronged, and hiding in plain sight. Western culture—broadly including the structures of how we gather information, do business, and communicate as well as our understandings of self and authority—has gradually drifted from its Enlightenment moorings over the past two hundred years. In contrast, legal systems arguably remain stubbornly rooted.

Institutionally, the Rule of Law has seemed almost impervious to its slow detachment from surrounding environment. Perhaps the established power of legal structures—their social respectability and command of resources—has blinded the law from a sense of urgency in responding to the widening gulf of world understanding. But flashpoints of tension are intensifying and accelerating, toward unknown ends.

The lack of visibility of legal/cultural divergence could change. If the institutions of law and democratic governance are pushed to some evident and broadly impactful brink in ways that clearly implicate personal freedom of everyday citizens—through, say, dramatic political upheaval or widespread street-level violence—perhaps ordinary people will rally intuitively toward strong rescue efforts. In an emergency, old loyalties may surface. Putting the best face on it, traditional legal institutions may suffer more from popular neglect than outright rejection, able to be resuscitated when in imminent peril.

That would be welcome; but even if it came, such a fix may be only temporary. The causes beneath the legal/cultural detachment are too deep to be easily swept away. We should not await some gripping political or social crisis, trusting that heroic instincts preserving our legal systems will prevail like the climax of an adventure thriller. The detachment of legal legitimacy from everyday life is ominous and real. If neglected too long a coming crisis may descend quickly and seriously, with the damage not easily reversible. Alternative forms of social control and problem solving could move quickly to fill the ensuing vacuum—strong-man tyrannical power masquerading as democracy, winner-take-all majoritarian rule, theocratic control, indirect manipulation by oligopolies or technocracies—all may begin culturally to seem more accessible, comfortable, or efficacious as the Rule of Law gradually recedes from perceived effectiveness and importance.[2]

Any of those substitutions, of course, would be deeply destabilizing for democracy and individual autonomy as well as against our better moral instincts. At their best, legal institutions represent the possibility for decisions that are procedurally regular, reviewable, and respectful of diverse minorities. The judiciary takes rule/values decisions that refuse to be assessed exclusively by efficiency metrics and instrumental gains. As Ronald Dworkin defines them, legal rights stand apart from utilitarian calculations.[3]

Courts do not solve all sorts of problems well, but they do act as a generalist default system that can buffer over-reach or failure by other methods. Formal legal

[2]"[L]arge shares of the public in many countries are open to nondemocratic alternatives. . . . Indeed, a median of 31% across 24 nations are supportive of authoritarian systems, according to a recent Pew Research Center survey." Laura Silver & Janell Fetterolf, *Who Likes Authoritarianism and How Do They Want to Change Their Government?* https://www.pewresearch.org/short-reads/2024/02/28/who-likes-authoritarianism-and-how-do-they-want-to-change-their-government/ , February 28, 2024.

[3]Ronald Dworkin, Taking Rights Seriously (1977).

authority needs to be available and strong, which can occur only when its methods and decisions are respected—both because they are efficacious in addressing social problems that people cannot otherwise seem to resolve, and because they are regarded as basically fair and broadly accessible. The law cannot safely compartmentalize itself fully outside of public support; to do so is to depend precariously on power rather than draw on reservoirs of respect. As a method of coping with social disputes and promoting a just order, the Rule of Law is unique and irreplaceable, even as it must grope toward stronger compatibility with constantly evolving sentiments and technologies, and the burgeoning complexities of contemporary problems.

What, therefore, can we do about a possible ever-widening rift between the Rule of Law and contemporary culture? Can the two domains find more stable common ground as they confront social and technological evolution, changing moral sensibilities, and geopolitical power shifts? How far can the fundamental assumptions underpinning legal institutions—manifested by day-to-day transactions and judicial decisions—bend toward modern cultural understandings without compromising their uniqueness or effectiveness? Can bridges between law and culture be forged by technical augmentations to legal systems, as may be offered by AI? Or—the risk must be faced—could abdication of the professional legal community from making proactive decisions about AI actually worsen the long-term threat to legal institutions?

The potentially corrosive severance of routine life and thought from legal aspirations creates three options for resolution:

- First, legal institutions could attempt to morph onto changing cultural norms.
- Second, a more muscular, assertive legal system could attempt to drag contemporary culture back to Western Enlightenment orthodoxy.
- Or, finally, a plausible outside mediator—perhaps a technology like AI—could build workable bridges between the gradually de-coupling legal institutions and cultural practices.

The first two options seem imprudent or unrealistic. An unreflective, full capitulation of legal thought and institutional methods to shifting cultural values—even if that could plausibly be accomplished—compromises a vital function of the Rule of Law. Legal institutions are meant to stand apart from, or at least buffer, wide swings in political causes and ideology. Hence the law cannot collapse into just another set of political tools even while, as elaborated in Sect. 3, law becomes more effective by finding common ground with cultural shifts.

The second possibility for reconciliation between law and contemporary culture envisions that legal institutions drag popular culture back to what we describe below as classic Enlightenment assumptions. But that is equally flawed, even apart from the self-destructiveness of reversing centuries of economic and technological progress. Such efforts would fail for lack of any sort of effective platform within legal systems that would substantially deepen their popular impact. Judges, even the few who attain a certain celebrity, will not become social media influencers. That would likely violate judicial ethics and be seen publicly as efforts toward pursuing specific agendas, an illegitimate use of the powers of a formally non-political branch of government.

Hence it does not seem feasible for the law to go fully toward culture, nor vice-versa. But legal systems must do something. They must somehow nod more directly toward cultural understandings and underlying economic/technological conditions not embraced inside the traditional formats or tools of its legal rules and procedures. The trajectory of the law/culture divergence is moving too quickly to be ignored. Purity is a dangerous option; in the long run, culture is indeed likely to win a pitched battle. But what that would mean for social order and individual autonomy is forbiddingly opaque. To date, however, the philosophical and institutional heritage of the law has seemed so central to its implementing professionals that legal systems do not know how or where to pull back from traditional structures and methods.

The third option, to find a previously unavailable technical bridge for reconciliation, is untested and largely unknowable in detail or ultimate outcome. I offer here only the briefest sketch of possibilities. Yet those possibilities seem real. AI could offer the sort of novel, tech-assisted breakthrough that might work—a way of exploring new methods and opening out legal norms without disavowing Enlightenment traditions or explicitly disrupting time-honored lawyering techniques.

If we can imagine what might be built—the goals we can envision—we can work toward compiling the data, algorithms, and training methods that might make possible a far stronger reconciliation. Conversely, if we do *not* consciously ask ourselves what we really want the legal system to accomplish for our lives and work toward that vision, then AI will almost inevitably be used non-reflectively, in ways that could *worsen* the current law/culture rupture through an endless closed loop of legal self-authentication. Ironically, the more that AI is used as a mere robotic retriever of legal orthodoxy and past decisions, the more entrenched those doctrines will become; and the more that the rift between the law and surrounding culture will be engrained.

Section 2 below attempts to sketch the origins of the deepening fault lines. Then, the concluding Sect. 3 expands on what I suggested above: how an advisory generative AI judicial assistant might gradually expand legal norms to take account of broader, more culturally attractive perspectives as well as easier, stronger, consumer access.

2 How Did Law and Culture Divide?

Western law and culture too often ignore or talk past one another on central ideas about people and their communities—issues about the meanings of equality, transactional choice, and social connectedness; perceptions of impartiality in the creation, application, and enforcement of legal rules; and the extent to which social goals should influence legal decision-making.

Addressing any of these questions is difficult in part because of their abstraction, but also because of the polarization and possible sensitivities among all of us as potential speakers. These issues seem increasingly delicate—which itself may be another symptom of the growing tension between an Enlightenment heritage of objectivity about truth and authority, and contemporary norms of authenticity, agency, and social constructions of reality. But these questions are crucial in exploring the possibility of expanding the contextual reach of legal norms—and implications of such broadening on fundamental Rule of Law values: transcendence of the law beyond the wealth, power, or charisma of any individual; formal equality; and regular, reviewable due process.

This section makes a brief attempt to understand the slow detachment of Rule of Law institutions and values from contemporary social thought and structures: philosophical, economic, and technological. It is organized by first looking at the abstracted, artificial concept of personhood and attendant human ideals born in eighteenth Century Enlightenment philosophy. Then, we explore the gradual real-world rooting of those ideals in Rule of Law methods and values. Building durability for an enlightened outlook on humanity through the law unquestionably advanced human freedom and well-being. But that same entrenchment now, arguably, threatens those very values.

2.1 Enlightenment Foundational Ideals and Their Contemporary Challenges

Writing in the nineteenth century, legal historian Henry Sumner Maine summarized the evolution of law and society as moving from "status to contract."[4] Anciently, humans were seen socially—and largely legally—as placeholders within an elaborate status hierarchy. Roles and social position were largely ascribed from birth, a system of privileges supported by differential laws, perpetuating a relatively static hierarchy.

But with the Enlightenment and ensuing scientific and industrial revolutions, humans were philosophically viewed as an amalgamation of the rationality advanced by Rene Descartes and the morality of Immanual Kant: disembodied, autonomous, homogeneous, fully rational individuals deserving of equal respect and dignity. They were imbued with an assumed capability (and accountability) for making choices detached from the pull of social relations. They were atomistic, possessed of transactional freedom and growing geographic mobility. Constraints placed on people were required to satisfy Kant's moral imperative: they were to be assessed by imagining the regulation as it would be applied to all of humanity, through universalist norms.[5] It was morally valid for one person only if morally valid for all. Ideally, norms were not to be differentiated among people based on status, community, or religious belief. Moral and legal rules did not particularize; rights and duties were to be universal and non-dischargeable.

[4] Henry James Sumner Maine, Ancient Law (1861).

[5] Immanuel Kant, Groundwork of the Metaphysics of Morals (1785).

However imperfectly realized, both the law and the broader culture used this philosophical foundation to embrace a free market model for the interactions of legally autonomous persons, a vision based on bargaining or contract rather than status. Law was to understand and hold humans accountable as detached, choosing individuals exercising rational free will. By so regarding personhood, Enlightenment law took its role as consistent with Adam Smith's contemporaneous *Wealth of Nations:* assuring social and economic progress through facilitating consensual, value-generating transactions.[6] No utopian endpoints were specified. Atomized individuals would mold an unpredictable world by the accretion of self-interested transactions measured through whatever values individuals were willing to place on their consensual exchanges. The invisible hand of the market would largely shape environments, and by definition would expand human welfare through the aggregation of mutually beneficial bargains.[7]

Legal ideas about truth and authority had similar Enlightenment roots. Validity was sought through the hierarchical arrangement of universalist norms, with higher courts overseeing basic consistency among lower courts. Reliability was to be ensured through imposing uniform courtroom procedures of information-gathering and a strongly reductivist, analytical style among lawyers and judges that pared away local influences—the hope being that in any given court, similar fact patterns and disputes would result in similar outcomes. Authority was imposed not only formally through the state powers of fines and confinement, but also through strong curation of information shared with the public, aided by a growing refinement of legal doctrine and legal vocabulary spoken fluently only by legal professionals. The legal system was built and operated by experts in a downward style of communication inviting little user participation or input—the opposite, say, of the more organic, reciprocal construction of the internet that harnesses user communication and creativity.[8]

Western culture, I believe, is fast leaving behind the transactional or contract-based vision of humanity, as well as its hierarchical, curated truth-seeking and non-participatory authority. Contemporary cultural emphasizes more subjective, constructed, and often polarized meanings formed through horizontal, individuated information retrieval guided by fragmented social media algorithms and influencers. Cultural norms seem to find legitimation easier when pronouncements reflect realistic opportunities for stakeholder participation; comprehensible decisional explanations; and latitude for recognizing exceptions.

If Maine chronicled the passage of personhood from "status" to "contract," I believe contemporary culture is ready to describe a new progression in the social understanding of humanity: from contract to "identity." By identity I mean that people increasingly embrace differences as well as sameness; acknowledge undeniable, constraining historical personal traits and economic circumstances as well as

[6] Adam Smith, The Wealth of Nations (1776).

[7] See also Jeremy Bentham, An Introduction to the Principles of Moral and Legislation (1780).

[8] Lawrence Lessig, The Future of Ideas: The Fate of the Commons in a Connected World (2001).

transactional choices; and demand a legal system that at least sometimes accepts and protects groups with diverging collective senses of equality, truth, and justness. People of course continue to demand equality in some abstract sense. But they also have strong needs for formal recognition and institutional respect toward diverse heritages, as well as the freedom to express chosen selves both individually and in association with others.

The move to identity as cultural self-understanding is most easily seen in widening political polarization. "Identity politics" is a label often used to describe calls among diverse or minority groups for legal recognition of their distinctive history. They feel on the wrong end of distributional consequences, economically and socially, over generations of nominally neutral markets and laws. Enlightenment rhetoric about formal equality can sound hollow, a promise that is not realistically available to those within environments not defined by atomistic free markets, but instead by biologically defined characteristics. These consequences are more visible and persuasive when aggregated at a group identity level. Disadvantaged groups may seek reparations for past injuries or legally protected affirmative action on their behalf; but short of that they want universalist legal rules pushed further and further down into realms of life that once may have been considered too intimate for legal control. Housing, workplaces, schooling, social clubs, childcare arrangements: all are urged to be included in stronger universalist legal protections that would, realistically, newly include their identity group.

On the other side of the political polarity, identity recognition is experienced as "erasure," "cancellation," or "replacement." As the law responds to calls by disadvantaged groups for broader and more strongly enforced universalist norms into more intimate spaces, this alternative group pushes back. Matters considered connected to religious or historically honored traditions in realms like procreation, child rearing practices, social associations, or gun ownership—all are considered part of a group heritage they feel should be immune from universalist legal regulation. They too want formal identity recognition. They experience universalist legal norms in these arenas as invasions of historic "free" spaces, undermining their heritage.

At their core, both emerging understandings of human identity, truth, and authority are rooted in stronger senses of the inter-dependence of people and their day-to-day circumstances: social, physical, and technological. Some demand protection or reconstruction of a range of traditional practices deemed at risk. Others articulate purposeful endpoints of building a sustainable, climate-stable, inclusive and supportive world. For each group, however, a sense of identity is expressed in the surrounding legal, as well as cultural and economic environments.

Western legal systems struggle to accept this sense of environmental embeddedness, much less incorporate it into everyday legal decision-making. Instead, separatist Enlightenment sensibilities are acted out in virtually every traditional legal proceeding, where life is largely viewed as a series of detached, segmented choices for which independent, rational minds are held accountable.

Why should that be? Why should the law and its implementing institutions be so resistant toward these ideas of a more flexible personal identity, while other basic structures of life—economic, technological, information sharing, even religious—seem more agile? Perhaps the answers for the long, persistent inertia of Enlightenment legal methods can be accounted for if we look at the role that Rule of Law institutions and methods played toward realizing the Enlightenment goals of formal equality and individualistic social progress.

As elaborated in the sections below, the law enabled tremendous progress in advancing Enlightenment values. It did so, however, by creating and operating a largely detached, self-enclosed system that has slowly cut itself off from vital cultural support.[9] Reversing this trend requires gradually opening up the norms of the legal system to diverse social, relational, economic, and technological contexts of modern life and to the probable distributional and ecological consequences of judicial decisions.

The normative style of the eighteenth and nineteenth centuries may have been dictated by scarcity of informational and communicative resources, as well as Enlightenment philosophies. But AI offers breakthroughs in each of those limitations on legal decision making. Western legal systems thus may choose now to embark, even if tentatively, on an AI augmented normative style. Doing so would advance human flourishing even as it rescues the Rule of Law from eventual cultural abandonment.

2.2 Implementing Enlightenment Values Through Rule of Law Methods

The Enlightenment philosophical concept of personhood as abstracted, environmentally detached consciousness was essential to furthering the articulated fundamental values of formal equality and transactional individualism. To the modern eye, espousing universal freedom and dignity seems strangely discordant with the then-prevailing realities of an eighteenth century world replete with enslaved people and caste rankings. But, looking back, how else could such ideals possibly have taken hold, but through articulation of such socially disconnected but nonetheless high-minded ideals? A philosophy of shriveled personhood was perhaps an unlikely vehicle toward more genuine equality and freedom. Slowly, however, it worked—and not in small part through the evolution of legal methods that supported these as-yet-unrealized aspirations.

This evolution required the law to employ two basic tools, both of which ultimately found expression in the basic legal material of binary, universalistic, behavioral norms. Such norms were the building blocks of both the substance and the procedures of our inherited Western legal systems. The transcendent quality granted to such norms through Rule of Law values, floating above local practices, aristocratic whim, and religious edict, was an immense breakthrough toward human freedom.

[9] See generally Barton (2016), p. 1.

Crucially, however, we must distinguish this transcendence of legal norms—which must be preserved along with formal equality and due process—from the shape, specific qualities, or taxonomic rigidity of the norms themselves. As we shall see in Sect. 3, AI has the possibility of opening legal norms to stronger context, even while the basic principles and methods of our legal ordering are preserved.

More immediately, however, I examine in greater detail below how Enlightenment-inspired binary, universalist norms took the shape they did in our traditional legal systems—and why they now are so sticky.

Translating the Enlightenment human and moral outlook to operating legal systems within the economic and technological constraints of the period required two basic design features. First, the law narrowed its focus to judging discrete human behaviors—describable manifestations of individual will. Second, the law needed appropriate technology for announcing in advance its standards, transporting those standards across the geography of a given jurisdiction, and applying them in procedurally regular ways. Both aims took shape in discrete universalist, binary norms with their relatively easy evidentiary requirements, low information and transmissibility costs, and simple money transfer remedies.

2.2.1 An Enlightened, But Narrow, Legal Focus

Both philosophically and technically, the Enlightenment legal system did not attempt to judge the moral or social worth of individuals; or any distinctive ethnic, geographic, or domestic relational environments in which they historically lived; or, largely, either the motives for the human actions taken or their ultimate consequences. Courts had the resources—perhaps only barely—of uncovering reasonably objective evidence proving whether particular human actions were or were not taken. Assessing larger historical identities, or the variable influence of environmental settings or underlying human motives, or the probabilistic impacts of human conduct, were all beyond the law's capacities as well as offensive to Enlightenment values. Rule of Law institutions instead largely narrowed their field of inquiry to discrete behaviors, based on assumptions of the possibility of detached, rational, individual choices. This, of course, paired nicely with the disembodied, contextually starved personhood and accountability of Descartes and Kant.

This narrowed focus is unrealistic, however, about what actually propels or constrains human behavior. Social action is comprised of environmental antecedents and resulting outcomes, as well as behaviors. Rather than address social action more comprehensively, the law focused almost exclusively on the middle section: the behaviors, with little serious attention to the contexts surrounding the immediate conduct or its longer risks and consequences.

Leaving off the antecedents and consequences of behaviors not only ignores the influence that environments have on people's thoughts and motivations,[10] but also relinquishes the opportunity to adjust decisions by monitoring real-world outcomes of judicial determinations. Judging decontextualized behaviors and imposing freeze-

[10] See generally B.F. Skinner, Freedom and Dignity (1971).

frame remedies is arguably artificial and may result in less morally nuanced decisions.

Further, and paradoxically, the strongly individualistic focus may also slowly undermine the normative power of alternative, non-legal social influences. Legal philosopher Ralf Dahrendorf observed this tendency. "The law took the place of more pervasive traditional prescriptions and the absolute power that often went with them. Formalised law implies *limitations* which are absent from older and other types of normative structure."[11] This is how Enlightenment legal systems are traditionally said to supply both freedom and equality. The freedom was to offer choices where few previously existed, by de-contextualizing people. Humans were conceptually ripped from the historic cultures in which they were captured and held, cultures that shaped aspects of their everyday lives toward ascriptions of status and role as reinforced through powerful belief systems and communal ritual.

Formal equality logically followed: people were conceived abstractly as vessels of consciousness, made human by their endowment with rationality. As such they were the subjects, the designers of environments—not its objects. Environmental influence on human behavior violated Descartes' separation of mind from all else. Disconnected, humans were deemed responsible fully and individually for their decisions—but also entitled to Kantian equal dignity and respect. Ironically, however, this formal equality came with the attached cost of homogenization. People could be treated equally because they were regarded as all the same. Neither their origins, nor their futures, nor the integrity of their communities were the focus of the Enlightenment-built legal systems.

2.2.2 Decontextualized Rules as Appropriate Technology

In building this system of Enlightenment values, the law had to work with what it had—which were constrained economic and technological resources. Simple binary, universal, behavioral norms carrying predictable, easily enforced remedies were feasible to be communicated widely throughout a dispersed, often illiterate, general population. More particularized norms would have required not only better communication methods of dissemination than were available, but their breach would require more nuanced investigations. That in turn would mean gathering evidence from local sources with risky reliability and possibly self-interested stances. Legal systems which may have depended on itinerant, circuit-riding judges could not afford from either a resource or reputational perspective to work with culturally differentiated norms. Further, judges often had to be able to hear evidence and pronounce judgment and remedies within a strongly contained time period. De-contextualized, broadly applied behavioral norms once again were uniquely well suited to the tasks; procedures were conformed to available technologies.

Human accountability for the rules was often supported by signaling rituals of entry into the legal realm, as in swearing oaths, passing twigs, or impressing signet rings onto wax—so that people would become aware, and self-protect, when

[11] Ralf Dahrendorf, *Law and Order,* The Hamlyn Lectures 43–44 (1985) [emphasis supplied].

entering legally regulated relationships. It is as though the law wanted to ensure the image of atomized, freely choosing persons inside the legal transactional spaces of commerce and property. In those arenas it set boundaries which were both enabling and confining (as in Contract or Property Law). The law was more cautious, however, in setting rules for the more intimate confines of domestic households or family relations. There, the legal boundaries were set at a higher threshold: threats to external public order, through Criminal Law. Only slowly were the more private, non-transactional, non-consensual interactions of Tort Law developed.

Finally, the universality of the law within a given geographic territory was an important political tool of nation-building. Overcoming local differences and local aristocratic controls may have been one of the few articulable goals of the developing national legal systems. Clear, universalist legal norms served the purpose well, advancing broad political goals along with Enlightenment philosophies of personhood and human progress. The format of discrete behavioral rules thrived. So much, in fact, that legal professionals can scarcely imagine them now broadening to include stronger cultural context.

Left on their own, legal systems now seem unlikely to devise significant procedural or intellectual reforms that would reliably widen popular access or appeal. It is difficult for lawyers to relinquish the specialized vocabulary and procedures they have labored to master, and which for them carry necessary precision and rigor. The use of legal terminology and analytical methods imply, for many, a mandate of professional ethics. Relaxing the exactitude of language or classification not only feels sloppy, but also raises fears of liability for professional negligence. What may seem to outsiders as small, sensible steps inside private transactions, like adding supplemental visual icons or explanatory charts and graphs to a commercial contract, can raise instinctual discomfort in lawyers, even indignation. At minimum this is not how they were trained, they may say, and at worst it suggests to them an abdication of professional judgment or authority to unreliable popular interpretation. Things are no easier on an institutional level: the decentralized nature of many national judicial systems and diffusion of authority over procedural reforms impedes significant structural changes.

Hence it is not easy for legal thinking or judicial systems to bend toward contemporary trends. And the opposite also seems true. Popular culture is unlikely to develop a taste for parsing canonical texts as a way of interpreting what is right and good with the world. The hierarchical order and curated discipline of legal thought, plus costly access to decisional structures, seem to differ fundamentally from the vertical, individuated/iterative querying, crowd-source authentication, and elective qualities of the electronic/social media world.

If culture and law are locked in a contest, the players are differently equipped and seem to play in different stadiums. Popular culture can appeal easily, through multiple channels, to emotional and inspirational connections. The law, in contrast, thrives in the rarefied air of rational skepticism. While the cultural can soar rhetorically toward visions of a better future or self-fulfillment, legal systems stress process values, seeking typically only to ensure channeled, probative argument toward narrowly confined questions. Popular culture can elaborate and advocate bold, purposeful social ends. Legal systems settle for—often insist upon—slow accretion of social structure. Popular culture esteems breakthrough creativity in methods, as well as uniqueness of messages. Legal systems seek replicability through strongly channeled rules of proper procedure. Popular culture celebrates winners and victims. Legal systems instead depend on people being willing to self-limit as well as self-defend, affording procedural opportunities toward those who might easily be exploited, even an opponent.

Without some sort of substantial outside intervention or influence, we can foresee more of what we have now: the Rule of Law, as a set of institutions and aspirational ideals, struggling to maintain its cultural stature as a source of wisdom and legitimate authority, with its principles of fair, considered deliberation. One might imagine that two realms of life—a more formally legal and a more everyday cultural—could live peaceably apart, compartmentalized but largely complementary to one another. That does not seem the trend, however. Instead, as alternative social control systems wither or polarize, more and more weight is placed on the shoulders of the legal system, to address universally an ever-wider array of problems for which it is not well suited.

We thus turn, in Sect. 3 below, to one possibility for softening that polarity: a way for legal systems to broaden the scope of their judgments to reflect larger possibilities urged by contemporary culture. We propose using AI as a non-binding advisor for bringing stronger context, pattern recognition, and remedy supervision to legal judging.

3 What Can We Do? Seeking a "Constitutive Rationality" Through AI

As explored above, our inherited legal systems are the handmaidens of the Enlightenment outlooks on personhood, truth, authority—with their attendant ideas about human agency and social progress. Legal and Enlightenment values evolved together and are together being stressed by modern life. It is difficult to tease one from another, leading to these questions: can we engage in a strong re-design of legal assumptions and methods, perhaps aided by technology, without threatening the underlying Enlightenment thought that underpins the Rule of Law? If we tried to design a bridge toward contemporary human understandings, what would that be and with what risks?

The question is not new. Fifty years ago, Harvard law professor Lawrence Tribe presciently described the need to transcend our prevailing instrumental rationality. By that he meant the transactional mentality which posits a radical separation of ends and means, the idea that humans are far less affected by *how* they achieved their ends, than the content of the goals themselves. Describing this as a "discontinuity" between human identity and the technologies humans have created, Tribe sought a more immanent or "constitutive" rationality based on a starting point assumption of connection, rather than separation, of humans and their objectives. He wrote:

> It has been said that mankind stands today at the brink of a precipice as deep as the three ego-smashing divides that our species has already traversed in its intellectual history. The first crossing, signaled by the Copernican revolution if not earlier, dislodged man from his seat at the center of the universe by establishing a continuity in his perception between the earth he inhabited and the physical bodies he observed in the heavens. The second, heralded by Darwin, dethroned mankind from its secure place at the pinnacle of life by bridging the gap that had separated it from the rest of the animal kingdom. And the third crossing, due largely to the work of Freud, challenged the supremacy and autonomy of the human ego by linking the primitive and archaic in man with the civilized and the evolved. But this sequence is not yet complete.
>
> There remains, it is said, a fourth great discontinuity--that between man and his machines--which must be bridged if man is to live in harmony with his tools, and hence with himself. The only alternative to such unified coexistence, according to this view, is the dilemma of either rejecting man's technologies in Luddite panic--or becoming their slaves.[12]

Recent conversations about Chat-GPT 4 and related generative AI models reflect growing sophistication about what may be an inevitable blending of human identity with tools that enhance our biological capabilities. Ultimately, our sense of personhood as well as of truth and authoritative control may be merged into everyday lives by employing augmented intelligence. Tribe's bridging of the fourth discontinuity—reconciling humans and their tools for thinking as well as affecting environments—may be upon us. We must imagine the possibilities and work toward the best of them. We will not reject AI; it will permeate our lives. We must decide not whether, but how it will shape us. We must decide what we want to be and design institutions of decision making that gradually and durably constitute us accordingly.

We should imagine how AI could reforge a sense of personhood that may work acceptably—morally, politically, and practically—within a legal system that will itself be an intense user of AI tools. And hopefully this emerging personhood will also be assimilated into popular cultural understandings. The process may be reciprocal: the law may soften its Enlightenment assumptions, but so also may popular culture begin to move past its post-enlightenment personhood toward values largely shared with modernized legal institutions. The power of AI may forge reconciliation by, to some degree, remaking both legal institutions and popular beliefs in its own image.

In a few limited contexts, legal methods have historically departed from their focus on de-contextualized, individual human behaviors. In indeterminate criminal sentencing, for example, or in child custody proceedings, courts are faced with a need to "judge the whole person:" personal attributes, past tendencies, predicted trajectories, life prospects, moral reflectiveness, and regard for others. Such inquiries are not part of conventional judicial training, however, and reliance on social worker or psychologist assessments can be strong. Recently, valuable experiments with "problem solving courts" divert guilty-pleading defendants into a quite different style of tribunals that address underlying issues of alcohol or drug addiction,

[12] Tribe (1973), p. 617.

homelessness, or domestic violence.[13] In these state-sponsored courtrooms, judges work collaboratively with helping professionals, and often come down from their benches to speak directly, personally, supportively, and periodically over time with defendants, marking with them their hopeful re-integration into society. Again, however, these courtrooms are out of the norm—and the problem-solving judges sometimes report resistance from their colleagues who remain in traditional courtrooms. "We are not social workers," these more traditional judges sometimes object, explaining that they do not judge persons as embedded in their personal, family, and social histories or life circumstances, and as burdened with psychological vulnerabilities or addictions. In their view they judge instead the discrete behaviors of presumably choosing individuals who are equally capable and responsible for rising above their settings.

Hence environments and their potential causal influences on behavior are not part of the typical judging process—and procedures have not developed to assess them. In truth, judges have struggled with these "judge the whole person" issues, sometimes limiting themselves through strong presumptions that may change with changing cultural beliefs, as in the maternal custody presumption giving way to joint custody under a "best interests of the child" standard. Or judges may impose minimum/maximum sentencing requirements in criminal law to prevent suspicion of arbitrariness or class/ethnic biases.

But the converse is also true: legal procedures have not been well designed to consider options for affecting environmental design. Consider, for example, if the issue is the route that a planned new highway should take to minimize costs or a variety of spill-over effects on existing traffic patterns or neighborhood impacts. Traditional methods cannot easily judge one design proposal against others to optimize outcomes. As detailed in Sect. 2 above, legal processes are instead designed to frame questions as binary alternatives with binary solutions: a boundary has been trespassed, or not; a contract has been breached, or not—and typically with money remedies rather than efforts at in-kind environmental restoration.

A bridge-building AI suggests a stronger *structural* joining of legal institutions with the surrounding culture. The law could be brought to people in far more accessible ways—blunting popular criticisms that legal language seems almost purposefully dense, driving people into the arms of expensive attorneys. A freely accessible summarizing and explanatory generative AI chat could help to bolster broad-based social perceptions of the integrity and fairness of law. People could engage in a dialogue with an official, judiciary-sponsored generative AI site that offers stronger methods of information sharing, easier comprehensibility of the content of the law, and perhaps better affordability of helping professionals and forums.

That much seems relatively easy and non-controversial. It could employ a database of existing precedent, legislation, and regulations within nested

[13] See generally the description and citations in U.S. National Institute of Justice, https://nij.ojp.gov/topics/articles/problem-solving-courts.

jurisdictions. Second, however, I propose something far more difficult, but potentially far-reaching: bringing contemporary culture and probabilistic outcome analysis to the law. The stickiness of legal traditions, we saw in Sect. 2, largely follows from the entrenched Enlightened outlook on human beings, coupled with historical limitations in communication, information retrieval, and predictive technologies. But AI can change each of those. AI can bring environmental antecedents into legal judgments of human behavior, through its powers of causal pattern recognition. AI analytics based on longitudinal studies as well as massive databases of historical instances of similar problems could offer a perspective to legal decision-making that is more like psychology or epidemiology, designed to address patterned root causes as well as immediate symptoms. What, for example, are the correlations and causal connections among mental illness, homelessness, addiction, and child abuse? Or the connections among nondisclosure agreements, non-compete employment contracts, and rates of innovation? Or between intellectual property rights and technology diffusion? Through accessing a far broader range of human normative and policy thought, an LLM-based AI could suggest morally nuanced, non-binary decisions.

Further, AI offers a vastly more efficient technology to monitor long-term, adjustable remedies that historically would have been unthinkable from the standpoint of available judicial resources. Even the nature of the problems that could be considered by courts might expand, as systemic connections become more visible. Sustainability as a value, for example, becomes far more feasible to introduce into court decisions where follow-on consequences of court determinations become more visible. AI's computational powers of alternative scenario evaluation could better enable the judicial determination of multi-variable problems like the highway planning issue, or multi-jurisdictional problems like regional pollution or global climate change issues. AI could even help with thorny "judging the whole person" issues, by moving evaluation of alternative outcomes toward stronger, more objective, assessments of comparable risks.

I thus propose that governmental judiciaries also create a distinct generative and predictive AI system addressed solely to legal professionals, especially judges. It would be purely advisory, not a substitute for human judicial decision making, so as not to jeopardize the formal legitimacy of judgments. Judges could consult it by entering details of a particular controversy, with multiple queries and follow-ups as desired. Conceivably, litigating or even other attorneys could also query the LLM to help with advice about advising clients or finding a possible realistic negotiation range in a dispute. The AI outcomes would offer non-binding opinions, like a law clerk assigned to a judge, about how the case should come out; under what rationale; and with what proposed remedy (or multiple alternative possible remedies) along with suggestions for implementation.

But: the professionally directed database would not be restricted (as in the public-facing legal information LLM above) to existing laws. Indeed, if the database were so restricted its operation would seriously risk consigning judiciaries to perpetuating an ever-more powerful and self-referential status quo. This tendency would become more pronounced as gradually more and more AI-generated content (based on existing laws and case outcomes) joined the database on which the LLM based new advice. The judicial system should therefore strongly resist any urging that AI be employed solely as an efficiency-enhancing search and retrieval system, or even as an easy writing tool. Doing so would be *worse* than the opportunity costs of foregoing the stronger potentials of AI for finding justice in patterns, avoiding future problems, and implementing creative ongoing remedies. It would be worse than all those opportunity costs, because using AI robotically for search and retrieval risks making the law/culture divide ever wider and more insurmountable.

The database from which the judicial assistant based its advice should consciously seek to expand the idea of the legal norm from its individualist, transactional heritage toward a recognition of contemporary connectedness. AI would seek to bring the possibility of constitutive rationality to judicial decisions—a way in which judicial pronouncement could work toward recognizing, and strengthening, the positive bonds of our communities. It could identify risks that we as humans cannot discern. It could identify environmental interventions that, where appropriate, might shift the focus from individual defendant liability toward feasible solutions that might prevent recurrence of the problem for many more people than just this one defendant.

The database would be designed to offer wisdom, beyond pure fidelity to precedent. Clearly, the database could not be completely divorced from existing laws or decisions. Judges obviously must remain within boundaries of predictable stability. But for centuries our most revered judges have found creative ways to see underlying purposes and sensible exceptions in their interpretations of existing laws. Wisdom has always been sought, historically through institutionalized courts of Equity and its ongoing heritage in Anglo-American jurisprudence, and modernly in the interstices of Civil Law systems. That aspiration can be preserved, and hopefully expanded, in an AI tool that helps legal systems speak more saliently to evolving culture. Within the database for an AI assistant, we would want room for the recognition of stronger social purpose as well as more finely grained distinctions in the environments and predictable outcomes of decisions.

For the access-controlled judicial assistant LLM, I thus suggest a database that includes all of the materials of the public-facing database, but also resources arguing policy points, social goals, and evolving values: the full texts of law reviews and journals; the full texts of important daily newspapers, including opinion and analysis pages, and reflective monthly magazines; and the full texts of the thousands of monographs published each year devoted to psychology, human relationships, social and economic conditions, and technical/policy discussions that address particular problems. Such materials contain the serious, diverse reflections of evolving culture, plus identification of chronic problems as well as attempted solutions gone wrong.

The materials could be jurisdiction-limited, as in U.S. only or EU only, etc.; but I would recommend a global database. That would expand the possible inventiveness and readability of a language generative LLM as well as improve the likely accuracy of a pattern-recognition, predictive form of AI. Again, the AI judicial assistant would only be advisory; it should not raise concerns about the formal legitimacy of ensuing judicial opinions, even if those decisions took the AI suggestions into account. The judicial assistant could simply help spark the imagination, conscience, and common sense of judges and attorneys toward decisions that are more effective problem solvers as well as more popularly resonant.

Finally, though, might even an advisory AI system inadvertently pose difficulties for maintaining the Rule of Law? Could its use backfire, undermining confidence in legal systems? In making my proposals I am fully aware of the potential for unintended consequences, especially in matters that may depend on public perceptions. Does consideration of AI suggestions alter any of the fundamental qualities or values of the Rule of Law, either for short-term case decisions or longer-term norm flexibility? Could its use fuel arguments that legal transcendence, formal equality, or due process of law are irrelevant or corrupted?

These are serious issues. But the fundamentals of Rule of Law values, as well as the competency of legal institutions, are arguably strengthened rather than undermined through use of an AI advisor as I have outlined. Expanding the idea of legal norms to include broader and stronger consideration of contexts brings the possibility of a somewhat different, though not inconsistent, legal rationality and order-seeking.

Listening to, and sometimes adopting, an AI recommendation about a case outcome or remedy adds an ecological quality to the traditional taxonomic style of legal analysis. An ecological orientation to the natural world does not fight the idea, or undermine the value of, identifying and classifying organisms through taxonomy. Taxonomy and ecology simply pay attention to different data, and sometimes ask different questions. Taxonomy advances knowledge by bringing known classificatory attributes to an identified plant or animal—as it can to a legal issue. Classification is not useless sorting. It answers the questions: "what is this specimen? And what, therefore, do we know of its structure and functioning?" Ecological connections address different questions with different data. In the natural world it may ask, "how did this specimen come to occupy this niche? How does it contribute to its surroundings? What will it require for this specimen to flourish?" And so also could AI address legal problems differently than traditional courtroom procedures: "How did this case make it to a courtroom? What are the antecedents of this problem? Could the problem have been avoided? To what else is the problem connected, and what might the outcome in this case further affect? What decision in this case might best contribute generally to healthy relationships and human thriving?" These, for me, are the questions of constitutive rationality—asking how individual legal decisions affect us collectively.

Even when adding these ecological, constitutive qualities to legal rationality, the Rule of Law fundamentals would remain stable. As elaborated below, law would still be transcendent; formal equality could be preserved even while real-world disparities could be given stronger consideration; and due process could be enhanced through greater accessibility and the likelihood of future institutional reforms.

"Transcendence" does not mean that norms float disconnected above society, applied obliviously to the diverse contexts in which a norm may apply. Instead, transcendence concerns the relationship of individuals to the law. It is assured by maintaining the principle that *no person is above the law*. Contexts can be variable and affect judgments, even while all persons are subject to the laws.

So also with formal equality: assessing and respecting expanded contexts can be compatible with applying the law even-handedly. Formal equality does not mean that legal outcomes are always the same; it means that *all persons are treated under the law with equal dignity and respect.* Legal personnel at nearly every level have historically enjoyed some degree of discretion, even as the system takes steps to prevent its abuse. As a value, formal equality is one of the few unifying concepts of Western societies. It should be guarded carefully.

Finally, nothing regarding the AI judicial assistant need disrupt the regularity or trustworthiness of legal procedures. Indeed, the public-facing LLM system hopefully would make their operations—both with and without the AI component—more transparent and accessible. Would court outcomes become either less valid or less reliable by using the AI suggestions of the judiciary AI? Would the people subject to the laws be less confident about the legality or risks of their behaviors? I think not. If anything, offering an advisory second opinion to a judge may buffer unconscious biases or otherwise imprudent judgments before they are recorded; use of the AI advisor might lower reversal rates on appeal. Further, if people are confident in the justness and fairness of the system, they will be confident about the risk of their behaviors. Awareness that a community pulse and vast set of past experiences are available for consultation by judges may build public support for the judiciary, not unlike the procedure in some countries of including a public representative who participates formally alongside judges in some proceedings.

Both predictive and generative AI hold promise for the sort of bridge-building between law and culture that has not been possible over the past 300 years. The public-facing AI tool should make information and access to legal systems easier and more affordable. The professional AI assistant should enable more flexible, wide-ranging competencies within the judiciary and associated legal practice. If AI does not currently possess these capabilities, it likely will soon. These new tools are simply too powerful and useful to be ignored, in any domain. We should not design retrieval robots. We should use this breathtaking technology to reach toward something beyond ourselves, something in our collective that we cannot see. That, after all, is what makes the Rule of Law valuable. It is of us, even as it is beyond any one person's grasp.

Liquid-Legal-Waves to Other Chapters, Written by the Editors

Thomas outlines how non-binding generative pattern recognition AI-tools might help to reintegrate law and culture. What might sound "soft" or oriented towards private persons, initially, becomes a pressing business need in *Stuart's* chapter on *"Closing the E-Justice Gap Fed By Lawyerless Micro-Entities."*

As we focus on the opportunities that come with AI and its introduction into the legal ecosystem, it is timely that *Erion* takes us on a journey towards

(continued)

"Decoding Public and Private AI Legal Tech: Autonomy, Liability, Legal and Ethical Risk".

With the big picture around the (positive) effects of AI in Law in mind, the next chapter by *Marcel* focuses on the fundamental pre-condition for that: Data. He discusses the questions around the concept of 'open legal data', i.e. the free access to relevant legal data by any stakeholder: *"Towards Access to Justice through Generative AI and Open Legal Data: Between Utopia and Dystopia".*

References

Barton TD (2016) Re-designing law and lawyering for the information age. Notre Dame J Law Ethics Public Policy 30:1

Dauer EA (2006) The role of culture in legal risk management. Scand Stud Law 49:98

Tribe LH (1973) Technology assessment and the fourth discontinuity: the limits of instrumental rationality. South Calif Law Rev 46:617

Thomas D. Barton is a Professor Emeritus at the California Western School of Law in San Diego. He received his professional legal training at Cornell Law School and practiced law briefly in antitrust and taxation in New York state before beginning a Ph.D. in law at the University of Cambridge, England. His dissertation assessed the constraints and creativity of judicial problem solving, a theme to which he returns in this LLI Rule of Law chapter.

Professor Barton has published many articles, book chapters, and reviews on legal decision making, problem prevention and resolution, legal visualization, artificial intelligence, and contracting. He is the author of *Preventive Law and Problem Solving: Lawyering for the Future* (2009).

Towards Access to Justice Through Generative AI and Open Legal Data: Between Utopia and Dystopia

Marcel Hajd

Contents

Abstract

Interest in ensuring both access to justice and impartial resolutions through legal and justice institutions continues to be crucial, especially in contexts where public legal assistance is limited, self-help and self-representation are common, and outcomes are influenced by legal awareness and capability. The access to justice, influenced by individual, situational, and systemic factors, raises important questions about who can access it and how to improve it for others. However,

M. Hajd (✉)
LexRatio | MARIFARM d.o.o., Maribor, Slovenia
e-mail: marcel@lexratio.eu

K. Jacob et al. (eds.), *Liquid Legal – Sustaining the Rule of Law*, Law for Professionals, https://doi.org/10.1007/978-3-031-78596-2_3

access to justice remains unattainable or unachieved for many who require it for various reasons. With the public release of one of the fastest-growing applications in history—ChatGPT, OpenAI demonstrated powerful capabilities of Generative Artificial Intelligence (Generative AI) through digesting a vast amount of information and generating original and unique content. For legal practice, Generative AI demonstrated that legal problems can be solved differently and with higher efficiency. Generative AI can be used to provide legal assistance not only to legal experts but also to people and organizations who may have limited resources to afford traditional legal services. As a result, Generative AI might help increase access to justice and ensure people and organizations can understand their legal rights and options. On the other hand, Generative AI can help legal professionals provide legal aid services more effectively. The essential condition for training Generative AI models in the legal domain is access to legal data. Ironically, the law generates an enormous amount of legal data and legal content, while access to legal information is often limited for different reasons, this is why access to legal, especially judicial data, plays a vital role. Open Legal Data means anyone can freely access, use, modify, and share legal data for any purpose. Availability of the Open Legal Data can bring many benefits to individuals and society through increasing transparency and by enabling informed decisions by individuals and organizations. However, mere opening of legal data is not enough, since legal information is rarely organized in a way to be ready for machine processing. The obstacles related to the lack of public and free access to judgments and decisions made by courts and other official authorities have long been a concern. It is clear, that training Generative AI on relevant documents, such as judgments and other court decisions, can dramatically improve the accuracy of its responses. We believe that the opening of legal data and Generative AI can together create a powerful alliance in facilitating greater access to justice, but only if other requirements are also satisfied, such as the legal capability of subjects seeking solutions to their legal problem.

1 Introduction

Access to Justice is a critical challenge faced not only by numerous individuals but also many organizations. Our discussion begins with an introduction of Generative AI by unveiling its technical capabilities and limitations with continuation of discussion on its legal problems-solving abilities. Having gained an understanding of how Generative AI operates, our focus will shift to the Open Legal Data, exploring its significance and influence. In the third part, we bring these elements together, evaluating how the combination of Generative AI and Open Legal Data influences can transform the landscape of Access to Justice. The objective of this work is to provide an overview of Generative AI and Open Legal Data in the context of challenges relating to Access to Justice.

2 Generative AI

Recent advancements in Generative AI systems, introduced by platforms like ChatGPT, have reached a stage where their ability to generate textual and visual content is increasingly indistinguishable from human-produced work. The rapid evolution of Generative AI has taken the public by a surprise, particularly due to its proficiency in creative endeavours such as composing poetry and creating artwork. These developments signify a notable leap in the capabilities of Artificial Intelligence (AI) in mimicking human-like creativity and expression. Generative AI is a specific subset of AI used to create new content based on training on data taken from massive data sources—primarily the internet—in response to a user's prompt, or to replicate a style used as an input.[1] Additionally, its capability to generate realistic synthesized representations of real individuals has been notably impressive.[2] Significant advancements in this field also include a substantial reduction in the costs associated with the collection and storage of training data, alongside enhancements in the technology used for constructing large-scale training datasets.[3] The initial methodologies employed in Generative AI were based on a text-to-text paradigm, wherein a user would input a textual prompt or question, and the AI would generate a text-based, often narrative, response. This was achieved by the AI predicting subsequent words, or more accurately token,[4] in a sentence to formulate its reply. Numerous large language models (LLMs)[5] have been developed by prominent Silicon Valley technology companies. These include Google's Language Model for Dialogue Applications (LaMDA or Bard),[6] Meta's Large Language

---

[1] See for example Giorgio Franceschelli and Mirco Musolesi, Creativity and Machine Learning: A Survey, (last revision July 5, 2022), <https://arxiv.org/abs/2104.02726>; Ian J. Goodfellow et al., Generative Adversarial Networks, arXiv:1406.2661, (June 10, 2014) <https://arxiv.org/abs/1406.2661>.

[2] Grossman et al. (2023), p. 8, <https://ssrn.com/abstract=4460184>.

[3] See for example Leo Gao et al., The Pile: An 800GB Data Set of Diverse Text for Language Modeling, arXiv:2101.00027, (Dec. 31, 2020), <https://arxiv.org/abs/2101.00027>.

[4] A "language token" refers to an individual unit of text that has been extracted from a larger corpus during the process of tokenization. Tokenization is the process of splitting text into smaller pieces, which can be words, phrases, symbols, or other meaningful elements, depending on the granularity required by the specific application or the algorithm being used.

[5] Large Language Model (LLM) is a type of artificial intelligence that processes and generates human-like text by learning from a vast database of existing textual content. These models use deep learning techniques, particularly neural networks, to understand and predict language patterns, enabling them to compose coherent and contextually relevant text. LLMs like GPT (Generative Pre-trained Transformer) are known for their ability to perform a variety of language tasks, from translation to content creation, with a high degree of proficiency.

[6] Eli Collins, LaMDA: our breakthrough conversation technology, The Keyword Blog, (May 18, 2021), <https://blog.google/technology/ai/lamda/>.

Model Meta AI (LLaMA),[7] Microsoft's Bing AI (Sydney),[8] and arguably the most renowned, Open AI's Generative Pre-trained Transformer (GPT) series.[9]

2.1 (R)evolution

Although Artificial Intelligence (AI) has become a prominent topic in the public discourse quite recently, its notable surge in awareness can be largely attributed to the launch of ChatGPT[10] in late November 2022.[11] Nonetheless, significant advancements in the field of GenAI can be traced back to early as the year 2010. In 2014, the Generative Adversarial Networks (GAN) framework marked a significant advancement in the Generative AI field, enhancing the creation of authentic-seeming images, videos, and audio. This innovative framework operates through a dual-network system where one network, the generator, creates candidates, and the other, the discriminator, evaluates these against actual data to differentiate between them. On the generative network's side, this leads to generated content that is more authentic. On the discriminative network's side, this leads to new findings about the characteristics that improve accuracy in matching the training data.[12] In 2017, Google introduced the transformer architecture,[13] which was another advancement in computer processing of natural language.[14] Transformers do not require pre-labelled training data and can be trained in parallel, allowing much faster training than previous AI architectures. A multitude of well-recognized models, such as those in the GPT series, have been developed using transformer architectures. Each successive model in this series is trained on an increasingly larger dataset, enhancing its capacity to emulate human language more precisely than its predecessors. Another important change that began with GPT-3 is the use of reinforcement

[7] Introducing LLaMA: A foundational 65-billion parameter large language model, Meta AI Blog, (Feb. 24, 2023), <https://ai.facebook.com/blog/large-language-model-llama-meta-ai/>.

[8] Introducing the New Bing (2023), <https://www.bing.com/new#features>.

[9] GPT-4 is OpenAI's most advanced system, producing safer and more useful responses (2023), <https://openai.com/product/gpt-4>.

[10] ChatGPT is a variant of the GPT-3.5 AI large language model developed by OpenAI, specifically optimized for conversational responses and capable of generating contextually relevant, human-like text across a variety of topics.

[11] OpenAI, Introducing ChatGPT (Nov. 30, 2022), <https://openai.com/blog/chatgpt>.

[12] Grossman et al. (2023), p. 9.

[13] Transformer architecture is a type of model design in machine learning that revolutionized the way algorithms process sequential data like language. It is based on self-attention mechanisms, allowing the model to weigh the significance of different parts of the input data independently, leading to more efficient and effective processing of sequences. Transformers have become the foundation for many state-of-the-art natural language processing models, including large language models like GPT and BERT, due to their ability to handle long-range dependencies and contextual nuances in text.

[14] Ashish Vaswani et al., Attention is All You Need, arXiv:1706.03762, (Dec. 6, 2017), <https://arxiv.org/abs/1706.03762>.

learning,[15] which represent a process where external (e.g. human) feedback is used to change the output of an AI model. In the case of large language models (LLMs), the addition of the reinforcement learning allowed the creator of the GPT models (OpenAI) to avoid having its models produce improper or offensive outputs.[16] At the time of preparing this work, Generative AI continues to evolve, with ongoing research focusing on enhancing the system's efficiency, ethical considerations, and its ability to handle increasingly complex tasks.

2.2 Mechanics of Generative AI

Generative AI models come in many different shapes, utilizing varied statistical and computational techniques to target various modalities, ranging from code and text to audio and video. Within the realm of addressing legal problem-solving challenges, the most pertinent (language) models are those designed to generate new text based on textual inputs. Hence, it is evident that not every Generative AI model is suitable for effectively addressing tasks within the legal domain. At its essence, the operation of a language model is fundamentally focused on predicting the subsequent word (or language token) in a sequence, guided by a context window that consists of preceding words. More specifically, the language model like ChatGPT produces a probability distribution across its entire vocabulary, assigning probabilities to each word, or more accurately language token, to indicate its likelihood of following the established sequence of words.[17] ChatGPT and other similar large language models operate in three basic stages. Initially, the model processes the input sequence of tokens, which represent the existing text, and converts it into an embedding,[18] essentially a numerical array symbolizing these tokens. Following this, the model engages this embedding using typical neural network[19] operations, where values propagate through successive layers in the network, resulting in the generation of a new embedding, or a modified numerical array. The final step involves extracting the latter part of this array to form a different array comprising approximately 50,000

[15] See generally, e.g., Wiering and Otterlo (2012), <https://link.springer.com/book/10.1007/978-3-642-27645-3>.

[16] Grossman et al. (2023), p. 9.

[17] Karan Singh, Principles of Generative AI: A Technical Introduction, Carnegie Mellon University (Tepper School of Business), p. 3, <https://www.cmu.edu/intelligentbusiness/expertise/genai-principles.pdf>.

[18] Embedding is a numerical representation of words or phrases. It transforms text data into a format that the model can process, often as a vector in a high-dimensional space. Each word or phrase is mapped to a point in this space, with the position determined by the word's meaning and context derived from the training data. These embeddings capture semantic relationships, allowing the model to understand language nuances and perform tasks like text generation or sentiment analysis.

[19] A neural network in the context of AI is a computational model designed to process and analyze data in a way that mimics the human brain's approach, learning from examples to make decisions or predictions.

values. These values are then transformed into probabilities corresponding to various potential subsequent tokens. Notably, the number of tokens roughly equals the count of common words in the English language, though only about 3000 of these tokens represent entire words, with the remaining tokens being fragments. A critical point is that every part of this pipeline is implemented by a neural network, whose weights are determined by end-to-end training of the network. In other words, in effect nothing except the overall architecture is "explicitly engineered", everything is just "learned" from training data.[20]

2.3 Generative AI and Legal Problem-Solving

For the legal sector, the emergence of Generative AI models like ChatGPT might signify a more profound transformation than even the introduction of the internet. Much of the work in the legal profession is encapsulated in written form, such as emails, memos, motions, briefs, complaints, discovery requests and responses, and various transactional documents. While current technologies have simplified aspects of this work, for instance, through the use of templates and automated document assembly tools, these advancements have only modestly impacted the majority of legal practices. Contrarily, Generative AI based tools like ChatGPT offer the potential to revolutionize the creation process of a broader array of legal documents and information. Indeed, within just months following the release of ChatGPT, numerous law firms and legal (technology) companies have already begun exploring and announcing innovative applications of Generative AI tools in their operations.[21]

Although chatbots have been in existence for several decades, the advent of advanced language models like GPT-3 has heralded new frontiers for their application across various sectors, including the legal field. These sophisticated models have significantly expanded the capabilities and potential uses of chatbots, opening up a range of possibilities for enhancing services and operations within these industries. Generative AI tools like ChatGPT can be used in a variety of ways in the legal industry. Utilizing tools like ChatGPT in legal problem-solving space extends beyond simply offering content-based answers. It also encompasses the organization and structuring of data based on legal principles. Some potential use cases include:

- **Legal Research**: Generative AI can be used to assist legal practitioners and others seeking for legal help by quickly scanning through large amount of text data and providing relevant information on a given legal topic;

[20] Stephen Wolfram, What Is ChatGPT Doing . . . and Why Does It Work?, Wolfram Media Inc. (Feb. 14, 2023), <https://writings.stephenwolfram.com/2023/02/what-is-chatgpt-doing-and-why-does-it-work/>.

[21] Chris Morris, A Major International Law Firm Is Using an A.I. Chatbot to Help Lawyers Draft Contracts: 'It's Saving Time at All Levels,' FORTUNE, (Feb. 15, 2023), <https://fortune.com/2023/02/15/ai-chatbot-law-firm-contracts-allen-and-overy/>.

- **Legal Document Generation**: Generative AI can be used to generate legal and other law related documents such as contracts and briefs, saving time and effort;
- **Providing General Legal Information and Guidance**: Generative AI can be used to provide general legal information to the public, such as answering frequently asked questions or providing basic legal advice;
- **Legal Analysis**: Generative AI can be used to assist in legal analysis by providing suggestions and insights based on its understanding of the relevant legal rules;
- **Legal Data Structuring**: Generative AI can be used to organize and structure legal data based on the given instructions (e.g. preparing chronology of facts);
- **Legal Data Visualisation**: Generative AI can be used to generate computer code which can be used to generate visual content for easier data interpretation (e.g. creating visual scheme of corporate structure in dot language code, decision trees generation in python language).

Responses from Generative AI models like ChatGPT are surprisingly sophisticated, however they are still incomplete and sometimes problematic. This is why using Generative AI for legal problem- solving should be done with caution, especially in cases which contain a higher degree of complexity and whenever the impact of the result is high. The following section will explore the concept of Open Legal Data and its significance in enhancing the capabilities of Generative AI.

3 Open Legal Data

Following the inception of open data initiatives, there has been a continuous and systematic evolution in the accessibility of governmental data sets. Opening of government data represents an important factor in increasing transparency, participation, and collaboration of citizens and civil society. To the same extent this applies also to the data produced by law, especially by the judiciary. Open judicial data could therefore potentially help to close the justice gap. With other words, data opening is an integral part of open justice. However, considering the amount of data sets being published by legislative and executive branches of government, the progress in opening judicial data sets has been slower than expected.[22] Open Legal Data is a broader concept in comparison to open judicial data, since it includes legal data adopted and published by other official authorities, such as legislation, government interpretations of legislation, decisions published by local communities, statistical data related to the law. In addition, legal service providers produce unimaginable amount of legal data, whereas this data is at most confidential and not accessible to the public. When discussing about Open Legal Data, we will have in mind primarily legal data which is available to the public on valid legal grounds.

[22] Marković and Gostojić (2018), p. 295.

3.1 Open Data Principles

Open knowledge defines open data as “data that can be freely used, re-used, and redistributed by anyone—subject only, at most, to the requirement to attribute and share-alike.” Approach established by Tauber and Lessig suggests eight basic principles when opening governmental data,[23] which can be fully applied also when opening legal data. Data is considered open, when and if particular data is:

- **Complete:** all public data are made available, preferably in electronic information resources and if possible, in bulk;
- **Primary:** data as collected at the source, with the highest possible level of granularity, not in aggregate or modified form;
- **Timely:** data are made available as quickly as necessary to preserve the value of the data;
- **Accessible:** data are available to the widest range of users for the widest range of purposes;
- **Machine processable:** for maximal access, data must be released in formats that lend themselves to easy and efficient reuse with the support of technology;[24]
- **Non-discriminatory:** data is available to anyone, with no requirement of registration, thus the data should not be hidden behind “walled gardens.”
- **Non-proprietary:** data is available in a format over which no entity has exclusive control;
- **License-free:** Data is not subject to any copyright, patent, trademark or trade secret regulation, if not it is important to be clear about what data is available and what licensing (e.g. Creative Commons Licenses), terms of service, and legal restrictions apply.

To summarize above principles, open data must satisfy two main conditions for the data to be considered as open, namely the open data is required to be legally and technically open. Data is often subject to a variety of sometimes conflicting legal regimes (e.g. copyrights, trade secrets, personal data protection, access to public information) and often times voluntarily shared through different contractual mechanism with purpose to establish flexible data ecosystem.[25] Data is legally open, if data licences allow anyone to freely access, reuse, and redistribute the data. Data is technically open, if it is available in a machine-readable format[26] and in a bulk for a price that is not greater than the price of the reproduction. Therefore, open

[23] Eight principles of open government data, (8 Dec. 2007), <https://opengovdata.org/>.

[24] Open Data Policy Guidelines, Open Data Policy Hub, <https://opendatapolicyhub.sunlightfoundation.com/guidelines/>.

[25] Cf. YANIV BENHAMOU/LAURENT TRAN, Circulation des biens numeriques: de la commercialisation a la portabilite, in: sic! 2016, p. 572; JACQUES DE WERRA, Perspective “Inside-Out“. Defis du droit d’auteur dans un monde connecte, in: sic! 2014, p. 206.

[26] Machine-readable format is a structured format that enables automatic data processing and data is available in bulk if the user can download the complete data set.

governmental data is data produced or contracted by the government, including entities controlled by the government, that anyone can freely access, reuse, and redistribute. By analogy, open judicial data represents data produced or contracted by judicial system that anyone can freely access, reuse, and redistribute.[27]

3.2 Open Justice

The foundation of the open justice principle is rooted in common law and in Article 6 of the European Convention on Human Rights, which asserts that "'everyone shall be entitled to a fair and public hearing by a competent, independent and impartial tribunal established by law".[28] The rationale behind the concept of open justice is an important democratic and constitutional principle.[29]

Since common law forms the basis of this principle, it permits the definition to evolve and provides the judiciary with the latitude to apply it flexibly according to the specifics of each case. Open justice principle does not embody merely content relating to public judicial process, but also access to information on judicial records.[30] Opening judicial data sets increase transparency of judiciary that represents integral part of open justice and open judiciary.[31] Therefore, open judicial data is *conditio sine qua non* and important factor that contributes to open justice and open judiciary. As legal technologies continue to advance, particularly in the realm of Generative AI, open judicial data is increasingly valuable for training datasets. Training Generative AI models on these datasets enable Generative AI to more accurately and efficiently predict legal outcomes and offer accurate legal solutions at a greater speed. Consequently, legal knowledge is becoming accessible to a much broader audience. On the other hand, the progress of technology also raises concerns about privacy and national security when opening judicial data.[32] As a consequence, some countries have even taken the extreme measure of banning the publication of certain data analysis pertaining to judicial decisions.[33]

[27] Marković and Gostojić (2018), p. 296.

[28] Open Justice: the way forward, Ministry of Justice (UK), (2023), p. 6, <https://assets.publishing.service.gov.uk/media/645ba3532226ee00130ae5fb/open-justice-cfe.pdf>.

[29] Marilyn (2019), p. 46, <https://doi.org/10.26180/5db803e6bacd9>.

[30] Jiménez-Gómez and Gascó-Hernández (2017), pp. 1–15, <https://doi.org/10.4018/978-1-5225-0717-8>.

[31] Marković and Gostojić (2018), p. 296.

[32] McLachlin, B., Openness and the rule of law, At the Annual International Rule of Law Lecture. Retrieved from <http://www.barcouncil.org.uk/media/270848/jan_8__2014__12_pt._rule_of_law_annual_international_rule_of_law_lecture.pdf>.

[33] In 2019 France prohibited the data analysis to judges rulings', while the violation can lead to up to five years prison sentence. The rule from new article 33 states: "No personally identifiable data concerning judges or court clerks may be subject to any reuse with the purpose or result of evaluating, analyzing or predicting their actual or supposed professional practices." The adoption

To realize the goal of open justice, simply providing open access to judicial data is not sufficient. This is merely the first and probably the most important component among many, and it cannot substitute for other essential aspects of democratic societies, such as strong access to information legislation, whistleblower safeguards, and regulations that uphold the freedom of expression, press freedom, and the right to assemble.

3.3 Open Judicial Data

As the trend of opening the access to government data is becoming commonplace in societies, some courts are still progressively overwhelmed with requests for data access—especially the ones which do not have in place the system for publication of majority of court decisions and are therefore struggling to meet their obligations for disclosure. These requests could be better served by proactively releasing the court data on the web.[34] The minimum standard to achieve transparency, judicial control and principle of public hearing should be publishing majority of court decisions online, excluding the ones which are most sensitive for the involved subject, whereas the exclusions for data publication should be established on legal grounds, carefully weighing the privacy concerns that are central to the debate against the opening of the access to judicial data. Following the eight basic principles on opening of data (see Sect. 3.1 above), such approach requires technical resources for developing and maintaining on-line court decision repository, while having in place the system to anonymize sensitive information (e.g. personal data) in accordance with the applicable laws. Referring to the open data 5-star deployment scheme created by Tim Berners-Lee, simply posting judicial data online in any computer format whatsoever, such as a non-machine-readable PDF (Portable Document Format) scan of a judicial decision, would meet the criteria.[35] For more advanced data processing with aim to transform judicial data into legal knowledge, data should satisfy at least second level according to Tim Berners-Lee model. Second level (second star) means that judicial data is not only publicly available for human eyes but also machine processable, so the user can "directly process judicial data to generate legal texts like summarisations, subsumptions, etc." Some countries like Estonia, Netherlands and Germany are publishing almost all judicial data, while others only summaries from supreme and higher courts decisions, like Slovenia. Furthermore, part of the countries like Greece, additionally publish procedural information such as stage of the procedure, results of appeal, irrevocability of the decision, etc., so not only the

of new law was a result of deviations in judges' decisions in comparable legal matters based on different Legal Technology service providers.

[34] Open Government Partnership, Open Justice: Justice Policy II Open Court Data, (2020), retrieved from <https://www.opengovpartnership.org/wp-content/uploads/2020/12/Open-Justice_Justice-II_Open-Court-Data_Dec2020.pdf>.

[35] 5 Star Open Data. (n.d.), retrieved from <https://5stardata.info/en/>.

judicial decision content, but also supporting data.[36] In terms of machine processability and technical aspect are commonly used formats PDF and HTML (HyperText Markup Language) which are primarily meant for visually presenting legal information without any particular internal structure of data (second star according to 5-star Tim Berns-Lee model). France for example is publishing supreme court decisions in more advanced XML (Extensible Markup Language) format which include information structured in a way to enable easier data transferability between different software systems. Therefore, it is surprising that France imposed certain serious limitations relating to judicial data analysis.[37] From the technical perspective and considering the data maturity level according to Tim Berns-Lee scheme, XML represents third level on the 5-star open data maturity model. The fourth and fifth level represent form RDF (Resource Descriptive Framework) and LOD (Linked Open Data).[38]

Court decisions, case registers, filed document records, and statistical data are being of a paramount relevance. However, not all countries are publishing judicial data equally. The main drawbacks in published data sets include data not being available in bulk, not being available in machine readable formats and not being released in the public domain, not being published with an open license, or not having the publication license explicitly specified. Publishing statistical data about judges and courts is an initial step to accomplish before implementing a full opening of judicial data sets. Some actions to consider for enabling more effective and efficient opening of judicial data sets are anonymisation and redaction of data before their publishing to support the protection of privacy and confidentiality, to publish legal documents and legal data in standardized machine-processable formats, to assign standardized metadata and identifiers to the published documents, to provide

[36] For more information visit: European e-Justice Portal. (n.d.), <https://e-justice.europa.eu/6/EN/national_legislation>.

[37] See Footnote 32.

[38] Tim Berners-Lee's 5-star Open Data Maturity Model provides a simple framework for assessing the quality of open data. Each star level represents a step towards more open, interconnected, and useful data, with the goal of maximizing the ease of access, integration, and reusability of data on the web. (1) One Star: The data is available on the web in any format, but with an open license. It's just accessible online, possibly in a non-machine-readable format like a scanned image or a PDF. (2) Two Stars: At this level, the data is still open but now in a structured format, like an Excel spreadsheet. It's more usable than a simple image or PDF, but not yet in a format that's easily processed by a machine. (3) Three Stars: The data is available in a non-proprietary open format, such as CSV or XML, which makes it easier for machines to process. This is a significant step up in terms of reusability and ease of access for users who want to analyze the data. (4) Four Stars: In addition to being in an open, non-proprietary format, the data now uses standards from the Resource Description Framework (RDF). This means it can be linked to other data to provide context, which is a big step towards the semantic web. (5) Five Stars: The highest level of open data maturity. Here, the data is not only in an open format and linked to other data but also links back to other data. This reciprocal linking enriches the data ecosystem, making it part of a broad, interconnected web of data.

bulk access to documents, and finally to introduce a central portal enabling retrieval and browsing of open data sets from a single source.[39]

3.4 Other Open Legal Data

Even though judicial data is probably the most valuable source to train Generative AI models, it is not the only source of legal data. One needs to take into account also other legal sources like publicly available legal information under different licences, such as legislation and statues, regulatory decisions, legal commentaries, governments gazettes and notices, international treaties and agreements, patents and trademark information, etc. In addition to the publicly available data under open licences, legal organisations control their own private legal information which can also be used to train private Generative AI models for internal usage with the objective to support external clients and thus help to fill the justice gap.

4 Access to Justice

In an environment characterized by a higher demand for public legal assistance than what is available, a common reliance on self-help and self-representation, and an emerging understanding that legal outcomes are influenced by one's legal awareness, confidence, and capability, raise fundamental question, namely who has access to justice and how to enhance this access for others. A significant number of individuals handle legal matters, especially civil ones, on their own. Whether they make use of law, accessing legal assistance and other justice institutions, however, depends on personal, situational, and systemic factors.[40] As a result, access to justice has become a key concern for all involved in the legal sector, including governments, regulatory bodies, bar associations, academics, and educators. The time has come for this issue to gain more attention not only from the people it directly affects, but also for the organisations that cannot afford legal services. The notion of access to justice is two folded. Firstly, under ideal conditions, access to justice should represent a system by which legal subjects would be encouraged to exercise their rights and/or resolve their disputes under the general sponsorship of the state. As a result, the access component of the notion expands not only to access of legal subjects to relevant legal information, but also embodies the access to formally established and recognized systems according to which legal subjects are able to receive an official decision on their rights effectively. Secondly, the systems must lead to a result that are individually and socially just.[41]

[39] Marković and Gostojić (2018), pp. 310–311.

[40] McDonald (2021), p. 696, <https://escholarship.org/uc/item/3qg5249t>.

[41] Garth and Cappelletti (1978), p. 183, <https://www.repository.law.indiana.edu/cgi/viewcontent.cgi?article=2140&context=facpub>.

The notion of access to justice has evolved over time. In its initial and conventional understanding, access to justice was predominantly viewed as the ability to utilize lawyers and court systems. Early access to justice reform thus tended to be focused on providing equal access to lawyers and courts through "top-down" expenditure on legal aid schemes.[42] Later, the concept of access to justice has been extended to include access to legal information, legal education, non-court-based dispute resolution mechanisms and law reform. In the evolving understanding of access to justice, which now extends beyond traditional legal and formal justice institutions to include the influence of non-legal and informal sectors on legal efficacy, there is a corresponding need for a broader empirical methodologies and measurements.[43]

4.1 Legal Capability

Legal capability in its broadest sense represents wider consciousness and understanding of the law and legality, entailing what may be needed to frame, characterize, or perceive law as relevant to troubles of everyday life, in the mundane as much as adversity, and events and circumstances that are potentially justiciable.[44] Legal capability on the more individual level refers to the individual personal characteristics or competencies required to effectively and purposefully function in the legal sphere, including purposeful use of law and legal institutions. It encapsulates the ability to perceive potentially justiciable issues, access or obtain appropriate legal information and assistance, apply law to their circumstances, assess available options, and take appropriate steps to assert and defend rights.[45] What a person can be and do may be affected by a wide variety of factors, such as whether or not they are healthy, are literate, have a well-paying job, live free from violence, have personal efficacy, have trust and confidence in institutions, etc. Having a substantive opportunity to do certain activities—such as acting to effectively resolve legal problems—may in turn depend on having capability in one or more domains. Importantly, capability can also be undermined in multiple ways (e.g., through ignorance, illiteracy, poverty, oppression, starvation, etc.).[46] Aforementioned explanation signals that personal legal capability is in its nature multi-dimensional. Therefore, the mere legal awareness and understanding is not sufficient for legal subject action and resolution. Beyond the legal framework, subjects must also

[42] See generally: Coumarelos et al. (2012), p. 1.

[43] McDonald (2021), p. 708, <https://escholarship.org/uc/item/3qg5249t>.

[44] Sandefur (2016), p. 443; Pascoe Pleasence, Nigel J. Balmer & Catrina Denvir, How People Understand and Interact With The Law, (2015), section v–vi; Hazel Genn, Paths to Justice: What People Do and Think About Going to Law 12 (1999).

[45] McDonald (2021), p. 708, <https://escholarship.org/uc/item/3qg5249t>.

[46] Pascoe Pleasence, Nigel J. Balmer & Catrina Denvir, How People Understand and Interact With the Law, (2015), p. 123, supra note 4.

possess the necessary skills, such as legal awareness or legal literacy, to effectively make use of law, legal services, and the justice system. At its most rudimentary, adequate literacy, language, communication, and information-processing skills are just some of the abilities providing a foundation for legal capability.[47] Moreover, legal capability involves not only the necessary mindset, psychological readiness, and confidence to utilize law, legal services, or the justice system, but also the resilience to persist until a resolution is reached. Another crucial aspect of capability is the access to resources. Resources such as financial, technological, social, and human capital can significantly enhance one's capability. For instance, in legal matters, having more financial resources typically translates into an increased ability to obtain private legal assistance and thus exercise rights more effectively.

Empirical studies revealed that individuals are unlikely to seek legal assistance or try to make use of the justice system unless they perceive the circumstances as somewhat legal in nature and, more broadly, see the law and its institutions as potentially relevant.[48] Among people who seek legal advice, only some people resolve their legal problems, in particular civil legal problems, by purchasing fully bundled casework and representation services from private legal practitioners.[49] On the other hand, in addressing their legal issues, the majority of individuals either attempt to utilize various forms of public legal assistance, including legal information, self-help resources, and legal advice when eligible, managing their justiciable issues independently without any legal aid, or they choose to overlook and endure these issues without seeking resolution. Nevertheless, it should be acknowledged that not all legal issues will simply disappear on their own. For instance, while certain legal disputes might be resolved passively through inaction, this approach often fails if the opposing party in the dispute actively pursues the matter. The actions and outcomes individuals experience in legal contexts hinge on their awareness and recognition of the legal nature of their situation, the potential relevance and benefits of the law, available legal assistance, institutional processes, and options, as well as understanding the steps required to utilize these resources. Additionally, the institutional landscape, particularly the availability and accessibility of assistance, plays a crucial role in shaping how individuals can engage with the law and justice system institutions.[50] We agree with Balmer et al. that legal capability can be divided into four distinctive stages: recognition of issue, accessing information or assistance, resolving the issue, and wider influences and law reform (i.e. law-making and regulatory processes).[51]

[47] McDonald (2021), pp. 704–705, <https://escholarship.org/uc/item/3qg5249t>.

[48] Pascoe Pleasence, Nigel J. Balmer & Catrina Denvir, How People Understand and Interact with The Law, (2015), p. 140.

[49] Coumarelos et al. (2012), p. 1, supra note 4.

[50] McDonald (2021), p. 698, <https://escholarship.org/uc/item/3qg5249t>.

[51] Pascoe Pleasence, Nigel J. Balmer & Catrina Denvir, How People Understand and Interact with The Law, (2015), p. 7, supra note 32.

4.2 User-Centric Approach

Technological advancements, economic shifts, and demographic changes have significantly altered the expectations legal subjects have of services, systems, and institutions. The collection and examination of detailed data on users, customers, and clients across various service sectors have led to a more refined understanding of diverse needs, preferences, and behaviours. This enhanced understanding has prompted a shift from the traditional, uniform "one-size-fits-all" method of delivering legal services and processes towards more customized and adaptable approaches. These new methods are increasingly designed to cater to the specific interests, needs, and situations of niche groups of customers, clients, and users.

The transformation from standard to increasingly segmented and personalized user-centric services and processes is also observed with respect to access to justice issues. Standard "one-size-fits-all" legal service models are now seen as likely to be ineffective and ill-suited to the legal needs and capability of some users. Standard service approaches can also create access to justice barriers and increase service inefficiency, especially when they fail to take account of diverse legal needs and capability.[52] Diversity of experience, handling, and outcomes of a various legal matters suggest that access to justice approaches must be multifaceted. This approach includes the following: legal information and education, self-help strategies, accessible legal services, non-legal advisers as gateways and pathways to legal services, integrated legal services, integrated responses to legal and non-legal problems, tailoring of services for specific legal problems, and tailoring of services for specific demographic groups. A more holistic approach to access to justice involves potentially reshaping legal services and justice systems to target resources more effectively and efficiently, streamline access to justice, and enhance legal resolution.[53]

4.3 Digital Transformation

As the global reach of the internet continues to grow, users are increasingly able to swiftly access and utilize information and data online. One of the strategies to improve court administration is through the adoption of information and communication technologies.[54] Access to information does not only transform the justice system as such, but also the legal services market in general. This includes effectively accessing the untapped market for legal needs and enhancing access to justice overall through the introduction of innovative services. Nonetheless, the digital transition within the justice system and legal services has progressed more slowly

[52] Pleasence, P., Coumarelos, C., Forell, S., & McDonald, H. M., Reshaping Legal Assistance Services: Building on the Evidence Base, (2014), p. 121.

[53] Coumarelos et al. (2012), p. 243, supra note 4.

[54] See generally: Gomes et al. (2018), pp. 480–490.

than initially anticipated.[55] One widely held and repeated prediction is the view that much legal assistance and dispute resolution can, and will, eventually and inevitably move online.[56] Additionally, online legal assistance services can empower people with everyday legal problems and provide access to justice through digital forms of legal help that they would otherwise be unable to obtain in a timely and cost-commensurate way offline.[57] New interactive and responsive technology holds the promise of better supporting self-help actions, legal problem resolution, and access to justice. This mirrors the promise of a successful bottom-up access to justice strategies,[58] which are accessible and affordable for people and organisations. On the other hand, when discussing about top-down approach of digital transformation of the justice system, such as public legal assistance services, the motivation to invest in technological advancements differs significantly. Additionally, this investment is accompanied by added concerns involving the allocation of limited public resources, whereas the use of digital technology in the provision of access to justice services is highly dependent on the availability of and access to technology in specific countries and/or areas.[59] We are not proposing that the bottom-up approach is the only way to increase access to justice and legal services, but merely stating that this strategy of digital transformation has greater potential for wider use, since governments and public legal institutions are normally more conservative and wary of technology and change.

McDonald, Forell, and Wei identified three distinctive evolution phases of innovation in the area of legal self-help resources in the provision of legal self-help resources that point of digital—based[60] and, unbundled[61] legal assistance. First wave of self-help legal resources represents hardcopy formats in form of factsheets, leaflets, step-by-step "do-it-yourself" guide, and the like. Targeted dissemination also sought to facilitate access to and use of legal self-help materials where potential users ware likely to need and seek such material. With more information being produced to help lay users help themselves, the second wave involved the

---

[55] McDonald (2021), pp. 711–712, <https://escholarship.org/uc/item/3qg5249t>.

[56] Susskind (2017), p. 111.

[57] Susskind (2017), pp. 96–100.

[58] McDonald (2021), p. 712, <https://escholarship.org/uc/item/3qg5249t>.

[59] Beqiraj, J., & McNamara, L., International access to justice: barriers and solutions, (2014), pp. 33–34.

[60] This aspect involves the use of digital technologies to provide legal services. This can include online platforms, software applications, and other technological tools that allow individuals to access legal information, resources, and services through the internet or digital devices. The digital approach aims to make legal assistance more accessible, efficient, and often more affordable.

[61] Traditionally, legal services have been offered as a comprehensive package where a lawyer handles all aspects of a case from start to finish. Unbundled legal assistance, also known as limited scope representation, breaks this down. Instead of a full-service approach, clients can choose specific services based on their needs and budget. For example, a client might hire a lawyer only for legal advice, document preparation, or representation in court, rather than for an entire legal matter.

development of more comprehensive and user-friendly materials, including more sophisticated websites, online databases with the focus on making self-help resources more accessible and practical, allowing individuals to take more significant step in handling their legal issues independently. With the second waive the rise of the internet the hardcopy legal self-help materials ware transferred online. Improved Internet connections and performance subsequently saw Web2.0 applications, development of guided pathways to assist self-represented litigants, such as A2J Author and the like, and, subsequently, improved online audio, video, and interactive communication. The third phase, taking place currently, involves the integration of advanced digital technologies and the concept of unbundled legal services. This wave sees the creation of highly sophisticated online platforms, mobile apps, and other digital tools that not only provide information but also facilitate access to specific legal services. Rather than simply reproduce legal self-help material online and use basic decision trees as introduced by second wave, legal self-help blurred distinction between legal information, legal advice and legal resolution while also being capable of integrating triage, tailored legal information and access top expert advice, guiding users through intake, and canvasing possible solutions and resolution. This is partially possible through unbundled legal services, where a client can choose particular services rather than full representation, are made more accessible through these digital platforms. This wave represents a significant shift towards more personalized, flexible, and cost-effective legal assistance.[62] With the rise of Generative AI, the third wave of self-help resources has advanced significantly. Generative AI is concentrating information and knowledge like no other tool before in the history. With the rise of Generative AI in the legal sphere, there is a high demand to make available more of legal data, which is necessary to train its models with goal to produce better results.

4.4 Challenges of Access to Justice

Despite all extensive discussions and ongoing reforms, numerous challenges within legal assistance and the justice system still hinder access to justice, as well as the availability of resources needed to develop a solid empirical evidence base.[63] Next, we will explore various challenges encountered in accessing justice:

- **High Demand for Public Legal Assistance:** demand for public legal assistance exceeds supply in many jurisdictions.[64] Service eligibility and scope are the

[62] Mcdonald et al. (2019), pp. 16–22.

[63] McDonald (2021), p. 716, <https://escholarship.org/uc/item/3qg5249t>.

[64] Source: Civil Legal Aid 101, U.S. DEP'T JUST., <https://www.justice.gov/olp/civil-legal-aid-101> (last updated Nov. 20, 2020) (stating that "63 million Americans qualify for free civil legal assistance" but "50% of those seeking civil legal help are turned away for lack of resources").

primary tools available to public legal assistance within available resources.[65] Due to limited funding tightening of services scope and eligibility usually results in narrowing the areas of law and particular types of legal matters for which legal assistance is available, restricting the level of services provided for different types of legal matters. Public legal assistance service providers typically provide legal assistance in defined areas of law, to certain types of people, and in particular circumstances. For example, legal representation provided under a grant of legal aid in most jurisdictions is mostly provided for criminal matters. Fewer grants of aid are typically provided for administrative, civil, and family areas of law.[66] With hight demand for public legal assistance on one side and tight financial resources, improved understanding of different legal needs and capabilities across the community, what services models "work," for whom, for what, when, and under what circumstances, to what end and at what costs, are vital for building the economic business case for investing in bottom-up legal assistance strategies.

- **Socioeconomic Risks:** Legal problem commonness is normally higher for disadvantaged groups.[67] In particular, legal problems are usually prevalent among those with compounding health and welfare needs, such as those with chronic ill-health/disability, who are single parents, unemployed, and live in disadvantage housing. Individuals commonly identified as socially and economically disadvantaged, socially excluded, marginalized, or living in poverty frequently exhibit a confluence of multiple and complex legal and other needs. Additionally, they tend to have lower personal capabilities across various socioeconomic indicators. Corelation between legal and related needs and socioeconomic risks point towards direction of potential benefits of more intensive and integrated forms of legal assistance to meet the access to justice and legal needs of those at greater risk of multiple legal and related social problems. Therefore, when deciding to whom provide legal services under legal aid programs, one should consider following criteria: reaching those with the highest legal need and lowest capability, joined-up legal services with other services to address complex life problems, provide services on time to minimize the impact of problems and maximize utility of services and the disadvantaged people required legal services that are appropriate to the needs and capabilities of users.[68]
- **Legal Capability**: the most vulnerable to legal problems are those who lack legal knowledge, self-help skills, motivation, confidence, and resources necessary to effectively deal with legal problems without assistance. This results in delayed, crisis-driven help seeking and consequently add additional barriers when

[65] Hagan (2016), pp. 412–413, supra note 94.

[66] Pleasence, P., Coumarelos, C., Forell, S., & McDonald, H. M., Reshaping Legal Assistance Services: Building on the Evidence Base, (2014), p. 13.

[67] Mcdonald et al. (2019), pp. 3–4.

[68] Pleasence, P., Coumarelos, C., Forell, S., & McDonald, H. M., Reshaping Legal Assistance Services: Building on the Evidence Base, (2014), pp. 5–12.

accessing to justice.[69] The strongest predictor of legal problem solving tends to be legal problem characteristics, whereas the demographics are also important.[70] It is perhaps not surprising that having more access to financial and other resources, such as the support of a friend, colleague, or family member who is a legal practitioner, is linked with a higher probability of taking the right action to address a justiciable issue.[71] Higher levels of socioeconomic disadvantage are correlated not only with increased vulnerability to legal issues but also with less effective legal problem-solving behaviours. This includes a greater tendency to ignore or lump together legal problems and to take action without any legal information or advice. As socioeconomic disadvantage increases, the likelihood of self-help action informed by legal self-help materials, such as hardcopy and website materials, has recently been shown to decrease.[72]

- **Growing "justice gap"**: Justice gap represent the gap between those who are eligible for public legal assistance and those able to afford legal assistance privately.[73] In the jurisdictions with public legal aid schemes, an analysis of legal representation status in relation to income or financial resources reveals that individuals who are typically represented in formal dispute resolution processes are often located at either the lower or higher extremes of the financial spectrum.[74] Those in the middle are often called "missing middle". Consequently, a persistent challenge in ensuring access to justice involves accurately identifying strategies to maximize the impact of limited services. This entails assisting a larger number of individuals in ways that are proportionate, appropriate, and effective, while simultaneously ensuring that public resources are not diverted away from supporting the most disadvantaged.[75]
- **Unbundled Public Legal Assistance**: In the traditional lawyer—client relationship, lawyer takes on the carriage of a matter and acts on the client's instructions, usually from the beginning to the end when solving legal problems or providing legal advice. Considering the hight demand and insufficient number of public lawyers to go around, access to legal services has to be rationalized and prioritized by particular types of matters and people.[76] A prevalent strategy employed by public legal assistance providers to manage the discrepancy between service demand and capacity is the unbundling of legal services. This

---

[69] AUSTRALIAN GOV'T PRODUCTIVITY COMM'N, ACCESS TO JUSTICE ARRANGEMENTS 26 (2014), p. 20.

[70] Coumarelos et al. (2012), p. 1, supra note 4.

[71] McDonald (2021), p. 719, <https://escholarship.org/uc/item/3qg5249t>.

[72] Mcdonald et al. (2019), pp. 2, 8–10.

[73] Mcdonald et al. (2019), pp. 8–10.

[74] Mcdonald et al. (2019), pp. 8–10.

[75] Pleasence, P., Coumarelos, C., Forell, S., & McDonald, H. M., Reshaping Legal Assistance Services: Building on the Evidence Base, (2014), p. 122.

[76] AUSTRALIAN GOV'T PRODUCTIVITY COMM'N, ACCESS TO JUSTICE ARRANGEMENTS 26 (2014), p. 32.

approach, also referred to as "discrete task assistance" or "limited scope services," which involves dividing legal assistance into distinct, separate components. This is how "unbundled" legal services differ from "fully bundled" services, where legal advisors handle all the elements and tasks to achieve legal resolution. Unbundling is sometimes a way how to cut legal costs, but only to those subjects who possess enough legal capacity. Within the realm of public legal assistance, unbundling typically signifies offering only the level of assistance a client is eligible for. This may include providing solely legal information, advice, and minor task assistance, or a combination of these services, depending on the service model employed. Moreover, unbundling is sometimes also approach how to provide some form of legal assistance to more people.[77] With such approach there is ever-present dilemma what is better, to provide fewer people with more "heavier" legal services such as legal representation, or more people with "lighter" legal services such as legal information, legal advice, and minor task assistance. Various unbundled public legal information and education initiatives aim to assist lay individuals in addressing their legal requirements, manoeuvring through the justice system, and independently resolving justiciable issues. And finally, the utility and effectiveness of unbundled legal assistance depends on the ability of people to make effective us of that assistance. As a result, to meet legal needs, unbundled forms of legal assistance have to be sought, obtained, and actually used.[78]

- **Legal Problem-Solving Mindset**: Part of the surveys demonstrated that legal problem-solving behaviour is learned and can become entrenched and persistent. People and organisations who had used legal self-help resources for one legal problem that was solved successfully are more likely to also use legal self-help resources for other justiciable problem. The awareness that legal problem-solving behaviour and capability is patterned at the personal level has important impact on preparing access to justice strategies. Initially, this implies that improving access to justice could, to some extent, depend on initiatives aimed at altering deep-seated ineffective legal problem-solving behaviours, or alternatively, fostering and reinforcing more beneficial behaviours. Secondly, building legal capability and facilitating access to justice for one legal problem can endure and improve legal capability and access to justice for subsequent legal problems. Thirdly, the investment in fundamental legal capabilities, encompassing digital and other methods, to enhance access to justice from the grassroots level is anticipated to yield benefits both at the individual and systemic levels. Individuals possessing basic legal skills are more inclined to recognize and address their legal requirements. Fourth, strategies to increase public understanding of law, assist people to perceive when and how they may benefit from legal assistance, and how

[77] Pleasence, P., Coumarelos, C., Forell, S., & McDonald, H. M., Reshaping Legal Assistance Services: Building on the Evidence Base, (2014), pp. 141–142.

[78] McDonald (2021), p. 719, <https://escholarship.org/uc/item/3qg5249t>.

that assistance can be obtained appear to be beneficial.[79] To sum up, the ability of subjects to excursive their rights and act on legal needs may empower those who could otherwise not afford legal services.

– **Increasing Complexity and Lack of Available Information**: a significant challenge to enhancing access to justice is the lack of available information and data to monitor and assess access to justice and legal need. This issue arises from a combination of theoretical, practical, and technical complexity, as well as resource limitations, which complicate the process of accurately capturing the intricacies and outcomes of user experiences and legal issues. These complexities are necessary to firstly, understand the influence of individual legal needs and capabilities on the resolution and management of legal problems, and secondly, to facilitate a nuanced examination of effective strategies and solutions.[80] The judicial system produces a considerable amount of administrative and operational data. Nonetheless, there exist multiple systemic obstacles in utilizing this data for evaluating access to justice, both from the perspectives of individual users and at a broader system-wide level.[81] Furthermore, these challenges impede the effective evaluation of the impact and outcomes of legislative, policy, and institutional reforms on access to justice.[82] Such data could be used to form policies and tools to solve access to justice problem more efficiently.

5 Conclusion

Generative AI underscores the potential of Artificial Intelligence to impact our daily lives in both nuanced and significant ways. It suggests an imminent reimagination of how we access and create information, as well as obtain legal and other services. As information technology rapidly advances and changes sweep sector after sector, it is increasingly likely that people and organisations will expect legal information to be readily available, inexpensive, and available at a time and in a form that can easily be used to meet their needs. Generative AI is a powerful tool but only to people and organisations with sufficient level of legal capability, and only if the system itself provides reliable and accurate legal response. Latter is possible only and if it is trained on quality legal data, this is why open access to judicial and other legal data is of significant importance. The effectiveness and utility of self-help legal materials seem to be constrained by both the inherent nature of legal issues and the sociodemographic traits of certain user groups. A segment of the population demonstrates limited capability in effectively utilizing these materials, often either

[79] McDonald (2021), p. 728, <https://escholarship.org/uc/item/3qg5249t>.

[80] McDonald, H. M., McRae, C., Balmer, N. J., Hagland, T., & Kennedy, C., Apples, Oranges and Lemons: The Use and Utility of Administrative Data in the Victorian Legal Assistance Sector, (2020), pp. 93–94.

[81] See Sect. 3.3 (Open Judicial Data).

[82] McDonald (2021), p. 733, <https://escholarship.org/uc/item/3qg5249t>.

not attempting to access or use them or finding them unhelpful upon usage. Furthermore, there is an observable correlation where users who deemed these self-help legal resources as unhelpful were also more likely to experience less satisfactory and unfavourable legal outcomes. On the other hand, legal aid and public assistance organisations may use Open Legal Data publicly available and their own private legal information to train their Generative AI models with aim to provide legal support for most disadvantaged groups more effectively and thus supply services to more seekers of legal support. In addition, we are facing an expanding group of "missing middle" which represent a segment of the population that is better equipped with knowledge and skills to use legal self-help materials effectively. This segment of people and organisations can potential utilize well-designed, multifaceted service models that integrate targeted and tailored self-help materials with access to other complementary forms of legal assistance at much more accessible level. Here, Generative AI plays an important role. This observation underscores the significance of employing user-testing ("what works approach") and focusing on human-cantered design principles in the development of information and systems. This realization highlights the necessity for enhancing the ability to tailor legal self-help strategies specifically for distinct user groups and types of legal challenges, while also developing robust methods to assess and track user capabilities and the outcomes they achieve. And especially for the "missing middle" Generative AI has the greatest potential to make law more accessible.

There is a need for more theoretical development and research to explore the interconnectedness of legal capability with other areas, such as digital proficiency. This is particularly pertinent in light of the ongoing shift towards digital legal assistance such as Generative AI and the migration of some justice system processes to online platforms. A deeper understanding of the interplay between legal and digital capabilities will be crucial for evaluating the implications of digital transformation within access to justice in the future.

Liquid-Legal-Waves to Other Chapters, Written by the Editors

Based on current reality in the legal industry, the concept of 'open legal data' that *Marcel* just introduced seems close to a moonshot. Well—if you (seemingly) want to travel to Mars, read *Anita's* fascinating chapter on *"Digital Twins of Law. Embracing Complexity"*.

Marcel's article makes you wonder, how we ever get to overcome the traditional technical beliefs and boundaries in our industry. This is where *Bernhard* comes in, proposing a structured approach to *"Sustainable Digital Transformation as a pre-requisite for Sustainable Law"*—a Sustainable Digital Transformation Framework (SDTF).

If you want to explore a very concrete and practical example of what open legal data and AI-based digital transformation can do, just flip the page to the upcoming chapter by *Stuart* on *"OLRAS: Closing the E-Justice Gap Fed By "Lawyer-less" Micro-Entities"*.

References

Coumarelos C, Macourt D, People J, McDonald HM, Wei Z, Iriana R, Ramsey S (2012) Legal Australia-wide survey: legal need in Australia. Access Just Leg Needs 7:1

Garth BG, Cappelletti M (1978) Access to justice: the newest wave in the worldwide movement to make rights effective. Indiana University School of Law – Bloomington, p 183

Gomes ADO, Alves ST, Silva JT (2018) Effects of investment in information and communication technologies on productivity of courts in Brazil. Gov Inf Q 35:480–490

Grossman M, Grimm P, Brown D, Xu M (2023) The GPTJudge: justice in a generative AI world (May 23, 2023). Duke Law Technol Rev 23(1). Duke Law School Public Law & Legal Theory Series No. 2023-30

Hagan M (2016) The user experience of the internet as a legal help service: defining standards for the next generation of user-friendly online legal services. Va J Law Technol 20:412–413

Jiménez-Gómez CE, Gascó-Hernández M (eds) (2017) Achieving open justice through citizen participation and transparency. IGI Global, pp 1–15

Marilyn W (2019) Open justice in the technological age. Monash University, Journal contribution (29 Oct. 2019), p 46

Marković M, Gostojić S (2018) Open judicial data: a comparative analysis. Soc Sci Comput Rev 38(3) (May 20, 2018)

McDonald H (2021) Assessing access to justice: how much "legal" do people need and how can we know? UC Irvine Law Rev 11(3) (Feb. 1, 2021)

Mcdonald HM, Forell S, Wei Z (2019) Uptake of legal self-help resources: what works, for whom and for what? Law & Just. Found. of N.S.W., Issues Ser. No. 30

Sandefur RL (2016) What we know and need to know about the legal needs of the public. South Carolina Law Rev 67:443

Susskind R (2017) Tomorrow's lawyers: an introduction to your future, 2nd edn. Oxford Press

Wiering M, Otterlo M (eds) (2012) Reinforcement learning: state-of-the-art. Springer

Marcel Hajd is a fully qualified Slovenian legal professional and a LegalTech expert based in Slovenia. With an additional LL.M. in LegalTech from Mykolas Romeris University, Lithuania, Marcel has forged a path at the intersection of law and technology. He currently serves as the General Counsel at MARIFARM d.o.o., where he oversees the legal department, managing a broad range of legal affairs from commercial and corporate to labor law, all tailored to the pharmaceutical industry's unique regulatory environment. In his role, he is responsible for the integration of digitally supported agile methodologies and collaboratively supports the digital transformation of the company.

His professional journey is marked by the roles in distinguished law firms across the European Union, including the United Kingdom, Germany, Austria, and Croatia. These positions have deepened his legal expertise and enhanced his skills in strategic negotiation and effective communication.

Marcel regularly contributes scholarly articles and speaks at conferences in the field of Legal Technology. He is the founder of LexRatio, a Slovenian LegalTech research and consulting institute which goal is to democratize legal knowledge through innovative technology. His commitment to advancing the legal profession is evident through his active involvement in various professional associations and continuous professional development.

OLRAS: Closing the E-Justice Gap Faced by "Lawyer-less" Micro-Entities When They Are Negotiating Commercial Contracts Against Larger "Lawyered-Up" Parties

Stuart Weinstein

Contents

Abstract

This chapter explains the development of an app that is designed to assist micro-entities to address commercial contract legal risk. Micro-entities are the smallest of small enterprises. The impetus to undertake the production of this artefact stems from the need to address the lack of available legal risk management (LRM) advice tools for them. Micro-entities have significant problems when dealing with trading problems arising from the purchase or sale of goods or services between an individual and the business or with another business and constitute more than half the legal problems they face. It is in this spirit that Online Legal Risk Advisory Service (OLRAS) was developed. It follows the lines of a 1980s legal expert system using Prolog and "if-then" rules. Some preliminary insights which need to be confirmed by beta testing indicate the potential of OLRAS to be used as a tool that micro-entities can use to "lawyer up"

S. Weinstein (✉)
Aston University, School of Law and Social Sciences, Birmingham, UK
e-mail: s.weinstein@aston.ac.uk

K. Jacob et al. (eds.), *Liquid Legal – Sustaining the Rule of Law*, Law for Professionals, https://doi.org/10.1007/978-3-031-78596-2_4

against larger organisations with sophisticated legal functions. Once this further work is done, OLRAS could assist micro-entities in engaging in self-evaluation of their legal risk exposure in the context of negotiating commercial contracts for the purchase or sale of goods and/or services. As micro-entities cannot afford legal advice and usually enter into commercial agreements with larger enterprises without the benefit of LRM guidance, an app that can help closing this e-justice gap cannot come too soon.

1 Introduction

> No firm is too small to be sued, face other legal problems, or have risks that can eat up its resources and keep the owner awake at night. No firm, therefore, is too small to use [a] model for legal risk analysis.[1]

A micro-entity is defined as a small business that must meet at least two of the following conditions: (1) annual turnover must be not more than £632,000; (2) the balance sheet total must be not more than £316,000; and (3) the average number of employees must be not more than ten.[2] A large-scale survey of 10,228 small businesses in England and Wales completed in July 2021 (LSB 2022 Small Business Legal Needs Study) identified that trading problems, e.g., issues arising from the purchase or sale of goods or services between an individual and the business or with another business constituted more than half the legal problems they face.[3] Of the 5.5 million small businesses in England and Wales, micro-entities appear worse off across a series of measures in terms of having their legal needs met in that they are least likely to use professional help, have the lowest legal capabilities, and report worse outcomes.[4] Given this need, the development of a legal app that can help micro-entities address their unmet legal advice needs and assist them to undertake rudimentary legal risk analysis without the use of lawyers might help such micro-entities even out the score when negotiating commercial contracts against much larger companies that do have lawyers on hand to draft and negotiate such commercial contracts. There are other areas where this disadvantage plays out besides the area of legal negotiation power, most notably in the ability of organisations to evaluate real time data to engage in prospective risk analysis essential for long term planning.[5]

[1] Johnson and Swanson (2007), p. 29.

[2] Companies House (2023).

[3] Legal Services Board (LSB) (2022), p. 10. Available at: https://legalservicesboard.org.uk/wp-content/uploads/2022/05/20220406-Small-business-legal-needs-FINAL.pdf.

[4] Ibid.

[5] Marks (2022).

When the term "e-justice"[6] is used in this context, it refers to the responsibility of legal practitioners to ensure that digitalisation facilitates access to affordable legal expertise for micro-entities to ensure that the contracts these micro-entities enter into with vendors and customers are fairer and more efficient.[7] While "e-justice" is traditionally seen as a civic obligation to ensure digital access to courts and the justice system, the e-justice domain incorporates the duty to harness law and case-law through AI and other innovative information technology services and make it available to the general public. This function drove the development of legal expert systems decades ago in the 1980s and it is the driving force behind the development of OLRAS today.

An explication of (1) what is legal risk management (LRM) and (2) why micro-entities would benefit from engagement with this app as opposed to using other apps offer legal guidance to micro-entities is necessary at this point. LRM involves identifying issues such as legal liability and compliance failure, mitigation, and the balancing of risk in all forms.[8] The key point about the relationship of LRM with the risk management function is that it enables lawyers to set out to identify and tackle an organisation's overall legal risk, not simply specific manifestations of it arising in cases or transactions, important though they may be.[9] For an organisation such as a micro-entity which would have not have regular access to legal expertise, the app is designed to awaken the need in such an organisation to see the management of legal risk as a task separate and apart from dealing with legal problems as and when they arise on an ad hoc basis. The impetus for the development of this app stems from the author's work as the British Standards Institute subject matter expert to International Standards Organization (ISO)/Technical Committee 262 - Working Group 5 which developed this standard which was published in 2020 as BS ISO 31022:2020 (ISO 31022).[10] ISO 31022 is designed to "help organisations meet the legal and regulatory requirements, manage contractual risk, enhance the organisation's strategic decision-making and improve the organisation's capability of handling complex legal environments."[11] Management of legal risk involves more than meeting compliance obligations but going further and integrating legal governance (the management of legal concerns within an organisation) into the risk management function so that the organisation's culture and how it addresses everyday business operations are transformed.

OLRAS was developed along the lines of a 1980s legal expert system using Prolog (a general-purpose computer programming language used for developing

[6] Council of the European Union (2023).

[7] See Schwartz and Sepe (2023).

[8] Weinstein and Wild (2013), pp. 11–44.

[9] Whittaker (2003), pp. 5–7.

[10] ISO (2020).

[11] Ibid.

complex applications in the field of artificial intelligence)[12] (AI) whose main strengths are for symbolic rather than for numerical computation[13] and "if-then" rules ("the 'if-then' structure is at "its simplest, the 'IF' acts as a condition and the 'THEN' acts as a consequence").[14] Further evaluation is needed through beta testing with a representative sampling of the very micro-entities the app is designed to help. While in-house legal advisors recognise the potential of OLRAS as a tool that micro-entities can use to "lawyer up" against larger organisations with sophisticated legal functions, some limitations were raised with respect to OLRAS. OLRAS is not a machine learning (ML)[15] based AI where algorithms mine large datasets to uncover—or "learn"—latent rules and patterns that may help inform some future decisions. As such, it is not deep learning[16] (DL) (a subset of ML) which operates by learning (nonlinear) relationships between several input variables to produce predictions as accurately as possible by combining smaller neural networks together to form larger ones to tease out the complex and granular relationships between these inputs and outputs.[17]

A combination of a rules based expert system such as what was developed by OLRAS with an added element of natural language processing (NLP)[18] tools that takes advantage of recent developments in ML and DL would offer greater knowledge and accuracy when working with data such as contract language so that this data can be mined for additional insights to enable micro-entities to evaluate contract terms and conditions on their own. Moreover, while OLRAS seeks to provide qualitative holistic advice on likely exposure to unwanted situations due to poor positions in contract negotiations, the ability for it to engage in more rigorous quantitative legal risk analysis[19] would be a valuable addition to OLRAS to help it

[12] For purposes here, the most applicable definition of AI we found was contained in the *New Scientist* which "simply means software used by computers to mimic aspects of human intelligence." See Revell (Undated); Nilson (2010) defines AI as "activity devoted to making machines intelligent, and intelligence is that quality that enables an entity to function appropriately and with foresight in its environment." See Nilsson (2009), pp. xiii–xvi.

[13] Bramer (2013), p. vi.

[14] Neyland and Möllers (2017), pp. 45–62.

[15] ML is an automated process of discovering correlations (sometimes alternatively referred to as relationships or patterns) between variables in a dataset, often to make predictions or estimates of some outcome. Liebowitz (1995), pp. 601–607.

[16] DL is a new name for an approach to AI called neural networks which is a means of doing ML in which a computer learns to perform some tasks by analysing training examples. See Hardesty (2017).

[17] See Gillani et al. (2023), pp. 99–111.

[18] NLP involves gathering knowledge on how human beings understand and use language so that appropriate tools and techniques can be developed to make computer systems understand and manipulate natural languages to perform the desired tasks. See Chowdhury (2003), pp. 51–89.

[19] Legal risk is often identified as a subset of operational risk, and when such losses that may be related to litigation or legal disputes need to be captured in many organisations it will be in the operational risk event database and it must be considered in the risk and control self-analysis and scenario analysis activities. See Girling (2022), p. 308.

even out the score with micro-entities that can easily weaponize data to the detriment of these micro-entities. If OLRAS can address some of these issues in the future, it could prove an agile armamentarium that micro-entities can use when they step into the legal lion's den and face off much larger and better-resourced opponents and help close the e-justice gap when addressing legal risk challenges their businesses face.

2 Research Methodology

This chapter is one of a series of published outputs the author is producing as part of research on the use of legal expert systems (an area that was once at the centre of AI and law in the 1980s) to assist organisations in the evaluation and treatment of legal risk.[20] The first question that comes to mind is, namely, with all the developments taking place in AI, e.g., generative AI (Chat GPT) and extractive AI (Google's featured snippets), why is this research focused on what some may see as a such a quaint (and perhaps dated) type of computer program that uses AI to simulate the judgment and behaviour of a human that has expertise in legal risk analysis.[21] The growth of the Internet in the interim period (between the 1980s and today) has only increased the need for this sort of app. It is not enough that legal information be widely available (as it is over the Internet) but a mediation of the space between providing knowledge of the law and making the law more useful and usable by non-lawyers[22] may be available on offer through a legal expert system. Moreover, when such legal expert systems are combined with more advanced AI techniques that can mine data or recognise patterns so that outcomes may be predicted can put non-lawyers in a position that could be comparable to collaborating one-on-one with a lawyer. More work needs to be done in incorporating the value that NLP advances in recent years to make appropriate connections between the information the end user inputs into the interface, e.g., contract drafts, and the output retrieved from evaluation of this language against large data sets that contain comparable materials that might offer insights that can be extracted or generated from what is contained from these large data sets.

[20] See for instance Weinstein (2022).

[21] See Pilling (2023) where the author argues that the legal expert system is just coming into its own with no code platforms, more advanced NLP, integration with ML algorithms and explainable AI all of which bring heretofore unavailable exponential advances in their development and capability. See also Matheson (2023). Matheson argues that expert systems and their component 'decision trees' are readily adaptable for use in the legal sector with reasonable efficiencies in contrast to artificial neural networks (ANN) which may offer greater potential overall but are far harder to adapt in current practice settings at this point. For more on the state of AI in legal practice, see Jackowski and Araszkiewicz (2023).

[22] See Noel (2015), pp. 245–267, who argues that the "unbundling" of legal services through the Internet through legal advice sites may close the "e-justice gap" but there are problems when such advice is offered without professional constraints.

Legal expert systems are computer programs that incorporate a legal knowledge base ordered by an inference engine that provides specific solutions to legal questions as output in answer to the input of a set of legal issues and facts.[23] It is not novel to suggest that expert systems for legal decision making (a subset type of legal expert system) may have applicability in the management of legal risk. In the related discipline of risk management, expert systems are already in wide use where they incorporate decision-support programs containing a large body of knowledge from field experts[24] to assist risk managers "base their decisions on the synthesis of a broad body of knowledge which makes the field ideal for computerization."[25] A rule-based legal expert systems such as OLRAS gives the user the information as to what questions should be asked to solve a legal problem, rather than an actual solution to such concrete problem.[26]

The methodology employed here is that of applied research done in the form of developing an artefact, namely, a software program that models legal risk decision-making tasks. Applied research is directed primarily towards a specific, practical aim or objective using the existing stock knowledge with the appropriate methodology towards the resolution of a practical problem.[27] OLRAS is a prototype LRM expert system designed to be evaluated by a community of practitioners and users. While we have developed the artefact, a full-scale evaluation by practitioners and users has yet to be made. Such a large-scale examination of the efficacy of OLRAS to assist micro-entities to self-assess their legal risk profiles in respect of commercial contract matters needs to be done to further develop OLRAS and adjust it before it can be made available for general use. In this section, we set forth what is it we are attempting to accomplish with our work on OLRAS, how we intend to achieve it, what has been done thus far and what needs to be done.

Increasingly, technology is advanced as a potential solution to the unaffordability of conventional legal services.[28] And with the cost of legal services placing them out of reach for micro-entities and small to medium-sized enterprises (SMEs) in every circumstance except the direst ones, it becomes clear that cost is a massive driving force in the development of legal apps such as OLRAS. However, a pitfall in the process of developing legal apps is that they are "usually provider-driven, reflecting the interests and beliefs of those offering the service, rather than the wants and needs of the intended user populations."[29] Participatory design in the development of a legal app is optimal and it involves actively consulting and collaborating with a wide range of stakeholders in a system to understand their perspectives and incorporate

[23] Tantisripreecha and Soonthornphisaj (2016), pp. 315–328.

[24] Kangari and Boyer (1989), pp. 40–48.

[25] Jablonowski (1992).

[26] Bench-Capon (2012), pp. 11–20.

[27] de Mello and Wood (2019), p. 338.

[28] Scassa et al. (2020), p. 1.

[29] Sandefur (2019).

their priorities into system innovation.[30] Hagan (2017) states the problem more bluntly: "Lawyers aren't very good at getting non-lawyers to use their stuff...if you just build cool tech, you might get some lawyers in your circles to use it and love it—but you won't get wider adoption among lay people."[31] While the goal of a legal expert system is "really the robotisation of lawyers - that their skills and knowledge could be easily formalised, and that as a process was at heart a quite simple operation – if you knew the rules, then you could give advice,"[32] one must be realistic as to what can actually be achieved with apps like OLRAS. In the next section, we examine the legal design process involved with the development of OLRAS.

3 The Legal Design Process

This project is an outgrowth of a research project centred around an effort to establish what practice exists now that constitutes the assessment and treatment of legal risk by in-house lawyers using an LRM Expert System. To have a better understanding of what an LRM Expert System is and how it can assist in-house lawyers and other legal professionals as well evaluate to legal risk, an attempt was made to develop a prototype LRM Expert System that was to be evaluated by a community of legal practitioners and non-lawyer businesspersons who can assess its strengths and weaknesses from a practical perspective. An essential starting point for this discussion is a recognition that the author's background is that of a lawyer and that he does not have expertise as a coder or in legal design. While coding and design remain distinct skills and roles that are different from that of being a legal expert, there is an expectation that as the driving force behind this project the author will have equipped himself "with the necessary knowledge – or literacy – to seamlessly partner with and mediate between multiple perspectives and facilitate the successful interfacing of human and machine."[33] Human-centred design has long been the province of visionary product and systems designers but, realistically, this has never been the strength of a majority of lawyers.[34] Concern for user experience combined with an experimental and iterative approach to developing new solutions in legal risk should guide the design of this project.[35]

An optimal approach to the design work behind this project would be (1) to identify the core user requirements of micro-entities who might want to assess their own contract legal risk position without access to lawyers, (2) to define the key points of failure in undertaking contract legal risk analysis for micro-entities without

[30] Hagan (2019), pp. 120–127.

[31] Hagan (2017).

[32] Leith (2016), pp. 94–106.

[33] Corrales Compagnucci et al. (2022), pp. 421–444.

[34] Jackson (2016), pp. 82–97.

[35] Hagan (2018), pp. 199–239.

access to lawyers, and (3) propose a new app that could improve users' contracting experiences.[36] In terms of examining user needs, the author set about to examine the needs of micro-entities through individual conversations with micro-entities. Three micro-entities were introduced to the author by Aston University's Business Engagement Operations team who the author contacted for discussions.

Before speaking with potential end-users such as micro-entities to ascertain their needs, my employer, Aston University, who sponsored the research had concern as to whether any app or tool that would be produced would be offering end-users *legal advice* as opposed to *legal guidance*, or *legal information*. Legal guidance and legal information were seen as acceptable and would not expose Aston University to potential legal liability for offering legal services to the public. However, providing legal advice was seen as being too risky to offer as Aston University does not provide legal services to the public except in a very restricted and highly controlled environment through its Law Clinic. An Aston University created app that was freely available over the Internet where anyone could access it for legal advice was seen as being incompatible with the legal risk profile set by Aston University's Legal Services team. Thus, a clear instruction was given that the app could not offer "legal advice" but only "legal guidance" or "legal information."[37] *Legal information* is any information on a legal issue that is made available through the app that is not tailored to specific circumstances or an organisation. *Legal guidance* is where legal information is provided and specific knowledge, skill and/or expertise is applied to a generic legal issue. *Legal advice* applies where specific skill and expertise is applied to the same legal information considering the specific legal issue of the organisation seeking the advice and response is tailored to their specific requirements. Now with the institutional constraints as to what sort of legal output could be delivered through this app was resolved, the next step was to go out in the field and talk with micro-entities directly.

The author's decision to build a LRM app for the use of micro-entities was made *a priori*. Originally, the concept was that an app would be developed that would be suitable for use by in-house legal departments of any size to assess their own legal risk exposure. However, this soon proved to be a *fool's errand* as there were so many different sized organisations operating in different industries that it would be impossible to offer a *one size fits all solution*. Moreover, these legal departments are staffed with lawyers and legal operations teams and will have access to a variety of law firm and industry developed contract management, compliance systems and risk management tools many of which might be industry specific so that developing such an app for their use would be *like carrying coals to Newcastle*. Second, the author needed substantive rules upon which to build his expert system. While the author had thought that producing an app using actual language from ISO 31022:2020 would offer a framework and text for his app this route was not feasible given the

[36] Hagan (2018). This approach is adapted from the approach recommended at pp. 200–201.

[37] A clear explanation of the difference between legal advice, legal guidance and legal information can be found here: Michalsons (2020).

intellectual property rights management policies of ISO which would not allow for quotation of text from their standards. Moreover, the ISO standard covers several categories of legal risk, e.g., legal, regulatory, and contractual matters, and from non-contractual rights and obligations[38] and the transposition of such complex and lengthy guidelines into an app format was beyond the scope of what would be reasonably achieved given the timeframe available, the expertise of the author, the capacity of the software development team and the funding available for this project.

As if to confirm the author's hunch about the need to focus the app on micro-entities and their legal risk needs, the LSB 2022 Small Business Legal Needs Study was published. The key findings include a recognition that small businesses face a significant access to justice gap in that only a quarter of small businesses used professional help in response to legal issues while around half either sought to resolve their legal issues entirely on their own or took no action at all.[39] The study also noted that one-third of small businesses experience a legal issue annually with trading issues being the most common.[40] And, finally, and perhaps most important to this task was the fact that micro-entities appear worse off across a series of measures in that they are least likely to use professional help, have the lowest legal capabilities, and report worse outcomes.[41] The LSB 2022 Small Business Legal Needs Study framed the essential issues that the author needed to discuss with the micro-entities he was going to speak with as part of the legal design process. More specifically, the author was going to focus on how these micro-entities handle contractual legal risk faced in their day-to-day operations and how the app could help these businesses shape their contract negotiations so that they could "score points" against larger companies when negotiating contracts for the sale or purchase of goods/services without access to a lawyer.

Once the author was able to complete legal design talks with the three micro-entities it became clear that the points the author wanted to focus on were the same issues that they deal with when they enter contract negotiations. Most importantly, these micro-entities found that they were frequently given contract forms with language that they did not understand and that they did not have access to a legal advisor at a price point they could afford who could help them parse the language, rewrite it to their advantage and make the terms less one sided against their interests.

An additional issue that arose from the discussions with the micro-entities is that none of the micro-entities owners the author spoke with understood what is meant by "LRM" and why this is different from "legal advice" that they may receive from a solicitor or legal advisor. The author explained that 'legal risk' involves a threat and the possibility of suffering harm or loss or the risk of any penalty resulting from

---

[38] ISO (2020) BS ISO 31022:2020 Risk management - Guidelines for the management of legal risk, 3.2. Available at: https://www.iso.org/standard/69295.html.

[39] LSB 2022 Small Business Legal Needs Study, i.

[40] Ibid.

[41] Ibid.

non-compliance with legal requirements or from a losing a court action.[42] It means that "all legal advice should be risk-based and offer options for mitigating or avoiding risk."[43] The author was keen to frame the OLRAS app as a tool for proactive lawyering as "a way of fusing legal foresight and proactive (or preventive) legal skills with business management, especially with enterprise-wide quality and risk management."[44] The analysis OLRAS intended to offer was to be a combination of a more general enterprise-wide LRM which defines the overall risk criteria of the micro-entity involved which then can be used in a more specific risk assessment in relation to the specific contract being evaluated with the results of the contract specific risk analysis being a valuable input and feedback to the enterprise-wide process.[45] Of course, however, this approach proved too complex to design from a programming perspective and would require a systematic approach to risk management that many micro-entities lack. Thus, it was decided that OLRAS would operate in the manner of a traditional legal expert system whose knowledge consists of *facts* that constitute the rules of contract law and drafting and *heuristics* "that are the mostly private little-discussed rules of good judgment (rules of plausible reasoning, rules of good guessing)" that characterise expert-level decision making in contract legal analysis.[46] What OLRAS will do is to capture the domain knowledge from a legal risk expert with 35 years' experience in the field (the author) and provide legal guidance to micro-entities taking into account the author's heuristics to ensure a high level of accuracy and consistency on contract workflows for a wide-variety of micro-entities.[47] The use of such a legal guidance expert system could provide micro-entities with advantages in terms of increased contract making efficiency, supply greater consistency and accuracy, resulting in cost savings, and giving such micro-entities a competitive advantage.[48]

The marked difference in the way micro-entities dealt with legal issues as opposed to small businesses made it clear that the need was to develop an app exclusively designed for micro-entities. In the United Kingdom (UK) there are approximately 5.47 million small businesses (with 0 to 49 employees) constituting 99.2% of the total UK business population.[49] Of these 5.47 million small businesses, 4,061,035 had no employees, e.g., sole proprietorships, and an additional 1,187,045 had only 1 to 9 employees.[50] When these figures are correlated with the findings of the LSB 2022 Small Business Legal Needs Study, this finding stuck out and made the business case for an app aimed exclusively at micro-entities:

---

[42] UK Government Legal Department (2015).

[43] Ibid.

[44] Haapio (2006), pp. 149–194.

[45] Mahler and Bing (2006), pp. 338–357.

[46] US Department of Commerce (1982), p. 2.

[47] Pilling (2023) *Op Cit.*

[48] Ibid.

[49] UK Department for Business, Energy & Industrial Strategy (2022), pp. 3–4.

[50] Ibid.

> When responding to a legal issue, 8% of small businesses took no action, while 44% sought to resolve it entirely on their own. Small businesses with one employee were more likely to seek to resolve their issue entirely on their own when compared to businesses with 2-9 employees and 10-49 employees. Small businesses experiencing trading issues were most likely to deal with the issue entirely on their own.[51]

The LSB 2022 Small Business Legal Needs Study also found that the difference between one employee and 2-9 employee businesses was also marginally significant.[52] This finding was confirmed anecdotally by a discussion the researcher had with one of the micro-entities who had a trading dispute involving a contract with one of their suppliers.[53] When the micro-entity owner (a sole proprietor with no employees) approached a local solicitor in her town for a demand letter to be sent to their supplier in respect of the contract the fee quoted was £500 plus VAT at 20% (£600) which was simply unaffordable.[54] This conversation (and the discussions with two other micro-entities) led the author to conclude that the original intent to design an app for use by small business legal departments to assess their own contract legal risk needed to be set aside in favour of developing a suitable contract LRM app for the use of micro-entities. While small businesses (other than micro-entities) could afford contract risk management tools and obtain legal advice for specific legal problems on an "as and when needed basis," micro-entities struggle to find contract risk management tools scalable for their businesses and they cannot afford legal services at all. As part of the legal design process, it is useful to think of what types of tools are out there that might be available for a micro-entity to use to analyse their existing contract requirements. Corrales Compagnucci et al. (2022) note that incoming AI tools promise to help anyone—lawyers and clients alike—to prepare, review and monitor contracts and legal documents.[55] Some examples of the sort of services that are currently available on the include LegalSifter,[56] Maigon,[57]

---

[51] LSB 2022 Small Business Legal Needs Study, 33.

[52] Ibid.

[53] Phone conversation with Micro-Entity 1 held 15 August 2022. The owner requested anonymity in these circumstances.

[54] Ibid.

[55] Corrales Compagnucci et al. (2022) *Op cit.* p. 423.

[56] LegalSifter claims to negotiate contracts faster, affordably, and safely with its own self-service AI-powered app that provides contract guidance in a minute or two starting at a monthly cost of $28 a month. https://www.legalsifter.com/. LegalSifter® acquired Akorda on 18 September 2023 which was one of its competitors that offers contract lifecycle management (CLM) software. Akorda's CLM software claims to "supercharge contracts with AI, enabling enterprises to complete agreements faster and with less risk." See https://www.akorda.com/about-us.

[57] Maigon AB is a Stockholm based AI-driven contract review space that incorporates both GPT-4 (unveiled by OpenAI on 14 March 2023) for specific tasks and insights while relying on its in-house AI models to maintain the highest levels of accuracy and performance. https://maigon.io/.

Lawgeex[58]and LegalZoom.[59] Wolters Kluwers has Legisway Analyzer which is an extractive AI tool which helps a legal department automatically find and extract key data points in a large number of contracts and integrate it "in a single click."[60] These services make use of what Surden (2021) describes as an ML algorithm that is trained on sample contracts that have been properly categorized and labelled and that is capable of assisting with tasks such as identifying types of clauses across contracts, highlighting legal obligations, and extracting key terms, parties, or provisions.[61] The key here according to Surden is having computer algorithms that can reliably perform such analysis on natural language contracts which "is not a trivial task, given the variable, non-mechanized type of language in which it is composed."[62]

Many of the commercial contract review programs described hereinabove incorporate GPT-4 (OpenAI, 14 March 2023) which is described by OpenAI (2023) as a DL "large multimodal model (accepting image and text inputs, emitting text outputs) that, while less capable than humans in many real-world scenarios, exhibits human-level performance on various professional and academic benchmarks."[63] GPT-4 is seen as an improvement over its predecessor GPT-3.5 and it outperforms other state-of-the-art (SOTA) existing large language models (LLMs).[64] Nonetheless, GPT-4 like other SOTA LLMs "still is not fully reliable (it "hallucinates" facts and makes reasoning errors)"[65] and as such "great care should be taken when using language model outputs, particularly in high-stakes contexts, with the exact protocol (such as human review, grounding with additional context, or avoiding high-stakes uses altogether) matching the needs of a specific use-case."[66]

---

[58] Lawgeex is contract review automation (CRA) technology that claims to harness the power of AI to help in-house legal teams automate the contract review process during the pre-signature phase. CRA is designed for routine, high volume, low-to-medium complexity agreements such as non-disclosure agreements, service level agreements, statements of works, framework agreements, supply agreements, and others. CRAs work off an entity's existing playbooks and/or existing contracts so that new contracts can be assessed against positions such as standard and fallback language. See https://www.lawgeex.com/.

[59] LegalZoom offers Doc Assist on a free basis as part of a beta test. Doc Assist reviews small business-related contracts and other agreements in text-based pdf format that are less than 5 MB in size that are intended to be used within the US. See https://www.legalzoom.com/ai/doc-assist.

[60] Wolters Kluwers - Legisway Analyzer - https://www.wolterskluwer.com/en-gb/solutions/legisway/contract-review-for-legal-departments.

[61] Surden (2021), p. 177.

[62] Ibid. p. 177.

[63] OpenAI website, Research GPT-4. Available at: https://openai.com/research/gpt-4.

[64] Ibid.

[65] Ibid.

[66] Ibid.

3.1 Legal Zoom

Of these different applications available, the LegalZoom Doc Assist is the only one designed for someone who might need an occasional contract reviewed under the assumption that the person seeking the advice is someone who might run a micro-entity and would lack any sort of legal training or experience. Doc Assist is a beta test so there is no cost to use it at the present time. When the author uploaded a simple consulting agreement of 10 pages in length, the analysis offered by the LegalZoom Document Summarizer was to offer key facts and figures (names, dates, parties, length of contract term and sums involved), signatories, etc.), it identified twelve key contract provisions (Introduction, Scope of Services, Independent Contractor Status, Warranties and Representations, Compensation and Payment Terms, Term and Termination, Intellectual Property Rights, Confidentiality, Indemnification, Dispute Resolution, Notices and Assignments) and then it asks ten common questions and answers such as: what are the terms, covenants, and conditions of the engagement, what services will the Consultant provide to the Company, etc.[67]

The beta then offers for a fee legal document review whereby an attorney (it is a US based service only) will review your legal docs or the customer can pick from a library of more than 150 customisable legal forms. While there was no legal analysis offered, the key facts, breakdown of the twelve key contract provisions and the ten common questions are useful to give an end-user a better comprehension of the contract they need to have reviewed.

When one considers what is out there on the market for contract review and guidance, we see that the current SOTA approach to contract review programs involves the use of LLM DL algorithms that can engage with NLP review of contract language working massive datasets. Generative AI such as GPT-4 augments what companies have developed in house themselves with their massive datasets however the hallucination problem has not been resolved. While these CRM or CLM systems are optimal for use by in-house legal departments with legally trained minds available, they are not feasible for micro-entities to use if they lack legal training. A costly price point (subscriptions can go into hundreds of pounds a year) and scalability (the algorithms are trained with sophisticated lawyer-drafted documents, not the sort of documents that micro-entities need advice on in their day-to-day workday environment) point to the difficulty of using sophisticated CRM or CLM systems in the SME or micro-entity context. Finally, some micro-entities will struggle with a lack of technological capacity to use such online CRM or CLM systems proving the point that simpler solutions are essential for micro-entities.

---

[67] LegalZoom Document Summarizer Report for Consulting Agreement dated as of November 1, 2018 between TO Pharmaceuticals LLC and Broom Street Associates LLC (Consulting Agreement) available at: https://www.legalzoom.com/ai/doc-assist/documents/DOC-aExm4BXilsGD. The Consulting Agreement was a publicly available document available on JUSTIA (https://www.justia.com/) which is an American website specializing in legal information retrieval. Justia has been in business for 20 years.

3.2 Legal Utopia

In the UK, there is one app that performs a similar function to OLRAS aimed at a similar sort of clientele—small businesses and that is Legal Utopia.[68] Legal Utopia is an app for SMEs and individuals that uses AI to identify "more than 400,000 everyday legal problems through its Legal Checker function, and provides more than 5,000 legal documents, 24,000 FAQs and 10,000 pages of legal guidance."[69] Legal Utopia uses ML technology based on NLP which it claims can now identify the nature of a legal problem after the user inputs 100 words.[70] When the author used the Legal Utopia app to assist in identifying a legal problem namely *whether force majeure terminates a contract by operation of law as opposed to mutual agreement of the parties*, the technology asked me to identify my position the response the author chose was, e.g., "There is no issue or formal dispute at the moment, but I would like more information about a particular issue." It then asked the author the problem's status, so the response chosen was, e.g., "I am looking for advice to solve, or avoid, potential issues now, or in the future." Once the information the author typed in on force majeure was entered in the form of questions with the amount in total being limited to 100 words the result came out as follows: The Legal Checker AI identified the issue of force majeure and came up with an explanation of the specific area of legal practice involved (Contracts) and some general guidance on the topics and links on the Internet to find further resources. After this, legal help in the form of a selected range of lawyers that can help with the issue. After the list of lawyers was provided, a request for feedback on the result found and the service offered was requested based on a scale of one to five stars.

The author's impression of Legal Utopia was that its use of ML and its ability to search the data it has in its store enabled a quick response offering a general explanation of what force majeure was and where further guidance could be found on the Internet specific to English law. The app also has available forms and templates to use such as those for contracts for instance which might offer appropriate language to use if drafting of an agreement is required. In the estimation of the author, Legal Utopia provides a quick easily accessible and well-constructed legal app that could assist a micro-entity to find out appropriate legal guidance, resources, forms and templates and legal advisors to assist them to address legal issues.

3.3 Legal Beagles

A final legal resource for micro-entities in the UK that needs to be mentioned is the Legal Beagles website.[71] Legal Beagles is a free discussion forum, founded in May

---

[68] Legal Utopia website, available at: https://www.legalutopia.co.uk/.

[69] Rose (2021).

[70] Ibid.

[71] Legal Beagles website, available at: https://legalbeagles.info/.

2007, that provides legal guidance and support to consumers and SMEs across a range of legal areas. Information and forms are available on the forum; for those individuals or SMEs who wish personalised legal advice for themselves or their business this is available from the Legal Beagles team on a sister website on a fee-paying basis https://justbeagle.com/. The forum is a knowledge sharing exchange with information posted by members of Legal Beagles team and forum subscribers. It is a first stop resource for micro-entities that might want legal guidance on a variety of SME related issues including trading and contract matters.

4 Development of the OLRAS App

It is not so straightforward to develop a legal expert system from scratch as envisioned here. Huttner and Merigoux (2022) write of legal expert systems that "after more than 30 years of existence, they have now acquired all the general characteristics of legacy code: use of obsolete technologies, no longer taught in university courses, loss of expertise on critical portions of the source code, as original programmers retire, and a "plaster on a wooden-leg" approach to modification and maintenance."[72] What emerges from the design process is a recognition that a rule-based system that stores legal knowledge as rules and reasons directly with these rules through formal logical deductive and inductive methods[73] is the optimal way to present necessary legal guidance to micro-entities with respect to contract issues. Such an effort to design a LRM expert system requires a combination of expertise in knowledge engineering, the law and software architecture.[74] Muthuri et al. (2022) refer to this as the ITxLaw misalignment, namely, that the law is unable to keep pace with technological innovation and technical experts may be able to appreciate overarching legal principles but they may not be able to condense them to fit new scenarios.[75]

Dimyadi et al. (2019) identify the steps by which the legal expert system replicates the lawyering process through three main steps: firstly, the gathering of information via a machine based "interview"; secondly, the testing of that information against the logic built into the system; and thirdly, the generation of a report that provides an answer or some form of guidance.[76] The model for a rule-based system typically follows an "if–then" flow process that develops a solution based on alternatives.[77] The system designer must build in the laws, institutional knowledge and the "rules of thumb" that lawyers may use when addressing client requirements

[72] Huttner and Merigoux (2022), pp. 1–23.

[73] Dove (1995), pp. 1–28.

[74] Stevens et al. (2010).

[75] Muthuri et al. (2022), pp. 27–55.

[76] Dimyadi et al. (2019), pp. 93–111.

[77] Ibid. 97.

and then once this is done they then can proceed to the actual coding of the system that may then begin once the design parameters have been developed in detail.[78]

The plan was to start by building a simple prototype and then after review, build a more elaborate and complex version. OLRAS was designed to be an exemplar on how an LRM Expert System can be developed to help micro-entities to undertake their legal risk self-service assessment. It was also designed to be used as a teaching tool to train students to assess and evaluate legal risk exposure and advise such legal risk can be mitigated or eliminated. It was the author's original vision that OLRAS would be built to cover all the different elements of legal risk covered in ISO 31022: 2020 guidelines for the management of legal risk, namely, legal risk related to legal, regulatory, and contractual matters and from non-contractual rights and obligations.[79] The monumental size of such a task was indicated by the fact that the ISO 31022:2020 guidelines in and of themselves run up to 31 pages of single space pages including several annexes. The incorporation of so much "law" into an expert system would require hundreds of hours of programming time that could not be realistically achieved in the period and budget we had even if we were able to secure the intellectual property rights to ISO 31022:2020 from ISO. A more realistic solution was to focus on the legal risk elements micro-entities face when negotiating a contract for goods and/or services as a buyer or seller.

It is not without irony that the original plan for the design of OLRAS had to be amended because it implied too much risk and that is legal risk. First, my employer was not comfortable with the legal risk of OLRAS offering legal advice as opposed to legal guidance on the Internet without appropriate clinical controls. Second, ISO 31022:2020 is proprietary to the ISO and they are rightfully concerned that the text of its standards could be copied and used by others for commercial purposes without paying appropriate licence fees. Thus, in this regard, not only does the legal design process address how to incorporate LRM into the app being designed but the very design of the app raises legal risk at several levels and has had an impact on the legal design itself.

The need to avoid "boiling the ocean" when developing an app was explained to the author in the first development call with the system developers from Logic Programming Associates (LPA).[80] The work of LPA in the development of

[78] Ibid. 97.

[79] ISO (2020) - ISO 31022 – Risk Management-Guidelines for the Management of Legal Risk (ISO 2020) available at: https://committee.iso.org/sites/tc262/home/projects/published/iso-31022-guidelines-for-implem.html.

[80] Phone conference – 23 May 2022 - Clive Spenser and Alan Westwood. LPA was formed in 1980 to exploit the results emerging from the logic programming research team of Prof. Bob Kowalski at Imperial College, London, which, among others, included Brian D Steel, Clive Spenser, Diane Reeve, Phil Vasey, Paul French, and Jonathan Briggs, all under the directorship of Keith Clark and Frank McCabe. Since then, LPA has continued to develop and market advanced software tools and is a leading supplier of commercial software products and solutions in the areas of expert systems and artificial intelligence. Source: LPA website, "About LPA." Available at: https://www.lpa.co.uk/hom_lpa.htm.

OLRAS stems from their expertise in working with logic programming. Logic programming is different from that of conventional programming languages such as C++ and Java with the Prolog language being widely used for developing complex applications in the field of AI especially in the form of expert systems which are programs that 'reason out' the solution to complex problems using rules.[81] Leith (2016) notes that "Prolog became extremely influential in the UK, and was seen as offering a core methodology for .... legal expert systems...and was, in effect, perceived in the UK as the *de facto* standard for this kind of legal application..."[82]

Bramer (2013) notes that while Prolog is a very powerful facility for building programs to solve complex problems involving reasoning, Prolog programs themselves are simple in form with only three elements needed for logic programming: facts, rules and queries.[83] Another advantage of Prolog is that "in many cases algorithms that would require substantial amounts of coding in other languages can be implemented in a few lines in Prolog."[84] LPA makes available to the general public versions of Prolog for Windows, DOS and Macintosh on its website where its long involvement with Prolog can be found.[85] OLRAS makes two uses of Prolog. First, it uses Prolog to help parse and extract the (cell) data from the spreadsheet and populate a dynamic but generic questionnaire. Second, at run-time, Prolog is used to analyse the answers and work out what goes on the next screen (i.e., typically next questions and/or calculate scores and draw conclusions and results.[86]

LPA provided the programming expertise and the author functioned as the legal expert who provided the questions and answers for the expert system to address. A no-code or low-code software development platform entitled VisiRule which was developed by LPA was used to assist in the development of OLRAS. VisiRule is a graphical tool for non-programmers to develop and deliver rule-based and expert systems simply by drawing their decision logic:

> As a result, potentially complex business logic can be elegantly and clearly represented in a diagram comprising of interconnected boxes. These diagrams are easy to construct and quick to test. By laying out complex logic in a simple and coherent way, expertise can be shared and communicated with colleagues in a non-technical and platform independent manner. VisiRule charts are simply self-contained diagrams; they can be exported to and displayed within other applications such as Word, Acrobat, etc.[87]

The questions and logic behind OLRAS may evolve and be modified based on continuous review and user feedback. Even though OLRAS is a rule-based system it

[81] Bramer (2013), pp. v–vi.

[82] Leith (2016), pp. 94–106.

[83] Bramer (2013), p. viii.

[84] Ibid, ix.

[85] See http://www.lpa.co.uk.

[86] Email from Clive Spenser to Stuart Weinstein – 4 October 2023.

[87] LPA Website, "About VisiRule." Available at: https://www.lpa.co.uk/vsr_det.htm.

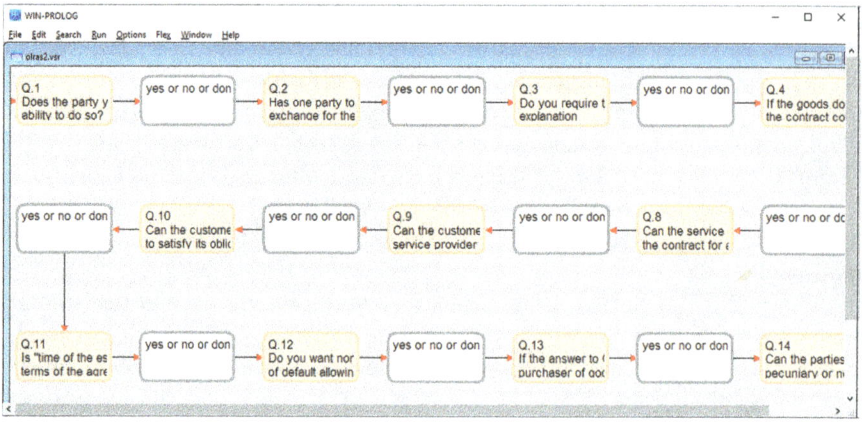

Fig. 1 Screenshot of VisiRule visualisation generated for OLRAS (Source: Technical Report: Designing a Legal Risk Management Expert System to Evaluate Contracts for Micro-Entities (10 October 2024))

incorporates longstanding heuristic rules based on longstanding English contract law practice with LRM guidance but when these rules change updating work can and will be done.[88]

An example of a VisiRule visualisation generated for OLRAS can be found in Fig. 1 which is a reproduction of a flowchart generated by VisiRule in constructing OLRAS which maps out the process of answering the questions posed to users of OLRAS and mapping out response options along a "yes", "no" or "don't know" generating options based on each of these results. It is reproduced from a technical report on OLRAS that was produced by Stuart Weinstein and Clive Spenser[89]which offers a full explanation of the steps involved in the development of OLRAS. OLRAS itself and further explanation on how it works can be found on the OLRAS webpage platform located on the Visirule website.[90]

The original working premise of this project was to harness rules-based AI to provide OLRAS for micro-entities who lack affordable access to in-house or external LRM expertise to ensure that they are compliant and adhering to best practice. The purpose of OLRAS will be to help organisations assess and treat legal risk efficiently to meet their LRM obligations in contract risk. OLRAS will help provide these SMEs an appropriate tool to assist them to establish the relevant internal and external criteria for legal risk so that proper identification, analysis, and evaluation may be made to improve their operational performance by reducing legal risk through a self-evaluation process. In hindsight these objectives were too ambitious and require restatement considering what was realistically achievable. It was only

[88] Dimyadi et al. (2019), pp. 93–112.

[89] Weinstein and Spenser (2024).

[90] OLRAS. Available at: https://www.visirule.co.uk/visirule-demos/olras.

when the author sat down with the programmers did he get a sense for what was possible and what was fantasy.

While it is true that OLRAS does harness rules-based AI for micro-entities, and it might be useful for micro-entities who lack affordable access to in-house or external LRM expertise, it is not a compliance tool that ensures organisations are compliant and adhering to best practice. Such a tool would require an understanding of a particular organisation's existing technical infrastructure and current state analysis as a starting point.[91] Without an *ex-ante* analysis being done and the establishment of a bespoke control framework criteria such a compliance tool would not appropriately calibrate to the specific needs of the micro-entity it is designed to assist. Moreover, such a LRM compliance tool would benefit from the ability to assess quantitative data on a real-time basis as opposed to manually inputted information. In either case it is not clear that a micro-entity would be capable of assembling such data on their own or would be capable to assemble it in such a fashion as to enable a quantitative assessment mechanism.

It remains true that the purpose of OLRAS will be to help organisations assess and treat legal risk efficiently to meet their LRM obligations in contract risk. This it achieves to a certain limited extent. If a micro-entity uses OLRAS with a specific contract in hand and follows its steps it will receive legal guidance on how to avoid certain elements of legal risk associated with entering into the agreement. It may not be a full-scale quantitative analysis of legal risk, but it may offer some qualitative legal risk insights with respect to the particular contract at hand and when OLRAS is used. While the app does require to a certain extent "a self-evaluation process" in that a user must assess its economic position, the economic position of the other party entering the contract and the overall value of the contract itself, this is by no means establishing the relevant internal and external criteria for legal risk which requires a much broader and systematic evaluation. As such, the idea that OLRAS will enable a micro-entity to undertake a proper identification, analysis, and evaluation of legal risk to improve their operational performance is overstated. The tool helps an organisation assess from a LRM perspective some of the risks an organisation faces when it enters a specific contract, but such analysis will not in and of itself improve operational performance which requires a much more dynamic engagement with the micro-entity on a consistent basis over a period to achieve such improvements.

Granada Ribeiro (2021) writes "qualitative, heuristic judgment has until recently reigned absolute in the minds of lawyers and judges alike. Why has law "evaded" quantification thus far? One reason might lay in methodological barriers recently lowered by technology."[92] The way OLRAS was designed and how it operates is that it provides guidance on exposure to unwanted legal risk situations. However, the approach taken to legal risk is to offer a holistic qualitative approach because there is a lack of data from the micro-entities using OLRAS to derive anything meaningful in

[91] Papazafeiropoulou and Spanaki (2016), pp. 1251–1263.

[92] Granada Ribeiro (2021), pp. 51–67.

the way of statistics.[93] For instance, Annex D of ISO 31022:2020 suggest that quantitative analysis of legal risk consequences can be performed through use of a risk matrix by subdividing categories such as legal risk training, counterparty risk, categories, enforcement of laws and type of business activity into a spectrum ranging from no adverse consequence to severe consequences with an organisation developing its own weighting system to fit its needs.[94] This could be done but it would require each micro-entity that would use OLRAS to assemble meaningful data to back up construction of accurate and well-founded probabilities which cuts against the grain of how such micro-entities operate.[95] Even though risk matrices such as that suggested in ISO 31022:2020 have wide acceptance and some advantages, whether such risk matrices succeed in actually leading to improved risk management decisions is another matter.[96]

An excellent discussion on the nature of quantitative LRM was held between Alex Siderenko and Sam Savage as part of their RISK-ACADEMY—risk management and risk analysis blog.[97] Siderenko (2023) made the point that legal risks are often overlooked in risk registers because people are hesitant to document them due to the potential for court cases, similar to taxation risks; Savage notes that legal risks can be quantified in a risk register by simulating the potential conditional VAR[98] for each high-level legal issue, as it is an ideal metric to use in stochastic linear programming. Muthuri et al. (2022) focus on the following research question, namely, on how to identify and assess the impact of a legal risk on a business model in order to apply a specific legal interpretation to mitigate the risk.[99] In their analysis, Muthuri et al. (2022) conclude that there is difficulty with the quantification of legal risk in start-ups (a cohort not wholly dissimilar from our micro-entities) given that the perceived value of compliance is low among startups and that even with elaborate value modelling tools such as the value management platform it is challenging to estimate the legal risk.[100] They propose that future work needs to be done to develop a general method for quantification of legal risk in conjunction with either statistical or rule-based NLP methods.[101]

It was agreed between the author (the legal risk expert) and the programming team (Spenser and Westwood) that OLRAS would:

[93] Email from Clive Spenser to Stuart Weinstein – 4 October 2023.

[94] ISO (2020), BS ISO 31022:2020 Risk management - Guidelines for the management of legal risk, 3.2. Available at: https://www.iso.org/standard/69295.html.

[95] Email from Clive Spenser to Stuart Weinstein – 4 October 2023.

[96] Cox (2008), pp. 497–512.

[97] Quantifying Legal Risks: How to Make a Quantitative Risk Register - ChanceTALK 25 (2023). Available at: https://youtu.be/XKm5Yzf1Om4.

[98] Value at Risk.

[99] Muthuri et al. (2022), pp. 27–55.

[100] Ibid. 50.

[101] Ibid. 50. See also Kiriinya (2017).

[a]. ask general context questions
[b]. use [a] to determine which categories need examining, e.g., legal, regulatory, and contractual matters, non-contractual rights, and obligations, etc. and what their relative priority is [here for the prototype on contractual matters were covered]
[c]. ask the questions in the various question groups within each category [contractual matters only]
[d]. evaluate the answers by generating scores per question, per group, and category (see the discussion of the scoring algorithm which follows below
[e]. weights in the form of key risk indicators (KRIs) data points can be applied to consider the relative priorities of each category (which is influenced by the current business context)
[f]. make recommendations and pointers to useful resources can be provided per question, per group and per-category
[g]. online help can be supported by attaching explanations to individual questions (i.e., why is this question being asked, what is so important about this?)
[h]. document templates can be used to produce output documents that report on the session, answers, scores, and advice given.

While it was envisioned having 5 or 6 categories that would involve criteria such as KRIs that could assist in assessing elements of legal risk qualitatively or quantitatively depending on the elements of risk to be assessed, it was not implemented for the prototype but thought it might be better to implement in the event a second more sophisticated iteration was made.

Categories of law would include [as appropriate] national or international law such as statute law, case law or common law, administrative acts, regulatory orders, codified law, judgments and awards, procedural rules, memoranda of understanding, or contracts. OLRAS focused exclusively on contractual risk, simple black letter English contract and sales of good law with the recommendations incorporated into the analysis offered.

Duties and responsibilities such as best practice, soft law, and guidance will also have to be considered.

Additional guidance will be provided in the form of sound commercial practice guidance on contract management, etc.

Each category will have 4 to 6 groups (areas of interest/concern), each of which will comprise 4 or 5 questions. These questions will be designed to probe further into categories of likelihood, consequences, and evaluation of risk.

While it was discussed, weighting to allow one question or issue to be more important than another was not implemented, so as it stands all questions and all issues impact the score equally producing a "flat" result. This last point might need to be reissued in subsequent versions of the app as the development process becomes more sophisticated to consider that certain issues, e.g., breach of a warranty issue might be more significant and deserve more weighting than an issue of a penalty for late arrival of goods. The ability to assign a score for each answer is advantageous

Table 1 If-then rules

IF	THEN
IF the parties can predict with certainty the damages or loss that would be payable in the event of a breach	THEN the parties can fix a sum to be payable as agreed upon liquidated damages
IF there is information between the parties that should be kept confidential and not disclosed to others	THEN this information should remain confidential after the termination or expiration of the agreement
IF the goods are required to be delivered on a certain date	THEN the party who did not receive the goods on a timely basis should be compensated for this late delivery

from a programming cost and time point of view. A free text input approach would involve writing an NLP system which is not easy to do.

Insight into the nature of legal expert systems can be gleaned from this exchange between the author (the legal risk expert) and the lead programmer (Spenser). When I stated that "what we have done here is taken a set of rules derived from legal risk expertise in contracts and codified them into a set of logical statements that the system can use to reason about new situations,"[102] the lead programmer responded by saying that "I would say instead we have rationalised legal risk experience and expertise and applied it to contracts."[103] Critical to the success of a rules-based legal expert system such as OLRAS is the reasoning engine it employs which is an "if-then" flow process that develops a solution based on alternatives.[104]

Some simple examples of IF-THEN are shown in Table 1.

There was a steep learning curve on the part of the author to learn the 'power' of the algorithmic system to asymmetrically divide relevant data from irrelevant data in that the consequences of the algorithmic system (for example, damages should be paid) cannot be achieved without the conditions (a failure to make timely delivery).[105] As one researcher aptly noted, "you know, the rules don't fall from the sky, someone has to specify them... But really, the core of the problem is this... there is a knowledge gap between theory and practice. Experts are capable of certain classifications that you simply cannot imitate with technical means."[106] The caveat to this statement would be that it can take some time before an expert can learn to write in a manner that can be capable of being translated into an "If-Then" statement that can translate into a sound algorithm. One caveat on the implication of "If-Then" statement is that an "If-Then's conditional statement....suggests one more thing: what now?"[107]

[102] Email exchange - Clive Spenser and Stuart Weinstein – 5 October 2023.

[103] Ibid.

[104] Dimyadi et al. (2019), p. 97.

[105] Neyland and Möllers (2017), p. 54.

[106] Ibid., 52.

[107] Kramer (2021).

The starting point for this project was to work off a structure of analysis as suggested by Table E1 - Annex E – ISO 31022:2020 (Key clauses to consider when reviewing contracts) and to rationalise the legal risk guidance one would give in respect of the specific issues raised by each clause taking into accounts the specific dynamics such clauses might give a micro-entity. Once the legal risk expert "signed off" on what would be the required advice, it had to be able to be represented in a spreadsheet with columns dealing with each consideration. This process could be characterised as devising a systematic way of questioning the end-user about existing contracts and making legal risk recommendations based on the above. This gives the benefit of using a single question mechanism as all the questions and answers adhere to the same schema. The result was to codify some rules in a decision table to assess and quantify the answers given. The summary is then generated by using the answers from the initial context questions to determine which text fragments to use using a decision table.

Once OLRAS was completed some preliminary feedback was obtained from lawyers and legal tech specialists who were willing to "test run" the app. Seventeen individuals were solicited to make an evaluation of OLRAS to date but to date only three responses were received.[108] Of the feedback received one response offered extensive commentary and merits reproduction here:

> I think that your app would be a great tool for smaller businesses when reviewing contracts as it provides comprehensive feedback on the importance of clauses and the risk in the absence of them. It is also helpful for those businesses that lack a legal team, as I can understand that sometimes it is difficult to gauge the importance and content of varying different contractual clauses and how to go about negotiating these...I particularly liked how the app let me know that as a large business, we would be well placed to negotiate the contract – as this is generally the case. But it also let me know that the smaller company may get scared away from dealing with us. – I liked the inclusion of this information as it is correct and something we are working on! Often smaller businesses do not have the risk appetite to agree to some of the more important clauses within our contracts (such as indemnities and damages caps).[109]

The fact that out of 20 persons solicited, 17 did not respond at all raises concerns. Can any negative inference be drawn from their unwillingness to engage with OLRAS? Did they find this task too onerous or time consuming? These points remain unanswered. It should be noted that feedback received from individuals is the only way one can gauge the success or failure of OLRAS as OLRAS does not log usage of OLRAS and integrate the data associated with the visitor's session.

[108] Response rate confirmed as of 22 December 2023.

[109] Email from Contracts Manager at Pharma Research Company to Stuart Weinstein dated 25 May 2023.

5 Next Step: Beta-Test

The premise behind OLRAS is to help micro-entities address their unmet legal advice needs and assist them to undertake rudimentary legal risk analysis without the use of lawyers. OLRAS is designed to provide access to e-justice by helping micro-entities even out the score when negotiating commercial contracts against much larger companies that do have lawyers on hand to draft and negotiate such commercial contracts. One significant issue that remains is that a systematic beta testing with micro-entities is needed to fully evaluate OLRAS and offer feedback on what could be improved and what works well. Discussions are underway to collaborate with various institutions, e.g., regional business development agencies, professional regulators, contract management organisations, etc., which would enable a large-scale beta testing rollout of OLRAS and gain greater reach through getting an institutional partner. We believe OLRAS can help with access to e-justice for micro-entities to address the inherent imbalance between them and larger commercial entities they must negotiate against. However, this point may not be confirmed unless and until a full-scale roll-out takes place.

6 Conclusions and Future Work

The premise of OLRAS was that a 1980s legal expert system could assist micro-entities in closing the e-justice gap they face when negotiating commercial contracts against larger more sophisticated organisations that are able to use legal advisors to make the agreements more favourable to their own legal and commercial needs to the detriment of micro-entities. Apart from the immediate next step which is to undertake further evaluate OLRAS through beta testing with a representative sampling of micro-entities, other work needs to be done to improve the app. To use OLRAS to evaluate a contract, a micro-entity must complete a questionnaire that runs about eight pages in length with approximately 40 questions to answer some of which might be too complicated for someone without training in law to answer.

Apps like LegalUtopia and LegalZoom show that adding an ML based capability whereby OLRAS could work with actual contract provisions and mine them for additional insights or provide drafting suggestions could be especially useful for an app aimed at non-lawyers to help them evaluate contract provisions. More work could be done as well to enable micro-entities to self-assess and ascribe their own weighting to questions asked by OLRAS which may not be significant to their business operations or needs. At the present time OLRAS has a "flat" weighting giving each question the same weighting in its scoring algorithm. This does not consider that all issues do not merit same level of importance for every micro-entity using OLRAS. At the present time, OLRAS provides qualitative LRM guidance to the exclusion of quantitative LRM guidance. If beta testing reveals that the ability to add more quantitative tools to the app such as a risk register or the ability to assess conditional probabilities this might worth considering.

OLRAS covered only one small element of legal risk, namely, contractual risk arising from the sale or purchase of goods or services. It is hoped that OLRAS could be expanded to encompass the entirety of the categories of legal risk, e.g., legal, regulatory, and contractual matters, and from non-contractual rights and obligations[110] covered in the ISO 31022:2020 guidelines.[111] Recent research done in the field of AI and law shows the potential of using LLMs to support the development of legal expert systems. For instance, if Open AI's GPT-4 can accomplish the task of analysing legal rules and extracting a formal representation from the processing of legislative text with reasonable accuracy, the same could be done with ISO 31022:2020.[112] By allowing us to leverage the power of LLMs to support the creation of transparent and explainable legal expert systems using rule-based reasoning in LRM we could generate a draft pathway which can then be verified and completed by a legal risk expert.[113]

Several issues have been raised here in conclusions and future work with the idea that if these issues could be addressed OLRAS could prove an added asset to the agile armamentarium that micro-entities can use when they step into the legal lion's den and face off much larger and better-resourced opponents. Undoubtedly, OLRAS needs further work and beta testing with a wide sampling of micro-entities before it can be seen as ready. However, unlike other apps that are already on the market OLRAS offers micro-entities LRM guidance tailored to specific contract provisions that consider the contract's overall commercial value to the micro-entity and the micro-entity overall turnover or balance sheet position. What is unique to OLRAS is that it makes LRM recommendations in respect of commercial contracts utilising a traffic light system and a decision table in a way that enables these micro-entities to conduct their own legal risk evaluation without a legal advisor on hand and enables them to undertake a cost benefit analysis as to whether the benefit of commercial opportunity might outweigh the legal risk associated with accepting some contractual ambiguity.

Liquid-Legal-Waves to Other Chapters, Written by the Editors

Stuart has forced the abstract considerations about the risk associated with AI in Law to the concrete opportunity of addressing the mind-boggling access to justice-gap for the vast number of micro-entities. So, let's see if *Thomas*

(continued)

[110] ISO (2020), BS ISO 31022:2020 Risk management - Guidelines for the management of legal risk, 3.2. Available at: https://www.iso.org/standard/69295.html.

[111] ISO has not nor is it likely to authorise the use of such usage of ISO 31022:2020 for such purposes.

[112] Janatian et al. (2023), pp. 167–176.

[113] Ibid.

answers the question *"Can Artificial Intelligence Save the Rule of Law?"* with a clear 'yes'.

However, supporting the application of generative AI in order to address access-to-justice-gaps does raise very important challenges in deployment. Precision, reliability, quality of results—all of which is fundamental for sustaining the Rule of Law—very much depend on *"Legal Prompt Engineering and How it Will Change the Way Lawyers Work"*, explain *Philipp*, *Valentin* and *Alexander* in their chapter.

If you feel it is time to work through the fundamental challenges and risks that come with (generative) AI in Law, turn the page to *Bruno's* thoughtful chapter on *"AI in the Legal Market: The Dark Side of the Moon"*.

Acknowledgements
The author acknowledges with gratitude the feedback of Professor Tobias Mahler, Jelena Schidzig, and Clive Spenser for their advice and guidance on this chapter. The author appreciates the work of the programming team at Logic Programming Associates (https://www.lpa.co.uk/hom_lpa.htm) consisting of Clive Spenser and Alan Westwood who completed OLRAS on an expedited basis saving Aston University both development time and programming costs. Research funding for the development of OLRAS and subsequent beta testing was provided by Aston University. The author notes with sadness the passing of Professor Trevor Bench-Capon on 20 May 2024 whose work in the field of AI & law and computational models of argument has been a source of inspiration.

References

Akorda. Website https://www.akorda.com/about-us

Bench-Capon T (2012) What makes a system a legal expert? In: Schäfer B (ed) Twenty-Fifth Annual Conference Legal Knowledge and Information Systems, JURIX 2012. IOS Press, Amsterdam, p 19. https://www.research.ed.ac.uk/en/publications/legal-knowledge-and-information-systems-jurix-2012-the-twenty-fif

Bramer M (2013) Logic programming with prolog, 2nd edn. Springer-Verlag, London. ISBN 978-1-4471-5487-7 (eBook). https://doi.org/10.1007/978-1-4471-5487. https://drive.uqu.edu.sa/_/fbshareef/files/logic%20programming%20/Prolog.pdf

ChanceTALK You Tube page (2023) Quantifying Legal Risks: How to Make a Quantitative Risk Register, ChanceTALK 25 (31 July). https://youtu.be/XKm5Yzf1Om4

Chowdhury G (2003) Natural language processing. Annu Rev Inf Sci Technol 37:51. ISSN 0066-4200. https://strathprints.strath.ac.uk/2611/1/strathprints002611.pdf

Companies House (2023) Accounts Guidance, Update 5 April. https://www.gov.uk/government/publications/life-of-a-company-annual-requirements/life-of-a-company-part-1-accounts

Corrales Compagnucci M, Fenwick M, Haapio H (2022) Chapter 23: Digital technology, future lawyers, and the computable contract designer of tomorrow. In: Research handbook on contract design. Edward Elgar Publishing, Cheltenham, UK, p 421. Retrieved Dec 18, 2023, from https://doi-org.ezproxy.uio.no/10.4337/9781839102288.00035

Council of the European Union (2023) European e-Justice Strategy 2024-2028, 17 November (OR. en) 15509/23 LIMITE EJUSTICE 56 JAI 1487 JURINFO 12, Annex (I Introduction, para. 4). https://data.consilium.europa.eu/doc/document/ST-15509-2023-INIT/en/pdf

Cox ATL Jr (2008) What's wrong with risk matrices? Risk Anal 28:499. https://doi.org/10.1111/j.1539-6924.2008.01030.x

Dahlbeck M (2022) Spinoza, legal theory, and artificial intelligence: a conceptual analysis of law and technology. SN Soc Sci 2:156. https://doi.org/10.1007/s43545-022-00458-w

de Mello AM, Wood T Jr (2019) What is applied research anyway? Guest Editorial. Revista de Gestão 26(4):338. Emerald Publishing Limited 2177-8736. https://doi.org/10.1108/REGE-10-2019-128

Dimyadi J, Bookman S, Harvey D et al (2019) Maintainable process model driven online legal expert systems. Artif Intell Law 27:96–97. https://doi-org.ezproxy.uio.no/10.1007/s10506-018-9231-3

Dove IL (1995) Legal expert systems: the end of jurisprudence? J Leg Stud Bus 5:1–28. https://journaloflegalstudiesinbusiness.org/wp-content/uploads/2015/09/les_1996_1to28.pdf

Email exchange - Clive Spenser and Stuart Weinstein – 5 October 2023

Email from Clive Spenser to Stuart Weinstein dated 4 October 2023

Email from Contracts Manager at Pharma Research Company to Stuart Weinstein dated 25 May 2023

Email from Survey Monkey Outbound to Stuart Weinstein (Aston University) dated 11 May 2023. This survey can be found here: https://www.surveymonkey.co.uk/r/LPC7TPT

Feghali Vargas N, Padilla Casas C, Vanegas Herrera LV, Guzman-Abello L, de Francisco Vela S (2022) Designing legal interfaces: transforming the digital services of a legal aid clinic. In: Martins N, Brandão D (eds) Advances in Design and Digital Communication II. DIGICOM 2021. Springer Series in Design and Innovation, vol 19. Springer, Cham. https://doi.org/10.1007/978-3-030-89735-2_20

Gillani N, Eynon R, Chiabaut C, Finkel K (2023) Unpacking the "Black Box" of AI in education. Educ Technol Soc 26(1):100–103. https://doi.org/10.30191/ETS.202301_26(1).0008

Girling P (2022) Operational risk management – a complete guide for banking and Fintech, 2nd edn. Wiley Finance Series. John Wiley & Sons, Inc., Hoboken, NJ, p 308. ISBN 9781119836056 (epub)

Granada Ribeiro A (2021) The quantification of law: counting, predicting, and valuating. Law Technol Hum 3(1):57. https://lthj.qut.edu.au/article/view/1966

Haapio H (2006) Business success and problem prevention through proactive contracting. In: Wahlgren P (ed) A proactive approach, Scandinavian studies in law, vol 49. Stockholm Institute for Scandinavian Law, Stockholm, pp 150–151. Available at: https://scandinavianlaw.se/pdf/49-2.pdf

Hagan M (2017) The state of legal design: the big takeaways of the Stanford Law + Design Summit, Medium, 25 September 2017. https://medium.com/legal-design-and-innovation/the-state-of-legal-design-the-big-takeaways-of-the-stanford-law-design-summit-ee363b5bf109

Hagan M (2018) Human-centered design approach to access to justice: generating new prototypes and hypotheses for interventions to make courts user-friendly. Ind J Law Soc Equal 6(2):200. https://www.repository.law.indiana.edu/ijlse/vol6/iss2/2

Hagan M (2019) Participatory design for innovation in access to justice. Daedalus 148(1):122. https://doi.org/10.1162/daed_a_00544

Hardesty L (2017) Explained: neural networks - Ballyhooed artificial-intelligence technique known as "deep learning" revives 70-year-old idea. MIT News Office, 14 April. https://news.mit.edu/2017/explained-neural-networks-deep-learning-0414

Huttner L, Merigoux M (2022) Catala: moving towards the future of legal expert systems. Artificial Intelligence and Law, p 4. ff10.1007/s10506-022-09328-5ff. ffhal-02936606v3f. https://inria.hal.science/hal-02936606/file/paper.pdf

ISO (2020) ISO 31022 – Risk Management-Guidelines for the Management of Legal Risk. https://committee.iso.org/sites/tc262/home/projects/published/iso-31022-guidelines-for-implem.html

Jablonowski M (1992) Expert systems for risk management. Risk Manag 39(9). https://go.gale.com/ps/i.do?p=AONE&u=googlescholar&id=GALE|A12749533&v=2.1&it=r&sid=AONE&asid=17976153

Jackowski M, Araszkiewicz M (eds) (2023) Liquid Legal Institute Whitepaper, First Global Report on the State of Artificial Intelligence in Legal Practice. https://doi.org/10.38023/5501c854-14eb-4529-b6b9-44343e477f44. https://liquid-legal-institute.com/wp-content/uploads/2024/03/E-Book-First-Global-Report-on-AI-in-Legal-Practice.pdf

Jackson D (2016) Human-centered legal tech: integrating design in legal education. Law Teach 50(1):85. https://doi.org/10.1080/03069400.2016.114646. https://papers.ssrn.com/sol3/papers.cfm?abstract_id=2767486

Janatian S, Westermann H, Tan J, Savelka J, Benyekhlef K (2023) From text to structure: using large language models to support the development of legal expert systems. In: Sileno G, Spanakis J, van Dijck G (eds) Frontiers in artificial intelligence and applications, vol 379, p 168. JURIX 2024 – 36th Annual Conference Maastricht The Netherlands 18–20 December 2023. IOS Press, Amsterdam - 978-1-64368-473-4 (online). https://ebooks.iospress.nl/volume/legal-knowledge-and-information-systems-jurix-2023-the-thirty-sixth-annual-conference-maastricht-the-netherlands-1820-december-2023

Johnson K, Swanson Z (2007) Quantifying legal risk: a method for managing legal risk. Manag Account Q 9(1):29. https://www.google.com/search?q=Johnson+K+and+Swanson+Z+(2007)%2C+Quantifying+Legal+Risk%3A+A+Method+for+Managing+Legal+Risk%2C+Management+Accounting+Quarterly%2C+Fall%2C+Vol.+9%2C+No.+1%2C+22-30%2C+29.&rlz=1C1CHBF_en-GBGB1031GB1031&oq=Johnson+K+and+Swanson+Z+(2007)%2C+Quantifying+Legal+Risk%3A+A+Method+for+Managing+Legal+Risk%2C+Management+Accounting+Quarterly%2C+Fall%2C+Vol.+9%2C+No.+1%2C+22-30%2C+29.&gs_lcrp=EgZjaHJvbWUyBggAEEUYOdIBCDM2NzJqMGo0qAIAsAIA&sourceid=chrome&ie=UTF-8#vhid=zephyr:0&vssid=atritem-https://www.imanet.org/-/media/d01c97aeb8eb4d25a9db3dbe628a38be.ashx

JUSTIA website. https://www.justia.com/

Kangari R, Boyer LT (1989) Risk management by expert systems. Project Manag J 20(1):40–48. https://www.pmi.org/learning/library/risk-management-expert-systems-5480

Kiriinya RKM (2017) Designing compliance patterns: integrating value modeling, legal interpretation, and argument schemes for legal risk management. PhD thesis, Universita degli studi di Bologna. https://amsdottorato.unibo.it/8268/1/KIRIINYA_ROBERT_KEVIN_MUTHURI_tesi.pdf

Kramer MJ (2021) "History Does Not Compute": Michael J. Kramer on Jill Lepore's *If Then: How the Simulmatics Corporation Invented the Future* (4 December). https://s-usih.org/2021/12/michael-j-kramer-on-if-then-how-the-simulmatics-corporation-invented-the-future/

Lawgeex website https://www.lawgeex.com/

Legal Beagles website, available at: https://legalbeagles.info/

Legal Utopia website https://www.legalutopia.co.uk/

LegalSifter website https://www.legalsifter.com/

LegalZoom website https://www.legalzoom.com/ai/doc-assist

LegalZoom Document Summarizer Report for Consulting Agreement dated as of November 1, 2018 between TO Pharmaceuticals LLC and Broom Street Associates LLC (Consulting Agreement). https://www.legalzoom.com/ai/doc-assist/documents/DOC-aExm4BXilsGD

Leith P (2016) The rise and fall of the legal expert system. Int Rev Law Comput Technol 30(3):98. https://doi.org/10.1080/13600869.2016.1232465

Liebowitz J (1995) Expert systems: a short introduction. Eng Fract Mech 50(5–6):601–607. https://www.sciencedirect.com/science/article/pii/0013794494E0047K

Logic Programming Associates website, "About LPA." https://www.lpa.co.uk/hom_lpa.htm

LSB (2022) Small business legal needs – wave four survey 2021, April 2022. https://legalservicesboard.org.uk/wp-content/uploads/2022/05/20220406-Small-business-legal-needs-FINAL.pdf

Mahler T, Bing J (2006) Contractual risk management in an ICT context – searching for a possible interface between legal methods and risk analysis. In: Wahlgren P (ed) A proactive approach,

Scandinavian studies in law, vol 49. Stockholm Institute for Scandinavian Law, Stockholm, p 353. https://scandinavianlaw.se/pdf/49-20.pdf

Maigon AB Website, https://maigon.io/

Marks N (2022) Do smaller companies manage risk better than larger one? Governance, Risk Management and Internal Audit, 16 January. https://normanmarks.wordpress.com/2022/01/16/do-smaller-companies-manage-risk-better-than-larger-ones/

Matheson A (2023) Applied artificial intelligence for law: the use of expert systems and decision trees in legal practice and the potential of artificial neural networks. Leg Issues J 9(2), January–June 2023. legalissuesjournal.com/articles/i18-032023

Michalsons (2020) Legal guidance, or legal advice that is valuable, 29 July. https://www.michalsons.com/legal-services/legal-guidance

Muthuri R, Capecchi S, Sulis E et al (2022) Integrating value modeling and legal risk management: an IT case study. Inf Syst E-Bus Manage 20:28. https://doi-org.ezproxy.uio.no/10.1007/s10257-021-00543-2

Neyland D, Möllers N (2017) Algorithmic IF ... THEN rules and the conditions and consequences of power. Inf Commun Soc 20(1):45–62. https://doi.org/10.1080/1369118X.2016.1156141. https://www.tandfonline.com/doi/full/10.1080/1369118X.2016.1156141

Nilsson NJ (2009) Preface. In: The quest for artificial intelligence. Cambridge University Press, Cambridge, pp xiii–xvi. (Online publication date 2013) https://doi.org/10.1017/CBO9780511819346.001. https://www.cambridge.org/core/books/quest-for-artificial-intelligence/32C727961B24223BBB1B3511F44F343E

Noel K (2015) The unbundling of legal services and its implications for law librarianship. Legal Ref Serv Q 34(4):245–267. https://doi.org/10.1080/0270319X.2015.1102023. https://papers.ssrn.com/sol3/papers.cfm?abstract_id=2285052

OLRAS webpage. Available at: https://www.visirule.co.uk/visirule-demos/olras

OpenAI website, Research GPT-4. https://openai.com/research/gpt-4

Papazafeiropoulou A, Spanaki K (2016) Understanding governance, risk, and compliance information systems (GRC IS): the experts view. Inf Syst Front 18:1259. https://doi.org/10.1007/s10796-015-9572-3

Phone call between Stuart Weinstein and Clive Spenser and Alan Westwood held 23 May 2022

Phone call between Stuart Weinstein with Micro-Entity 1 held 15 August 2022. The owner requested anonymity in these circumstances

Pilling D (2023) Expert Systems, the other AI digital transformation solution for the legal vertical, Linked In, 11 April. https://www.linkedin.com/pulse/expert-systems-other-ai-digital-transformation-solution-david-pilling

Revell T (Undated) Artificial Intelligence (AI). New Scientist. https://www.newscientist.com/definition/artificial-intelligence-ai/

Rose N (2021) App launches with huge range of legal help to consumers and SMEs. Legalfutures, 17 May. https://www.legalfutures.co.uk/latest-news/app-launches-with-huge-range-of-legal-help-to-consumers-and-smes

Sandefur R (2019) Legal tech for non-lawyers: report of the survey of US legal technologies. American Bar Foundation, Chicago, p 15. https://www.americanbarfoundation.org/wp-content/uploads/2023/04/report_us_digital_legal_tech_for_nonlawyers.pdf

Scassa T, Salyzyn A, McGill J, Bouclin S (2020) Developing privacy best practices for direct-to-public legal apps: observations and lessons learned. CJLT 18(1):1. https://digitalcommons.schulichlaw.dal.ca/cjlt/vol18/iss1/1/

Schwartz A, Sepe S (2023) Fairness and freedom in contract law. Columbia Law School Law and Economics Workspace, 9 October. https://law-economic-studies.law.columbia.edu/sites/default/files/content/Schwartz%20&%20Sepe.%20Fairness%20&%20Freedom%20in%20Contract%20Law.%202023%2010%2009%20CLS%20L&E%20Wksp.pdf

Stevens C, Barot V, Carter J (2010) The next generation of legal expert systems: new dawn or false dawn? In: SGAI conference proceedings. https://link.springer.com/chapter/10.1007/978-0-85729-130-1_33

Surden H (2021) Chapter 8: Machine learning and law: an overview. In: Research handbook on big data law. Edward Elgar Publishing, Cheltenham, UK, p 177. Retrieved Dec 20, 2023, from https://doi-org.ezproxy.uio.no/10.4337/9781788972826.00014
Survey Monkey Outbound Email to Stuart Weinstein (Aston University) dated 11 May 2023
Tantisripreecha T, Soonthornphisaj N (2016) LegalEX: an expert system for law firm. Intell Decis Technol 10:315. https://content.iospress.com/articles/intelligent-decision-technologies/idt258
UK Department for Business, Energy & Industrial Strategy (2022) Statistical Release, Business Population Estimates for the UK, and the Regions 2022 (6th October) National Statistics, pp 3–4. https://assets.publishing.service.gov.uk/media/632d8197d3bf7f567394f7b3/2022_Business_Population_Estimates_for_the_UK_and_regions_Statistical_Release.pdf
UK Government Legal Department (2015) Legal Quality Committee, Guidance Note on Legal Risk, July 2015. https://assets.publishing.service.gov.uk/media/5b858a0eed915d7e1aa25744/Legal_Risk_Guidance_-_Amended_July_2015.pdf
US Department of Commerce (1982) William B. Gevarter, NBSIR 82-2505, An Overview of Expert Systems, May, p 2. https://ntrs.nasa.gov/api/citations/19820022023/downloads/19820022023.pdf
Visirule Examples Website, OLRAS Demo, https://visiruleexamples.com/olrademo.html
Weinstein S (2022) Lawyers' perceptions on the use of AI. In: Custers B, Fosch-Villaronga E (eds) Law and artificial intelligence. Information technology and law series, vol 35. T.M.C. Asser Press, The Hague. https://doi.org/10.1007/978-94-6265-523-2_21
Weinstein S, Spenser C (2024) Designing a legal risk management expert system to evaluate contracts for micro-entities (October 10). Available at SSRN: https://ssrn.com/abstract=4987650 or https://doi.org/10.2139/ssrn.4987650
Weinstein S, Wild C (2013) Developing the right formula for successful legal risk management, governance and compliance. In: Weinstein S, Wild C (eds) Legal risk management, governance and compliance: a guide to best practice from leading experts. Globe Law and Business, London
Westermann H, Benyekhlef K (2023) JusticeBot: a methodology for building augmented intelligence tools for laypeople to increase access to justice. In: Proceedings of the Nineteenth International Conference on Artificial Intelligence and Law (ICAIL '23). Association for Computing Machinery, New York, NY, USA, pp 351–360. https://doi.org/10.1145/3594536.3595166
Whittaker AS (2003) Lawyers as risk managers. Butterworths J Int Bank Financ Law (January), p 5. https://lexisweb.co.uk/sources/journal-of-international-banking-financial-law
Wolters Kluwers - Legisway Analyzer - https://www.wolterskluwer.com/en-gb/solutions/legisway/contract-review-for-legal-departments

Stuart Weinstein is an expert on the management of legal risk and the operation of corporate legal departments pursuant to governance, risk, and compliance frameworks. Since 2017, Stuart Weinstein has been Reader in Legal Risk Management, Aston Law School, Aston University, Birmingham. Aston University. Prior to joining Aston Law School, Stuart was professor of practise informed legal education at Coventry Law School (2014–2017). Stuart Weinstein is researching the use of AI and legal risk as part of a PhD by publication at the University of Oslo Faculty of Law – Norwegian Center for Computers and Law to be completed 2025. In addition to being admitted to the Roll as a Solicitor of the Senior Courts of England and Wales (non-practising), Stuart Weinstein is a member of the Bar of the States of California (active), New York (inactive) and the District of Columbia (active). Stuart Weinstein served as the United Kingdom subject matter expert for the British Standards Institute

Working Group on the development of BS ISO 31022:2020—guidelines for the management of legal risk (published June 2020). Stuart Weinstein earned a Bachelor of Honors in History of Ideas from Williams College, Williamstown, Massachusetts, a Juris Doctor from Columbia University School of Law in the City of New York, and a master's degree in business administration from the University of Hertfordshire, Hatfield, Hertfordshire.

AI in the Legal Market: The Dark Side of the Moon

Bruno Mascello

Contents

Abstract

The widespread emergence of artificial intelligence (AI) is expected to support the legal sector in its daily work and, most importantly, relieve it of laborious tasks. Both the promise and the temptation are very significant. Therefore, it is essential to adopt a critical perspective on this matter. This is not due to being against technology but rather to the fact that its use requires effective risk management that surpasses mere reliance on technology, or rather, a zero

B. Mascello (✉)
Executive School of Management, Technology and Law, St. Gallen University, St. Gallen, Switzerland
e-mail: bruno.mascello@unisg.ch

K. Jacob et al. (eds.), *Liquid Legal – Sustaining the Rule of Law*, Law for Professionals, https://doi.org/10.1007/978-3-031-78596-2_5

tolerance for errors. It is crucial to strategically position AI in the value chain of legal service providers and reflect it in the chosen business model. In addition, the impact on leadership must be analysed because, at the end of the day, there are still human beings at work. And it is imperative to focus on potential convenience traps: the loss of human creativity and negotiation skills, a reduction in valuable training exercises, a lack of plausibility checks for AI solutions, and a deterioration in service quality. Lawyers will have to face the fact that they have to think about the use of AI if they want to remain relevant to their internal and external customers. Legal professionals are strongly encouraged to pursue a well-informed and responsible approach towards AI with the aim of safeguarding their professional integrity and prepare themselves for potential changes at an early stage.

1 Introduction

When everyone is in raptures, one should stop and be critical,[1] especially when the originators of and experts on artificial intelligence (AI) themselves raise concerns regarding potential dangers, and others do not shrink from drawing comparisons with the nuclear bomb.[2] A comparison with the invention of the power loom would be more helpful, where a few benefitted while many lost their jobs and livelihoods as a result.[3] In any case, political authorities have already taken action to regulate the use of AI and to address any negative consequences in advance.[4]

I also become cautious, in particular, when students and practitioners are asked about AI in lectures and tutorials and then enthusiastically explain which of the many boring tasks they may finally delegate to AI. These include activities such as drafting

[1] AI has become a buzzword and is also used for machine learning. “It overly inflates expectations and distracts from the precise way ML [machine learning] will improve business operations” (Siegel 2023).

[2] In March 2023, over 1000 experts and tech companies called for a pause in the development of particularly advanced artificial intelligence (AI). Sam Altman, CEO of OpenAI, compared OpenAI to the Manhattan Project for the development of the atomic bomb by the USA (New York Times, 31 March 2023).

[3] The invention of mechanical looms enabled a small number of mill owners to replace experienced workers with cheaper, unskilled labour (often women and children) (Dibbits 2017). Cf. also European Route of Industrial Heritage (ERIH 2023). It must be mentioned, that in the long run new jobs were created as well, which may happen with AI as well.

[4] For Europe, on 8 December 2023, EU policymakers announced an agreement on the text of an AI Act which applies a risk-based approach (cf. the Proposal for a new Artificial Intelligence Act (European Commission 2021)). In the US, the Biden administration has issued initial guidelines for dealing with artificial intelligence, setting safety standards and requiring developers to test their AI models before publication and share the results with the government (The White House 2023). Cf. also the UK’s Bletchley Declaration agreed at the AI Safety Summit in November 2023 (UK Government 2023).

e-mails, creating presentations and drawing up contracts, writing summaries and minutes, analysing documents (especially in due diligence and e-discovery), proof-reading and editing contracts, assisting with research and knowledge management, and generally relieving them of monotonous work and other laborious writing chores. AI is expected to enhance efficiency and save a lot of time.[5] But for what purpose?

Sceptical non-experts, who do not tend to glorify hypes, regularly point out existing shortcomings in connection with generative AI: the incomplete and at best selective or biased database used for training, the inaccurate results, and disturbing errors (hallucinations) that rule out complete trust.[6] And of course, lawyers in particular like to point out other risks, such as the lack of confidentiality and data security when uploading data, the lack of transparency in the training data and algorithms used, the lack of legal training data, ethical questions, infringement of IP rights, and the difficulty of verifying sources.[7] These risks are real. Another problem is the principle of data minimisation enshrined in current data protection regulations, which prevents the data used to train AI from being representative and of high quality because training with as much data as possible is made impossible.[8]

AI and the innovations based on it are developing at an impressive speed, a fact we should treat with a certain amount of respect.[9] The issue of AI is developing very quickly, especially in the field of security. Solutions are already being offered for using ChatGPT in a company's own environment (Azure Open AI from Microsoft[10] being a case in point) and thus keeping prompts and results in-house. Further, databases are being developed that enable conclusions to be drawn about the sources used (such as Lexis+ AI). It is to be expected that all remaining reservations that currently exist will also be resolved in the foreseeable future. To everyone's complete satisfaction? Hardly. But if we waited until technology (and people) were perfect, we would not implement or change anything. And we do not want to wait until all teething troubles are ironed out before we start. Therefore, we must accept the residual risks and apply risk management. An everyday example: anyone who drives a car or flies knows very well that there is no such thing as 100% safety, but they still do it regularly.

[5] For example, efficiency gains of up to a quarter of working hours are expected (cf. Lips et al. 2023; Goldman Sachs 2023).

[6] Kravitz (2023). Cf. also Rodrigues (2020).

[7] There has already been a first case in the USA in which two lawyers submitted a petition to the court drafted by ChatGPT in which reference was made to fictitious court judgements. The lawyers were fined USD 5000 by the court (Shin 2023).

[8] Braun Binder et al. (2021).

[9] In 2019, more than three AI pre-publications per hour were submitted to arXiv, a curated research platform accessible to everyone—which is more than 148 times faster than in 1994 (Tang et al. 2020). This is also much faster than Moore's Law, which states that the computing power of integrated circuits has doubled approximately every two years.

[10] Microsoft (2023).

AI could indeed prove to be a game changer in the digital transformation of the legal market, which would lead to a clear separation between the time before and after November 2022. Today could mark a turning point, a tipping point that legal technology has not been able to achieve so far. AI could even overtake legal tech and simply leave it behind, because AI concerns a general competence, i.e. the writing skills, which applies to the entire value chain of legal services, and not just a single task. However, as we all know, no coin is thin enough not to have two sides. We should accept threats that cannot be changed rather than fight against them. In my opinion, this includes the latest stage of technological development in the form of AI.[11] While today's prevailing narrative surrounding AI tends to highlight its positive aspects, the focus here should for once—as a counterbalance and in the sense of acting as a *devil's advocate*—be deliberately placed on the "dark side" and critically examine various topics.

2 Risk Management

Risks include both, opportunities and threats. Responsible corporate governance requires careful risk management that takes appropriate account of both sides. In order to effectively manage future undesirable events, it is necessary to identify and assess them. Only then is it possible to react appropriately. As a first step, it needs to be critically considered what AI is all about, what potential pitfalls could evolve and how to thoroughly prepare in advance. I deliberately refrain from proposing any specific solutions here; rather, it must suffice to raise awareness when engaging with AI, thereby enabling everyone to effectively implement the necessary precautions. This focus on threats does not serve the purpose of discouraging the legal service providers in law firms, legal departments, and ALSPs from using AI. On the contrary, the many opportunities and advantages AI offers should not be belittled here; after all, I am also pleased about the many new potential applications. Nevertheless, I recommend an initial appropriate classification in the overall context, which lawyers should not find difficult. Thus in litigation, in particular, lawyers learn that there are always more ways than one of presenting the facts or interpreting the law, and that potential counterarguments must be considered well in advance when preparing for a hearing.

A realistic risk assessment is crucial. One must carefully assess the extent to which technologies can be used and for what purpose. Demanding both blind trust and zero tolerance for errors is not helpful and only helps to prematurely stifle a critical discussion.[12] Lawyers are therefore advised not to place any higher demands

[11] Cf. e.g., Artificial Intelligence Risk Management Framework (NIST 2023); DOE AI Risk Management Playbook (AITO 2023); EU's Proposal for a Regulation laying down harmonised rules on artificial intelligence (European Commission 2021).

[12] Mascello (2020).

on third parties—in this case, the machine—than they could and would like to satisfy themselves. After all, it is well known that lawyers and their contracts are not flawless and waterproof.[13] Striving for perfection is important, but it is rarely achieved. Therefore, it is important to work as well as possible with the available resources in given circumstances. When we deal with AI, we must accept that good is good enough to start with, and that any residual risks, which remains after thoroughly applying risk management, must be tolerated as background noise.

3 Strategic Positioning

The global confrontation with AI offers the opportunity to rethink one's own positioning in the legal market. This raises the question of who may emerge as a serious competitor in the future. So far, it has mainly been legal departments and law firms that have been visible. However, tech companies and tech law firms could increasingly cover all levels of the value chain. The competition will therefore not be AI itself, but rather the legal service providers that integrate AI into their advice and services. At best, it might be advisable to enter into sensible cooperation ventures to avoid having to re-invent the wheel. Law firms should view AI not solely as a new business opportunity or legal practice that enables them to provide more legal advice and to increase the hours billed. And AI can be considered a kind of magic potion which will lead to a levelling of lawyers, being in particular advantageous for small law firms and legal departments.[14]

In the initial stage of a strategy development process, a SWOT analysis is conducted to acquire an overview of the current framework conditions and the company's status. Based on this, the process addresses two key questions: which customer segment should the company target, and what specific services and products will be offered to them in the future?[15] It is assumed that a company's existing customer base will hardly be changed significantly as a result of the use of AI alone. External legal service providers could also tap into new technology-savvy customer segments through the deliberate integration and use of AI.

However, it is much more interesting to think about potential changes in the range of products and services when AI may cover entire value chains or parts of it. For example, highly AI-supported products could serve a cost-sensitive market demand. It is necessary to find an answer to the question whether and how a product which was originally created using only human resources, can and must be adapted to

[13] Henderson (2019). In this context cf. also the "issue spotting test" related to NDAs. In a study on the review of non-disclosure agreements (NDAs), the performance of lawyers varied widely, with the best human lawyer achieving an accuracy of 94.94%, while some were below 80%. AI achieved a similarly high accuracy of 94.55% and took just 26 seconds to complete the review, in contrast to the lawyers who took an average of 92 min (Aumann 2018).

[14] Mascello (2024b).

[15] For the development of strategy management as a discipline, cf. e.g., Müller-Stewens (2016, p. 324).

integrate AI. It is very likely that customers will demand the use of AI from their legal service providers for cost and efficiency reasons, or switch advisors or do the work themselves. Legal departments have clearly demonstrated in the past that they are willing and able to handle a large proportion of legal work themselves and no longer leave it to external service providers.[16] Moreover, the use of AI not only makes external service providers more comparable but also easier to replace. As a result, there is a risk that the use of AI tools by external service providers might lead to diminished customer retention and loyalty.

4 Business Model and Hourly Fee Model

Among other things, business models provide information on how a company generates income (revenue model). Law firms still widely use the hourly fee model. It is uncertain whether AI will deliver the long-promised death blow to this revenue model. The hourly billing model is based on two pillars: human labour and billing according to hours worked. In simplified terms, the income of the law firm owners, the partners, is calculated on the basis of four factors: the costs incurred (cost margin), the hours billed (utilisation), the hourly rates charged, and the number of associates (leverage; this value shows the number of associates per partner).[17] With this in mind, the use of AI will have the following effects: (1) Cost: the licensing of AI will have an impact on the cost margin as an additional expense. However, if associates will be replaced by AI, less salary cost will be incurred. (2) Utilization: if an increase in efficiency is expected because less time is required for a mandate, this will reduce the number of billable hours, at least for the mandate in question. However, AI could be expected to generate more work. (3) Hourly rates: what will not change immediately is the hourly rate, because this, at least today, only relates to a lawyer's human labour. However, if less junior associates can be charged, the average hourly rate will increase. (4) Leverage: AI will lead to a lower utilisation of associates and reduce the leverage rate. This will in turn lead to a reduction in turnover through leverage and ultimately to a reduction in profitability.

At first glance, one could conclude that the pyramid model of large law firms will change because technology will replace the associates and human resources in the lower level that were previously billed to customers (cf. the analogy with the looms in the industrial revolution). However, if the law firm has a well-filled pipeline of mandates and enough additional work available to offset the time savings achieved by using AI, this will result in a zero-sum game for the law firm because the same number of hours will still be billed. The only beneficiary is the customer, who will pay less for a mandate because the law firms cannot internalise the efficiency gains achieved for themselves based on the applicable hourly fee business model. In this context, law firms sometimes argue that the hours worked by young associates, and

[16]Mascello (2018).

[17]Staub (2012).

the hours which can be fully passed through to the customers are overestimated. Therefore, the use of AI would not result in a loss of billable hours.[18]

Legal services that are provided traditionally, i.e. with human resources, but fail to achieve efficiency gains, could soon become too costly for law firms and force them to look for new pricing and business models.[19] Customers will only be willing to pay hourly fees for work that AI cannot accomplish. Law firms will have to clarify how they can continue to work profitably when they use AI and whether and how they can pass on the costs of AI to customers. Customers may argue that they did not have to pay anything for lawyers using services like Google or ChatGPT in the past. Charging one-off fees or demanding an increase in hourly rates could become difficult if the cost that is incurred additionally cannot be accounted for transparently.

It remains to be seen how law firms will begin to "factor in" AI. Simply charging for licence fees and the consumption of data storage does not allow the internalisation of efficiency gains or scaling, and is more reminiscent of charging for hours and copies. And we know what the consequence was: customers started to insource. It will be interesting to see whether the use of AI will, eventually, lead to a change in the hourly fee model which is still favoured by law firms. Of course, it is possible to charge for the five minutes during which a lawyer uses AI and, at best, add a small usage fee for AI software.[20] However, depending on the law firm, this is no longer profitable, especially if there are not enough spare mandates in the pipeline. The use of alternative fee models is still available (for instance flat fees or value billing). Subscription models for proprietary services and tools could also be considered, for example, where customers log into the law firms AI independently, which enables law firms to reinforce the links with their customers again.

5 Operations

Once you know the strategic positioning you are aiming for and which business model to use, the process of implementation steps can be tackled. It has already been established that human lawyers cannot be completely replaced by technology. However, AI will be able to perform certain tasks in the legal value chain better, faster, and more efficiently than those currently performed by more cost-intensive human lawyers.[21] "The days when everything that was done by lawyers was

[18] Cf. e.g., Dipshan (2023).

[19] Thomson Reuters (2023).

[20] Harvey AI, similar to ChatGPT but specialised for legal applications, is enhanced with extensive legal data, including case law and reference materials, and further tailored with a law firm's own documents. This AI tool aids in contract analysis, due diligence, litigation, and compliance tasks, enabling lawyers to provide quicker, more economical client solutions (Rattray 2023).

[21] Cf. also Aumann (2018).

considered to be necessarily expensive legal work, are irretrievably gone."[22] Not lawyers but boring legal work is to be replaced by technology.[23] Routine tasks that are currently carried out by associates and paralegals at a cost, could in the future be taken over by AI. Goldman Sachs predicts that 44% of legal work will be replaced by AI.[24] Other studies similarly forecast unfavourable prospects for the legal market, including judges and lawyers.[25] The question is therefore not only how important lawyers, but also how important legal staff will still be in the future if the relevance of IT and data increases. The possibility of enabling multi-disciplinary partnerships (MDPs) could point in one direction. Such a development is moving more in the direction of an advisory model that does not focus exclusively on traditional legal advice and lawyers, but promises a more diverse and therefore more complex offering. This means that so-called legal professionals would no longer be important employees, but rather become business people who happen to have a legal education. And people with unconventional career paths and diverse educational backgrounds could become increasingly important in today's working world as they can network and link topics in a different way.

6 Leadership

The questions regarding the use of AI already present a significant challenge for executives. However, it is the combination with other elements that makes them really explosive from an employee management point of view: on the one hand, the combination with New Work, which includes topics such as working from home, working from anywhere, and part-time (working) models; and on the other hand, the experience gained during the pandemic, which acted as a catalyst for working from home, the search for meaning, and a new set of values. This requires not only more organisational talent but, above all, leadership and social skills.

The question arises as to what disciplinary measures a company can and should take to intervene in its employees' modus operandi. In this specific case, should the use of AI be permitted, and if so, to what extent, and how transparently must its use be labelled? How can a fair and appropriate assessment of performance be made if it is unclear how much of the result is due to the person "themselves", given that working hours and office presence (input) are no longer the decisive factors for promotion or pay rise, but rather performance (output)? Two critical trust issues now arise: do employees work as productively at home without direct supervision by

[22] Original quote: "Die Zeiten, in denen all das als notwendigerweise teure anwaltliche Arbeit angesehen wurde, was von Anwälten gemacht wurde, sind unwiederbringlich vorbei." Hartung (2018), pp. 5–18, point 14.

[23] A study that investigated the optimal delegation of tasks is interesting in this regard (Fügener et al. 2022).

[24] Goldman Sachs (2023).

[25] Cf. e.g., Felten et al. (2023).

superiors as they do in the office (keyword: proximity bias), and if so, does the use of unauthorised or non-transparent tools at home hinder an objective assessment of personal performance? It must not be forgotten that people are not machines. They need attention, appreciation, and communicative exchange in order to work powerfully, creatively, and enthusiastically. Reducing them to measurable performance targets makes it easier to compare them with machines. This could mean that instead of operating looms and conveyor belts, we become operators of AI and let it work for us.

A carefully managed transition period may be necessary initially to avoid major damage. New generations such as Alpha will grow up with AI as a matter of course, just as millennials/Gen Y took the internet and Gen Z took the social media for granted. What impact it will have on the war for talent and the various social and age groups is yet unknown.

7 Attention: Convenience Trap!

7.1 Loss of Human Creativity and Negotiation Skills

It is claimed that creativity distinguishes humans from machines and that we are superior to machines in this respect.[26] During the pandemic, many people turned to a creative hobby. But it is often the case that "the time we save with automation is often not used creatively."[27] So what happens if we do not utilise this creative power, for example, when we let AI create the first draft for us due to convenience reasons?[28] This places an initial "anchor" in our creative thinking process, and we lose the ability to think independently and develop our own creative thoughts. The same applies if we leave our critical thinking to AI. This could lead to a situation whereby AI impairs rather than supports our original creativity and critical thinking. We already know this effect from other areas: calculators have significantly reduced the ability to do mental arithmetic, and the constant distraction of smartphones not only reduces our ability to concentrate but apparently also our mental capacity by ten IQ points.[29] People who do not have a fund of their own examples, experience, and application possibilities, will inevitably find themselves at a disadvantage in negotiation situations that take place in the presence of the contracting parties or in court. There will neither be time, nor will they be allowed to quickly consult Google,

[26] Du Sautoy (2019).

[27] Original quote: "[. . .] die Zeit, die wir mit Automatisierung sparen, wir eben häufig nicht kreativ nutzen" cf. interview with Chamorro-Premuzic (Severin 2023).

[28] "Artificial general intelligence" (AGI) is the holy grail of AI. This is machine intelligence that surpasses the mental abilities of any human being. Softbank CEO Masayoshi Son explained that meanwhile more than 100,000 AI-generated proposals have been submitted and around 10,000 patent-worthy ideas have been developed. Thanks to generative AI, he said, he comes up with 30 ideas a day (Kölling 2023, p. 22).

[29] According to Chamorro-Premuzic (Severin 2023).

ChatGPT or another AI tool. Experienced negotiators will have an advantage in such situations.

7.2 Loss of Training Opportunities

Technology today does not only offer lawyers more flexibility but also the ability to work from anywhere. AI also holds the promise that we can increasingly focus on "pleasant", more productive, more challenging, and more complex work. Routine tasks that require less technical or human involvement can increasingly be delegated to AI systems. Despite these wonderful advances, the question remains as to how one can successfully play in the "Champions League" of professional life without having had the prior professional training and experience that, today, is developed through less exciting but instructive work and intensive training. Without sufficient basic knowledge and personal experience, you cannot do demanding jobs later. More senior lawyers will certainly remember the days when they spent hours and days in data rooms reading and summarising countless contracts. Malicious tongues called the related increase in profitability generated by law firms (keyword: leverage) also "internal education on the job". In any case, it was also training to gain experience and improve one's own attention and instinct for contract clauses. Today, this no longer exists because a small black box scans all contracts for the key clauses and produces a summary and final report in a fraction of the time previously spent. What is more, today's advanced AI is already able to identify more cross-disciplinary and cross-topical links in the documents. The following question remains to be answered: if AI will take over typical tasks from junior associates, how will they learn to handle high-value tasks, which by the way is anyhow not sufficiently available for all lawyers, and how do you train and develop them into senior leaders? This cannot be pushed back to law schools only, but all employers must provide opportunities to learn and develop, and each lawyer is responsible for their own further education to keep the employability.

To stick with the analogy of premier league of football: if lawyers are kept away from all repetitive, unproductive (i.e., unpaid), boring work, where will they learn to play football and score goals? Currently, I do not yet see a substitute for the loss of this valuable training time and who will pay for this time. It is, of course, possible to trust that they will learn how to use AI properly on their own in due course, and that AI will fully compensate for the loss. After all, nobody taught us how to use Google, either.

7.3 Impossibility of Reasonable Plausibility Checks

The outcome produced by AI is based on a limited and selective amount of data that is usually unknown to the user. This means that a result already contains an unknown and limiting bias (data, culture, age, etc.), which must be identified and verified. In order to be able to check the plausibility of an AI result, a reference value to compare is required.[30] It does not make much sense to ask an AI whether the solution it presents has been created with AI and is plausible. The reference must therefore be our human brain, which is constantly being filled with new knowledge and experience over time. This plausibility check is comparable to a senior lawyer or partner assessing a contract drafted by an associate.

I doubt that such plausibility checks by humans will be effective and possible in the future. Firstly, because of the lack of the qualitative component: the human brain as a reference point will only be equipped with selective training data (cf. Sect. 7.2), because the entire spectrum of experience and knowledge will no longer be found in the brain due to the shift in work. If you know nothing, you cannot validate and check plausibility. Secondly, because of the quantitative component: part-time work and the demand for more work-life balance inevitably mean that a person works fewer hours and consequently will accumulate less experience and knowledge. Combining both effects makes it impossible for a user to adequately assess the plausibility of a solution generated by AI. This gives the argument of not being able to trust AI a completely different weight due to the lack of suitable alternatives.

One can only creatively solve economic and legal problems by drawing on extensive prior experience and on this basis generating numerous new combinations and connections. However, anyone who does not regularly and broadly train their own thinking skills, which by the way is still associated with a great deal of (probably also boring) practice, time, and effort, will not be able to make a reasonable plausibility check of the AI-generated results. It will simply not be possible to recognise the AI's shortcomings. This is comparable to the increasing specialisation of lawyers, who lose their overall view and their position as trusted advisors. In the worst case, a lawyer will remain an overqualified project manager.[31]

7.4 Loss of Service Quality

Currently, the assumption is that customers should not sustain any loss of quality when services provided by human resources today are replaced by technology. There are various reasons why this may not apply to legal services. It is often not a question of carrying out simple work that can be done in a transactional manner, i.e. in analogy with a machine that performs an action repetitively in accordance with the commands it is fed. Furthermore, it is doubtful that isolated human work still has the same quality, especially if people work in a qualitatively and quantitatively reduced manner (cf. Sect. 7.3). A customer must therefore inevitably accept that, at least initially, the quality of legal work will decline. The decisive factor remains how and

[30] "Because such systems contain literally no mechanisms for checking the truth of what they say, they can easily be *automated* to generate misinformation at unprecedented scale" (Marcus 2022).

[31] "Lawyers will have to write less, read less, search less and, frankly, also think less. They will become hyper-augmented which might turn them into overqualified project managers." Brochner (2023).

by whom the two elements can be optimally combined again in a way that creates value. This becomes clear if one imagines a situation where three different law firms each work on a particular legal issue and the general counsel must then combine the three results into a coherent overall picture. If AI cannot independently compensate for the expected loss of quality, the quality of the result will be poorer. Nevertheless, this result may well be acceptable in a specific case, provided it is fit for purpose and perhaps even more cost-effective.

8 New USP for Lawyers

If the prophecies of doom come true, what will be left for lawyers in the end and what will be their future differentiator or competitive edge? Lawyers like to explain what makes them irreplaceable and why they cannot be replaced by machines. They seem to overlook the fact that they are already gradually manoeuvring themselves into self-imposed insignificance. The "holy grail of legal knowledge" no longer lies exclusively with lawyers. Since the introduction of the internet, legal knowledge has been democratised and made freely accessible, ChatGPT has also been made available for unrestricted and free use, customers already absorb the lion's share of legal work with their own legal departments, and legal tech has absorbed some legal tasks. In addition, certain tasks that still require legal expertise, such as drawing up contracts, can increasingly be taken over by technological resources. Contextual knowledge and negotiation skills are at risk of decline due to a lack of practical applications and training. Furthermore, even writing proficiency, a core skill that lawyers used to be quite proud of, will increasingly become redundant as AI enables everyone to produce well-crafted and error-free texts.

AI will further alienate customers from their legal service providers. This has an adverse effect on the often-desired partnership and relationship maintenance as a trusted advisor. Customers will no longer be forced to commission law firms or lawyers for initial drafts or evaluations. They will do this on their own, without asking their external advisors for permission in advance. Customers have also learnt that the initial assessment of a situation does not require 100% certainty. As a result, this means that law firms will probably have to carry out more verification work because the initial assessment has already been completed internally by the customer.

What currently bothers me most is that lawyers seem to put the client-attorney-privilege at risk. Customers naturally expect their legal service providers to work efficiently and, if possible, to use available technologies (e.g., internet services for research purposes). No customer would ever think to instruct their lawyers to do so or, even worse, to consent to their confidential information being shared on the web. Since ChatGPT, however, lawyers seem unsettled and are wondering whether they have to inform their customers if they (want to) use AI technology. Why? Nothing has changed in the applicable rules on legal professional privilege because of AI. Lawyers still have to treat their customers' information confidential. But now one can observe the following: lawyers are asking their customers for consent to process their mandates with AI. Legal departments are being asked by law firms to define the applicable rules for dealing with AI in the outside counsel guidelines. And some lawyers go even further and expect their customers to explicitly instruct them if they are not allowed to use AI. This brings us into the area of reversing the burden of instruction or burden of proof. I am surprised to see lawyers come up with the idea of actively encouraging their customers to waive their confidentiality rights, one of the most important competitive advantages. I am concerned that the professional secrecy seems to be about to be sacrificed unnoticed on the scaffold of AI.[32]

What is left for external lawyers? It might be an idea to place less reliance on their specific legal expertise and more on the non-legal competences. It is recommended that they should reconnect with their human roots and increasingly prioritise relationship-building, which includes a proper service delivery. When they deal with other people, then emotional intelligence, empathy, conflict resolution mechanisms, and negotiation skills, on the one hand side, and business acumen, strategy and risk management advice, and technology related knowledge, on the other side, will become much more important than the isolated legal skills that a customer takes as a given anyhow. Less legal and more social and soft skills are needed. The search for a valid unique selling proposition (USP) will become all the more urgent for lawyers who currently differentiate themselves through their specialist expertise.[33]

The call for "access to justice" has been heard in connection with court proceedings, as many people can no longer afford to go to court because of the expensive and lengthy legal proceedings. Perhaps AI-controlled court proceedings will be established, similar to the dispute resolution procedures on eBay.[34] And in connection with general legal advice, which is increasingly becoming the lawyers' financially relevant core activity (i.e., not litigation), service and relationship-related skills will become more important. One way or another, the judgement of an experienced lawyer will always be needed and appreciated.

9 Excursus 1: Admission as a Lawyer

Observing past trends in the development of human resources within the legal market, the following can be noticed: thirty years ago, Swiss citizenship was a prerequisite for admission to the bar examination in Switzerland. A federal court ruling subsequently expanded admission and included foreign nationals residing in Switzerland. Then, non-lawyers were increasingly employed in organisations to support lawyers (e.g., paralegals, assistants, secretaries, IT specialists, and legal operations specialists). However, the binary categorisation of "professionals and other employees" was maintained and only the turnover of professionals was

[32] Mascello (2024a).

[33] Mascello (2023).

[34] Cf. Susskind (2023), p. 138 ff.

relevant, as if the non-lawyers had not contributed to the generation of the financial result. In the wake of the growing demand for diversity and equal treatment, the profession has been called upon for some time to promote more women to partner and management levels. Now, non-legal experts (e.g., tax experts, doctors, engineers) are also being admitted to law firms, which is reflected in the so-called multi-disciplinary partnerships (MDP). Finally, the woke wave has sensitised people to the fact that not only women but also other minorities should be adequately represented in companies and in key management positions. The latest focus is on legal technology and AI, which are aimed less at the qualitative but more at the quantitative side of the legal value chain. Digitalisation in general is primarily intended to relieve the burden of certain activities without providing an answer as to whether and how the time freed up will be filled. At best, this could lead to the surmounting of cultural barriers and contribute to an increase in intercultural competence. It will be interesting to observe the continued liberalisation of the legal market.

10 Excursus 2: Self-test

Please use the following examples to test your acceptance of AI and how great the risk could be of yielding your ability to think independently and critically to AI.

Test 1 Do you still recalculate Excel results with a calculator or even in your head?

Test 2 How much do you trust your navigation system or Google to guide you to a destination?

Test 3 How much do you enjoy driving a vehicle? Initially, manual gear shifts were replaced by automatic transmissions. Subsequently, more and more driver assistance technologies were installed in a car, aimed at alleviating the burden of driving or to compensate for human errors. To what extent do you currently rely on driver assistance systems when overtaking or parking? When will we (have to) entrust ourselves to self-driving cars? Inevitably, due to these numerous conveniences, we will gradually lose the ability to manually steer and control a vehicle.

Test 4 Would you prefer your next blood analysis to be conducted solely by a machine, or will you insist on a human carrying out the examination conventionally by hand? And what about the subsequent diagnosis? Whom do you trust more for interpreting the results: the machine or a human?

Test 5 Would you trust a robot to analyse your X-ray images? Bear in mind that even a qualified radiologist will only see a limited number of images during her professional career due to time constraints. By contrast, the software has millions of X-ray images stored in its database, which it can continuously compare with each other. Ideally, the software should therefore only help the doctor with the findings (for example as a first or second opinion).[35] Yet this creates a secondary challenge: how great is the temptation and potential unease for doctors to contradict the machine? One thing should be clear in any case, namely that it is imperative that any adverse findings are conveyed by the examining and hopefully empathetic doctor.

11 Concluding Remarks

It is often claimed that an important difference between humans and machines is the machine's lack of consciousness ("mindless robots"[36]). The focus here is on what the machine cannot do. However, if we change the perspective, we could put forward the following hypothesis: the more humans delegate work to machines, the more they will disable themselves and ultimately lose mental awareness. The use of AI makes us predictable, and what is predictable can be standardised and automated.[37] And ultimately be replaced.

Regardless of whether you are enthusiastic or defensive about AI, an informed approach and the application of a responsible risk management are key for dealing with it objectively and preparing for possible effects in advance. It will not be possible to evade technological development. Moreover, it will not come free of charge for anyone. In this context, I agree with Richard Susskind: "Most of the current claims being made by enthusiasts and pundits about the impact of AI on the law *overstate* its likely *short-term* impact. However, and more importantly, most of the current claims about the *long-term* greatly *understate* the impact of AI on legal service."[38] In the context of strategic positioning, it is essential to determine along the timeline which areas—be it time, financial, human, or technical resources—should be prioritised and which tasks can be delegated or discontinued. This may also affect aspects of the professional identity within a profession.

[35] Google app to detect skin diseases (Bleiker 2021). At the annual congress of the American Urological Association (AUA) in Chicago, USA, a study was presented that examined the role of AI in aiding the detection and management of prostate cancer through radiology, histopathology, and support tasks (Biermann Verlag GmbH 2023). The study concluded that AI is as effective as trained radiologists in detecting prostate cancer using magnetic resonance imaging (MRI) (Bhattacharya et al. 2022). In 2019, radiology produced around 675 billion gigabytes of image data, the equivalent of 13.5 trillion slice images (Blume 2019). Modern CT or MRI devices measure organs to such an extent that a single lung screening produces 600 to 800 images that need to be viewed. Cf. also Jotterand and Bosco (2020).

[36] Attributed to video artist Nam June Paik.

[37] Interview with Tomas Chamorro-Premuzic, Chief Innovation Officer at Manpower Group, Professor of Business Psychology at University College, London, and Columbia University, New York (Severin 2023, p. 21).

[38] Cf. Susskind (2023), p. 256. Cf. Amara's Law: "We tend to overestimate the effect of a technology in the short run and underestimate the effect in the long run," coined by Roy Amara, former president of The Institute for the Future (Amara 2006).

It is still too early to talk about disruption today, and we will only be able to recognise it retrospectively. In my opinion, a major change will initially occur at the level of business models rather than in a changed product range. It will remain exciting to see whether and to what extent AI will also find its way into high-level and complex legal work.

However, the initial question remains unanswered: if the use of AI increases efficiency, what do we do with the time thus saved? Firstly, we could continue working in the same way which, however, requires sufficient other productive work that genuinely needs legal expertise and is also compensated for. Optimists like to point out that lawyers could then concentrate more on tricky, exciting, high-value, and complex challenges and by doing so, move up the value chain (and increase the hourly rates). I doubt that such work is available in sufficient quantity, and that so many rocket scientists will be required. A simple look at today's large law firms (keyword: leverage factor) shows: already now a large number of cases or sub-activities are handled by lawyers which do not even require a lawyer, let alone a rocket scientist. There is even a risk that the number of hours spent on so-called bespoke work will decrease in the future because customers will no longer accept a cross-subsidisation. Secondly, you could take more time for your customers, for example, to better understand the facts of the case and provide legal advice that is not only legally correct but also useful for the customer. Thirdly, the time available could be invested into own education, training, and personal development, to make whole for the loss of human creativity, to improve non-legal competences and skills, and to reconsider strategic positioning and the own USP. Fourth, the new freedom can be used for more free time. However, this will also raise the tricky question of whether you expect to continue to earn the same salary and who should pay for it. Ultimately, I assume that the number of human resources required to do the job will decrease.

Liquid-Legal-Waves to Other Chapters, Written by the Editors

Bruno's call-to-action for adequate risk-management by the stakeholders in the legal ecosystem provides a perfect basis to explore *Erion's* chapter on *"Decoding Public and Private AI Legal Tech: Autonomy, Liability, Legal and Ethical Risk"*.

However, focusing primarily on the risk-side of AI might push the pendulum to far on the restrictive side. How easily this might be the—unintended—result of regulation explain *Marco*, *Sharon*, *Christina*, and *Robert* in their chapter on *"Evaluating how the AI Act affects Systems in the Pharma and BioTech Sector"*.

So—can technology help mitigate the risks of technology? Good timing to next follow *Anita* into the vision of *"Digital Twins of Law. Embracing Complexity"* to see if technology's unique features might help us bring our rigid legal systems back to life—or sustain their longevity?

Acknowledgements
I would like to thank Amelia Amanda Bruderer, LLB (Hons), for her valuable thoughts and comments in the preparation of this article and her meticulous support in the literature research. It has been considered literature until the end of 2023.

References

Amara R (2006) Oxford Reference. In: Ratcliffe S (ed) Oxford Essential Quotations 2016, 4th edn. Oxford. https://www.oxfordreference.com/display/10.1093/acref/9780191826719.001.0001/q-oro-ed4-00018679

Aumann Y (2018) Artificial Intelligence vs. Human in the Legal Profession - AI vs. Legal Profession. In: LRZ E-Journal for Business Law & Digitalisation LR 2018, pp 74–76. www.lrz.legal/2018S74

Bhattacharya I, Khandwala YS, Vesal S, Shao W, Yang Q, Soerensen SJC, Fan RE, Ghanouni P, Kunder CA, Brooks JD, Hu Y, Rusu M, Sonn GA (2022) A review of artificial intelligence in prostate cancer detection on imaging. Ther Adv Urol 2022 Oct 10. https://doi.org/10.1177/17562872221128791

Biermann Verlag GmbH (2023) Artificial intelligence recognises prostate cancer in MRI as well as trained radiologists. https://biermann-medizin.de/kuenstliche-intelligenz-erkennt-prostatakrebs-in-der-mrt-so-gut-wie-ausgebildete-radiologen/#:~:text=Artificial%20Intelligence%20(AI)%20can%20detect%20prostate%20cancer,(USA)%20presented%20is%20presented

Bleiker C (2021) Google app to recognise skin diseases. Deutsche Welle. https://www.dw.com/de/ausschlag-oder-hautkrebs-google-app-soll-hautkrankheiten-erkennen/a-57625767

Blume E (2019) Man vs. machine - the benefits of AI in imaging. MEDICA. https://www.medica.de/de/digital-health/Mensch_vs._Maschine_-_der_Nutzen_von_KI_in_der_Bildgebung

Braun Binder N, Burri T, Lohmann MF, Simmler M, Thouvenin F, Vokinger KN (2021) Artificial intelligence: need for action in Swiss law. In: Jusletter 2021 Jun 28. https://jusletter.weblaw.ch/juslissues/2021/1072/kunstliche-intellige_aad585e523.html__ONCE&login=false

Brochner NM (2023) Will AI replace lawyers? Forbes Technology Council. https://www.forbes.com/sites/forbestechcouncil/2023/05/25/will-ai-replace-lawyers/

Dibbits K (2017) Richard Arkwright: Innovation and Controversy. Science and Industry Museum. https://blog.scienceandindustrymuseum.org.uk/richard-arkwright/

Dipshan R (2023) Is Generative AI Coming For Your Billable Hours? ALM Global, Legaltech news. https://www.law.com/legaltechnews/2023/09/26/is-generative-ai-coming-for-your-billable-hours/

Du Sautoy (2019) Can AI ever be truly creative? New Sci 242(3229):38–41. https://doi.org/10.1016/S0262-4079(19)30840-1

ERIH (2023) On the History of Textiles Production. https://www.erih.net/how-it-started/history-of-industries/textiles

European Commission (2021) Proposal for a regulation of the European Parliament and of the Council on laying down harmonised rules on Artificial Intelligence (Artificial Intelligence Act) and amending certain Union Legislative Acts (COM2021/0206 - C9-0146/2021 - 2021/0106 (COD). https://eur-lex.europa.eu/legal-content/EN/TXT/?uri=CELEX:52021PC0206

Felten E, Raj M, Seamans R (2023) How will Language Modelers like ChatGPT Affect Occupations and Industries? https://papers.ssrn.com/sol3/papers.cfm?abstract_id=4375268

Fügener A, Grahl J, Gupta A, Ketter W (2022) Cognitive challenges in human-artificial intelligence collaboration: investigating the path toward productive delegation. Inf Syst Res 33(2):678–696. https://doi.org/10.1287/isre.2021.1079

Goldman Sachs (2023) The potentially large effects of artificial intelligence on economic growth. https://www.gspublishing.com/content/research/en/reports/2023/03/27/d64e052b-0f6e-45d7-967b-d7be35fabd16.html

Hartung M (2018) Thoughts on legal tech and digitalisation. In: Hartung M, Bues MM, Halbleib G (eds) Legal Tech - the digitalisation of the legal market, pp 5–18, point 14

Henderson B (2019) American law firms in transition: trends, threats, and strategies (book review). Legal Evolution PBC. https://www.legalevolution.org/2019/08/american-law-firms-in-transition-book-review-110/

Jotterand F, Bosco C (2020) Keeping the "Human in the Loop" in the age of artificial intelligence. Sci Eng Ethics 26(5):2455–2460. https://doi.org/10.1007/s11948-020-00241-1

Kölling M (2023) "Wake up, Japan," says Softbank boss Son. Artificial intelligence will surpass human capabilities in ten years. In: NZZ, 2023 Oct 4, p 22. https://www.nzz.ch/wirtschaft/softbank-chef-son-erwartet-agi-in-zehn-jahren-ld.1759241

Kravitz A (2023) ChatGPT and the future of corporate legal work: insights and hallucinations. Fordham J Corp Financ Law. https://news.law.fordham.edu/jcfl/2023/03/25/chatgpt-and-the-future-of-corporate-legal-work-insights-and-hallucinations/

Lips M, Şahin F, Rosenauer P (2023) Efficiency enhancement opportunities through generative AI for legal services. Lawyers' Rev 8:323–327

Marcus G (2022) AI platforms like ChatGPT are easy to use but also potentially dangerous. Scientific American. https://www.scientificamerican.com/article/ai-platforms-like-chatgpt-are-easy-to-use-but-also-potentially-dangerous/

Mascello B (2018) Strategic positioning of law firms in times of LegalTech and digitalisation. Lawyers' Rev 1:18–24

Mascello B (2020) How a simple "or" becomes an innovation killer in the legal market. https://es.unisg.ch/de/blog/wie-ein-simples-oder-zum-innovationskiller-im-rechtsmarkt-wird

Mascello B (2023) Are lawyers threatened by a convenience trap? https://es.unisg.ch/en/blog/are-lawyers-being-threatened-by-a-convenience-trap/

Mascello B (2024a) Umgang mit KI überdenken und auf Konsolidierung setzen. Was den Rechtsmarkt 2024 prägen wird. Anwaltspiegel, 4 Januar 2024, pp 3–5. https://www.deutscheranwaltspiegel.de/wp-content/uploads/sites/49/2024/01/DAS-Online_Ausgabe-01-2024_L.pdf#page=3

Mascello B (2024b) Artificial Intelligence – Asterix' magic potion and a leveller of lawyers? German Law International, 1/2024, p 2. https://www.deutscheranwaltspiegel.de/wp-content/uploads/sites/49/2024/03/GermanLawInternational_01-2024_L.pdf#page=2

Microsoft (2023) What is Azure OpenAI Service? https://learn.microsoft.com/en-us/azure/ai-services/openai/overview

Müller-Stewens G (2016) Strategic management as a discipline - milestones and prospects for its development. Die Unternehmung - Swiss J Bus Res Pract. Nomos Verlagsgesellschaft mbH & Co KG 70(4):322–343. https://www.alexandria.unisg.ch/server/api/core/bitstreams/012e17dc-c082-4352-9daa-a8784b8860fa/content

Rattray K (2023) Harvey AI: What We Know So Far. Themis Solutions Inc (Clio). https://www.clio.com/blog/harvey-ai-legal/

Rodrigues R (2020) Legal and human rights issues of AI: gaps, challenges and vulnerabilities. J Responsible Technol 4. https://doi.org/10.1016/j.jrt.2020.100005

Severin Ch (2023) In this interview, industrial psychologist Tomas Chamorro explains why the digital world promotes narcissism, why the search for happiness in everyday working life is counterproductive. And why mobile phones make us stupid. In: NZZ, 2023 Oct 2, p 21. https://www.nzz.ch/wirtschaft/arbeitspsychologe-die-ablenkung-durch-das-smartphone-reduziert-unsere-geistigen-faehigkeiten-um-zehn-iq-punkte-ld.1757284

Shin R (2023) Humiliated lawyers fined $5,000 for submitting ChatGPT hallucinations in court: 'I heard about this new site, which I falsely assumed was, like, a super search engine'. Fortune. https://fortune.com/2023/06/23/lawyers-fined-filing-chatgpt-hallucinations-in-court/

Siegel E (2023) The AI hype cycle is distracting companies. Harv Bus Rev. https://hbr.org/2023/06/the-ai-hype-cycle-is-distracting-companies

Staub L (2012) Accounting and Billing. In: Staub L, Hehli Hidber Ch (eds) Management von Anwaltskanzleien, pp 525–614, point 61 ff

Susskind R (2023) Tomorrow's Lawyers, 3rd edn. Oxford, p 138 ff

Tang X, Li X, Ding Y, Song M, Bu Y (2020) The pace of artificial intelligence innovations: speed, talent, and trial-and-error. J Informetr 14. https://www.sciencedirect.com/science/article/pii/S1751157720301991

The Ezra Klein Show (2023) A Skeptical Take on the AI Revolution. In: The New York Times, 2023 Jan 6. https://www.nytimes.com/2023/01/06/opinion/ezra-klein-podcast-gary-marcus.html

The White House (2023) Executive Order on the Safe, Secure, and Trustworthy Development and Use of Artificial Intelligence. https://www.whitehouse.gov/briefing-room/presidential-actions/2023/10/30/executive-order-on-the-safe-secure-and-trustworthy-development-and-use-of-artificial-intelligence/

Thomson Reuters (2023) How AI is the Catalyst for Transforming Every Aspect of Work. Future of Professionals Report. https://www.thomsonreuters.com/content/dam/ewp-m/documents/thomsonreuters/en/pdf/reports/future-of-professionals-august-2023.pdf

UK Government (2023) AI Safety Summit 2023. https://www.gov.uk/government/topical-events/ai-safety-summit-2023

Bruno Mascello is adjunct (titular) professor of business law and legal management at the University of St. Gallen (HSG) and Director at the Executive School of Management, Technology and Law (ES-HSG) of the University of St. Gallen. He lectures at both the Executive School and the University of St. Gallen, is a keynote speaker at conferences and researches and publishes about various topics at the intersection of law and management.

Before joining the University of St. Gallen he served at an international insurance group in various leading management positions of the worldwide legal function (i.a., as Chief Operations Officer Group Legal/Compliance; Regional General Counsel), after having worked first as a senior attorney in law firm focused on international corporate and business law.

Bruno Mascello studied law at the faculty of law (lic.iur./masters of laws), earned a Ph.D. (Dr.iur.) and completed an Executive MBA at the University of St. Gallen. He holds an LL.M. in Comparative Jurisprudence from New York University School of Law. He is a qualified lawyer, admitted to the Swiss Bar and runs a private practice providing legal, legal management and strategy consulting services.

Digital Twins of Law: Embracing Complexity

Anita Lamprecht

The balance between order and chaos is complexity.

Contents

Abstract

We must update our legal systems to keep pace with technological progress and ensure the rule of law. For this purpose, this chapter introduces the idea of utilising digital twin technology. This technology's unique features could help us bring our rigid legal systems back to life and provide better access to justice. It allows us to learn from the past, manage the present, and design the future. We can ensure human agency by embracing society and law as complex adaptive systems. The chapter builds on the authors' previous work on the architecture of law as a neural network, digital twins of law and the convergence of reality in the Metaverse.

A. Lamprecht (✉)
DiploFoundation, Geneva, Switzerland
e-mail: drlamprecht@proton.me

K. Jacob et al. (eds.), *Liquid Legal – Sustaining the Rule of Law*, Law for Professionals, https://doi.org/10.1007/978-3-031-78596-2_6

1 A New Reality beyond Transformation

Digital technologies are changing our living conditions and environment at an accelerating pace. We increasingly realise that the anticipated change will be more profound than a transformation. "*The goal is not incremental improvement, but a step change towards total reinvention. Not everybody will be ready for this change* [. . .]" (Accenture 2023, p. 2). Our digital and physical realities are converging. While transformation describes a change process, convergence comprises a more **fundamental change**. The envisioned **convergence** is about the integration of different technologies, processes, or systems into a single entity. In our case, this is a **new reality**.

The Law in a New Reality

Whenever our living conditions change, the legal world must be alert and examine if and how the legal systems need to (re)act and adapt our laws. This is especially important when economic interests heavily drive and accelerate change. In the context of this chapter, 'the **law'** is used as an **umbrella term** for an ecosystem of legal systems with many different levels and interrelated layers governing human interaction and communication. The examples mentioned are based on the perspective of civil law. While companies are already working on a new reality (i.e. the convergence of digital and physical realities), our digital life still needs impactful, accessible and enforceable regulation. Impactful regulation is lagging since digital **space evolved** as the World Wide Web (www) 30 years ago. The latest developments, especially around artificial intelligence, give us a glimpse into the legal world's challenges in this emerging reality.

The Challenge of Governing New Realities

Technology allows us to manipulate the rules of space and time. It always has. Take the invention of script or the first handprint in a cave around 40,000 years ago. Since then, we have communicated **beyond our physical limitations of time and space**. We are detaching information from our biological lifespan and giving it a more eternal existence. For example, photography and video recordings keep a memory of a person alive. Thanks to the interplay of emerging technologies, we can go much further now.

Emerging technologies, for example, enable us to upload digitalised memories (i.e. information in the form of data) of deceased loved ones and pretend to resurrect a digital version of them. Moreover, we do not stop at the dead. We do the same thing to ourselves. Voluntarily as avatars, our digital representations in the digitalised environment of our new converged reality are also referred to as the Metaverse, Virtual Worlds or Web 4.0. We are **scaling ourselves** beyond our physical limitations of space and time.

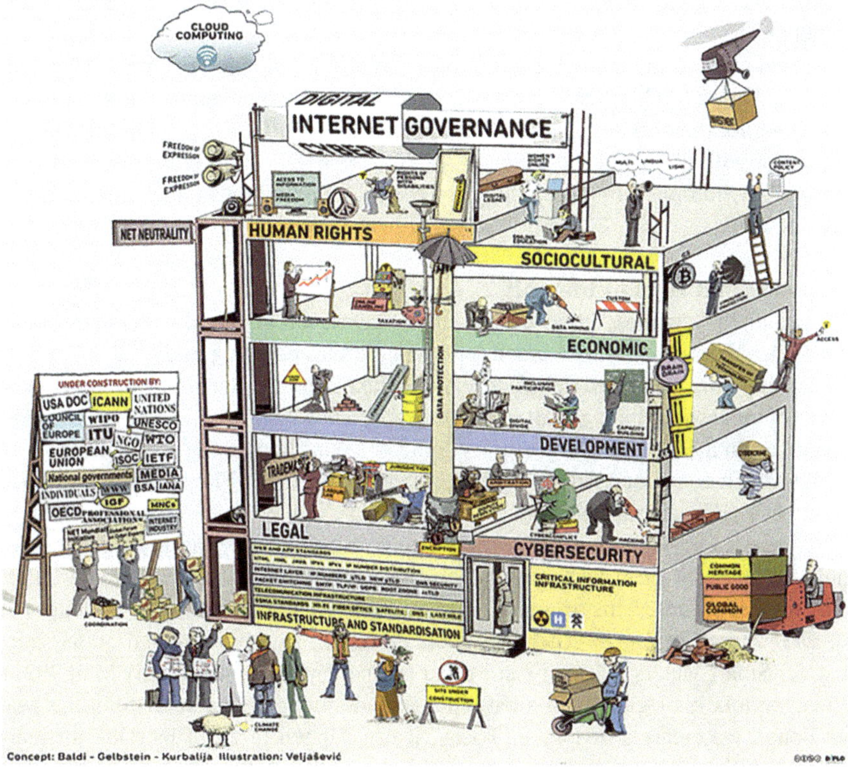

Fig. 1 Internet governance building under construction by DiploFoundation (Kurbalija 2016), licensed under CC

Law Lost in Digital Space?
We aim to put ourselves with a deep feeling of presence in a space we struggle to govern. We struggle to agree on a unified definition of this digital space, the internet or cyberspace. Internet governance is highly complex as it addresses a wide range of issues. The DiploFoundation, for example, has identified 40–50 main issues in infrastructure, security, legal, economic, development, and human rights, see Fig. 1 (Kurbalija 2016). This failure of the past is now haunting us.

A Call to Action: Protecting Humanity
In 2019, the www inventor Berners-Lee (2019) opened the International Governance Forum in Berlin with warning words. "*If we fail to tackle the threats we face, we risk a digital dystopia. We cannot leave the next generation a Web and a world that is darker than the one we have today.*" Berners-Lee highlighted several threats to the future of the web, especially the digital divide due to a lack of reliable access to the internet, the censorship and surveillance by governments, and the failure of

companies to stop misinformation and hateful content from spreading and polarising people. He warned of the effect of these threats on our trust in information and democracy.

A year later, at the annual meeting of the World Economic Forum in Davos, the historian Harari (2020) identified, besides inequality, another significant danger, '*the rise of digital dictatorships that will monitor everyone all the time*'. He summarised this threat with the danger formula: B x C x D = AHH. In other words, biological knowledge multiplied by computing power multiplied by data equals the ability to hack humans.

Deepfakes and Human Integrity

We can already witness how these dangers have become a reality (Adjeder et al. 2019). An alarming form of human representation is spreading in digital space with devastating consequences: deepfakes. A deepfake is manipulated or synthetic audio or visual media convincingly altered to misrepresent a person and deceive the media consumer. In a deepfake, the person is doing or saying something not done or stated by the person concerned. **Deepfakes** are not a new problem. They have been around for a while (European Parliament 2021).

A great example is Nobel laureate Albert Einstein. He has been resurrected multiple times. We can find him as a humanoid robot, a digital twin, and a digital human. In some cases, his resurrection is understood as a celebration of his legacy as by ETH Zurich (n.d.). In other instances, he serves as a promotional ambassador (e.g. for Smart Meters 2023) or some other form of entertainment (Daily Mail 2021). When we mix his legacy with alien input (i.e., doing or saying something that was not done), we create a deepfake. Today, it can happen to all of us. Due to freely available technology, everybody can quickly become a victim and a perpetrator in a digital reality of unlimited possibilities. The recent surge in their accessibility and scalability has motivated legislative action in countries like the US (Burga 2024) and the UK (Ministry of Justice and Farris J. 2024).

Human Rights Going Online

Deepfakes, especially in the form of deepfake pornography, are a massive challenge to our **human right to dignity,** as granted in Article 1 of the Universal Declaration of Human Rights (UDHR). Due to the devastating effects, especially on our mental integrity. Within the European Union, our physical and mental integrity is protected by Article 3 of the Charter of Fundamental Rights of the European Union (ECHR). In 2023, the citizens of the Swiss canton of Geneva voted to explicitly incorporate digital integrity into the Constitution of Geneva to ensure the protection of people's autonomy and freedom in digital space (Rochel 2023; digwatch 2020).

"*Digital integrity includes the right to be protected against the abusive processing of data related to digital life, the right to security in the digital space, the right to life offline, and the right to be forgotten.*" (EPFL 2023).

In March 2024, the United Nations (UN) affirmed that **the same rights that people have offline must also be protected online** as part of the newly adopted global resolution on AI (UN News 2024).

AI Relationships: Protecting Mental Integrity

Our mental integrity is not just challenged by the misuse of deepfake technology but also in our relationship with chatbots. Mental integrity is discussed in the context of neurotechnology and how it interferes with our brains. It protects "*mental life being in some sense whole, unimpaired or undivided*" (Zohny et al. 2023). Considering the manipulative potential of chatbots, equal consideration should be given to them, as in the fields of neurotechnology.

Current experience shows that we are not ready for a human-chatbot relationship (Reuters 2023; Brussels Times 2023). What seems like a dream can quickly turn into a manipulative nightmare. Chatbots can use persuasive language and psychological tactics to manipulate their human counterparts. Behavioural chatbots are intentionally made to mimic communication beyond words. Such communication is only possible if the system can 'read' a person in a similar way as we humans do.

Moreover, they are far more intrusive due to the nature of underlying AI systems. This raises the question of whether legislation like the EU's AI Act is sufficient to regulate this new form of human-machine relationship. In 2023, claims were raised that a chatbot encouraged a man to commit suicide (Bharade 2023). The system behind such artificial humans understands how to manipulate us, but we do not understand it (Harari 2023).

Challenges of Tomorrow

Why is such a development giving us a glimpse into the legal world's challenges in this emerging reality? Because it symbolises the profound and rapid effect of digital change on our lives and the law. It concerns the core of our existence and humanity at an accelerated pace, challenging our trust in digital communication, our relationships, the agency over our digital DNA (i.e. data), and the protection of the most basic human rights.

In this fast-converged reality, our human integrity heavily depends on our digital embodiments and our relationship with technology. Both follow different rules of nature and economics than our physical existence and human relationships. This rapid shift exposes the limitations of current legal frameworks.

2 Complexity and the Rule of Law

From a legal perspective, the rapid convergence of the physical and digital worlds presents a significant challenge due to the **high complexity** of the emerging interactions.

The Human Dimension

Human life is complex because humans, societies and even the law are complex adaptive systems. What is a complex adaptive system? It is a system where "*the action of the whole is more than the sum of the actions of the parts*" (Holland 2014). This **interaction between agents** is characterised by self-reinforcing cycles (called **feedback loops**) and the distinctive feature of the emergence of new, unexpected interactions between the agents. Such behaviour is **non-linear**, making governing complex adaptive systems challenging.

The Dimension of Sovereignty

Our legal systems are mainly based on their relation to physical entities such as land and the people acting on this territory or being connected to it (through citizenship) in specific frames of time and space. The principle of sovereignty, a state's right to govern its internal and external affairs without interference, has been and is still seen as a significant obstacle in fragmented (internet) regulation.

The lack of a unified, global framework makes safeguarding fundamental rights and the well-being of individuals beyond their own countries difficult. At the same time, the principle of sovereignty helps to reduce complexity by tailoring regulation to the specific needs of a country's citizens. The challenge is to **move beyond a binary view** of local versus international regulation.

The Dimension of Convergence

As highlighted earlier, our digital and physical realities converge, bringing a **fundamental change**. **Convergence** integrates different technologies, processes, or systems with human societies and nature. Through interaction, technological systems become agents in our systems and humans in them. **Feedback loops reinforce** certain behaviours, and **new, unexpected behaviour emerges**.

These **agents** are different from biological agents and behave differently. Therefore, we can especially expect the emergence of new, unexpected behaviour and a new form of tailored reinforcement. This will probably increase complexity at an unprecedented pace and scale, making governance and protection of even the most fundamental human rights more difficult.

It Is Not Complicated. It Is Complex

How do we solve this problem? This depends on the agents. Technological agents are introduced into our human system by humans, thus the discussion about guardrails. Human agents, on the other hand, need to be treated differently. We shouldn't regard human behaviour as complicated but rather as complex. So, how do we solve the problem of complexity?

We do not, at least not with the claim of finality. Instead, we should embrace complexity as a distinct feature of human life and shift our mindset from complicated problem-solving to managing complexity (Gordon and Williams 2020). The crucial question is how we can manage such an approach. This chapter proposes digital twin technology as a promising method to manage the complexity of life. By creating digital twins of our legal systems and embedding them in an even broader ecosystem of digital twins, we could find much quicker solutions for new challenges and even design a new way of international governance.

The Simplification Trap

By utilising digital twin technology, we try to avoid the trap of simplification. We encounter simplification in two ways. The first is the notion of re-establishing the rule of law and access to justice, especially in the borderless world of the internet, through a call for a unified, global framework. Secondly, technology tends to offer simplified solutions. Whenever new developments in artificial intelligence emerge, hopes are high that technology could help us solve the problem of access to justice.

Simplifying complex adaptive systems in human societies is a **dangerous trap**. The trap is to bring order into the alleged chaos. History is full of examples, in the form of secular and religious dominance, that demand following a single source of truth. Simplification has manipulation at its core, which requires the ability to hack humans, whether directly by humans or through machines.

Navigating Complexity: A Road Map to Humanity

Legal systems based on democracy and human rights try to embrace complexity through a **delicate network** of institutions. This complexity encompasses diverse cultures, individual needs, and evolving social structures. Remarkably, the experiences of the Second World War, an example of the dangers of over-simplification, led to the UN's Universal Declaration of Human Rights (UDHR) in 1948.

The UDHR acknowledges the inherent complexity of human life and its need to be protected by a framework of human rights. Our human rights are "*a road map to guarantee the rights of every individual everywhere*", considering that "*there is more than one kind of ultimate reality.*" (United Nations 2023). The problem with road maps is that we need to acquire the ability to read, interpret, and follow them. We also need road signs and landmarks to remain on the right path. **We quickly get lost without all this information and skills**, just like with human rights and our legal systems. The Pact for the Future and the transformed UN 2.0 show us a path to a better future for all, with technological progress at its heart. This article, while focused specifically on the potential of digital twin technology, leaves the analysis of its intersection with UN 2.0 to the author's future research.

From Traffic Lights to Digital Twins

However, the UN's **figure of speech of** road maps leads us directly to our digital twin strategy. Traffic has utilised technological progress for a long time and offers excellent learnings for our effort to update the law. We rely on an ecosystem of traffic lights, navigation systems, and speed traps to keep us on the desired path. Digital twin systems have already been developed and are used in many areas of logistics and public transport (Härdi 2021).

One of the agents in this new traffic ecosystem is automated, self-driving cars. They have been introduced into this ecosystem with the hope and promise to increase safety and improve traffic flow and mobility, even for people who cannot drive themselves. Tesla, for example, announced in 2016 that the automated car driving problem was solved (Tesla 2016). Despite this initial optimism, the technology remains under development. Legal investigations have been launched following fatal incidents involving Tesla vehicles equipped with self-driving features (Carter 2023).

Gaining Agency as co-Pilots

The example of self-driving cars highlights the need for continued development and rigorous safety testing before widespread adoption. Technology, as defined by Britannica, is "*the application of scientific knowledge to the practical aims.*" Without sufficient knowledge, the aim of autonomous driving remains out of reach, and drivers need to keep their hands on the wheel (BBC 2023). In such a case, technology can support humans as co-pilot. This means it assists the **human pilot** with specific tasks (such as lane control, parking assistance, etc.).

While full automation has yet to be reached in many areas, digitalisation already has a massive advantage. Objects such as cars, systems, and processes **emerge in different, "smart" ways** to help us deal with complex situations. Their value for humanity depends on how we establish this **relationship**. To get this relationship right, we must ask whether we are falling into the trap of harmful simplification or whether we could manage **complexity** through digital twin technology tailored to specific needs and mutual capabilities.

3 Digital Twins: Managing Complexity in Real-Time

Across industries, digital twin technology is employed and developed to tackle the most challenging and complex problems. The real-time exchange of data and the interaction between the twin entities makes digital twin technology so unique. The digital twin **becomes alive** through the information provided by the non-digital entity. Its purpose is (usually) not to become independent but to serve **as life support** for the other twin. It allows us to perform tasks beyond our physical limitations. This can be simply a remote update of the "autopilot" system of a car or the dynamic modelling of entire (smart) cities and the planning of medical treatments of humans.

What Is Exactly a Digital Twin?

A digital twin is a virtual, computer-generated representation of a physical entity. The physical entity can be an object, a subject, a process, and even an extraordinarily complex ecosystem like Earth. The digital twin is often described as a digital replica. The digital and non-digital twins are connected by constantly exchanging real-time data and interaction. They **evolve together**. The interplay of high-performance computing, machine learning, and data represents past, present, and future changes.

Digital Twins on a Space Mission

The US space agency NASA created the first digital twin as a "***living model***" of the Apollo 13 mission in the 1960s. After the explosion of an oxygen tank, the digital twin allowed the team based on Earth to conduct a virtual forensic investigation of the blast, find solutions, and perform remote maintenance on the system. Today, NASA develops systems with much more **independence** as constant connectivity and human intervention on demand are impossible for missions into deeper space. The scale and the **non-deterministic** nature characterise the digital twin models developed for such a purpose. As there will not be just one digital twin but many autonomous models, NASA speaks of "*a changing ecosystem, returning to the idea of a living model*". (NASA 2021).

A Galaxy of Digital Twins

In the EU project interTwin, leading scientists in CERN are even building a **blueprint for a digital twin engine** to "*connect the galaxy of sciences.*" (European Commission 2023). Such a **network of digital twins** could also fundamentally change the internet ecosystem if realised. Maybe we will witness another ground-breaking invention from the birthplace of our current www. A web that might even exceed the visionary plans of the Semantic Web from 2001 (see 'Back to the Future of 2001'). Meanwhile, digital twin technology is developed to tackle one of humanity's most complex and pressing problems, climate change.

Digital Twin Ecosystems of Earth

The US (NASA 2023) and the European Union (ESA 2023) have launched ambitious projects to build ecosystems of digital twins of the earth. Destination Earth is a flagship initiative of the European Commission. The initiative aims to develop highly accurate digital models or twins of Earth. The digital twins will **model, monitor, and simulate** complex natural development and human activities. To **anticipate** natural disasters and enable simulations to **develop solution** strategies and policies. Both projects were created with the affiliated space agencies.

Legal Climate Change

While climate change is a natural phenomenon and the law is a human construct, they share fundamental characteristics. Both climate and legal systems are complex adaptive systems. Natural disasters due to climate changes as well as a limited access to justice affect the most vulnerable disproportionally. Therefore, it is a social matter. They are equally.

global matters due to the borderless nature of weather phenomena and the digital space. Most of all, it is a human matter. Climate change and limited access to justice disrupt human life. The devastating consequence of the spread of deepfakes, especially in the deepfake pornography, are a neglected example of such a disruption.

This chapter supports the idea to utilize digital twins' technology to modernize the legal ecosystem.

The System behind the Bot

Like climate change, we need to monitor the effects of human activity, understand connections, simulate developments, and test solutions. Furthermore, we anticipate disasters and socioeconomic crises so that we can adapt our strategies and policies. Digital twins of law could be promising **because they enable humans** to make informed decisions on policies, governance, and laws, even for the most complex global challenges. Eventually, digital twins could be the **technological system behind the bot** we eagerly hope for. Such a bot could provide real-time access to up-to-date legal information and provide feedback to the legal system. (Lamprecht 2023).

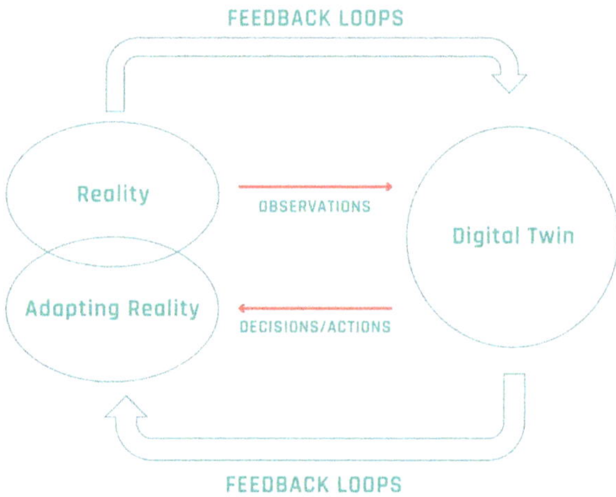

Fig. 2 Predictive Maintenance by ECMWF (adapted), licensed under CC

Combating Deepfakes: A Use Case

What if we could use digital twin technology to fight deepfakes by protecting, detecting, and prosecuting the misuse of technology to make and distribute them? We would need to create an ecosystem of information (data), knowledge, and processes. This would include identifying deepfakes, securing evidence, automated informing the responsible authorities, and supporting trial processing by identifying relevant documents and law.

A Digital Immune System

The development of protective systems, like a multi-dimensional digital immune system, should go hand in hand with creating digital humans, especially if they are the digital copy of an existing human being or even functioning as their digital twin with real-time data exchange. These digital twins could serve as a verifiable baseline for authentication and, therefore, detection of deepfakes. Such a system would require strong privacy protection, comparable to the human immune system.

Its design would depend on the existing technological capabilities and legal framework. The system would need to provide **feedback** to other connected twin systems. This would help align international cooperation, law enforcement, and the development of suitable legislation on a national and international level. It could help us anticipate **emerging** deepfake methods, legal and societal challenges as well as identify loopholes (compare Fig. 2. Predictive Maintenance by ECMWF (2024).

Ecosystems of Twins

Considering the ambitious efforts to build interTwin, a blueprint of digital twin technology to connect the galaxy of sciences, the legal world should take advantage of timely involvement in **shaping the future** worldwide web of digital twins. Imagine an **ecosystem** of distributed, independent, yet collaborative legal systems. Systems that can directly interact with the space they are supposed to govern. The twins need to remain connected but still independent entities. They are evolving together with progress but existing on their own. With a **backup system** in place to ensure resilience against manipulation. With clearly defined roles and realistic expectations. To achieve such a collaboration, we must be very clear about our relationship with technology.

4 Framing the Twin Relationship

This chapter introduces the **two-dimensional framework, Levels of Digital Twins** (LoDT), by Agrawal et al. (2023) to show a possible design of a (legal) twin relationship, see Fig. 3.

The First Dimension

The first dimension distinguishes between a digital twin (DT) 's four roles. It can fulfil the roles of (1) an Observer, (2) an Analyst, (3) a Decision-maker, and (4) an Action Executor. The concrete functions performed by each role depend on the task at hand. Table 1 outlines some examples of the expected functions for distinct roles.

The Second Dimension

The second dimension covers allocating these four roles between the human operator and the digital twin. The extent of automation by the digital twin is divided into four plus one different level, see Table 2.

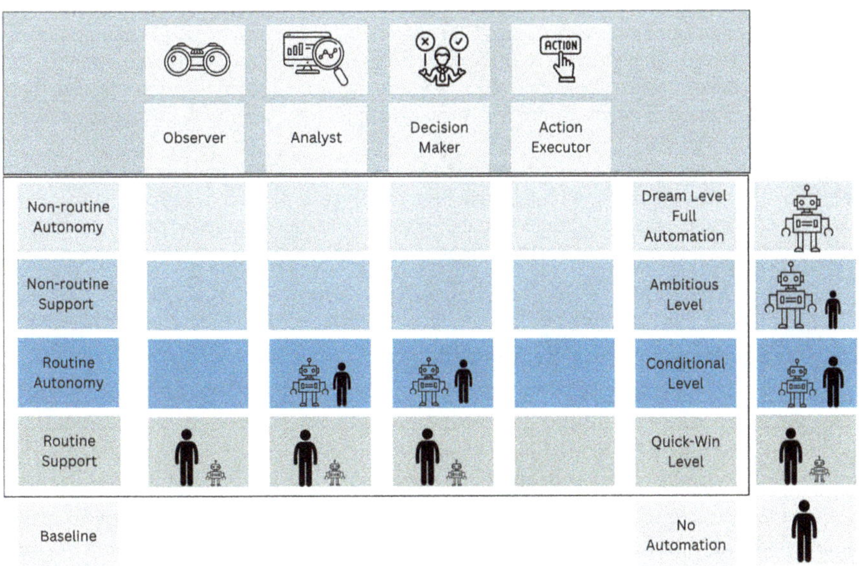

Fig. 3 Levels of Digital Twin framework

Table 1 First Dimension—Role Description

Role	Role description
Observer	Basic manipulation tasks are performed including sensing, representing, describing, visualising, and retrieving information. In the case of deepfakes, the twin could be employed to monitor online activities comparable to a virus scan.
Analyst	An analyst is responsible for analysing and monitoring data, recognising patterns, making predictions, interpreting data, diagnosing problems, optimising processes, simulating scenarios, forecasting outcomes, and prescribing solutions. In the case of deepfakes, suspicious content could be analysed and compared to the authentic data by the digital twin.
Decision maker	A decision maker is responsible for planning, taking physical action, communicating, and controlling. Action executors oversee these activities. The digital twin, in our example, could provide information to decide whether further steps need to be taken by reporting its findings to the person concerned or directly to the competent authorities, such as platform content moderators.

Table 2 Second Dimension—Role Allocation

Level	Role allocation
Baseline	**At the baseline** the human operator performs all tasks entirely manually. This means no automation by the digital twin takes place.
First level	**At the quick-win level** the digital twin helps to reduce human workload**.** For example, by performing online scans to detect potential deepfakes.
Second level	**At the conditional level, the human acts as a backup for the system. In this setting, the digital twin performs** *support*. Simple rule-based situations are automated with human support. In addition to scanning for potential deepfakes, the system would provide an analysis under human supervision.
Third level	**At the ambitious level** human(like) capabilities are extended. This means the digital twin handles simple rule-based situations autonomously. The human operator comes into play again to support the digital twin in (non-routine) complex and dynamic situations. In the example of deepfakes, the digital twin would automatically flag, secure and report deepfakes to the platform and notify relevant authorities to ensure the timely removal of harmful deepfakes, limiting their reach and impact.
Fourth level	**At the dream level full automation is achieved.** Non-routine autonomy is completed, and the digital twin handles complex, dynamic situations autonomously. In addition to the previous tasks, the digital twin would proactively take action to mitigate the damage. For example, by informing business partners, or in case of celebrities the press of the incident.

The Dark Side of the Twin Relationship

The LoDT framework leaves many research questions open. Especially the effect of this **allocation of roles** on the human-digital twin interface and other human and technological factors. The reliability, robustness, and resilience of the engineering of digital twins have considerable effects on humans' well-being, health, and safety.

The chapter suggests exploring a generalisable **framework** which should bring the legal world into play. (Agrawal et al. 2023). The legal world would not start from nothing. There is a rich debate about the capabilities and limits of technology from a legal, ethical and technological perspective. Such a framework could also use the research and experience of all related technologies and fields, such as the Internet of Things, AI, cybersecurity, and many more, to identify the dangers of digital twin technology. This chapter focuses on utilising **digital twin** technology for better access to justice and the rule of law.

5 Managing Expectations

Respect your Partner

To improve access to justice and the rule of law, we need to establish a healthy balance or rather **relationship between technology and humans**. Both extremes, from no automation at the "Baseline" to full automation at the "Dream Level", are not serving our purpose of providing better access to justice. At the Baseline, all tasks such as monitoring, legal research, drafting, case management, communication, judgements, and legislation are performed by humans. The Dream Level is the final level. On this level, the digital twin performs full automation even for complex, dynamic situations such as conflict resolution, decision making and legislation without any human operator.

At the Dream Level, it would mean the **replacement of the legal profession, including the judicial system,** by technology. Replacing court services with technology requires re-thinking, among other things, the right to a fair trial and a public hearing. Considerations that can build on the experiences from online platforms to conduct remote hearings during the COVID-19 pandemic (OHCHR 2023). With the advent of ChatGPT, the replacement of legal services by technology seemed to become possible in 2022. Lawyers were once again leading the list of professions to be replaced by AI.

History keeps repeating itself. In the 1980s and 1990s, legal expert systems promised to digitalise legal knowledge through a rule-based logic. By 2000, the expectations were downsized to mere support systems instead of replacing human legal experts. (Leith 2010). Another promising system was IBM's Watson around 10 years ago; however," *Connecting concepts and building taxonomies for every word are monumentally tricky tasks. It is so difficult that despite IBM's Watson spending billions to advance this technology, it never truly came to fruition.*" (Silver 2020).

Superior Intelligence or Agents of Change

Generative AI systems such as GPT-4, LaMDA, and PaLM are the latest promising methods. The downside of these models is that they "*make things up*" (Ray 2023; Heikkilä 2023) due to their pseudo non-deterministic nature. Such systems only give the **illusion of human-like semantic understanding**. Despite impressively progressive AI systems, they still **miss the crucial requirement of "*common sense*"**. "*Common sense is the basic understanding of the world and humans. An "ability to use models of the world to fill in information about the world that is unavailable form perception or memory (e.g., to predict the future).*" (Dawid and LeCun 2023,

p. 5). Nonetheless, some are pushing the notion of a **superintelligence** that will somehow emerge from such systems at some point.

So far, the legal world is **trying to comprehend** the opportunities and challenges of generative AI for law. The predicted fall of the legal profession has not taken place. Instead, we are defending professionals from the creative and information sector, who are forced to fight for the survival of their professions and indirectly for human integrity in digital space (deep fakes). The situation in the relationship seems obvious. Those behind the technologies demand that the rest of us accept and adapt to the new reality after building and introducing the technologies to the world, leaving us to wonder about the **quality of our relationship**.

Reframing our Relationship

The framework of the digital twin relationship offers a **nuanced approach** to a human–technological collaboration. Although developed for the construction industry, the two-dimensional framework of Levels of Digital Twins is a great starting point for **designing the relationship** properly. After briefly analysing what went wrong, the next step is to take a deeper look at the nature of the law to establish the distinct roles properly.

6 The Nature of Law

At its very core, law is the attempt to regulate interpersonal and **social behaviour**. Law is, in its essence, about **human relations**. Humans form societies, which are complex adaptive systems. This means they are composed of interconnected agents which interact with each other in unpredictable ways. Those agents can learn and change their behaviour. (Winston 2023, p. 2). Law provides a specific stability to ensure a **peaceful co-existence**. Legal norms are ideally formulated in such a general and abstract way that they enable the broadest possible and long-term applicability. In addition, formal law provides some concrete, almost static **framework** for the enforceability of substantive law. If we act in a certain way, we can ideally predict what will happen in the future.

As per the complex nature of law, the system also includes **unanswered questions and inconsistencies**. The art of legal interpretation by legal experts allows us **to adapt** the law to everchanging values and the emergence of unexpected situations and, therefore, to balance the complexity of human societies. Law is a **social contract** that determines what kind of reality we want to live in. An **intersubjective reality,** as Harari (2017) calls it. A reality that only exists because people believe and **commit to** it. Ideally, by accepting that there is more than one reality, as agreed 75 years ago through the Declaration of Human Rights by the UN (as discussed above).

Lost in Translation

This social contract is constantly re-negotiated, weighing interests. The Human Rights and National Constitutions are building the guardrails for it. Our values are only sometimes logical or straightforward. Moreover, they are not homogeneous. Laws are **artificially created models of the world** based on a shared common sense or unwritten rules of reality. Let us look at a simple example. Imagine a (non-legal) friend. Let us call him Bob. Bob wants to get married in Austria. Before he ties the knot for life, he wants to know what to expect legally. He reads the definition of the legal term «marriage» in the Austrian Civil Code, §44 ABGB (2017). Does Bob now know what marriage means in legal terms? Probably not. "*The family relationships are established by marital contract. In the marital contract, two persons lawfully declare their will to live in inseparable union, to conceive children, to educate them, and to support each other.*"

We lawyers know that §44 consists of a series of legal terms that must be considered. Bob, on the other hand, does not see it this way. He sees this one paragraph. The term "*inseparable community*" will confuse him. Some of his friends are probably already divorced. The situation is even more tricky for his partner, Alice. She comes from another country. For example, from Dubai. Her legal and, especially, **cultural understanding** of marriage is quite different. Bob might translate the definition of marriage for her. However, the specific legal community's **underlying social concept** and consequences remain **hidden**. Anne and Bob do not share a common legal sense. This is noticeably clear on an international level. And their different values on marriage.

§ 44 is especially interesting, as it is also a notable example of the **inconsistency in the interpretation** of the law. At one time, we ignore the precise meaning of terms such as "inseparable community;" at other times, we insist on the literal meaning and modify the wording. For example, in the previous version of §44, marriage was still limited to persons of "*different sexes*". The reason? You find it out by interpreting the social, unwritten values behind written code. Especially in the international context, we quickly find ourselves alien to the unwritten laws of other cultures and societies. (see Lamprecht 2022a, 2022b).

When Law Froze into Code

As technological progress rapidly changes our reality, we find ourselves in a legally challenging, if not unknown, **space where** adequate, timely human intervention is no longer possible. Like NASA, we should consider developing an **adequate system** for these challenges. Let us follow NASA's example and examine how to return to the idea of a living model of law. Legal systems were once living models consisting of human agents before humans invented one of the most potent tools: script.

Before the codification, or rather, transfer of law into a written format, people created and **communicated** their rules of conduct **directly** among themselves. The interaction took place in a shared space and time. Those rules of conduct were embedded in a cultural human community. The law was created, communicated, and executed within a defined human network. (Lamprecht 2021). A closed system with a **shared, intersubjective reality** (Harari 2017, p. 144f) and relatively straightforward shared social values and expectations.

The invention of **script** and the subsequent codification of the law allowed to **scale the reach of the law** in content and range. However, it also controls the content to a certain extent due to the written format. This control function has become so convincing that people fall into the simplified perspective of a law. While script was invented as merely a communication tool, written text is no longer just describing reality but has even become **more powerful than reality** itself (Harari 2017, p. 167). Codification also led to a significant interruption in the system, resulting in a loss of information and flexibility, as our example with Bob and Alice has shown. How can we change our legal ecosystem to return to a more living law model with digital twins?

7 Digital Life

Back to the Future of 2001

To answer this question, we briefly return to a point when an essential part of our future started. In 2001, the inventor of the www, Tim Berners-Lee, and colleagues envisioned the **next big step** in developing the Internet, Web 3.0. An internet that enables **agents** (i.e. software) to carry out sophisticated tasks for human users. The idea resembles current AI assistants. The difference is that the Semantic Web was envisioned as quite the opposite of these assistants. It was envisioned as a decentralised **and open web** of computable meaning.

"The Semantic Web is not a separate Web but an extension of the current one, in which information is given well-defined meaning, better-enabling computers and people to work in cooperation." "And it will "know" all this without needing artificial intelligence on the scale of 2001's Hal or Star Wars's C-3PO. Instead, these semantics were encoded into the Web page [...]." (Berners-Lee et al. 2001). The title «Semantic Web« is confusing. It does not refer to a human understanding of content. Rather, it refers to «*comprehension*» by computers. The article explains the shortcomings of knowledge trees and suggests an approach that **embraces complexity**. *"[...] any system that is complex enough to be useful also encompasses unanswerable questions, much like sophisticated versions of the basic paradox [...]. Semantic Web researchers, in contrast, accept that paradoxes and unanswerable questions are a price that must be paid to achieve versatility."*

Breathing Life into a System

This sounds very much like our legal system. Our simple example of Anne and Bob clearly shows the complex challenge of regulating human life and how our legal system accepts paradoxes and unanswerable questions. As highlighted above, **Law is a complex adaptive system** because it is a part of our societies, which are also complex adaptive systems. Interactions of **agents determine the behaviour** of the system. The agents have (relatively) free choice in their decisions, so the system's behaviour is pseudo non-deterministic and non-linear. It is a result of the **negotiations** between its agents. Objects like cars are not complex adaptive systems as they lack interacting parts. This, however, is changing when "smart" cars are embedded in an intelligent ecosystem that allows parts of the vehicle to “talk” to each other and its environment (Skobelev 2023).

Skobelev’s research translates these evolutionary principles of complex adaptive living systems into a new form of artificial intelligence called **Emergent Intelligence.** Emergent Intelligence is defined “*as the property of a self-organizing multi-agent system, operating on principles of virtual market with competition on the cooperation of agents, to solve complex problems through identification and resolution of conflicts, with mutual trade-offs, until the state of consensus is reached that meets the interest of both individual elements (agents) and the system as a whole. The consensus is understood as such a state of a “competitive equilibrium” between the whole system and the agents of its elements.*” (Skobelev 2023, 377f) It is a **paradigm shift** from centralised data-centred Digital Systems to distributed, self-organising and knowledge-centred Digital Twins systems—a form of **digital democracy**.

Digital Democracy

Suppose we want to uphold the democratic values of our society as a self-organising, complex adaptive system. In that case, we must embrace complexity equally for our digital twin of law and demand **agency** over the digital twin of our human system. **Our legal system is already a web of meaning**. They are an ontology, a model of the world expressed through an expert language. But flexible, not rigidly deterministic. Instead, it is **alive through its agents**, who we all are as we constantly influence our legal systems through our behaviour. Some agents have determined roles in legislature, judicature, execution or, for example, as negotiators at an international level.

Winston (2023) recently developed a theory in international law based on the phenomenon of emergence in complex adaptive systems. Winston demonstrates that **norms are emergent properties** of complex adaptive systems. In complex adaptive systems, agents can learn and change their behaviour. Norms are emerging properties of such a system as they evolve within the system. Complexity theory enables the identification of **legal norms about the system** they are embedded in, including its composition, structure, and effects. It “*reminds us to see the forest rather than just the trees.*” By taking the nature of the legal system into account, this theory of norms as emerging properties helps us to get new insights and find much-needed innovative solutions. (Winston 2023 p. 6).

Emerging Legal Intelligence

Legal systems have a **shared common sense** at their core. A form of legal intelligence that emerges from the system itself. With certain biases, society agrees to accept an ***unstable equilibrium*** for an agreed period and in a particular space. A kind of **social balance** that will be challenged by new events (inspired by Skobelev 2023). This chapter discusses such deep fakes as an example of such new or emerging events. By creating a digital twin of our legal systems, we could find much quicker solutions for new challenges and even design a new way of international governance by overcoming the limitations of sovereignty.

8 Conclusions

By new events and thriving for simplification, technology can help us **embrace the complexity of life**. After the Second World War, the global community agreed that there was more than one ultimate reality. The United Nations enshrined this notion in the Declaration of Human Rights. Human Rights is a milestone in the evolution of law and humanity. Now, we need a **new strategy to update** our legal systems and translate this milestone of humanity in line with technological progress. Putting the **law into the framework of digital twins** could be the urgently needed leap in the evolution of a digitally **transformed ecosystem**. It is a promising technology that can provide an ecosystem of human-centric collaboration, communication, and decision-making.

The digital twins could serve as **life support** for the other twin. Helping the legal world to understand the past, manage the present and design the future of law. Eventually, digital twins could be the **technological system behind the bot** we eagerly hope for. Such a bot could provide access to up-to-date legal information in real-time and in an understandable way, with the ability to **adapt the output to the user's needs**. However, to ensure human agency, we must **acknowledge our relationship** with law and technology by clearly defining our roles and capabilities. This way, we can **remain the agents of change** in the complex adaptive system of our human societies. Maybe all we need to do is to breathe **digital life into law** and follow the UN 2.0's path to a better world for all.

Declaration on the Use of AI

This chapter is the genuine product of the author. The author used traditional search engines and conversational Bing to conduct the research. Microsoft Bing and Copilot, Google Gemini and Grammarly served as cross-readers and helped improve the English writing style of a non-native English author. AI was not used as a co-author. As the system learns from its users, any similarities might emerge as the product of this relationship.

Liquid-Legal-Waves to Other Chapters, Written by the Editors

Anita has taken us to new digital places, passing fundamental questions like 'is the Law lost in digital space?' and the challenging aspects following from the convergence of new technologies. Is 'Open Legal Data' then adding to the challenges, or a necessity to master them?—Read *Marcel's* chapter *"Towards Access to Justice through Generative AI and Open Legal Data: Between Utopia and Dystopia"*.

Human life is complex and unique in its complexion. Are Generative AI and immersive technologies a way to embrace that reality and to transport it into digital space? *Barbara* masterly leads us to reflect on the abyss of human

(continued)

nature and the question if it can—and should—be fenced in by modern technology: *"If a machine, a Terminator can learn the value of human life, maybe we can, too."*

If we want to secure human agency in the digital age, as *Anita* reminds us, let us read on and have *Shân* and *Tatiana* take us through ways of *"Codifying Corporate Cultural Intelligence to Mitigate Culture Risk in AI"*.

References

Allgemeines bürgerliches Gesetzbuch (ABGB), in the version of BGBl. 161/2017. (*translated by the author*)

Accenture (2023) Technology vision 2023. When Atoms meet Bits. https://www.accenture.com/content/dam/accenture/final/accenture-com/a-com-custom-component/iconic/document/Accenture-Technology-Vision-2023-Full-Report.pdf

Adjeder H et al (2019) The state of deepfakes, landscapes, threats and impact. September 2019. https://enough.org/objects/Deeptrace-the-State-of-Deepfakes-2019.pdf

Agrawal A et al (2023) Digital twin: where do humans fit in? In: Automation in construction, vol 148. https://doi.org/10.1016/j.autcon.2023.104749

BBC (2023) Elon Musk's Tesla recalls two million cars in the US over Autopilot defect. https://www.bbc.com/news/technology-67693935

Berners-Lee T (2019) Rede am Internet Governance Forum Berlin 2019. Launch of the CONTRACT FOR THE Web. https://www.intgovforum.org/en/content/igf-2019-%E2%80%93-day-0-%E2%80%93-saal-europa-%E2%80%93-launch-of-the-contract-for-the-web-0

Berners-Lee T et al (2001) The semantic web. Sci Am 284(5) http://www.jstor.org/stable/26059207

Bharade A (2023) A widow is accusing an AI chatbot of being the reason her husband killed himself. Business Insider. https://www.businessinsider.com/widow-accuses-ai-chatbot-reason-husband-kill-himself-2023-4

Britannica. Technology. https://www.britannica.com/technology/technology

Brussel Times (2023) Belgian man commits suicide following exchanges with Chatgpt. https://www.brusselstimes.com/430098/belgian-man-commits-suicide-following-exchanges-with-chatgpt

Burga S (2024) How a new bill could protect against deepfakes. Time. https://time.com/6590711/deepfake-protection-federal-bill

Carter T (2023) Evidence shows that Elon Musk knew Tesla's Autopilot system was faulty but still let cars run, judge says. Business Insider. https://www.businessinsider.com/elon-musk-aware-of-tesla-autopilot-defect-driver-death-judge-2023-11

Daily Mail (2021) Albert Einstein comes alive at World Robot Conference in Beijing. https://youtu.be/jjHamjpjd5E?si=g33ltR5ruPCUPWFw&t=96

Dawid A, LeCun Y (2023) Introduction to latent variable energy-based models: a path towards autonomous machine intelligence, arXiv:2306.02572

Digwatch. Geneva Internet Platform (2020) Digital human rights: Digital integrity of the human person. November 17, 2020. https://dig.watch/event/igf2020/digital-human-rights-digital-integrity-human-person

ECMWF (2024) Understanding destination DestinE's digital twin. Predictive Maintenance. https://stories.ecmwf.int/explainer-digitaltwins/index.html

EPFL Center for Digital Trust (2023) 'Big News from Geneva: Making sense of the fundamental right to digital integrity and its potential implications on digital sovereignty and beyond. June 21, 2023. https://c4dt.epfl.ch/geneva-digital-sovereignty

ESA (2023) Destination earth. https://www.esa.int/Applications/Observing_the_Earth/Destination_Earth

ETH Zurich. Digital Einstein. https://ethz.ch/en/the-eth-zurich/global/events/digitaler-einstein.html

European Commission (2023) An interdisciplinary Digital Twin Engine for science. https://cordis.europa.eu/project/id/101058386

European Parliament (2021) Tackling deepfakes in European policy. https://www.europarl.europa.eu/RegData/etudes/STUD/2021/690039/EPRS_STU%282021%29690039_EN.pdf

Gordon M, Williams S (2020) What is the difference between complicated and complex systems... and why is it important in understanding the systemic nature of risk. United Nations Office for Disaster Risk Reduction. https://www.preventionweb.net/news/what-difference-between-complicated-and-complex-systems-and-why-it-important-understanding

Harari Y (2017) Homo Deus. A brief history of tomorrow. Harper-Perenneal

Harari Y (2020) How to survive the 21st century—Davos 2020. https://www.youtube.com/watch?v=gG6WnMb9Fho&t=1s

Harari Y (2023) Human Nature, Intelligence, Power, and Conspiracies. In: Lex Fridman Podcast #390. https://youtu.be/Mde2q7GFCrw?si=LniACa33-2MhtDX0

Härdi R (2021) Deutsche Bahn. Digital Twin: Ein Fundament für die Zukunft der Bahn. https://www.system-bahn.net/aktuell/digital-twin-ein-fundament-fuer-die-zukunft-der-bahn/

Heikkilä M (2023) Four trends that changed AI in 2023. In: MIT technology review. https://www.technologyreview.com/2023/12/19/1085696/four-trends-that-changed-ai-in-2023

Holland J (2014) Complexity: a very short introduction. Oxford University Press. https://academic.oup.com/book/417?login=false

Kurbalija J (2016) An introduction to internet governance, 7th edn. DiploFoundation

Lamprecht A (2021) Digitale transformation: Recht als neuronales Netzwerk, in: Jusletter IT 16. December 2021. https://www.researchgate.net/publication/357207158_Digitale_Transformation_Recht_als_neuronales_Netzwerk

Lamprecht A (2022a) Recht als neuronales Netzwerk. Der digitale Zwilling des Rechts. In: Brown Bag Legal Tech. https://www2.weblaw.ch/de/academy/brownbags-legaltech/recht-als-neuronales-netzwerk.html

Lamprecht A (2022b) The Architecture of Law. Law as a Neural Network. Conference Paper. IRIS 2022. https://www.researchgate.net/publication/376885644_THE_ARCHITECTURE_OF_LAW_LAW_AS_NEURAL_NETWORK

Lamprecht A (2023) Digital Twin of law. Enabling converging realities. AWE conference, Vienna 2023. https://youtu.be/KAW0-jE0BZE?si=o_wH-RayiHM7iOVS

Leith P (2010) The rise and fall of the legal expert system. European Journal of Law and Technology 1(1):179. https://www.researchgate.net/publication/309708513_The_rise_and_fall_of_the_legal_expert_system_Previously_published_in_Leith_P_%27The_rise_and_fall_of_the_legal_expert_system%27_in_European_Journal_of_Law_and_Technology_Vol_1_Issue_1_2010View_all_notes

Ministry of Justice and Farris L (2024). Press release. Government cracks dowon on 'deepfakes' creation. https://www.gov.uk/government/news/government-cracks-down-on-deepfakes-creation

NASA (2021) Digital twins and living models at NASA. https://ntrs.nasa.gov/citations/20210023699

NASA (2023) Earth system digital twin

OHCHR (2023) Trial monitoring to protect the right to a fair trial. August 17, 2023. https://www.ohchr.org/en/stories/2023/08/trial-monitoring-protect-right-fair-trial

Ray T (2023) ChatGPT is 'not particularly innovative' and 'nothing revolutionary', says Meta's chief AI scientist. ZDNET. https://www.zdnet.com/article/chatgpt-is-not-particularly-innovative-and-nothing-revolutionary-says-metas-chief-ai-scientist/

Reuters (2023) What happens when your AI chatbot stops loving you back? https://www.reuters.com/technology/what-happens-when-your-ai-chatbot-stops-loving-you-back-2023-03-18/

Rochel J (2023) Digital integrity—A new lense through which to assess the impact of digital technologies. https://www.lextechinstitute.ch/digital-integrity-a-new-lens-through-which-to-assess-the-impact-of-digital-technologies/?lang=en
Silver C (2020) What is Web 3.0? Forbes online. https://www.forbes.com/sites/forbestechcouncil/2020/01/06/what-is-web-3-0/?sh=5ec9fa8258df
Skobelev P (2023) Emergent intelligence of digital twins: from concept to application. In: Kovalev S, Kotenko I, Sukhanov A (eds) Proceedings of the seventh international scientific conference "intelligent information technologies for industry" (IITI'23). IITI 2023, Lecture notes in networks and systems, vol 776. Springer, Cham. https://doi.org/10.1007/978-3-031-43789-2_35
Smart Meters (2023) Albert Einstein. https://youtu.be/6VK71D8ZsKA?si=lCH_gBcWDQqw8XpM
Tesla (2016) Full self-driving hardware on all Tesla cars [Video]. Tesla. https://www.tesla.com/videos/full-self-driving-hardware-all-tesla-cars
UN News (2024) General Assembly adopts landmark resolution on artificial intelligence. https://news.un.org/en/story/2024/03/1147831
United Nations (2023) The Universal Declaration of Human Rights. History of the Declaration. https://www.un.org/en/about-us/udhr/history-of-the-declaration
Winston C (2023) International norms as emergent properties of complex adaptive systems. Int Stud Q 67:063. 10.1093/isq/sqad063
Zohny H et al (2023) The mystery of mental integrity: clarifying its relevance to neurotechnologies. Neuroethics 16(3):20. https://www.ncbi.nlm.nih.gov/pmc/articles/PMC10442279

Anita Lamprecht is an international lawyer and Futures Literacy expert at the DiploFoundation, Geneva. She combines her legal background with a focus on internet governance, AI, the Metaverse, and UN 2.0 exploring the impact of these emerging trends on society and the law.

Codifying Corporate Cultural Intelligence to Mitigate Culture Risk in AI: UK Insurance as a Case in Point

Shân M. Millie and Tatiana Caldas-Löttiger

"AI technology brings major benefits in many areas, but without the ethical guardrails, it risks reproducing real-world biases and discrimination, fueling divisions, and threatening fundamental human rights and freedoms." Gabriela Ramos, Assistant Director-General for Social and Human Sciences of UNESCO.

Contents

S. M. Millie
Bright Blue Hare, Cambridge, UK
e-mail: Shan@brightbluehare.com

T. Caldas-Löttiger (✉)
Universidad El Rosario, Bogotá, Colombia, USA

International Business & Trade Law, University of Illinois Chicago School of Law, Chicago, USA

European Law, Stockholm University, Stockholm, Sweden
e-mail: tati.lottiger@iwib4ai.com

K. Jacob et al. (eds.), *Liquid Legal – Sustaining the Rule of Law*, Law for Professionals, https://doi.org/10.1007/978-3-031-78596-2_7

Abstract

Regulating AI means addressing issues that could harm public trust in AI systems and the organizations (public and private) using them. Financial Services firms are prolific users of, investors in and insurers of AI and Emerging Tech, such as algorithmic social scoring, and biometric identification. As key pillars of functioning economies and society-at-large, the responsibility for Financial Services firms is to be not just operating within the rule of Law but operating to the highest Cultural standards—especially where the rule of Law is lacking, inadequate or a work-in-progress (as is the case with AI). This is a matter not just for the firm but for systemic stability, globally.

This chapter explains the concept of Cultural Intelligence (CQ), and how it can be applied to ethical issues around AI in the organisation; and using these ideas as context and a reference point, presents a snapshot view of the experience and views of UK Insurance (owned by or owning EU firms, embedded in supply chains, servicing customers globally, and facing legislative and regulatory developments well beyond the UK and EU Insurers offer an excellent window into the realities of digital commerce within a (sectoral) regulated context for Legal professionals.) Legal professionals, how they're navigating the gaps between the rule of law and the realities of AI in the firm today, and what developing the firm's ability to 'do' CQ for AI could look like. A 'How's our ability to 'do' Culture (CQ)?' lens is applied inwards, to the firm's own internal communities of functions and experts and societal stakeholders, drawing out key themes from the Insurance's sector experience with (Personal) Data, automated profiling (**social scoring**) and decisioning. An analysis of UK Consumer Duty is offered as both an example of failed CQ, and an opportunity to ensure that Insurance firms do a better job of navigating similar gaps between the 'rule of Law' and what's happening on the ground in the firm now, for AI in Financial Services.

1 Introduction

It's been said that Artificial Intelligence (AI) will be the last great human invention because AI will create a new form of discovery which in turn will create a new form of discoverer.[1] This opens the possibilities for extreme good or extreme bad; the

[1] See MIT Article *"AI is reinventing the way we invent"* by David Rotman (2019). Available at: https://www.technologyreview.com/2019/02/15/137023/ai-is-reinventing-the-way-we-invent/

basic difference between the two is that one is ethical and the other one is not. Therefore, AI Ethics is the critical enabler of ethical AI because it will protect what it means to be human, particularly when it comes to algorithmic recommendations and decision making.

For corporate leaders, senior managers, and advisors in all disciplines (not just Legal professionals, Risk Management, and Compliance colleagues) when it comes to AI and Emerging Tech, although the near future is undoubtedly about consistent, tighter regulation, the rule of Law is currently lacking, inadequate and/or a work-in-progress. In this relative vacuum, whilst uncertainty and debates on whether existing sectoral legal and regulatory frameworks and AI policies are adequate or not continue, life (and business) goes on, and organisational Culture comes to the forefront.

As author Silvia Carreta states on the upcoming book "the fast pace of innovation in the development of AI technologies is mirrored by the fast pace of development of the emerging field of AI governance, where traditional legislation by public bodies is complemented with more innovative approaches, such as hybrid and adaptive governance, **ethical alignment**, **governance by design** and the creation of regulatory sandboxes."[2]

Thus, in times of dynamic change, uncertainty and fast moving risks and opportunities, arguably it is the firm's ability not to add Culture into the equation—or as Tatiana calls it, Corporate Cultural Intelligence (CQ)—that can enable **ethical alignment**, superior adaptation, and better outcomes for the firm, its people, investors and customers.

This chapter explains the concept of **Cultural Intelligence**, and how it can be applied to **AI ethical issues** in organisations; and using these ideas as context and a reference point, presents a snapshot view of the experience and views of **UK Insurance Legal professionals**, how they're navigating the gaps between the rule of law and the realities of AI in the firm today, and what developing the firm's ability to 'do' CQ for AI could look like.[3]

---

[2]Carretta (2023). Available at: https://www.ysec-yearbook.eu/current-volume/

[3]Shân spoke with 8 individual Legal practitioners (labelled in the piece as 'contributors') with current or recent experience as in-house Counsel for established Insurers and/or for early-stage firms (InsurTechs), including two interviewees providing niche outsourced regulatory and General Counsel services specifically for InsurTechs. Over the past 10 years or so, the label 'InsurTech' has become synonymous with disruptive Innovation in Insurance and applied to new, Tech-specialist firms targeting Insurers as customers (and investors) operating as (1) specialist Tech/Data vendors and/or (2) specialist distribution partners. It was important to reflect the Legal practitioner experience from within both 'established' Insurers and these new entrants (Disruptors), who have become such an important part of the Insurance value chain. Quotes are an anonymised amalgam of different voices, capturing the essence of views, but preserving the privacy of contributors. Any errors in understanding of in subsequent analysis are Shân's.

2 Applying Cultural Intelligence (C.Q) in Artificial Intelligence (A.I)

2.1 What Is Cultural Intelligence?

To define Cultural Intelligence we need to first understand the concept of culture. Broadly speaking, culture refers to the beliefs, behaviours, norms, traditions, arts, customs, and habits that a group of people share. The term does not necessarily refer to an individuals' country of origin so much as the societies or communities they are a part of.[4]

Individuals who learn about C.Q are not just aware of different cultures, but how culture influences the behaviour of humans and **determines their moral and ethical values.** Their C.Q level makes them able to culturally adapt, effectively work and relate with people across a variety of cultural contexts, including working or socialising with people from their own country. These characteristics are part of **cultural sensitivity**, which is defined as *"an awareness of, and willingness to, investigate the reasons why individuals of another culture act as they do"*.[5] In the workplace, empathy is a significant trait and skill that facilitates cultural sensitivity and political correctness. Empathy allows you to place yourself in the other person's perspective. Thus, **Cultural Intelligence (CQ)** is an advanced aspect of cultural sensitivity and is understood as *"an outsider's ability to interpret someone's unfamiliar and ambiguous behaviour the same way that people from that culture would"*.[6]

2.2 Corporate Cultural Intelligence & Emotional AI

Besides individual's C.Q there is Corporate Cultural Intelligence. Culturally intelligent organizations establish better trust, tolerance and understanding, and a better reputation—both internally and externally. They are more capable of working well across cultures because they understand the impact of cultural background in terms of both an individual's and group's behaviour which is essential for good business.

However, in the corporate world, it is widely acknowledged that Culture has been identified as an often-overlooked barrier. A lack of C.Q has been blamed for many scandals that have hit organisations in general, and financial services organisations in particular.

Cultural consideration would increase awareness of identifying and reading **non-verbal codes** that are not regulated by law such as assumptions, the **feeling** of fear, doubt, trust, manipulation, or **emotions** like the sense of inclusiveness and

---

[4] See definition of Culture by the Britannica dictionary. Available at: https://www.britannica.com/topic/culture

[5] DuBrin (2014), p.176.

[6] DuBrin (2014).

belonging, resentment and anger. In this regard, countries like the United States are already using **AI-driven emotional recognition technology**, which is being procured by insurance firms to 'improve' their customers' experience and determine how much you should pay for your insurance premium.[7]

The EU AI Act in Annex III classifies post biometric identification and **emotional inference** for law enforcement as high-risk. In contrast, the private sector seems to be allowed to exploit these technologies more flexibly. It is noteworthy that Art. 52(2) defines that emotion detection is considered a medium-low risk application with only transparency obligations.

As discussed earlier, C.Q pertains to an individual's capability to comprehend and navigate diverse cultural contexts. Emotional AI will play a crucial role in enhancing AI tools with Cultural Intelligence by imbuing technology with the ability to discern and respond to culturally nuanced emotional cues.

For instance, in scenarios where cultural norms dictate distinct emotional expressions or responses, Emotional AI can facilitate a more accurate interpretation, thereby aiding in cross-cultural communication.

This alignment can be achieved through the incorporation of diverse cultural perspectives in the training data, ensuring that the AI system recognizes and respects the variability in emotional expression across different cultures.

2.3 Foundations of a Corporate Cultural Intelligence Strategy

Regardless, what AI is capable of doing in order to read human cues, human interactions will remain, and corporations will hire individuals to serve as human agents to oversee and validate the algorithmic recommendations in the AI systems used by the firms. Today, we are in urgent need of setting the foundations of a Corporate Cultural Intelligence Strategy. Thus, organizations, from top to bottom, should consider;

- addressing their own cultural biases by recognizing and considering their own cultural assumptions and biases, as well as how they may influence interactions with others.
- developing cultural sensitivity by putting themselves in the shoes of others and trying to understand their points of view, feelings, and motivations.
- preparing a plan for how to approach a situation before engaging in cross-cultural interactions and being ready to adjust as needed.

[7]Rovella (2023). The Future With Hannah Fry: Emotional Recognition. Available at: https://www.bloomberg.com/news/articles/2023-03-02/emotional-ai-can-artificial-intelligence-accurately-detect-human-feelings

3 Human-Centric AI, Governance and Ethics

3.1 Diversity Is not Enough for Human-Centric AI

In every organisation people are expected to work harmoniously and ethically, but sometimes cultural differences can be a challenge for organisations and this is why Diversity, Equity & Inclusion (DE&I) policies are supposed to be implemented. However, evidence shows that biases, conscious or unconscious, inhibit an organization's ability to hire, promote and reward diverse employees, and even expose organizations to compliance risk (e.g., discrimination against a job applicant or an employee due to that person's race, country of origin, religion, age or gender). In the same line, when insurance firms procure and use AI systems, individuals writing the algorithms and validating the outputs from the system (human agency) may also have bias. One way to mitigate the risk is to help hold human-agents to a higher standard not only on DE&I but also on Cultural Intelligence, to better address and mitigate the risk and not to perpetuate their biases upon the systems.[8]

From the AI governance and organisational perspective, C.Q should be ingrained in the firm's values and ethical principles to better establish human-centric AI frameworks and policies. This is valuable not only from the ethical perspective but also from the business perspective. For instance, understanding customer's cultural preferences may uncover why customers prefer one product over another, make certain decisions or demand certain services.

3.2 Ethical use of Artificial Intelligence in Insurance

AI Ethics refers to the principles and guidelines that govern the ethical development and deployment of AI systems. It involves addressing concerns such as transparency, fairness, accountability, privacy, and bias mitigation. Implementing ethical practices in AI is vital to maintain public trust, protect individuals' rights, and promote responsible innovation, particularly in the insurance sector.

When it comes to ethical frameworks for AI, there are as many frameworks as cultures. Actually, there are over 400 ethical frameworks around the world and most of them include the principle of **fairness** and **non-discrimination**.[9] According to the majority of these frameworks, AI algorithms should be designed and implemented in a way that prevents discrimination or bias based on personal characteristics such as gender, race, or age. For instance, **The EU Ethics Guidelines for Trustworthy AI**, in chapter one states that "AI shall be based on an approach founded on fundamental

---

[8]For example, some studies indicate that diversity is associated with positive outcomes such as improved innovation and productivity, while some show that diversity is related to negative outcomes such as conflict and turnover. IBM—The role of AI in mitigating bias to enhance diversity and inclusion. Available at: https://www.ibm.com/downloads/cas/2DZELQ4O

[9]OECD (2022).

rights, and identifies the ethical principles and their correlated values that must be respected in the development, deployment and use of AI systems in a way that adheres to the ethical principles of: a) respect for human autonomy, b) prevention of harm, c) fairness and explicability".[10]

Relevant to the Insurance sector is the risk of algorithmic bias. The principle of **fairness,** which ensures that the AI model is fair towards everybody, especially vulnerable groups that have historically been disadvantaged (such as women and children, people of colour, neurodiverse persons and/or with disabilities) as well as others who are at risk of exclusion because of their country of origin or social-economic status. Then, the principle of **explicability** ensures that AI models are explainable. For example, if an organisation gets a request from an end-user or an authority, that organisation should be able to explain the **outcome** and what data sets were used in order to curate that model, what methods, what expertise was the data lineage originally associated with, including the capability to explain how that model was trained to explain the outcome.

3.3 How to Earn Trust in AI Systems When It Comes to Culture Risk in AI?

AI risk management frameworks and standards are not enough to address ethical issues derived from Culture Risk.

Usually, AI frameworks, policies and standards provide guidance to mitigate risks related to the design, development, and deployment of AI systems. However, they are not specific to Culture risk but rather provide a high-level structure for assessing risks and developing strategies for addressing them. Consequently, organizations need to create **the use case for Culture Risk** for the specific AI systems and applications to effectively manage and mitigate the risks, and earn trust in AI-driven systems that are being made or procured by an organization. The starting point for the firm should be to apply the **foundation model** and align its Corporate Culture Intelligence with the identified alien cultural ethics and values.

Ensuring **trustworthy AI** is not about ticking boxes, but about continuously identifying and implementing requirements, evaluating solutions, ensuring improved outcomes throughout the AI system's lifecycle, and all involving stakeholders in this. One has to also consider the **human factor** and alien cultural ethics and values derived from it. Earning users' trust in AI is not a technological challenge but a socio-technological challenge. This means that besides tooling and governance there is the human factor which is reflected in the culture of an organization and the human culture. This includes thinking not only about the **diversity of**

---

[10] See Ethics Guidelines For Trustworthy AI revised on the draft published on 18 December 2018 by the High Level Expert Group building on the work of the European Group on Ethics in Science and New Technologies, taking inspiration from other similar efforts. Available at: https://www.europarl.europa.eu/cmsdata/196377/AI%20HLEG_Ethics%20Guidelines%20for%20Trustworthy%20AI.pdf

its teams, particularly the data science team but their cultural and ethical values. Who is curating that data to train that model? How many cultures do they represent? How many minorities are on that team? How many women are on that team? The more data you gather about how diverse these teams are, and everyone involved feels that the target end-users are represented, the less chance for error in AI-systems.

These Are Some of the Results of Applying Culture Risk Mitigation in AI Ethics

1. **Cultural Contextualization**: By understanding different cultural contexts, businesses can not only adapt their business model depending on the target market but also tailor their AI systems to align with specific societal norms and values. This ensures that AI technologies respect cultural sensitivities and avoid generating biased or offensive outputs.
2. **Bias Detection and Mitigation:** CQ can help identify biases embedded within AI algorithms by considering cultural nuances. By incorporating diverse datasets and involving individuals with different backgrounds during the training phase, businesses can reduce bias and enhance fairness in AI decision-making processes.
3. **Ethical Decision-Making**: CQ can provide organizations with the necessary insights to address ethical dilemmas and make ethical decisions regarding AI development and deployment in complex cultural landscapes by considering cultural implications and societal expectations.
4. **Acknowledgment of other Values.** The transfer of AI Western values to the East, for example, can be inappropriate, and corporate culture and management practices as well as AI development may need modifying to suit local conditions. By implementing these measures, organizations not only align with the EU AI Act's principles of trustworthy and accountable AI but also demonstrate a genuine commitment to cultural intelligence (CQ) and AI ethics. This provides a solid foundation for developing and tailoring an AI Policy that incorporates Cultural Intelligence and Ethical AI Guidelines. This policy would help organizations to implement a code that helps navigate the organization's actual **culture** and the culture the employees belong to, and the culture they **aspire** to belong to. To gain this knowledge, cultural and ethics assessments should be conducted before drafting the code. The code could help build consensus about the organization's ethical standards. It does this by specifying the organization's mission, core values and other standards. A well-written AI ethics code combined with training programs, Socratic-style[11] debate clubs to address ethical dilemmas around Culture Risk, and other methods of reinforcing

[11] The Socratic Method—"Socrates (470–399 BC) was a Greek philosopher who sought to get to the foundations of his students' and colleagues' views by asking continual questions until a contradiction was exposed, thus proving the fallacy of the initial assumption. This became known as the Socratic Method, and may be Socrates' most enduring contribution to philosophy". Socratic Method is not used to intimidate, nor to "break down" inodivual opinions, but instead for the very reason Socrates developed it: to develop critical thinking skills in students and enable them to approach the law as intellectuals. Available at: https://www.law.uchicago.edu/socratic-method

the code will make Cultural Intelligence & Ethics a regular topic of discussion, encourage employees to seek guidance when they are unsure about the proper course of action, and raise awareness about the ethical dimensions not only in the AI systems but in the workplace. And it legitimises their interest in CQ and Ethics in AI.

4 UK Insurance, AI and Legal Professionals: CQ and Individual Experiences

The following examines how the gaps between the rule of law and ongoing business are being understood and navigated by Legal professionals, whose roles mean they're involved every day in bridging the gaps between the 'rule of Law', and how business and AI is done. The reference point is the concept of CQ presented above: how organisations can build a Cultural Intelligence & AI Ethics Code for thinking and doing on AI-related issues (such as Trust, human-centric AI, algorithmic-bias) by using existing (Diversity Equity & Inclusion) toolkits for international business (e.g. how firms can excel at building trust of/with customers and partners through excelling at cross-cultural interactions) and Tatiana's proposed approach to AI Ethics (based on 5 core elements of Fairness, Explainability, Robustness, Transparency, and Privacy).

The following analysis aims to provide useful inputs for how UK Insurance, and its in-house legal practitioners, might go about putting the process into practice by:

- turning the 'How's our CQ?' lens inwards, to the firm's own **internal** communities of functions and experts; and to that other 'home' community in which the firm sits—Civil Society, and what Society will or will not tolerate (manifested as Regulation or 'the rule of Law').
- examining what this means for Insurance on the question of 'How's our AI CQ?' now, so providing an indicative operating context for Legal colleagues practitioners.
- understanding the lived experience of Legal colleagues, and their organisational 'action list' (or how they define key elements of organisational AI CQ), so contributing to the foundational thinking that would be needed to build a Cultural Intelligence & AI Ethics Code that would put theory into practice.

4.1 UK Insurance: No Strangers to Personal Data-Led Profiling, Automated Decisioning and AI

Insurers are, in many ways, the original experts in Personal Data-led profiling and automated decisioning. Insurance 'runs' on Personal Data, and proprietary modeling whether it's for mandatory covers like Home and Motor for consumers; Employer's and Public Liability for SMEs; or for opt-in covers such as Life, Home, and Income Protection.. Moreover, despite stereotyped perceptions to the contrary, Insurance sees prolific use of AI and Emerging Tech, Corporate Venturing, and underwriting (i.e. insuring) of AI and Emerging Tech products and services, directly and through partnerships. So whilst ChatGPT et al. has brought AI into the societal mainstream, Data-enabled Value Generation has been a constant thread in Insurance for years: from 2011/12 under the label of InsurTech, which itself was layered onto an existing familiarity with automated processing and latterly Machine Learning[12] notably for risk pricing and underwriting.

However: whilst the building, procurement and deployment of AI **is** happening in UK Insurance, it is broadly bereft of structure, standards, policies or frameworks, including the kind of detailed voluntary Codes like that presented by Tatiana above.[13] It is widely recognised that much of the fundamental data across Insurance (used in/with AI or not) is poor quality. In short, there is a widespread cultural obsession with quantity, not quality. In M&A due diligence, for instance, Data Quality is frequently an afterthought, or a 'nasty surprise' for the successful vendor once the transaction is done. The 'size of the book' is factored into the valuation, but not, seemingly, the quality of the underpinning Data. Unsurprisingly, Data Governance as a core business competency is under-developed and Data Culture patchy to non-existent. As Personal Data is completely fundamental to AI (as well as Insurance), it's no surprise that a core feature of all AI regulation already is or will be focused on Personal Data i.e. Governance and Data Culture.

4.1.1 Culture: Why and How?

For UK Insurance, a firm's competency on Culture (let's call it, 'CQ competencies') is a requirement, not optional. The UK regulator, the Financial Conduct Authority (FCA), explicitly calls out **firms' cultures as a major root cause of conduct failures**, non-financial misconduct, and consequent, unacceptable impacts on consumer protection and systemic stability.[14]

UK Insurance is done through a diverse and multifaceted web of partnerships, supply chains, and intermediary entities. The regulatory structures for Insurers to do business through these intermediaries and partners effectively makes them accountable (to the regulators) for the impacts on Customer of how those partners operate. In July 2023, a new regulatory standard was set with the coming into force of the UK's new Consumer Duty, explicitly designed "…to set higher and clearer standards of consumer protection across financial services and require firms to put their customers' needs first".[15] Arguably, Consumer Duty was an unprecedented

[12] Machine learning in UK financial services: second survey into the state of machine learning in UK financial services. Bank of England, Financial Conduct Authority, Oct 2022. https://www.bankofengland.co.uk/report/2022/machine-learning-in-uk-financial-services

[13] In February 2024, the Association of British Insurers, the trade association for insurance and long-term savings industry, the largest sector in Europe and the third largest in the world, produced AI Guide: Practical ideas for getting started with responsible AI https://www.abi.org.uk/globalassets/files/subject/public/ai/ai-guide.pdf. It is instructive that this is NOT a code, but 'ideas'.

[14] The FCA and Culture https://www.fca.org.uk/firms/culture-and-governance

[15] "The FCA's Consumer Duty will lead to a major shift in financial services", FCA press release, 27/2/23

regulatory intervention to protect Customer, required because Insurance could not be trusted to do the job for itself.

Significant parts of Civic Society agree. Insurance has betrayed a chronic lack of CQ, displaying a long-lived, widespread, institutionalised 'tuning out' of consistent and persistent concerns of Civic Society about Fairness, Access and Exclusion,[16] exacerbated (not eradicated) by the sector's embedded use of Data and Technology. (These issues are explored in detail in Shân's 2023 research piece, **Insurance, technology and data: Trust through a regulatory lens**.[17]

Although not specifically highlighted in Consumer Duty, organisational excellence in Customer Personal Data is a very strong indicator of how seriously the business really prioritises Customer, so Consumer Duty will surely drive change here, too, and increase the importance of Insurers fixing not just their own Data Culture issues but those entrenched (and obscured) in their webs of intermediaries, partnerships and supply chains. Amongst a plethora of transformational impacts, **Consumer Duty** should be seen as a monumental test of the firm's competency to verify customer-centered Culture in action—every day, across every function, as standard (remember: the ultimate accountability for supply chain and partners meeting the standards set by Consumer Duty rests with the Insurer).

4.1.2 The CQ Lens

In many ways, Consumer Duty's disruptive impacts and strategic challenge dwarfs those posed by AI and Emerging Tech on Financial Services firms, at least in the short to medium-term. In short, probably every part of UK Insurance is playing 'catch-up'. How (and at what costs) firms leverage, augment or build CQ competencies to respond to arguably the most material piece of cross-sectoral conduct regulation in the UK of the 2000s—aka a NEW 'rule of Law' will be hugely instructive. What lessons will be recognised and applied as firms navigate the gaps between the rule of Law and the here-and-now for AI and Emerging Tech in UK Insurance?

The following is worth noting:

- For Insurers, the AI CQ challenges are not simply about mastering the internal Culture, but the competency to understand, monitor and, if necessary, require change to the CQ of their partners, agents and suppliers. There will be contractual risks for other parties in the supply chain, but most Regulatory experts agree that in most situations, it is the Insurer who will have ultimate regulatory

[16] See "Citizens Advice sounds the alarm on £280 car insurance ethnicity penalty", Citizens Advice press release, 22/3/22 https://www.citizensadvice.org.uk/about-us/about-us1/media/press-releases/citizens-advice-sounds-the-alarm-on-280-car-insurance-ethnicity-penalty/ For an expert but accessible example of how Civic Society activists see the big risks presented by the increased adoption of AI in FS, and what is needed to protect citizens, AI in Financial Services: How to avoid the big risks, Finance Innovation Lab and Financial Inclusion Centre 6/12/23 https://financeinnovationlab.org/insights/ai-in-financial-services-how-to-avoid-the-big-risks/

[17] Insurance, technology and data: Trust through a regulatory lens, Chartered Insurance Institute Feb 2023 https://www.cii.co.uk/media/10129225/insurance-tech-data-report.pdf

accountability for the effective implementation, management and oversight of AI. And the insurer who will be held solely responsible for any risks that materialise—just like Consumer Duty.

- In today's dynamic global AI regulatory environment, trade bodies and associations are (broadly) making the case that existing regulation and 'the way we do things' is sufficient, that there is no need for the specific sectoral scrutiny (like the approach set out in the EU AI Act, where significant volumes of Insurance AI (now and next) use cases are likely to fall into their 'High Risk' category.[18] Can UK Insurance safely 'bank on' being allowed to 'mark its own homework' on AI and Emerging Tech? Or more likely that Insurance will face intervention on AI, just as it has with Consumer Duty?

5 AI in UK Insurance: What Do Our Legal Colleagues See?

Legal professionals in Insurance, notably in-house Counsel, are the expert problem-solvers and essential advisors on a range of business-critical agenda items, from commercial due diligence to liaison with regulators, from disputes and litigation to setting up Equity Share Incentive Schemes. These senior leaders and functional experts should be at the heart of (if not leading on) understanding and scenario planning for emerging AI-specific regulation, and bridging the here-and-now gaps in how firms are operating—from proposition and business development to Corporate Venturing, supplier management and procurement, and beyond.

This is not, however, the experience right now.

The Legal professionals contributing their views confirm that the persistence of the deeply-entrenched, siloed approach to Innovation in Insurance, where Legal (and Data and Compliance) colleagues are typically excluded from the proposition development process or the procurement of Emerging Tech (often labelled 'Transformation (Projects)') until the very end of the process, if at all. This means they are consigned to the role of trying to help the organisation be 'compliant in retrospect'—interestingly, analogous to the role many are currently playing with regard to Consumer Duty 'catch-up' compliance.

> Legal is viewed as Back Office: is this actually ok for a regulated sector?
> Source: interviewee, anonymized

Contributors are (1) aware of (2) sometimes users and/or (3) beneficiaries of, or (4) (in the event of 'issues') consulted on, tactical experimentation with and/or deployment of AI within the firm like:

– HR functional purposes involving employee (Personal) data
– Contract management (in the Legal Team)

[18] AI Act—Insurance spotlight, Sinead Lynch, A&L Goodbody 22/12/23 https://www.lexology.com/library/detail.aspx?g=0ca8071d-6867-46d2-b9bf-9a64208686a6

- (Through third-parties) document scraping for litigation work
- In private practice firms, bespoked Generative AI (like ChatGPT) being made available to juniors and interns for both internal operational purposes and as the enabler for the packaging up and selling of reference or insight services for clients
- GenAI (e.g. ChatGPT) plug-ins for internal email management and corporate intranets
- Potential for advancing research in mental health and wellbeing e.g. using AI for clinical studies and trials

Far from being essential to strategic evaluation, planning and action for AI in Insurance, involvement often comes as a de facto 'emergency first responder', called on after the event. The majority of contributors observed that strategic thinking on AI in Insurance is not being done—at the Board or elsewhere. The expert, well-funded sales efforts of Big Tech et al. tend to go unchallenged in the places in the organisation where it is most needed (arguably, at Board).

> If AWS or Microsoft or Google say, 'It works and everything's ok', that seems to be good enough.
>
> Source: interviewee, anonymized

> I absolutely know that AI will change Financial Services (FS), and what it means to be a lawyer in FS. I'm excited! I also know that the understanding of the technologies and issues I have now is superficial, which means I can't help my firm or my (insurance) clients how I'd like to, i.e. proactively. That's frustrating for me but it doesn't seem to be a priority for the Board, either.
>
> Source: interviewee, anonymized

All the contributors were independently, proactively developing their knowledge, contacts and perspectives through a variety of (re)sources, they all felt that this was not enough.

> This is so important, it should be a concerted effort that allows me to be involved and trained on specifics ahead of time. Otherwise, we'll be dependent on external (consultants) and playing constant catch-up. A bit like we see on Consumer Duty.
>
> Source: interviewee, anonymized

> I think within 6 months there will be in-house demand for advice on writing AI Risks, and selling them, including on Privacy and Data Protection. I want to be in the best position to meet this demand.
>
> Source: interviewee, anonymized

6 Insurance (Legal) Corporate CQ on AI: What Does It Look Like?

When asked about the practical questions needing answers within the firm from their professional perspectives—what could be viewed as key indicators of an internal Culture on AI that would be more fit for purpose—contributors identified the following:

Organisational Commitment to

- Being "excited in an informed way" about the potential of AI technologies that are "…untested and bring with them due diligence and negligence risks".
- Developing a systematic approach to understanding the reach and limitations of AI for internal and external (i.e. direct client-facing) purposes
- Deciding whether incorporating AI into client servicing aims to augment, not replace, the human experts

Organisational Ability to Answer These Questions

- How do we educate/upskill internal leaders, including (especially) the Board, so they can take a strategic view?
- What capabilities (skills, knowledge, etc) do we need to be able to advise client (s)?
- How should individual Legal professionals best be supported for the coming (in-house & client-driven) demand for advice on writing and selling AI risks (including Privacy & Data Protection)?
- What kinds of events involving AI would create a litigation event?
- What is the best solid, sustainable framework for secure operationalisation, Governance and Regulation that incorporates control, accountability and monitoring?
- Can Machine Learning in decisioning ever really be compliant with GDPR?
- What can we use to input into pricing and models so that: (a) it's 'fair' and 'relevant' (b) incorporating automated decisioning but compliant with GDPR?
- How do we make Privacy Impact Assessments BAU?
- Expertise on Bias in AI is needed throughout the firm, especially at Board: how do we make this happen?

7 Conclusion

Automated profiling and decisioning using personal data is the very foundation of insurance. Under the rules of The EU AI Act, classifying people based on behaviour, socio-economic status or personal characteristics, **(social scoring)** impose an **unacceptable risk** as they are considered a threat to people and will be banned. Therefore, before insurance and financial institutions procure AI systems, they need to assess if the algorithmic recommendations pose an **unacceptable risk, across their lifecycle**. The same applies to **all** high-risk AI systems.

Across all sectors, there is a power imbalance which cannot be addressed by simply giving consumers more information or giving them individual rights of complaints. What firms are ultimately going to have to do is to change the kind of structural ways in which these technologies are designed is to push the responsibilities back on to designers, back on the organizations who are relying on technologies to change their practices. This requires an introspective into their corporate culture, including the human culture, as it influences the behaviour of employees that impacts the organization's ethical values. To address this challenge, we conclude that developing an organisational **Cultural Intelligence & AI Ethics Code** is required to enable firms to mitigate ethical Culture risks in AI-systems.

As this analysis shows, when asked, individual professionals' views on their real-world experience can be interpreted into a consolidated 'action list' or starting point for developing foundational Corporate CQ on AI that covers:

- organisational 'commitments' or principles for they AI policies;
- specific 'questions to be answered' ranging from:
  - technical e.g. can Machine Learning-led decisoning ever be compliant with GDPR for retail customers?
  - talent and training e.g. how do we upskill leaders and Boards?
  - and process e.g. how do we make Privacy Impact Assessments standard?

Finally, our chapter calls for Legal & Compliance departments at insurance firms to create use cases for Culture Risk in AI; start assessing their Corporate C.Q level in alignment with existing AI Policy and Ethics Codes; to foster an ethical culture for AI in the firm; and make a commitment to trustworthiness and **ethical quality** in insurance services relating to AI. It is necessary for Legal & Compliance to find ways to explain to colleagues, boards and partners that ethics is not about abstract principles: it is a practical, dynamic system of doing and learning, both mandated from the top and lived from the bottom up within the firm, that is also experienced by customers and partners and measurable in superior outcomes for them.

Liquid-Legal-Waves to Other Chapters, Written by the Editors

Shân and *Tatiana* have explained the concept of Cultural Intelligence (C.Q.), and how it can be applied to AI issues in an organization. A perfect segway to *Bernhard's* concept of a Sustainable Digital Transformation Framework (SDTF), looking at *"Sustainable Digital Transformation as a Prerequisite for Sustainable Law"*, resting on sustainability in five dimensions: economical, technical, ergonomical, ecological, and regulatory.

As *Shân* and *Tatiana* underline the cultural dimension of sustaining the rule of law, it is important to look at it from a purely human dimension and hear *Ulf* answer the question: *"AI is here. But is the legal profession ready for it?"*

After understanding the importance of cultural and ethical standards, it is timely that *Erion* lays out the origin of AI legal tech, its positive impacts, a taxonomy of autonomy levels, correlated legal and ethical risks, and finally legal regimes for AI liability in the following chapter on *"Decoding Public and Private AI Legal Tech"*.

Brief Further Reading
For an extended definition of **Culture** see the Britannica dictionary. Available at: https://www.britannica.com/topic/culture

Sources used on The European Artificial Intelligence Act (EU AI Act)
"Regulatory divergences in the draft of The EU AI act: Differences in public and private sector obligations". This study identifies and examines sources of regulatory divergence within the AI act regarding the obligations and limitations upon public and private sector actors when using certain AI systems. The study is specifically focused on three AI application areas: manipulative AI, social scoring and biometric AI systems. Questions regarding how and when those systems are designated as prohibited or high-risk and the potentially diverging obligations towards public versus private sector actors and the rationale behind it, are described.
https://www.europarl.europa.eu/stoa/en/document/EPRS_STU(2022)729507
AI Ethics

- Silvia A. Carretta "*Everybody wants to rule the world. The relevance of the rule of law for private law, in the context of algorithmic profiling of online users.*" (2023), in: Eduardo Gill-Predro and Andreas Moberg (eds.), "Law and the Governance of Artificial Intelligence", Yearbook of Socio-Economic Constitutions (forthcoming). Silvia A. Carretta is a DLI Fellow at Cornell Tech and Doctoral Candidate at Uppsala University & WASP-HS. Chief Legal Officer at Women in AI. https://www.ysec-yearbook.eu/current-volume/
- AI Ethics: What It Is And Why It Matters - Forbes https://www.forbes.com/sites/nishatalagala/2022/05/31/ai-ethics-what-it-is-and-why-it-matters/
- Ethics of Artificial Intelligence | UNESCO. https://www.unesco.org/en/artificial-intelligence/recommendation-ethics.p
- Responsible AI Institute https://www.responsible.ai/post/eu-ai-act-explained
- Ethics Guidelines for Trustworthy AI https://digital-strategy.ec.europa.eu/en/library/ethics-guidelines-trustworthy-ai

References

Carretta SA (2023) Everyone wants to rule the world. The relevance of the rule of law for private law, in the context of algortithmic profiling of online users. In: Gill-Predro E, Moberg A (eds) Law and the governance of artificial intelligence. Yearbook of Socio-Economic Constitutions

DuBrin AJ (2014) Human relations: interpersonal job-oriented skills, 12th edn. Pearson, London, p 176

Rovella D (2023) The race to build AI that can read your emotions. Bloomberg. The Future With Hannah Fry: Emotional Recognition. Available at: https://www.bloomberg.com/news/articles/2023-03-02/emotional-ai-can-artificial-intelligence-accurately-detect-human-feelings

OECD (2022) OECD framework for the classification of AI systems. OECD Digital Economy Papers, No. 323. OECD Publishing, Paris. https://doi.org/10.1787/cb6d9eca-en

Shân Millie is a Corporate Innovation specialist for Insurance and FinTech, an independent voice of authority on AI in Financial Services (FS) and a proud 'accidental teccie'. She delivers human-scale, hands-on support through her purposely-micro firm, Bright Blue Hare. Shân has spent most of her professional life doing, studying, analysing and advising on FS Corporate Innovation, but, from the outside-in. Since 2018, her focus has been the intersection of innovation, Emerging Tech/AI and Governance, notably regulatory and data governance issues and asking: what is the best approach to supporting NEDs and executives in the firm who are liable and accountable but NOT subject matter experts to make informed decisions?)

Tatiana Caldas-Löttiger is a renowned legal futurist and international business lawyer legally trained in Colombia (J.D), the United States (LL.M in International Business & Trade Law), and Sweden (LL.M in European Law). Since 2012, she has been at the forefront of the intersection between business, law, and technology. Recognized for her *pro bono* work in empowering foreign women and foreign lawyers in Sweden, Tatiana was nominated for the King Carl Gustav Foreign Entrepreneur Award of 2024. Tatiana was also recognized in 2024 by The Global Legal Skills Institute for her expertise as an international keynote speaker and her contributions to teaching global skills to law students and lawyers, particularly in cross-cultural education, international skills training and Artificial Intelligence (AI) Ethics.

As the founder and CEO of International WoMenX In Business for Ethical AI (IWIB4AI) Think-Tank, Dr. Caldas-Löttiger leads a global non-for-profit organization, dedicated to fostering ethical discussions with civil society around the development, deployment, and use of AI. Her commitment to ethical AI and her leadership have positioned IWIB4AI as a critical voice in the AI ethics discourse.

In addition to her role at IWIB4AI, Tatiana serves as the Partnerships Lead for Women in AI (WAI) Spain, where she supports initiatives to bridge gender gaps in the AI sector. She also represents the Nordic countries as an Ambassador at The Liquid Legal Institute, further showcasing her dedication to advancing legal innovation and ethical AI practices across diverse regions. Tatiana's multifaceted career and leadership in ethical AI, combined with her international legal expertise, make her a pivotal figure in shaping a trustworthy AI on a global scale.

Decoding Public and Private AI Legal Tech: Autonomy, Liability, Legal and Ethical Risks

Erion Murati

Contents

Abstract

The convergence of digitalization and artificial intelligence (AI) is transforming the legal landscape through applications like legal chatbots, virtual legal assistants, e-justice systems, compliance platforms, contract analysis tools, predictive crime analysis, and automated dispute resolution. AI technology, divided into engineering AI and cognitive AI, focuses on creating cognitive systems that can generate outputs like predictions or decisions based on inputs, varying in autonomy and adaptiveness. Despite the benefits, AI legal tech raises ethical, social, and economic concerns, requiring a thorough evaluation of its impact and legal adjustments. This research investigates how legal professionals in both the

E. Murati (✉)
Berlin School of Law and Economics, Berlin, Germany
e-mail: e_murati@doz.hwr-berlin.de

K. Jacob et al. (eds.), *Liquid Legal – Sustaining the Rule of Law*, Law for Professionals, https://doi.org/10.1007/978-3-031-78596-2_8

public and private legal domain use AI technology, identifying the associated legal, ethical, and practical challenges. It outlines the origins of AI legal tech within computational law field, introduces a framework for comparing AI legal instruments, develops a taxonomy of autonomy levels and risk models, addresses related legal and ethical risks, and identifies legal regimes for AI liability.

1 Introduction

The legal landscape is being innovated by the convergence of digitalization and artificial intelligence (AI) technologies. Emerging trends in AI legal applications, such as legal chatbots, Chat-GPT, virtual legal assistants, e-justice management, compliance-platforms, contract creation and analysis, predictive crime analysis, automated online dispute resolution are just some of the tools that are automatizing the legal sector. AI is the research field dedicated to understanding, designing, and constructing cognitive systems.[1] Unlike cognitive psychology, AI's primary methodology involves exploring cognitive theory through the creation of intelligent computers or computer programs artifacts. AI research can be categorized into *engineering* AI, which designs intelligent artifacts without mimicking natural processes, and *cognitive* AI, which aims to create artifacts that think like humans.[2] Since a common universal definition of AI is lacking,[3] for the purposes of this research the OECD definition of AI is used: "*An AI system is a machine-based system that, for explicit or implicit objectives, infers, from the input it receives, how to generate outputs such as predictions, content, recommendations, or decisions that can influence, depending on their level of autonomy and adaptiveness, physical or virtual environments.*"[4]

AI refers thus to computer programs or computational systems that vary in their levels of autonomy and adaptiveness after deployment and comprise five (different) disciplines:[5] Machine Learning, Automated Reasoning, Computer Vision, Affective Computing, and Natural Language Processing. The novelty of the AI new generation of information technologies lies in their capacity for *self-learning*, enabling systems to independently identify patterns, discover information, and predict future events,

[1] Goel and Davies (2021), p. 468.

[2] Ibid. pp. 468–469.

[3] Historically, Alan Turing, known as the Godfather of AI, introduced the idea of creating AI and proposed the Turing Test—today applied, for example, at ReCAPTCHA—to gauge human-like intelligence in machines: König et al. (2022), pp. 18–19.

[4] OECD (2023) Recommendation of the Council on Artificial Intelligence, OECD/LEGAL/0449.

[5] If traditional programming can achieve it, it is not AI: Ng (2022), p. 36; Häuselmann (2022), pp. 47–65; Mik (2022), p. 48.

coupled with the ability to *act autonomously,* and make non-pre-programmed decisions.[6]

As further detailed below, the emergence of computer in general, and the rise of AI in particular, have given rise to the computational law field that covers various disciplines such as '*Cyberlaw*' (dealing with legal issues in the digital age such as privacy, data protection and cybersecurity), '*Legal Tech*' (enhancing public and private legal processes with technology), and '*Computational Legal Studies* (the application of computational research methods to study the law).[7] These areas often intersect,[8] and research primarily focuses on the 'legal tech' category. I use for this the general term of '*AI legal tech*' that encompasses legal applications that are based on different AI technology with the aim of developing AI to replace humans to a lesser extent by automating legal services, legal reasoning, and adjudication.

The shift to AI legal tech simplifies access to legal information, services, and resources, empowering users and enhancing efficiency through automation. However, the ethical, social, and economic implications of AI technologies warrant an in-depth evaluation of their impact and an audit of existing laws to address challenges posed by digitization.[9] This research focuses on comprehending how legal professionals (will) utilize AI technology and aims to pinpoint various legal, ethical, and practical challenges associated with automating public and private legal tech through AI. It illustrates the origin of AI legal tech within the computational law field (Sect. 2), improves the understanding of potential positive impacts by introducing a topological framework that streamlines the comparison of different public and private AI legal instruments (Sect. 3), builds a taxonomy of autonomy levels and risky models (Sect. 4), addresses correlated legal and ethical risks according to the relevant area of law (Sect. 5), identifies legal regimes for AI liability (Sect. 6).

2 The Rise of Computational Law and AI Legal Tech

Leibniz believed that even the most difficult questions of morality or law could be solved with an adequate formal system of computation. This aspiration to eliminate human involvement in legal reasoning has fascinated philosophers, lawyers, and, more recently, computer scientists. This has risen the discipline of law-as-computation, or code-driven law that aims to address legal norms that have been articulated in computer code, either by a contracting party, law enforcement authorities, public

[6]Custers and Fosch-Villaronga (2022), p. 8.

[7]Whalen (2020), pp. 1–3.

[8]For example, a study might explore the legal implications of emerging technologies, such as smart contracts (intersecting cyberlaw with legal tech), or it might employ computational techniques to investigate legal issues associated with technology (intersecting cyberlaw, legal tech, and computational legal studies).

[9]Hoffmann-Riem (2020), p. 5.

administration or by a legislator.[10] Indeed, (AI) computers and the law intersect in a variety of ways since these two fields share method and subject matter, and they intersect due to their shared use of semi-formal modeling which seeks a balance between formal and informal elements.[11] They aim to coordinate human behavior, with AI relying on intelligence (or better code) and law on the rule of law.[12] This shared method and subject matter result in the development of a science of hermeneutic pragmatics, which combines the goals of behavior coordination, understanding, and interpretation in an engineering science context. AI and law are highly interdisciplinary, benefiting from insights from various scientific areas, including the humanities, empirical sciences, and social sciences. Both fields involve theoretical systems, such as mathematics and legal theory, to learn about artificial systems, like software and statutes, while remaining rooted in natural systems, such as human intelligence and legal practices.[13] In particular, AI technologies, such as network analysis and machine learning systems, have revolutionized legal information analysis. Network analysis clusters legal cases, exposing connections, while machine learning-based natural language processing (NLP) improves accuracy in predicting human rights case outcomes, optimizing resource use. Applying computational and quantitative techniques for textual analysis addresses descriptive inquiries about jurists, courts, and jurisdictions, allowing exploration of connections with other variables of interest, including demographics.[14]

In the intersection of law and computer science, the question arises: do these fields share a common programming language, and if not, can alignment be achieved through a new legal programming language? While recognizing the potential of programming languages in legal writing (e.g., XML, Lawgood, Blawx, Lexon), it's essential to highlight their limitations and ensure they serve as tools for enhancing the legal landscape without fundamentally altering (contract) law.[15] Among the different forms of AI, the use of natural language categories, with their imprecision and adaptability, is argued to be more advantageous in juridical reasoning in s AI

[10] Livermore (2022), p. 238; Hildebrandt (2020), p. 67.

[11] As AI deals with uncertain reasoning, adaptive behavior and context-dependent knowledge, while Law involves rules, exceptions, reasoning, and principles. Bench-Capon et al. (2012).

[12] Law addresses how contracts, punishment, compensation and authorities can guide human society and its inhabitants in doing the right thing.

[13] Bench-Capon et al. (2012). The AI & Law research aims thus to create computer programs, known as Computational Models of Legal Reasoning (CMLRs), capable of making legal arguments and predicting legal dispute outcomes. Some CMLRs focus specifically on legal argumentation and are termed Computational Models of Legal Argument (CMLAs). Ashley (2017), p. 4.

[14] Varsava (2022), p. 46.

[15] Ma (2021), p. 180.

legal tech compared to mathematical functions in Machine Learning.[16] However, further efforts are needed for code to truly evolve into a legal language.[17]

Nevertheless, researchers believe that the final progression of computational and AI law is "*legal singularity*". It is a concept derived from Ray Kurzweil's[18] technological singularity, envisioning a scenario where increasingly powerful machines, trigger an 'intelligence explosion' leading to the emergence of a 'superintelligence' surpassing human understanding and control. Accordingly, legal singularity is seen as a state where legal disputes become rare due to clear legal consequences mapped onto agreed facts, resulting in a functionally complete legal system. It presumes thus the elimination of all legal uncertainty (by elimination of juridical reasoning as a basis for dispute resolution and the allocation of powers, rights and responsibilities).[19] Advocates contend that automating legal processes would enhance certainty and enable impartial application by overcoming human biases and errors.[20]

However, the rise of code-driven law and the (danger) scenario of the legal singularity has been heavily criticized, as it raises concerns about the loss of human oversight and emphasizes the contextual and reflexive nature of law, arguing that automated processes could undermine the intricacies of legal reasoning, potentially compromising fundamental ethical and human-centred principles.[21] Indeed, coders effectively act as quasi-legislators ("code is the law"), but there is a need for legal transparency and safeguards to ensure legal and ethical practices.[22] Additionally, researcher believe that law is not computable in any final sense, because due to its text-driven multi interpretability it can be computed in different ways and these different ways will make a difference for those subject to law.[23] A comprehensive description of the legal and ethical changes raised by AI is provided below (Sect. 5).

---

[16] Despite advancements in machine learning, its limitations, including being backward-looking, prone to lock-in effects, and having fewer error correction options than legal decision-making techniques, make natural language categories superior in representing complex social information and adapting to new data. Deakin and Markou (2020), p. 66.

[17] Ma (2021), p. 180.

[18] Kurzweil (2006).

[19] Deakin and Markou (2020), pp. 18–27, 66; Cobbe (2021), p. 67.

[20] Livermore (2022), p. 238.

[21] Ibid. pp. 19–27, 67.

[22] Di Matteo (2022), p. 11.

[23] Hildebrandt (2020), pp. 70, 83.

3 A Topological Framework for Navigating AI Legal-Tech

The legal tech concept encompasses AI algorithm-based technology utilized in both public and private legal sectors,[24] evolving beyond digitizing the work environment to empowering machines to undertake essential legal activities in both spheres.[25] While Sect. 3.1 provides a description of AI public legal tech, Sect. 3.2 describes use cases for AI private legal tech.

3.1 Public AI Legal Tech

Legal tech in public administration and justice spans predictive policing, AI in administrative decisions, road traffic management, tax proceedings, automated debt collection, dispute resolution, criminal investigations, and enforcement.[26] This section, however, specifically concentrates on AI tools in law enforcement and justice administration. It emphasizes that while AI can mitigate biases and influence discretion in public agencies, it also raises negative legal implications addressed in Sect. 5.

3.1.1 Law Enforcement and Predictive Justice

Technology, notably AI, plays a vital role in addressing societal issues,[27] particularly in law enforcement. It has the potential to predict and prevent crimes through A/B optimization, deepfake technologies, and algorithmic profiling. In procedural criminal law, AI functions as a predictive policing tool and serves as cyber agent technology.[28] AI is being used thus to analyze crime data, predict criminal activity, and optimize law enforcement resources. It autonomously builds patterns and detects suspicious (illegal) activities. Some techniques of smart smart' law enforcement are categorized as:[29] (a) *Watching* systems that include intelligent video surveillance software that, among other, provide facial recognition systems;[30] (b) *Reading* systems that complements or replaces human officers when it comes to filtering social media posts, police and commercial databases, financial transaction as well as metadata from hotline calls requesting help or reporting child abuse; (c) *Listening* systems that encompass software that provides aural surveillance (i.e., early recognition of mass shootings) that 'listens' for suspicious acoustic patterns; (d) *Predictive justice* systems such as COMPAS (Correctional Offender Management Profiling for Alternative Sanctions) and HART (Harm Assessment Risk Tool) that are based on a

[24] Buchholtz (2020), p. 177.

[25] Wagner (2018), pp. 2–3.

[26] Hermstrüwer (2020), p. 201; Buchholtz (2020), p. 180; Custer (2022), pp. 207 and ss.

[27] Cooman and Petit (2023), p. 16.

[28] Asimov (1959).

[29] Rademacher (2020), pp. 227–232.

[30] Liu et al. (2022), pp. 132 and ss.

set of predictors, where a score is calculated that indicates the risk of reoffending (i.e. assesses the likelihood of recidivism in a criminal defendant).[31] They proactively find suspicious patterns indicating past, ongoing, or various kinds of future criminal law infringements.

3.1.2 Justice: From Online Dispute Resolution to Judicial Automation, and "Robot-Judges"

The digitization of the justice system has been encouraged by significant growth in online dispute resolution (ODR)—encompassing both online alternative dispute resolution (ADR) and online court systems.[32] The motivation for technological change in the justice system includes cost savings, efficiency gains, increased openness, and potentially higher quality justice by enhancing access to justice by reducing costs, delays, and various barriers. This technological innovations in the justice system can be categorized into *supportive* technologies (informing and advising), *replacement* technologies (replacing human tasks), and *disruptive* technologies (transforming processes e.g. 'Judge AI').[33] 'Judge AI' encompasses various AI branches contributing to judicial tasks, ranging from technology use in pre-trial processes to playing a (administrative) supportive (*'supportive Judge AI'*) or even substitutive role in decision-making (*'Judge AI'*)[34]—especially in the beginning in lower court levels and certain categories of cases.[35] Automated systems are indeed suggested for sentencing matters where facts are predetermined, while Judge AI is seen as beneficial in civil and minor commercial matters but poses risks in administrative disputes.[36] Furthermore, efforts have been made to algorithmically predict court case outcomes, and (Chinese) courts use AI to ensure consistency in judgment criteria among similar cases and supervise judges through corrective functions.[37]

However, and as further developed below, the rise of replacement and disruptive AI technologies poses ethical and legal challenges, including the absence of the 'human element,' transparency issues, the need for public trust, and the prevention of algorithmic bias that have surfaced notably in criminal law (e.g., predicting recidivism,) and automated administrative decision-making (e.g., student welfare, China's social credit, Australia's 'rob debt' scheme).[38]

---

[31] Van Der Haegen (2023), p. 78; Erdoğan (2022), p. 100.

[32] Sourdin (2021), pp. 6–7.

[33] Ibid. pp. 2–3.

[34] Ibid. pp. 16, 154.

[35] Ibid. p. 154.

[36] Ibid. pp. 252–255.

[37] Ibid. pp. 12–14.

[38] Ibid. pp. 19, 49, 209, 235.

3.2 Private AI Legal Tech

3.2.1 From AI-Driven Legal Research to 'Robot Lawyers'

The global legal services industry is principally focused on the first wave of AI application, whose goal is to address the significant inefficiencies within the legal profession by creating reliable automation tools that simplify tasks like paperwork and case management. Examples of first-wave AI applications in the legal field include cloud-based document storage for easy retrieval, computer programs for rapid searches in regulatory registers, and natural language-processing engines for speedy contract review. The advantages of the first wave are transforming how lawyer-hours are utilized, ultimately improving performance.[39] Second-wave technologies in the legal industry include AI tools that enhance lawyers' capabilities, such as creating a "robot lawyer," AI software for contract interpretation, and AI systems trained to think like lawyers and extract key due diligence findings from legal documents. Some vendors are already working on third-wave AI, focusing on prediction analysis tools in big data analytics to aid in intelligent search and predicting litigation outcomes based on aggregated data from court decisions, particularly relevant to civil litigation practices.[40]

AI private legal has therefore the potential to equalize the legal landscape, diminishing the workforce disparity between large and small law firms, transforming revenue generation through modified billing practices, and streamlining the job market for lawyers by enhancing efficiency and possibly reducing the demand for numerous associates.[41] But measuring the tools' value for a competitive advantage is difficult due to the absence of industry-wide metrics.[42] The Stanford Law School CodeX Tech Index hosts a curated list of 1742 legal companies "changing the way legal is done".[43] Table 1 illustrates a taxonomy of AI functions, values, and AI providers for explanatory purposes.

The AI providers mentioned are examples, and there may be various other providers offering similar services in the legal tech space. AI, illustrated by DoNotPay's chatbot assisting users in contesting parking tickets and filing data breach-related suits, has the potential to make legal services more accessible by automating document generation and lowering litigation costs. However, concerns arise about potential misuse, leading to an influx of frivolous AI-generated lawsuits and prompting the need for legal updates to prevent abuse.[44]

[39] Ng (2022), pp. 37–39.

[40] Ibid. pp. 37–39.

[41] The Economist (June 6th, 2023) Generative AI could radically alter the practice of law.

[42] Weinstein (2022), p. 429.

[43] Stanford Law School, CodeX Techindex: https://techindex.law.stanford.edu/

[44] John Villasenor (March 20, 2023) How AI will revolutionize the practice of law. Avalable at https://www.brookings.edu/articles/how-ai-will-revolutionize-the-practice-of-law/

Table 1 Nomenclature of AI functions, values, and providers

AI functions	Description and value	AI-providers
Legal Research Assistance	AI can assist in legal research by quickly analyzing vast databases and providing relevant case law and statutes. AI can also translate legal documents.	ChatGPT, Ross Intelligence, Westlaw Edge, LexisNexis, Casetext, Ravel Law
Legal Education and Facilitation of Access to Legal Services	AI-based tools enhance legal education with interactive simulations, research support, and personalized learning. It has the potential to increase access by automating the generation of legal documents, reducing costs for initiating and pursuing litigation. AI can also provide "legal service" to clients, as seen with the DoNotPay chatbot contesting parking tickets and aiding in data breach-related suits.	ChatGPT, DoNotPay, Lex Machina, Ravel Law
Contract Automation, Analysis and Management	AI enables the automation of contract creation, review, and management, reducing time and errors.	eBrevia, Kira Systems, ROSS Intelligence CoCounsel, Harvey AI, DocuSign Insight, Ironclad, LinkSquares, Kira Systems, Contract Lifecycle Management (CLM), LawGeex, DeepL.
Predictive Analytics for Case Outcomes	AI algorithms can predict case outcomes, judge behaviour (except France),[a] witness testimony, and litigation trends based on historical data, enabling lawyers to make more informed decisions and strategies. AI significantly improves the speed, accuracy, and efficiency of document analysis, employing techniques like predictive coding, which has been widely accepted by US courts since the 2012 *Da Silva Moore v. Publicis Groupe* decision. AI could even prevail at predicting (Supreme) Court (s)decisions.[b]	Lex Machina, Kira Systems, Premonition AI, Blue J Legal, Ravel Law
Virtual Legal Assistants	AI-powered virtual assistants can handle routine tasks, schedule management, and basic client interactions.: AI-driven analytics help law firms understand client behavior and preferences to tailor marketing and services effectively.	LawGeex, Cognitiv+, Luminance

(continued)

Table 1 (continued)

AI functions	Description and value	AI-providers
Compliance Monitoring and Reporting	AI assists in monitoring legal compliance by analyzing regulations and generating reports on potential risks.	ComplyAdvantage, Onna, Legatics
Intellectual Property Management	AI helps in managing and monitoring intellectual property portfolios, including patent creation and analysis.	Anaqua, IPfolio, PatentSight
Legal Billing and Invoice Automation	AI can automate billing processes, generate invoices, and track billable hours, improving efficiency.	Brightflag, SimpleLegal, TimeSolv
Cybersecurity for Legal Data	AI enhances cybersecurity by detecting and preventing potential threats to sensitive legal data.	Darktrace, Cylance, Symantec
Online Dispute Resolution / AI Arbitrator[c]	AI-driven ODR platforms facilitate the resolution of disputes through online mediation, arbitration, or negotiation.	Tyler Technologies

[a]In France where it is no longer allowed to use data to evaluate or predict the behavior of individual Judges. LOI no 2019–222 du 23 mars 2019 de programmation 2018–2022 et de réforme pour la justice (1) - Article 33

[b]Guimerà and Sales-Pardo (2011), p. e27188

[c]If an AI adjudicator becomes feasible in the future, it would likely be developed based on litigation data rather than arbitration data: Ongenae (2023), pp. 111, 121

4 Developing a Taxonomy for AI Autonomy Levels and Risk Models

As technology accelerates, future AI is expected to exhibit increased autonomy, advanced machine learning, and physical robotics, posing challenges to our way of life by rising different risks.[45] Indeed, the "*alignment problem*," akin to the agency problem in corporate law (where director–officer–employee interests may diverge with the interests of the corporation and its shareholders), highlights the fear that AI's value judgments may not align with human values. This section aims therefore to create a taxonomy standard for Autonomy levels and Risk models applicable to AI public and private legal tech, with the goal of enhancing understanding of the connections between the degree of autonomy and associated risks.

[45]Di Matteo (2022), pp. 4, 7.

4.1 AI Legal Autonomy: Unveiling the 3A Model (Assisted, Advisory, Autonomous)

While current legal automation lacks autonomy, ongoing advancements, integrating AI capabilities, aspire to achieve autonomous operation.[46] To enable autonomy in legal tasks, AI systems must translate and incorporate existing legal reasoning capacities into computable terms (code as the law).[47] Drawing inspiration from AI literature and established autonomy standards in industries like automotive, this section sets forth an autonomy standard for AI-Based Legal Reasoning (AILR) systems. An AI system is described as autonomous when it takes decisions without further input from a human.[48] Autonomy in AI is typically classified into levels, leading to three AI roles:[49] assisted AI, advisory AI, and autonomous AI. Even in legal tech, the AI autonomy follows the **3A model** (*Assisted, Advisory, Autonomous*), structured as follows.

4.1.1 Manual and Controlled Autonomy (Level 1: Assisted Legal AI)

At this level, AI has lower level of autonomy and it requires continuous human control, intervention, and oversight. It encompasses basic NLP, simple ML, and statistical analysis tools in legal activities—such as simple document management systems or basic legal research platforms that can analyze and predict cases—aiding human-based legal reasoning without significant autonomy. Productivity gains are more limited.

4.1.2 Partial and Conditional Autonomy (Level 2: Advisory Legal AI)

Legal tech tools at this level feature AI systems capable of limited autonomy, such as document review tools that can handle routine tasks like identifying common or drafting new clauses, draft but for complex or unforeseen legal scenarios require human intervention and final assessment. Advisory AI has a heightened level of autonomy, which leads to increased productivity compared to assisted AI. Still, decision-making rights either remain with human users or are at most shared between humans. It includes the use of advanced Knowledge-Based Systems

[46] Autonomy is the capacity of an agent to achieve a set of coordinated goals by its own means (without human intervention) adapting to environment variations. When defining levels of autonomy, there are a multitude of factors that should be employed, doing so to systematically arrive at a parsimonious set that is logically sound and inherently robust. Scope, Sufficiency of Reason, Completeness, Applicability, Usefulness, Understandability, Foolproofness, Observe Occam's Razor, Differentiable, Logical Progression: Eliot (2021).

[47] Tools for argument analysis and evaluation that have been developed in informal logic and refined in artificial intelligence are applied to some central problems of defeasible reasoning in law. AI regarded as the main area of application of argumentation theory, including the legal reasoning. Argumentation is based on a pragmatic approach in which the use of an argument is studied in a dialogue context: Walton (2005), p. xii.

[48] Chesterman (2021), pp. 60–62.

[49] Petrin (2022), pp. 64–65.

(KBS) for legal reasoning, the use of ML and DP for legal reasoning, advanced NLP, etc. AI legal reasoning capabilities can function independently, either entirely or within specific limited legal domains, such as family law or data protection.

4.1.3 High and Full Autonomy (Level 3: Autonomous Legal AI)

At this juncture, AI systems exhibit legal reasoning comparable to humans, with high autonomy involving advanced contract drafting adaptable to diverse scenarios and full autonomy encompassing general legal advice, adjusting to evolving legal landscapes. Autonomous AI, allowing for occasional human intervention,[50] is positioned as the superset of Advisory AI, extending beyond legal domains, such as an IP Management AI system capable of autonomously identifying and addressing IP right violations on a large scale.[51]

In this context, autonomy refers to machines assuming more tasks, capable of achieving user goals without supervision, marking a crucial shift from '*automated*' to '*autonomous*' systems—with the ability to learn and adapt over time.[52] While this transition in the car industry—out of five levels of autonomy—occurs at 'level three' (i.e. conditional automation),[53] in the AI legal tech, this transition occurs at level 2, signifying a move from independent operation with human intervention to oversee complex legal matters as AI progresses. Advancing autonomy involves sophisticated AI technologies that make independent and unpredictable decisions, requiring ongoing updates for learning components and automations.

From a practical perspective, the evolution from manual operation to full autonomy highlights AI systems' increasing ability to handle legal tasks, necessitating a shift in the role of legal professionals from direct execution to overseeing and intervening in complex legal matters as AI technology advances. New legislation shall make it mandatory for AI developers and deployers to determine the level of autonomy of their AI systems. This enables clear distinctions in the autonomous capabilities of tools like, for example, e-Discovery at different levels (e.g., Level 2 and Level 3),[54] promoting fair competition, informed decision-making, and transparency for users.

However, it's crucial to recognize that achieving higher autonomy levels requires advanced AI technologies, varying based on the specific task or domain, with an increasing focus on safety and ethical considerations to ensure systems make sound decisions without human guidance. Moreover, the presence of learning components in AI systems,[55] introduces a level of independence and unpredictability, that

[50] Di Matteo (2022), p. 4.

[51] However, deploying AI systems for detecting and prosecuting IP infringement necessitates a comprehensive framework of rules and processes to maintain overall trust and address potential errors or unforeseen situations. Seng (2021), p. 320.

[52] Galdon et al. (2021), pp. 199–211.

[53] Chesterman (2020), pp. 210, 212; See also Kerrigan (2022), pp. 33–24.

[54] Eliot (2021).

[55] König et al. (2022), p. 33.

requires that these tools degree of autonomy need to be updated. In conclusion, as automation rises, the debate arises on whether legal personality, liability and rights should be granted to AI systems. The shift towards full automation (or realization of law-as-computation or legal singularity) may undermine democratic participation, disrupt the educative function of legal processes, and diminish the familiar forms of reasoning in law practice and scholarship, turning legal scholarship into a historical discipline rather than an active contributor to ongoing social projects.[56] The ethical, legal and liability aspects of AI autonomy are further developed below.

4.2 Risk-Based-Models of AI Systems According to the EU AI Act

The categorization of risk levels plays a vital role in the conscientious development, deployment, and continuous management of AI systems. It serves to tackle safety concerns, instil user confidence, adhere to regulations, and guarantee the ethical and efficient operation of AI technologies. The EU draft for AI Regulation follows this risk-based approach with four risk levels:[57] '*unacceptable risk*', '*high risk*', '*low risk*' and '*minimal risk*'. The focus of regulation is on high-risk AI.

4.2.1 Legal Tech with AI Systems of Unacceptable Risk

A limited set of AI applications that violate EU values, including causing harm, such social behaviour classification, risk assessments for law enforcement, specific biometric identification systems, and the use of manipulative techniques, are to be prohibited.[58] The AI Act underlines that these AI systems may lead to discriminatory outcomes and violate fundamental rights.[59] This is why, for instance, the application of 'real-time' biometric identification is restricted to cases of public interest, necessitating a thorough impact assessment on fundamental rights and requiring authorization from judicial authorities.[60] The precautionary principle used in environmental protection is used to regulate these categories of AI System.[61]

While specific use cases of legal tech are not explicitly outlined in this list, the prohibitions are formulated to encompass legal tech users as well. Consequently, providers of both public and private AI legal tech applications must guarantee that their applications do not incorporate or employ any of the practices restricted under Article 5 of the AI Act.

---

[56] Livermore (2022), p. 261.

[57] EU Commission (2021) Proposal for a Regulation harmonised rules on artificial intelligence (AI Act); Engelmann/Brunotte/Lütkens: Regulierung von Legal Tech durch die KI-Verordnung. RDi 2021, 317, para. 13.

[58] Art. 5 of Regulation Proposal on AI Act.

[59] Recital 7, 16, 20–21, 38–38.

[60] Recital 20–21.

[61] The consequences of a technological advancement pose potential dangers to human dignity, human rights, or democratic processes then it should be prohibited despite its perceived benefits.

4.2.2 Legal Tech with High-Risk AI Systems

AI systems, including those used in legal tech applications, are categorized as high-risk under Article 6 II in conjunction with Annex III of the AI Regulation. The classification depends on the specific purpose and application modalities, particularly in legal tech. Relevant categories for public legal tech applications involve the use by authorities and courts, falling under the term E-Justice:[62]

1. **Category 5** includes AI systems for assessing eligibility for public benefits and services, potentially covering legal tech applications checking social benefit eligibility;
2. **Category 6** covers law enforcement, including AI applications for evidence reliability assessment and criminal analysis, such as eDiscovery and Technology Assisted Review (TAR) for use by law enforcement authorities;
3. **Category 7** relates to migration, asylum, and border control, encompassing AI systems assisting authorities in examining asylum, visa, and residence permit applications;
4. **Category 8** concerns the administration of justice and democratic processes, involving AI systems supporting judicial authorities in determining facts, interpreting legal provisions, and applying the law. This may include legal tech applications aiding courts in analyzing statements of claim.

The AI Act designates legal tech as high-risk AI systems, focusing specifically on those employed in public legal tech. But the AI systems for purely ancillary administrative activities that do not impact the actual administration of justice, such as anonymization or pseudonymization of judicial decisions, communication, administrative tasks, or resource allocation are excluded (so called *supportive* technologies).[63]

Apparently, AI platforms in private legal tech are not explicitly outlined in the Act as highly risky. However, some private AI legal tech platforms, especially those handling sensitive legal information or impacting critical decision-making processes, may pose significant risks like their public counterparts. To prevent the rise of future AI platforms that are not underlined by the AI Act, the EU legislator grants the EU Commission the authority to update the list of high-risk AI systems in Annex III through delegated acts.[64] Legal tech providers and AI users must monitor updates to this list, considering potential impacts on their business models.

The AI Regulation imposes rigorous compliance requirements on covered high-risk AI systems and their providers. Unlike Article 22 of the GDPR, the AI Regulation specifies extensive technical requirements, requiring clarification by courts and supervisory authorities. Before launching a high-risk AI system, providers must

[62] See Annex III of the AI Regulation: https://eur-lex.europa.eu/resource.html?uri=cellar:e0649735-a372-11eb-9585-01aa75ed71a1.0001.02/DOC_2&format=PDF

[63] Recital 40 of the Regulation Proposal on AI Act.

[64] Article 7 of Regulation Proposal on AI Act.

undergo a conformity assessment[65]to demonstrate compliance with trustworthy AI standards.[66] Additional requirements encompass risk management (Article 9), cybersecurity (Article 15), documentation, and transparency obligations (Article 11 ff.), and quality management (Article 17). Transparency requirements include providing users with instructions for use in a digital format, including information on the provider's identity and system characteristics by providing explanations for AI-based determinations.[67] The AI proposal Regulation extends obligations to importers (Article 26), traders (Article 27), and users (Article 29) of high-risk AI systems.

4.2.3 Legal Tech with Low-Risk AI Systems

AI systems with low risk are only subject to special requirements regarding the transparency (e.g. if there is a clear risk of manipulation) and users should be aware that they are dealing with a machine, unless this is obvious due to the circumstances and context of use.[68] For instance, user shall know that they are not being consulted by a human lawyer in case of legal chatbots. It is expected that most AI-based legal tech applications that are used by companies, law firms and end users are included in this category because they are intended precisely for interaction with natural persons, namely to help answer legal questions. These are likely to include legal chat bots, applications for the automation of documents (e.g. based on an interactive questionnaire that is filled in by the user of the application), automatic filing of law suits, generation of legal documents, etc.

5 Identifying and Addressing Challenges in AI Legal-Tech

Advancements in AI systems have led various government sectors to delegate decision-making authority to automated systems in critical areas such as social welfare, law enforcement, and notably, judicial proceedings. However, autonomy in the AI systems raises questions about whether, how, and with what safeguards human decision-making authority is being transferred to a machine. Algorithmic decision-making runs the risk of treating human subjects as a means rather than an end (morality and legitimacy concerns).[69] Automation biases affects under-represented populations, and AI generates broader legal, social, and ethical

[65] Article 19 of Regulation Proposal on AI Act

[66] Article 48 mandates a declaration of conformity with information specified in Annex V. The product is labeled with the CE mark and registered in a new EU database: Article 49 and Article 51 in conjunction with Annex VIII of the AI Act.

[67] Ibid. Art. 13.

[68] However, it remains unclear when such obviousness should be given. Neither Art. 52 I nor the recitals of the AI Regulation provide further details. As things stand at present, it will therefore be up to the authorities and courts to provide clarity. Art. 52 of the AI Proposal Regulation

[69] Algorithmic decision-making, for example, raises directly the question of the extent to which public authorities can outsource their responsibilities: Chesterman (2021), p. 168.

challenges.[70] Indeed, the higher the degree of AI-system 's autonomy, the higher the risks that it might cause to society and nature.[71] However, the specific AI risks tied to its applications emerge from a combination of purpose-specific, context-specific, and technical factors.[72] Therefore, the aim of this section is to unpack some of the most prominent ethical, legal, and regulatory challenges arising from the practical application of AI Legal technologies, which are then accompanied by possible measures.

5.1 Opacity (*in dubio contra reum ex maschina?*)

Many arguments warning of opaque AI systems determining the fate of humans conjure a dystopian world without explanations, epitomized by Franz Kafka's *The Trial.*[73] AI entails algorithmic use as mathematical instructions to address problems via opaque and non-deterministic decision-making processes which hinders comprehension even among programmers (the so called *'black box'* problem).[74] The opacity of decision-making in the legal domain, especially the public domain (e.g. crime prediction), raises ethical concerns due to the potential for bias and discrimination in inputs, processes, outputs, and outcomes.[75] Opening the black box (*explainability*), so it is argued, is indispensable to identify encroachments on user privacy, to detect biases and to prevent other physical, emotional and legal harms. However, (achieving) interpretability challenges arise from deliberate design choices, insufficient literacy, or inherent complexity, especially given the prevalent hierarchical and nonlinear structures in most deep learning models.[76]

In response to the black box problem and in adherence to transparency and fairness principles, a new research field called explainable AI (xAI) has emerged. Its goal is to enhance the understandability and accountability of algorithmic decision aids by providing explanations for their outputs or the processes leading to those output.[77] In this context, transparency, accountability, and the need for human review (and intervention) in automated decision-making systems are emphasized to address these ethical challenges and prevent the delegation of excessive moral

[70] Liu et al. (2019), pp. 122–141; Liu et al. (2022), p. 138; EESC Opinion on AI and society (INT/806, 2017).

[71] Noto La Diega (2022), p. 3; UN Security Council, 'Letter Dated 8 March 2021 from the Panel of Experts on Libya Estab-lished Pursuant to Resolution 1973 (2011) Addressed to the President of the Security Council' (S/2021/22).

[72] König et al. (2022), pp. 28–29.

[73] Chesterman (2021), pp. 60–62.

[74] Janssen (2022), pp. 60–61; König et al. (2022), pp. 30–31.

[75] Shaw (2022), p. 400.

[76] Häuselmann (2022), pp. 55–56.

[77] Mik (2021), p. 56–57.

agency to AI, which could undermine human autonomy and confidence in decision-making.[78]

5.1.1 Transparency and Other Methods to Fight Opacity

While a transparency requirement is desirable, what is less clear is how the call for AI transparency can be translated into reasonable regulation (example from human partially opaque decision-making systems can be drawn).[79] But, efforts to achieve complete transparency in AI decision-making are impractical and undesirable. Instead, transparency obligations should provide stakeholders (citizens, consumers, the media, parliaments, regulatory agencies, and courts) with the necessary information for reviews (either administratively or judicially) and accountability, and empowering those directly affected by decisions to foster trust in the process.[80] Transparency requirements for AI systems should therefore be considered as a means to counteract the widespread ignorance and the diffuse sense of disenfranchisement that accompanies the rise of AI. Regulators must consider several factors when balancing interests in AI transparency and secrecy with fundamental rights.[81] Transparency is the informational dimension of accountability and, as such, both a precondition for and a product of the control framework for decision-making processes. However, neither are all AI-based systems inscrutable black boxes nor does transparency all by itself guarantee accountability.[82] To establish a comprehensive transparency strategy for AI systems, several crucial measures should be implemented.

First, the use of opaque AI systems, particularly in judicial decisions concerning criminal law process, should be avoided or limited due to concerns about *inferior decisions, impermissible biases, and illegitimacy* resulting from opacity.[83] The authority entrusted and exercise of discretion by judges (i.e. the authority granted to judges to make decisions based on their judgment and interpretation of the law) and other public officers, should not be outsourced to private AI actors anyone else.[84]

Second, the opacity problem should be addressed by improving decision quality through robust testing and verification and ensuring clarity on how and why

---

[78] Shaw (2022), p. 400.

[79] Wischmeyer (2020), p. 75.

[80] Wischmeyer (2020), p. 78.

[81] These include the criticality of the sector, the significance of the system operator, the impact on individual and collective rights, the type of data involved (especially special categories under GDPR), the integration of technology into decision-making processes, and the feasibility of protecting system operators' legitimate interests in AI secrecy through various means. Moving beyond the formalist approach of Article 22 GDPR is suggested, encompassing all AI-based systems using personal data in decision-making processes: Wischmeyer (2020), p. 94.

[82] For a comprehensive discussion of AI's accountability problem, of which transparency is one dimension, cf. Busch Busch (2018).

[83] Chesterman (2021), pp. 81–82.

[84] Chesterman (2021), p. 245.

algorithms are used to avoid (impermissible) biases. In cases where public authorities make decisions affecting individuals' rights, the need (or the right) for explanation becomes crucial for process legitimacy, aligning with calls for transparency and explainability in AI systems to hold human decision-makers accountable.[85]

Third, granting individual access to information rights is another important step, with public authorities extending existing freedom of information laws. Ensuring accountability for AI systems involves providing supervisory agencies and courts with access to information. The black box technical problem in legal decision-making, arising from the proprietary nature of statistical models protected by trade secret statutes, could be thus addressed through limited public disclosure conditions or restricting trade secret protection for private firms involved in essential public services to prioritize transparency and accountability in the public interest.[86]

Finally, accompanying measures, such as documenting AI system operations, impact assessments *before*, audits *during*, and an independent advocate *after* those decisions will lead to better decisions as well as increasing trust within courts and agencies in those decisions.[87]

5.2 Ethical and Legal Concerns of AI Legal Tech

AI systems, commonly employed in critical decisions like parole, loan approvals, and imprisonment determinations, often lack consistent integration of ethical considerations in their design, neglecting the interests of those beyond the development or deployment team.[88] This oversight, akin to trusting decisions to someone indifferent to ethical concerns, leads to adverse consequences for individuals, ethnic groups, and society as a whole.[89] There is a high risk that increasing reliance on machines for legal tasks sidelines human (intelligence) empathy and (judges) creativity in the field of law.[90] Indeed, computers make mistakes. For example, the UK Post Office scandal was marked by the Horizon IT-Software system's errors causing false accusations and legal challenges for thousands of employees who fired and accused of fraud and stealing. Some even killed themselves.[91] But AI might make things worse: the US COMPAS Recidivism Risk AI Model, introduced to aid judges and parole boards, discriminatorily (due to biased data training) revealed higher risk

[85] Chesterman (2021), pp. 81–82.

[86] Liu et al. (2019), pp. 122–141

[87] Wischmeyer (2020), pp. 95–97.

[88] Tsamados et al. (2021), p. 98.

[89] Liu et al. (2022), p. 40; O'Neil and Gunn (2020), pp. 251–252; Graham (2021).

[90] Schafer (2022), p. 305.

[91] Nature (January 2024) Computers make mistakes and AI will make things worse—the law must recognize that. Available at https://doi.org/10.1038/d41586-024-00168-8

scores for black male defendants and a disproportionately higher false positive rate.[92]

Furthermore, research highlights that human tendency to view algorithms as impartial leads to the "technology effect," characterized by excessive optimism in technology-related decisions, and "automation bias," where judges might adopt automated decision recommendations, bypassing additional confirmation and potentially relinquishing decision-making authority to the machine.[93] The infallibility of computer systems, including those employing AI, shall not be presumed since is placing an unjust burden on individuals to prove inaccuracies; instead, creator and deployers of AI shall share that obligation via data test publication and access to ensure transparency without compromising trade secrets and to prevent miscarriages of justice.

Therefore, in the context of AI, alongside security and privacy issues, there's a pervasive risk to essential values like self-determination, dignity, freedom of expression, contract freedom, and equality.[94] However, the envisioned future of a cold, objective, precise, predictable, and emotion-free robot-adjudicator is not an unavoidable destiny. In the following sub-sections I will provide different measures on how to avoid and/or mitigate ethical and legal concerns in both public and private legal tech.

5.2.1 Possible Remedies

It is essential to develop intelligent systems that adhere to moral behaviour to establish trust and enable their integration into critical domains, where adherence to ethical principles is crucial. To address thus ethical and related legal issues the AI literature has identified a set of possible solutions.

5.2.1.1 AI Need to Learn to Achieve Human Value Alignment

Addressing the AI control problem, to prevent human existential risk from superintelligent AI, involves redefining AI from optimizing objectives to ensuring machines are demonstrably beneficial for humans.[95] As for like huma specie, AI systems should evolve into complex social agents by acquiring by design ethical learning by collaborating with humans and understating human nature.[96] However, a challenge arises as human-friendly values are too intricate, vague and complex to be explicitly hardwired or programmed. That is why one must design the machine *to learn* to

---

[92] The imbalance is concerning, as higher risk scores may lead to longer sentences, posing potential civil rights issues for false positives (e.g. right to due and fair process). The asymmetry presents challenges, with false negatives raising concerns for judges accused of leniency, highlighting a complex set of interests for courts, judges, and defendants: O'Neil and Gunn (2020), p. 256.

[93] Gravett (2024), pp. 288–289; Sourdin (2021), pp. 92–93.

[94] Noto La Diega (2022), p. 3; UN Security Council, 'Letter Dated 8 March 2021 from the Panel of Experts on Libya Estab-lished Pursuant to Resolution 1973 (2011) Addressed to the President of the Security Council' (S/2021/22).

[95] Russell (2020), p. 339.

[96] Railton (2020), pp. 52, 66.

achieve human *value alignment*.[97] From a technical perspective, existing preference modelling and reasoning frameworks, such as hard constraints (e.g. Don't hurt humans, obey humans, and self-preserve—Asimov's law) and CP-nets (Conditional Preference Networks), can be utilized to model, learn and compare ethical priorities, ensuring that AI systems align closely with human values and community guidelines.[98] This will also allow to achieve trustworthy AI by asserting that value alignment must be the guiding principle throughout the design for achieving *value alignment* and *value learning*.[99] These two principles shall be thus implanted in computation legal reasoning.[100]

Therefore, while acknowledging the importance of laws and regulations, researchers argue that the most effective way to address ethical challenges posed by algorithmic decision-making is to implement ethical algorithms.[101]

5.2.1.2 Development of Standards for Structuring Qualitative Legal Data(Sets) to Avoid

AI is pivotal in ensuring a fair interpretation of the law, countering biases in manual methods, and establishing transparent digital laws for equitable treatment. However, the effectiveness of AI hinges on its input quality. Automated legal processes can inadvertently discriminate against vulnerable minorities since they heavily rely on the assumptions and biases present in the training datasets, including gender, racial, and social status biases. Therefore, and to prevent these issues, those involved in AI must be vigilant about data quality and integrity during the training process.[102] Developing computational and linguistic standards for structuring legal data is thus crucial to unlock the full potential of advanced AI techniques, including big legal data analytics.[103]

However, currently, the legal industry lacks unified standards for AI-ready data, leading to varied and often ineffective approaches. But the "Logical English" (LE) can serve as a valuable tool for structuring legal data by aligning legalese

[97] A superintelligence, adept at calculating coherence, may develop a value system perceived as more coherent than our own by addressing three problems: learning a final goal through coherence calculation, constructing a complex yet determinate final goal from simple goals with relation constraints, and acquiring the right final goal by seeding it with simple values conducive to coherent reflective equilibrium and plausible ethical principles: Petersen (2020), pp. 413, 428.

[98] Loreggia et al. (2020), p. 145.

[99] Wallach and Vallor (2020), p. 407.

[100] Ashley (2022), p. 213.

[101] There will always be **trade-offs** that we need to manage. Once we can precisely specify what we mean by "privacy" or "fairness," achieving these goals necessarily requires giving up on something else that we value—for example, raw predictive accuracy. It is the goal of algorithmic research not only to identify these constraints and embed them into our algorithms but also to quantify the extent of these trade-offs and to design algorithms that make them as mild as possible: Kearns and Roth (2020).

[102] Liu et al. (2022), p. 40; Sourdin (2021), pp. 9, 19, 22, 187.

[103] Ng (2022), p. 42.

with natural language, promoting compatibility with legal reasoning logic, enabling the creation of AI training data and reducing inconsistencies. Its disciplined use imposes standards on data structuring, preventing arbitrariness and inaccuracies, which is crucial for establishing consistent AI-ready data standards in the legal industry.[104] Furthermore, the effective structuring of legal data involves organizing information to mirror legal reasoning, making legalese machine-readable for AI programs to extract clear rules. Structuring tasks include refining fuzzy logic, defining legal terms, and physically reorganizing contract information.[105] If the AI legal output is proved to be biased due to bias on data or due to any other technical issue, the AI legal tech system must be designed to *unlearn* the prejudice. This will ensure transparency and foster trust.

But in addition to technical barriers, the standardization of legal data might also face legal barriers. For example, in the private law domain contracts, legal expertise and other acts are heavily subject to copyrights;[106] privacy and data protection also pose a limit to use them for training. In the public domain, all court data, defined inclusively to include lawsuit-level metadata, docket sheets, and party-filed and judge-filed court documents, should be provided by the court systems in machine-readable electronic format, to the public, for free. They need to be anonymized to protect privacy and other interests of the affected parties. Likewise, in the law enforcement context, the indiscriminate police data collection poses a risk to privacy and human rights since it might involve indiscriminate data collection from different purposes on everyone (e.g. daily routines, social networks, biometrics, and thoughts feed private and public databases), neglecting distinctions between suspects and non-suspects, overlooking data transparency and blurring (the much needed) lines between public and private domains.[107]

5.2.1.3 Development of an Ethical and Data Science Matrix

O'Neil and Gunn (2020) have developed an *ethical matrix* and a *data science ethical matrix* as a practical tool for intentionally analyzing the ethical consequences of AI and for avoiding discrimination. The *ethical matrix* requires us to consider the interests of a range of stakeholders (e.g. Court, Defendants, Public,) with general types of moral goods (e.g. wellbeing, autonomy, and justice).[108] AI design (e.g., data

---

[104] Ibid. p. 41

[105] Ng (2022), pp. 39–41.

[106] There are four machine learning categories based on data usage: (1) involving uncopyrightable training data, (2) incorporating copyrightable material under permissive licenses, (3) market-encroaching uses posing a threat to data markets (e.g. AI-generated soundtracks for media producers), and (4) non-market-encroaching uses utilizing copyrighted training data for purposes unrelated to copyright's monopoly. Despite only market-encroaching uses being subject to copyright control, copyright law appears paradoxically ill-equipped to effectively regulate them: Sobel (2021), pp. 228 and ss.

[107] Erdoğan (2022), p. 100.

[108] Given that data and computer scientists are not ethical experts, the construction of the matrix can be simplified according to the application sector (i.e., when the AI-system is used for crime

scientists or programmers) and deployer (e.g., a court, a local government) teams shall use the matrix to assess the broader impact of their choices on a diverse range of stakeholders, thereby enhancing transparency in the AI design process and promoting accountability.[109]

5.2.1.4 Establishing an AI Overarching Ethical Framework for AI Core Values

The efficiency principle urges the use of digital automated systems, emphasizing the necessity for a "digital check" to evaluate their impact on fundamental rights based on expected efficiency gains.[110] However, there is widespread agreement on the need for algorithmic fairness, particularly to mitigate the risks of direct and indirect discrimination (i.e. 'disparate treatment' and 'disparate impact').[111] However, translating ethical principles for digital technologies into practice faces challenges, including unethical risks (such as ethics shopping, ethics bluewashing, ethics lobbying, ethics dumping, and ethics shirking) and the development of different standards and AI principles which can undermine even the most diligent efforts.[112]

Therefore, Floridi has underlined that an overarching ethical framework for AI (shall) consist of five core principles: beneficence (do good), non-maleficence (do not harm), autonomy ('decide-to-delegate' model: humans should retain the power to decide which decisions to take), justice (avoid unfairness, promote prosperity and accountability) and explicability (tell how it works and who is responsible for the way it works).[113] Thus, the core AI values are guided by four key ethical principles: respect for human autonomy, prevention of harm, fairness, explicability, and human intervention to monitor and overturn decisions.[114] These principles are rooted in a fundamental rights-based approach, reflecting the core of international and EU human rights law.[115]Additionally, it is recemented that the governance of AI requires the creation of centres, oversight agencies, and other infrastructure which will contribute to securing the benefits and mitigating the risks of AI.[116] The OECD even recommends national priorities, emphasizing investments in interdisciplinary research and development for trustworthy AI and open datasets that are unbiased and

preventions, the matric can be based on Efficiency, False Positives, False Negatives, and assessing the interest of Court Black and White Defendants): O'Neil and Gunn (2020), pp. 251–252, and 260–261.

[109] Ibid. p. 266.

[110] Pfister (2021), p. 132.

[111] Tsamados et al. (2021), p. 107.

[112] Floridid (2021), p. 81.

[113] Flroidi and Cowls (2021), p. 13; OECD, Recommendation of the Council on Artificial Intelligence, OECD/LEGAL/0449 (2020), pp. 5–7.

[114] Di Matteo (2022), p. 5.

[115] European Commission's AI HLEG, *Ethics Guidelines for Trustworthy AI* (April 2019), p. 11–12; See also Di Matteo (2022), p. 5.

[116] Floridid et al. (2021), p. 38.

privacy-respecting.[117] To conclude, AI legal tech shall thus focus on ensuring fairness, mitigating algorithmic biases, and safeguarding human rights (e.g. freedom from technological experimentation, manipulation, or surveillance) in the development and deployment of AI systems.[118] Trust in AI is essential, as depicted in Asimov's stories showcasing strong bonds between humans and robots, and achieving transparency involves defining goals and understanding for end-users, evaluators, and regulators.[119]

5.2.1.5 Protection of Fundamental Rights by Adopting a Multifaceted Protection Governance

Constitutional democracies rely on fundamental principles like legality, accountability, and transparency, embodying the checks and balances inherent in the rule of law. This means that neither the legislature nor public administration has ultimate authority over legal interpretation and application. Judges do.[120] However, utilizing algorithms in the justice system presents risks, as it may jeopardize human dignity by potentially objectifying individuals through algorithmic decision-making, resulting in a less just system ('dehumanization').[121] Issues like the right to appeal AI Judge decisions, transparency, and the suitability of automation in criminal sentencing raise concerns about individual liberty and human rights protection.[122] Advanced AI automated decision can compromise due process rights by limiting challenges to decisions, stressing the need for accessible information,[123] undermine the fundamental values of due and fair process, equal protection, and transparency, responsibility, privacy.[124] Indeed, criminal law principles, such as the presumption of innocence, equality of arms, immediacy with regard to the contestation of evidence, and the legality of criminal investigation that requires probable cause, proportionality and a range of other safeguards whenever fundamental rights are infringed in the course of a criminal investigation may be violated in case of, for example, 'smart policing' or 'smart sentencing'.[125] Judges, who play a dual role in applying and creating law,[126] face a contrast with 'Judge AI', which relies on past legal data and applies only existing rules, lacking the ability to create or improve

---

[117] OECD, Recommendation of the Council on Artificial Intelligence, OECD/LEGAL/0449 (2020), pp. 5–7.

[118] To ensure trustworthiness, control should not be delegated to AI (processes to monitor and evaluate the integrity of AI systems): Di Matteo (2022), pp. 8, 12.

[119] To ensure trustworthiness, control should not be delegated to AI (processes to monitor and evaluate the integrity of AI systems): Di Matteo (2022), pp. 8, 12, 32; Cooman and Petit (2023), p. 16; Di Matteo (2022), p. 32.

[120] Hildebrandt (2020), pp. 70, 83.

[121] Sourdin (2021), p. 187

[122] Ibid. pp. 151 and 227.

[123] Sourdin (2021), pp. 246–249.

[124] Liu et al. (2019), pp. 122–141; Sourdin (2021), p. 227.

[125] Hildebrandt (2020), p. 70.

[126] Sourdin (2021), p. 34

legal interpretations—a fundamental role of judges. Additionally, judges' responsiveness, whether adhering to classic or progressive models, incorporate societal changes into their decision-making[127]—however, AI judges may lack the ability to recognize and factor in these changes.

Automated detection of suspicious activity and AI law enforcement tools in general shall be thus constitutionally clear. While Germany is stricter on allowing their use,[128] the EU and, especially, US Courts are more open to their use—even without prior suspicion—if some conditions of accountability and proportionality are meet.[129] A multifaceted protection approach is required. To that end, Rademacher (2020) proposes a three-step governance approach to ensure compliance with constitutional frameworks, prevent unjust State intrusion, and address discriminatory patterns in law enforcement. This includes establishing regulatory provisions for human accountability (the essence of democracy rests on the delegation and exercise of power and decisions by humans), exploring AI integration to counter discrimination and rectify long-standing discriminatory patterns observed in human policing in specific jurisdictions, and critically assessing the idea of a 'perfect' rule of law that may compromise the freedom to dissent.[130] Additionally, Biber et al. (2023) suggest that judicial interpretation is a key in protecting fundamental rights and understanding the intricate dimensions of AI automated decision-making by highlighting three key aspects: *epistemic* (focused on comprehending the purpose and functioning of the algorithms like fraud prevention), *substantial* (clarifying socio-technical and legal aspects, emphasizing legislation clarity for human understanding), and *methodological* (examining the normative interaction between both national and international legal provisions). It proves essential in bridging the gap between machines and humans, as well as between law and the built of a better digital society.[131]

5.2.1.6 Protection of Private Law Principles in Private AI Legal Tech

The adoption of legal tech software in contracting is transforming contracts and contract law by introducing AI creators acting as new intermediaries that simplify,

---

[127] Ibid. p. 46

[128] The conditions for deeming automated detection of **suspicious activity constitutional**, requires three criteria: the technology needs to work well (not to many false positives or negatives); the respective statute may only allow the use of the technology if police can demonstrate, beforehand, some form of person- or place-based suspicion that crimes or other infringements of the law might occur or might have occurred, in the given circumstances, with sufficient likelihood; surveillance must not be allowed to be 'flächendeckend', i.e. locally all-encompassing: Rademacher (2020), pp. 233–235.

[129] Ibid.

[130] Society must engage in thoughtful consideration of whether, where, and when it desires to preserve the **freedom to dissent** from established legal norms. Ibid. p. 250.

[131] Biber, Dr. Sümeyye Elif, Between Humans and Machines: Judicial Interpretation of the Automated Decision-Making Practices in the EU (December 12, 2023). University of Luxembourg Law Research Paper No. 2023–19, pp. 35–36.

monitor, execute, analyses, regulate and govern relationships.[132] AI techniques, such as ML and NLP, optimize the full contract lifecycle. For example, they enable personalized pricing in the *pre-contractual* stage, enhance negotiating, drafting, transaction efficiency, and risk management *during performance*, and aid in legal dispute resolution and court outcome prediction in the *post-contractual* phase.[133] The exploration of AI-based contracting highlights the potential benefits, making the process faster, more effective, and efficient, with AI-driven systems offering more accurate and less biased predictions and decisions than humans.

However, the use of AI in contracting introduces new challenges, including power imbalances, information asymmetries, issues with price discrimination and exploitative contracts, defects in consent, interpretation, and review of coded contracts, and determining contractual liability for damages caused by AI systems.[134] Indeed, the complexity of certain AI programs may lead to situations where their operations result in the conclusion of contracts that are commercially unfavourable (i.e. a website offers goods far below their market price or when a trading algorithm purchases a large amount of stock at an unreasonably high price). However, adopters (or deployers) of AI systems might be liable for the inefficiency of the implemented AI systems. For example, Air Canada reluctantly issued recently a partial refund to a passenger who, misled by the airline's chatbot on its bereavement travel policy, followed inaccurate advice to book a flight immediately and request a refund within 90 days, with the airline asserting that it should not be held liable for the chatbot's misleading information, a defense deemed "remarkable" by the tribunal member who ruled in favor of the passenger.[135]

However, the law generally does not require the statements made by contracting parties to be understandable or explainable, highlighting a potential gap between technological advancements and legal frameworks. The only exception concerns situations where a reasonable addressee of a statement knows or should know that such a statement does not represent the actual intention of its maker.[136]

Furthermore, private AI Legal Tech platforms could be misused leading to an influx of frivolous AI-generated lawsuits. Even imposing additional obligations on AI Legal Tech tools by Member States might be limited due to the legal status of these tools. Highly automated legal tech services, like chatbots or contract generators, often fall under information society services rather than legal services, allowing them to benefit from the country-of-origin principle of the E-Commerce Directive and potentially avoiding national authorization requirements, except for

[132] Martinelli and Chauvenet (2021), p. 96.

[133] Ebers (2021), pp. 21 and ss.

[134] Ibid Ebers, p. 39.

[135] ASHLEY BELANGER (17, 2024) Air Canada Has to Honor a Refund Policy Its Chatbot Made Up. Available at https://www.wired.com/story/air-canada-chatbot-refund-policy/

[136] A classic example is an offer to sell a high-end printer for S$67, while its market price exceeded S$2600,66 or the exchange of cryptocurrencies at 150 times the market rate: Mik (2022), pp. 56–57.

specific measures related to consumer protection or public policy purposes under Article 3(4) of the E-Commerce Directive.[137]

In short, private law principles—like freedom to contract and dispose of one's property, prompt inquiries into the constitution of contracts, addressing issues of information provision, investigations, voidability due to lack of information, and considerations of duress, fraud, or deception—might be harmed by private AI Legal Tech tools.[138] To address these concerns, the measures—algorithm human value alignment, development of qualitative legal data standards, development of overreaching ethical principles, right to opt out, and use of ethical matrix proposed developed in this section shall be used to identify, assess and address ethical and legal concerns that arise from private legal tech.

5.2.1.7 Right to Opt Out

A way to solve the black box problem and to avoid adverse impact, people shall have the right to opt in or to opt out from AI Legal Tech platforms.[139] For example, the use of automated risk assessment tools in criminal proceedings shall only be allowed if the defendant agrees for its use. Likewise, people shall retain the right to get consulted by a human lawyer and judged by a human. Indeed, human intelligence remains indispensable in areas like jury presentations, contract-strategic decision-making, client relationships, and leadership roles.[140]

6 AI and Liability Regimes

Scholars argue that the rise of AI has given rise to "liability gaps" (i.e., a situation in which, in the presence of damages, the allocation of legal liability based on the existing remedies to the parties involved is disrupted by certain circumstances).[141] This rise due to the intricate nature of AI systems (i.e., autonomy, self-learning capability, opaqueness, complexity, interoperability, unpredictable interactions,

[137] Sein (2022), pp. 153–154.

[138] Hildebrandt (2020), p. 70.

[139] Liu et al. (2019), pp. 122–141 (141).

[140] John Villasenor (March 20, 2023) How AI will revolutionize the practice of law. Available at https://www.brookings.edu/articles/how-ai-will-revolutionize-the-practice-of-law/

[141] Janssen (2022), pp. 59–60; De Conca (2022), pp. 241 and ss; While common law is adaptable in addressing liability regardless of human or AI involvement, civil law primarily follows a (human) fault liability model. With the increasing autonomy of AI, the duties of care of the operator of AI systems (especially the monitoring duties) are reduced, while that of the creator of the AI system correspondingly increases. The operator may therefore rebut the presumption of fault found in section 280(1) s. 2 BGB and thus escape liability. This causes a shift of liability from the operator to the creator of AI systems, whose duties of care intensify with the increasing autonomy of their systems. The challenge in civil law lies in attributing AI conduct to operators, given that its norms are designed for human actions. To resolve this issue, one option is to apply existing attribution provisions analogously, or to create new provisions specifically for AI system: Möslein (2022), pp. 62–80; EDPS Opinion 42/2023 on the Proposal for two Directives on AI liability rules.

multiple stakeholders like manufacturers, providers, and developers, potential vulnerabilities introduced by updates, etc.) that introduces disruptive elements, including the involvement of multiple responsible parties and the added unpredictability in interactions with diverse components, technologies, and human involvement.[142] Closing the liability gap could involve holding developers accountable, fostering control incentives. Alternatively, assigning legal personality to AI would make the system, rather than the creator, responsible.[143]

In short, the liability landscape for AI is multifaceted and the literature in AI has identified different cumulative, existing, new, and alternative legal liability regimes that could be applied to AI-systems such as:

(a) **strict liability framework** by holding creators or owners directly accountable for AI-related harm without the need to establish negligence since it is supposed as dangerous activity. This approach is complemented by negligence-based liability, which emphasizes fault and requires evidence of a breach of duty of care, foreseeability, and a causal link between negligence and harm.[144] This regime is particular claimed for the fact that the development of self-learning AI algorithm provides difficulties on explaining decision making since they change continuously overtime due to its self-learning capabilities.[145]
(b) **No-fault liability** models that seek to compensate victims without establishing fault, and hybrid approaches combine elements of various regimes to navigate this complex legal landscape. Here is taken into account that the dangerousness of certain objects or methods directly linked to State action in the public interest and capable of causing serious harm to a significant number of persons. Compensation is based on the collectivisation of risk through the use of public funds. This system remains based on liability but not on fault.[146]
(c) **Product liability** laws—such as the EU proposal on "AI Liability Directive"—may treat AI systems as products, holding manufacturers, distributors, and sellers responsible for defects.[147] This regime is similar with agency and vicarious liability that attribute actions of the AI to its owner or controller.[148]

[142] De Conca (2022), p. 242.

[143] König et al. (2022), p. 33.

[144] Focus on AI Operators: The person deploying AI should have a central role in ensuring AI safety. They can control the environment in which AI operates and establish security measures and controls. The researcher suggests that operators should contract with developers to ensure responsible AI development: Tjong and Tai (2022), pp. 116 and 130.

[145] Howells and Twigg-Flesner (2022), p. 193.

[146] Monot-Fouletier (2022), pp. 173 & 178.

[147] EU Commission (2022) Proposal for a Directive on adapting non-contractual civil liability rules to artificial intelligence (AI Liability Directive) COM/2022/496 final.

[148] When applying agency rules to AI agents, challenges emerge, as AI agents lack legal personality and contractual capacity. Even if an AI agent is found solely responsible for its actions, it lacks legal standing and cannot be sued or held liable in court: Çağlayan Aksoy (2022), p. 160.

(d) **contractual liability** that is rooted in agreements dictating AI system performance and behavior, with breaches leading to accountability. In consumer transactions, liability is based on strict contractual terms, and liability arises if the AI algorithm does not conform to the contract. Manufacturers, for instance, may be held responsible for failing to meet promised standards outlined in warranties. However, this regime might raise **asymmetries of power issues.** For example, firms may require their customers or users to sign exculpatory clauses in contractual limitations on liability, waiving their right to sue.[149] They validity shall not be.

(e) **tort liability**: authors contend that AI should continue to be subject to tort liability if we wish to avoid alarmism or anti-technological panic-mongering.[150] A statutory leap embracing one of the extremes—immunity from liability or strict liability—would preempt that development of tort law and its ability to provide a measured response. Such a leap may provide a degree of certainty, but it would be at the cost of preventing tort law from providing a better solution.[151] Tort liability covers civil wrongs causing harm due to negligence, intentional misconduct, or strict liability, involves AI producers, operators, and end-users. For example, manufacturers are accountable for defects, operators for negligence in monitoring AI systems, and end-users may share liability for misuse.

(f) **Sectorial Approach**: Researchers argues that AI is too diverse, with diverse consequences, to have a single liability approach. Instead, they suggest that liability should be tailored to specific AI applications and sectors, with varying degrees of liability based on the potential consequences of AI malfunctions. Thus specific liability regimes, such as result-oriented or strict liability, could be imposed in areas where there is a pressing need for accountability.[152]

(g) **Beyond Liability:** the above legal regimes are not the only legal tools proposed to mitigate the uncertainty in the allocation of liability or to redistribute the economic damages, with regard to AI. The most notable other legal solutions proposed are mandatory insurance schemes and creating an *ad hoc* type of legal personality for AI systems and/or robots. Regardless of the allocation of liability, insurance schemes are already in use to make sure that individuals carrying out certain activities can keep possible victims indemnified in case of damages, as is the case for cars.[153]

[149] Pasquale (2022), pp. 211–212.

[150] This stance is supported by the inherent adaptability of the tort system and its capacity for gradual evolution, which makes it advisable to afford the tort system the time it needs to address AI-related harms effectively. Robert (2022), p. 98; See also Knetsch (2022), p. 100.

[151] Robert (2022), p. 98.

[152] This research primarily focuses on cases involving economic loss in the context of AI, excluding situations where physical injury or property damage is typically caused by robots. For such cases, various specific torts and grounds of liability may apply, making compensation more likely: Tjong and Tai (2022), pp. 116 & 130.

[153] De Conca (2022), p. 252.

AI liability regimes involve a range of concurrent legal approaches, leading to a fragmented debate on the most suitable framework for addressing these changes. This fragmentation is understandable and, to some extent, desirable due to the varied economic sectors applying different levels of risk and harm. Efforts to bridge AI-related liability gaps must acknowledge the diverse applications of AI across industries. A universal solution may fall short, potentially leading to fragmented protection for affected parties.

In summary, a brief contemplation of the most fitting AI liability regime for both public and private legal tech is essential. For private AI legal tech used within organizations, emphasizing contractual liability ensures accountability based on internal agreements and performance standards, though careful attention is needed to avoid potential power imbalances arising from liability-limiting clauses and information asymmetries. For fully autonomous AI systems, such as those involved in securities trading, liability criteria should have a lower threshold and focus on evidence of constraints, design flaws, and limited data access.[154]

In the context of public AI legal tech, adopting a no-fault liability model aligns with compensating victims without establishing fault, especially in situations where the technology impacts many individuals (e.g. the UK Post Scandal is a good example). Simultaneously, treating AI systems as products under proposed directives ensures responsibility lies with manufacturers, distributors, and sellers, effectively addressing public safety concerns. In cases where AI supports human decision-making, greater weight should be given to human intent and foreseeability, with lesser emphasis on algorithm constraints, design nature, or available data in determining liability.[155] Any legal solution to it should put humans at the center, focusing on the damaged individuals, their rights, and interests.[156]

7 Conclusion

AI holds the potential for various positive externalities such as improving legal efficiency, democratizing legal services, facilitating access to justice, and reducing costs. However, severe negative consequences can arise. Computers are prone to errors, and AI may exacerbate them. Ethical considerations are paramount, highlighting the importance of safety, transparent handling of failures, fairness, designers' and implementers' responsibility, alignment with core human principles (dignity, freedom, rights, cultural diversity), safeguarding personal privacy and

[154] Bathaee (2018), pp. 889, 897.

[155] Bathaee (2018), pp. 889, 897.

[156] This will guarantee uniformity and maintain internal systemic coherence by: distributing the loss connected to the damages in a fair and efficient way; granting access to justice to the damaged party; addressing in a similar way situations which present comparable risks; the duty of producers to ensure transparency of the technology and its functioning/ use; introducing, besides insurances, compensation funds to support victims even in situations in which insurances are absent: De Conca (2022), p. 255; Portinale (2021), p. 18.

liberty, ensuring fair distribution of benefits and economic prosperity, maintaining human control over AI activities, preventing subversion of societal processes by advanced AI systems, and ultimately avoiding the development of prohibited AI tools. The right to opt-out is integral to these ethical principles. The future of law practice lies in a balanced integration of AI and human expertise. As the legal industry evolves with diverse AI technologies, judges and lawyers must transition into decision-makers and managers of legal technologies.

Liquid-Legal-Waves to Other Chapters, Written by the Editors

Erion has dissected the opportunities and risks of AI in legal tech, underlining that the future of legal practice lies in a balanced integration of AI and human expertise. In his chapter on *"AI in the Legal Market: The Dark Side of the Moon"*, *Bruno* has analyzed the risk side of things, reminding us that the current hype and the hopes around AI in law must not push aside adequate controls.

Against the background of *Erion's* analysis, it is fascinating to follow *Thomas* deep thoughts around the question, *"Can Artificial Intelligence Save the Rule of Law?"*. He ultimately outlines how non-binding generative and pattern-recognition tools might actually help reintegrate law and culture, by bringing law closer to the people and to its surrounding culture.

Following *Erion's* close-up on the theoretical foundation of AI in legal tech, *Marco, Sharon, Christina,* and *Robert* apply a very insightful analysis on the practical challenges AI applications face in an emerging legal landscape in their upcoming chapter: *"Evaluating how the AI Act affects Systems in the Pharma and BioTech Sector"*.

References

Ashley KD (2017) Artificial intelligence and legal analytics - new tools for law practice in the digital age. CUP, p 4

Ashley KD (2022) Accounting for legal values. In: Whalen R (ed) Computational legal studies. The promise and challenge of data-driven research. Edward Elgar, p 213

Asimov I (1959) All the troubles of the world. Super-Science Fiction. (Apr. 1958, reprinted in Isaac Asimov, Nine Tomorrows 137, 137–153)

Bathaee Y (2018) The artificial intelligence black box and the failure of intent and causation. Harv J Law Technol 31(2):889–897

Bench-Capon T et al (2012) A history of AI and law in 50 papers: 25 years of the international conference on AI and Law. Artif Intell Law 20:215–319. https://doi.org/10.1007/s10506-012-9131-x

Buchholtz G (2020) Artificial intelligence and legal tech: challenges to the rule of law. In: Wischmeyer T (ed) Regulating artificial intelligence. Springer, p 177

Busch Busch C (2018) Algorithmic accountablity. Gutachten im Auftrag von abida

Çağlayan Aksoy P (2022) AI and agency law. In: Di Matteo LA et al (eds) The Cambridge handbook of artificial intelligence global perspectives on law and ethics. CUP, p 160

Chesterman S (2020) Artificial intelligence and the problem of accountability. J Emerg Technol 1(2):210–212

Chesterman S (2021) We the robots? Regulating artificial intelligence and the limits of the law. CUP, pp 60–62

Cobbe J (2021) Legal singularity and the reflexivity of law. In: Deakin S, Markou C (eds) Is law computable? Critical perspectives on law and artificial intelligence. Hart, p 67

Cooman JD, Petit N (2023) Asimov for lawmakers. J Bus Technol Law 18:1

Custer B (2022) AI in criminal law: an overview of AI applications in substantive and procedural criminal law. In: Custers B et al (eds) Law and artificial intelligence: regulating AI and applying AI in legal practice. Springer, p 207

Custers B, Fosch-Villaronga E (2022) Humanizing machines: introduction and overview. In: Custers B et al (eds) Law and artificial intelligence: regulating AI and applying AI in legal practice. Springer, p 8

De Conca S (2022) Bridging the liability gaps: why AI challenges the existing rules on liability and how to design human-empowering solutions. In: Custers B et al (eds) Law and artificial intelligence: regulating ai and applying AI in legal practice. Springer, p 241

Deakin S, Markou C (2020) Is law computable? Critical perspectives on law and artificial intelligence. Hart, p 66

Di Matteo LA (2022) Artificial intelligence. The promise of disruption. In: Di Matteo LA et al (eds) The Cambridge handbook of artificial intelligence global perspectives on law and ethics. CUP, p 11

Ebers M (2021) Artificial intelligence, contracting and contract law: an introduction. In: Ebers M et al (eds) Contracting and contract law in the age of artificial intelligences. Bloomsbury Publishing, p 21

Eliot L (2021) Identifying a set of autonomous levels for AI-based computational legal reasoning. MIT Computational Law Report

Erdoğan I (2022) Algorithmic suspicion in the era of predictive policing. In: Borges G, Sorge C (eds) Law and technology in a global digital society. Springer, p 100

Floridid L (2021) Translating principles into practices of digital ethics: five risks of being unethical. In: Floridi L (ed) Ethics, governance, and policies in artificial intelligence. Springer, p 81

Floridid L et al (2021) An ethical framework for a good AI society: opportunities, risks, principles, and recommendations. In: Floridi L (ed) Ethics, governance, and policies in artificial intelligence. Springer, p 38

Flroidi L, Cowls J (2021) A unified framework of five principles for AI in society. In: Floridi L (ed) Ethics, governance, and policies in artificial intelligence. Springer, p 13

Galdon F, Hall A, Wang SJ (2021) Designing trust in highly automated virtual assistants: a taxonomy of levels of autonomy. In: Dingli A, Haddod F, Klüver C (eds) Artificial intelligence in industry 4.0, Studies in computational intelligence, vol 928. Springer, pp 199–211

Goel AK, Davies J (2021) Artificial intelligence. In: Sternberg RJ, Barry Kaufman S (eds) The Cambridge handbook of intelligence. CUP, p 468

Graham J (2021) Risk of discrimination in AI systems. In: Lui L, Ryder N (eds) FinTech, artificial intelligence and the law. Routledge

Gravett WH (2024) Judicial decision-making in the age of artificial intelligence. In: Sousa Antunes H et al (eds) Multidisciplinary perspectives on artificial intelligence and the law. Springer, pp 288–289

Guimerà R, Sales-Pardo M (2011) Justice blocks and predictability of U.S. Supreme Court Votes. PLoS One 6(11):e27188. https://doi.org/10.1371/journal.pone.0027188

Häuselmann A (2022) Disciplines of AI: an overview of approaches and techniques. In: Custers B et al (eds) Law and artificial intelligence: regulating AI and applying AI in legal practice. Springer

Hermstrüwer Y (2020) Artificial intelligence and administrative decisions under uncertainty. In: Wischmeyer T (ed) Regulating artificial intelligence. Springer, p 201

Hildebrandt M (2020) Code-driven law: freezing the future and scaling the past. In: Deakin S, Markou C (eds) Is law computable? Critical perspectives on law and artificial intelligence. Hart, p 67

Hoffmann-Riem W (2020) Artificial intelligence as a challenge for law and regulation. In: Wischmeyer T (ed) Regulating artificial intelligence. Springer, p 5

Howells G, Twigg-Flesner G (2022) Interconnectivity and liability. In: Di Matteo LA et al (eds) The Cambridge handbook of artificial intelligence global perspectives on law and ethics. CUP, p 193

Janssen A (2022) AI and contract performance. In: Di Matteo LA et al (eds) The Cambridge Handbook of Artificial Intelligence global perspectives on law and ethics. CUP, pp 60–61

Kearns M, Roth A (2020) The ethical algorithm. The science of socially aware algorithm design. OUP

Kerrigan C (2022) An introduction to artificial intelligence. In: Kerrigan C (ed) Artificial intelligence: law and regulation. Elgar, pp 33–24

Knetsch J (2022) Are existing tort theories ready for AI? A continental European perspective. In: Di Matteo LA et al (eds) The Cambridge handbook of artificial intelligence global perspectives on law and ethics. CUP, p 100

König D et al (2022) Essence of AI. What is AI. In: Di Matteo LA et al (eds) The Cambridge Handbook of Artificial Intelligence global perspectives on law and ethics. CUP, pp 18–19

Kurzweil R (2006) The singularity is near: when humans transcend biology. Gerald Duckworth & Co.

Liu HW et al (2019) Beyond State v Loomis: artificial intelligence, government algorithmization and accountability. Int J Law Inf Technol 27(2):122–141

Liu C et al (2022) Understanding artificial intelligence fundamentals and applications. Wiley, p 132

Livermore MA (2022) Rule by rules. In: Whalen R (ed) Computational legal studies. The promise and challenge of data-driven research. Edward Elgar, p 238

Loreggia A et al (2020) Modeling and reasoning with preferences and ethical priorities in AI systems. In: Liao M (ed) Ethics of artificial intelligence. OUP, p 145

Ma M (2021) Contracting in code. In: Ebers M et al (eds) Contracting and contract law in the age of artificial intelligences. Bloomsbury Publishing, p 180

Martinelli S, Chauvenet KR (2021) From document to data: revolution of contract through legal technologies. In: Ebers M et al (eds) Contracting and contract law in the age of artificial intelligences. Bloomsbury Publishing, p 96

Mik E (2021) AI in negotiating and entering into contracts. In: Di Matteo LA et al (eds) The Cambridge handbook of artificial intelligence global perspectives on law and ethics. CUP, pp 56–57

Mik E (2022) AI in negotiating and entering into contracts. In: Di Matteo LA et al (eds) The Cambridge Handbook of Artificial Intelligence global perspectives on law and ethics. CUP, p 48

Monot-Fouletier M (2022) Liability for autonomous vehicle accidents. In: Di Matteo LA et al (eds) The Cambridge handbook of artificial intelligence global perspectives on law and ethics. CUP, p 173

Möslein F (2022) AI and corporate law. In: Di Matteo LA et al (eds) The Cambridge handbook of artificial intelligence global perspectives on law and ethics. CUP, pp 62–80

Ng C (2022) AI in the legal profession. In: Di Matteo LA et al (eds) The Cambridge handbook of artificial intelligence global perspectives on law and ethics. CUP, p 36

Noto La Diega G (2022) Internet of Things and the law, 1st edn. Imprint Routledge, p 3

O'Neil C, Gunn H (2020) Near-term artificial intelligence and the ethical matrix. In: Liao M (ed) Ethics of artificial intelligence. OUP, pp 251–252

Ongenae K (2023) AI arbitrators 'does not compute. In: De Bruyne J, Vanleenhove C (eds) Artificial intelligence and the law. Intersentia

Pasquale F (2022) Liability standards for medical robotics and AI. In: Di Matteo LA et al (eds) The Cambridge handbook of artificial intelligence global perspectives on law and ethics. CUP, pp 211–212

Petersen S (2020) Machines learning values. In: Liao M (ed) Ethics of artificial intelligence. OUP, p 413
Petrin M (2022) Corporate governance. In: Kerrigan C (ed) Artificial intelligence: law and regulation. Elgar, pp 64–65
Pfister J (2021) Are we obligated to employ algorithmic decision-making? In: Borges G, Sorge C (eds) Law and technology in a global digital society. Springer, p 132
Portinale L (2021) Mapping artificial intelligence: perspectives from computer science. In: Ebers M et al (eds) Contracting and contract law in the age of artificial intelligences. Bloomsbury, p 18
Rademacher T (2020) Artificial intelligence and law enforcement. In: Wischmeyer T (ed) Regulating artificial intelligence. Springer, pp 227–232
Railton P (2020) Ethical learning, natural and artificial. In: Liao M (ed) Ethics of artificial intelligence. OUP, p 52
Robert A (2022) Heverly are existing tort theories ready for AI? An American perspective. In: Di Matteo LA et al (eds) The Cambridge handbook of artificial intelligence global perspectives on law and ethics. CUP, p 98
Russell S (2020) Artificial intelligence: a binary approach. In: Liao M (ed) Ethics of artificial intelligence. OUP, p 339
Schafer B (2022) Legal tech and computational legal theory. In: Borges G, Sorge C (eds) Law and technology in a global digital society. Springer, p 305
Sein K (2022) Contracting in code. In: Ebers M et al (eds) Contracting and contract law in the age of artificial intelligences. Bloomsbury Publishing, pp 153–154
Seng D (2021) Detecting and prosecuting IP infringement with AI. In: Jyh-An L et al (eds) Artificial intelligence and intellectual property. Oxford Press, p 320
Shaw P (2022) Ethics. In: Kerrigan C (ed) Artificial intelligence: law and regulation. Elgar, p 400
Sobel BA (2021) Taxonomy of training data: disentangling the mismatched rights, remedies, and rationales for restricting machine learning. In: Jyh-An L et al (eds) Artificial intelligence and intellectual property. Oxford Press, p 228
Sourdin T (2021) Judges, technology and artificial intelligence. Elgar, pp 6–7
Tjong E, Tai T (2022) Liability for AI decision-making. In: Di Matteo LA et al (eds) The Cambridge handbook of artificial intelligence global perspectives on law and ethics. CUP, p 116
Tsamados A et al (2021) The ethics of algorithms: key problems and solutions. In: Floridi L (ed) Ethics, governance, and policies in artificial intelligence. Springer, p 107
Van Der Haegen M (2023) Quantitative legal prediction: the future of dispute resolution? In: De Bruyne J, Vanleenhove C (eds) Artificial intelligence and the law. Intersentia, p 78
Varsava N (2022) Computational legal studies, digital humanities, and textual analysis. In: Whalen R (ed) Computational legal studies. The promise and challenge of data-driven research. Edward Elgar, p 46
Wagner J (2018) Legal Tech und Legal Robots: Der Wandel im Rechtsmarkt durch neue Technologien und künstliche Intelligenz. Springer, pp 2–3
Wallach W, Vallor S (2020) Moral machines from value alignment to embodied virtue. In: Liao M (ed) Ethics of artificial intelligence. OUP, p 407
Walton D (2005) Argumentation methods for artificial intelligence in law. Springer, p xii
Weinstein S (2022) Lawyers' perceptions on the use of AI. In: Custers B et al (eds) Law and artificial intelligence: regulating AI and applying AI in legal practice. Springer, p 429
Whalen R (2020) The emergence of computational legal studies: an introduction. In: Whalen R (ed) Computational legal studies. The promise and challenge of data-driven research. Edward Elgar, pp 1–3
Wischmeyer T (2020) Artificial intelligence and transparency: opening the black box. In: Wischmeyer T (ed) Regulating artificial intelligence. Springer, p 75

Erion Murati completed his law studies Italy in 2018 and obtained his Ph.D. at the University of Hamburg in Germany in 2023. His research focuses on exploring the impact of digitalisation on various EU legal frameworks, and he publishes his findings in English and German in international publishers and peer-reviewed journals. He has a wealth of teaching experience in EU and international law in Germany and abroad. He also works as a consultant in Berlin in the areas of data privacy protection, information security and cybersecurity. He is fluent in Albanian, Italian, English and German.

Evaluating How the AI Act Affects Systems in the Pharma and BioTech Sector

Explaining the Current Framework, Trends in Systems and Possible Solutions

Marco Rau, Sharon Naomi Reichl, and Robert Müller

Contents

Abstract

In 2021 the EU proposed harmonized rules on Artificial Intelligence (AI Act) as currently most countries have national AI strategies and regulations. The EU is set to become the global hub for trustworthy artificial intelligence (AI), so-called ecosystem of trust. Based on the upcoming regulation there is a high probability future IT-applications in the Pharma and BioTech sector could be considered as

M. Rau · R. Müller (✉)
CureVac N.V., Tübingen, Germany
e-mail: marco.rau@curevac.com; robert.mueller@curevac.com

S. N. Reichl
Rittershaus Rechtsanwälte PartmbB, Mannheim, Germany
e-mail: sharon.reichl@rittershaus.net

K. Jacob et al. (eds.), *Liquid Legal – Sustaining the Rule of Law*, Law for Professionals, https://doi.org/10.1007/978-3-031-78596-2_9

high-risk AI-applications and therefore need to meet considerable legal requirements of the AI Act. Especially in the Biotech and Pharma sector with the analysis and processing of biological data, DNA and RNA the AI Act needs to be evaluated with regard to its effects on the use and development of sophisticated selection processes based on IT-applications, which rely on AI-techniques.

A possible solution to strike the delicate balance between the regulatory need to provide safety and the high pace of technology development can be generated by the application of so called sandbox regimes. In its current form, the far-reaching risk-based approach reflected in the AI Act may impede the rapid development of AI-applications in the EU. Therefore, the design of innovation friendly and effective Sandbox-Regimes is key in order to keep innovation in the EU as well as to help cure human diseases by using modern AI systems for faster and more efficient development of biopharmaceuticals.

The AI Act includes many challenges and legal requirements for the use of AI systems in the BioTech and pharmaceutical sector. This may impede the creation of innovative AI systems to facilitate the development of drug products for human health. One possible solution to keep innovation and startups in Europe is the implementation of so-called sandbox regimes in order to comply with the regulatory framework and support the development of AI-systems.

1 Introduction

Artificial Intelligence is expected to provide enormous economic and social benefits to a wide range of sectors, including the healthcare sector.

AI systems do not only undergo rapid development but are also extremely diverse. Innovation is generally driven in the pharmaceutical sector, particularly in healthcare, and as part of the pharmaceutical sector also in the BioTech industry. Adopting AI in the healthcare sector holds immense innovative potential to revolutionize drug discovery as well as its development cycle.

The use of AI systems could e.g. cut costs by improving overall efficiency. It could also be used to answer recurring questions in the drug development cycle, such as to determine which patients should best be included in clinical trials or which molecules are the most promising targets. Nevertheless, innovation never comes without challenges which need to be mastered to fully develop its potential. From a technical perspective, data-driven innovations such as the machine-learning approaches of AI depend on the amount and variety of datasets used for training.

The innovation potential of Europe and the need to establish a global competitive AI ecosystem should not be prevented by an overburdening regulatory system while still protecting individual rights. Europe must create conditions for a competitive AI infrastructure, which is not yet the case. This is illustrated by an AI Act[1] Impact survey from the end of 2022, where AI start-ups are only considered partly ready for a global market.[2]

However, the EU is no longer alone in its regulatory plans. In August 2023 China passed a new law which aims to regulate generative AI. With its entry into force this law is internationally pioneering as it is the first law specifically targeting generative AI.[3] Other countries are following suit, as Canada has proposed the Artificial Intelligence and Data Act (AIDA) as foundation for the responsible design, development and deployment of AI systems.[4] The United States are currently taking a decentralized approach in the absence of comprehensive federal legislation.[5] Besides these regulatory frameworks there are various international projects underway with the G7 Hiroshima AI Process[6] and initiatives at United Nations level, such as the "Principles for the ethical use of Artificial Intelligence in the United Nations System"[7] or the Interim Report "Governing AI for Humanity" from December 2023.[8] This makes it even more important how the EU positions itself in this highly dynamic environment.

Especially focusing on the lawful implementation of BioTech AI systems, the specific technical background and BioTech use-cases are important to understand the technical challenges AI systems are facing. Afterwards the book chapter illustrates the AI Act and the resulting legal challenges, including the GDPR, resulting from the processing of personal and genomic data. To mitigate the resulting legal requirements of the AI Act and to support innovative projects to comply with the regulations the so-called AI Sandbox-Regime is explained and the future application frame for AI systems is proposed. The book chapter closes with a final outlook and summary of current developments of AI systems in the BioTech sector.

[1] Proposal for a Regulation of the European Parliament and of the Council laying down harmonized rules on Artificial Intelligence (Artificial Intelligence Act and amending certain Union Legislative Acts, COM/2021/206 final, 21.4.2021; The authors acknowledge the draft of the AI Act, but for simplification the authors use the short form "AI Act" for citation.

[2] AI Act Impact Survey, Pan-European survey of AI Startups and VCs about the impact of the AI Act, https://www.appliedai.de/assets/files/AI Act-Impact-Survey_Slides_Dec12.2022.pdf, from 12.12.2022.

[3] https://www.eastasiaforum.org/2023/09/27/the-future-of-ai-policy-in-china/; see also: Li / Kolling, CRi 2024, 33, 35.

[4] https://ised-isde.canada.ca/site/innovation-better-canada/en/artificial-intelligence-and-data-act.

[5] https://www.bclplaw.com/en-US/events-insights-news/2023-state-by-state-artificial-intelligence-legislation-snapshot.html.

[6] https://digital-strategy.ec.europa.eu/en/library/g7-leaders-statement-hiroshima-ai-process.

[7] https://unsceb.org/principles-ethical-use-artificial-intelligence-united-nations-system.

[8] https://www.un.org/techenvoy/sites/www.un.org.techenvoy/files/ai_advisory_body_interim_report.pdf.

2 Background Information and Illustration of BioTech-Systems

2.1 General Technical Background

There is not just one single AI application, but many different technical models and approaches to the use of AI, which is why the individual use-case is crucial. The specific AI application must be developed or determined based on each individual use-case. This subchapter shall provide a summary of general technical mechanisms and background of AI systems.

AI systems and the perception of what an AI system must be able to do are constantly changing. Former rule-based or so-called expert AI systems have now been replaced by AI systems that learn different sets of rules to solve problems themselves. These neural networks can use unstructured and structured data.

There are two main pillars of AI systems: supervised and unsupervised learning mechanisms. Supervised learning mechanisms rely on cooperative human-machine interaction in which human knowledge is manually fed into decision trees or the AI decision is manually corrected by humans. In contrast to human-guided supervised learning, unsupervised learning models (machine-learning models) make statements based on the clustering of interesting data or abnormal patterns using statistical methods.[9] However, these predictive analyses derive from hypotheses that are based on systemic statements about normalities, considering certain framework conditions. The machine learns from training data and applies the learned generalized statements to new and/or unknown datasets. This means that the statement of an AI using an unsupervised learning mechanism can only be a probable statement. However, the accuracy of this statement is increased by the quality and availability of the underlying training data.[10]

One method to train AI systems is the so-called deep learning attempt which aims to adapt human thought processes using neural networks and make them usable for machine-learning. Deep learning mechanisms are used to process large data volumes and recognize pictures as well as written text. The process of machine-learning is initially divided into the selection of a suitable model, the training of the learning algorithm using existing data, and finally the application to new cases (interference).[11] Large amounts of data are required for machine learning. At the same time, however, the importance of data quality for the AI results should not be underestimated in comparison to the size of the data sets.[12]

---

[9]Glauner (2021), p. 3, 4.

[10]In this way: Géron (2017), S. 22 ff.

[11]Géron (2017), p. 22.

[12]Regarding the text classification: Zheng and Jin (2018).

2.2 BioTech, Pharmaceutical AI Systems

There are already numerous use-cases and potential applications for AI in the healthcare sector. AI is particularly suitable in the following areas:[13]

- Manufacturing process improvement
- Drug discovery and design
- Processing biomedical and clinical data
- Personalized medicine and drugs
- Identifying potential clinical trial candidates and design[14]
- Predicting treatment results
- Drug repurposing, adherence, and dosage.

The mentioned areas do not cover the whole research process of drug discovery. AI is currently predominantly used to improve the drug discovery process regarding its costs, efficiency and velocity. The scope of applications is not limited to a specific therapeutic area, but is strongly oriented towards the market potential, e.g. the oncology sector.[15]

To achieve this improvement AI is used in the following phases of the drug discovery process:[16]

- Protein folding,
- Target discovery,
- Molecule discovery,
- Refining the target molecules,
- Identifying biomarkers in preclinic or clinical studies.

The average costs for drug development range from less than $ 1 billion to more than $ 2 billion.[17] Therefore even minor cost savings by using AI systems results are highly relevant.

One remarkable use-case in the BioTech and pharmaceutical sector is the development of so-called precision medicine by using individual human DNA.[18] The relevance of that use-case is reflected e.g. in AstraZeneca's genomic initiative and

[13] See for an overview: https://www.sartorius.com/en/knowledge/science-snippets/the-trending-role-of-artificial-intelligence-in-the-pharmaceutical-industry-599278.

[14] See early trends and techniques: Harrer et al. (2019).

[15] For example: Park et al. (2023), pp. 218 ff.

[16] Szalay (2023), p. 160 ff.

[17] Congressional Budget Office, Research and Development in the Pharmaceutical Industry, Chapter: R&D Costs of a New Drug, from April 2021, https://www.cbo.gov/publication/57126.

[18] *Statista*, Artificial Intelligence: in-depth market analysis – Market Insights report, April 2023, p. 100.

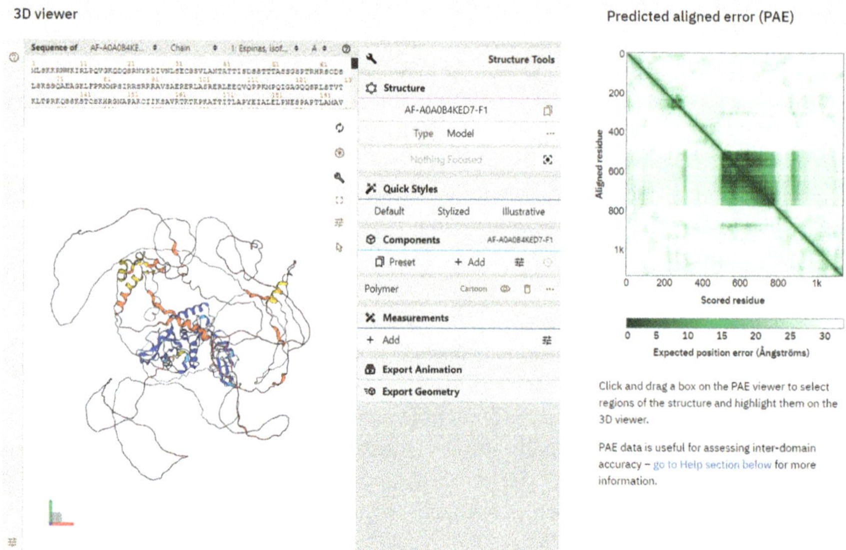

Fig. 1 Example AlphaFold, structure prediction - Espinas, isoform C (https://alphafold.ebi.ac.uk/entry/A0A0B4KED7)

the company wide establishment of the Centre for Genomics Research to analyze and process two million genome sequences.[19]

Another well-known AI example for identifying protein folding and structure is the free-to-use software AlphaFold by Google DeepMind.[20]

AlphaFold is used to understand the 3D structure of proteins, the underlying amino acids and the way a protein works, as the folding is decisive for their function and interaction, see Fig. 1. Machine-learning is also used to identify and visualize the target molecules.[21]

Training AI systems requires accurate patient data that is non-biased and is of high quality in general. In the area of drug discovery for the oncology sector genomic data is crucial. Necessary AI patient training data is gathered in silos. Therefore, it is difficult to gather large data volumes with a high quality for AI training purposes. It is also important to obtain relevant patient data from more than just one group (e.g. white male residing in western Europe).

[19] *AstraZeneca*, AstraZeneca launches integrated genomics approach to transform drug discovery and development, https://www.astrazeneca.com/media-centre/press-releases/2016/AstraZeneca-launches-integrated-genomics-approach-to-transform-drug-discovery-and-development-22042016.html#.

[20] https://deepmind.google/technologies/alphafold/.

[21] Goodsell et al. (2021), p. 31 ff.

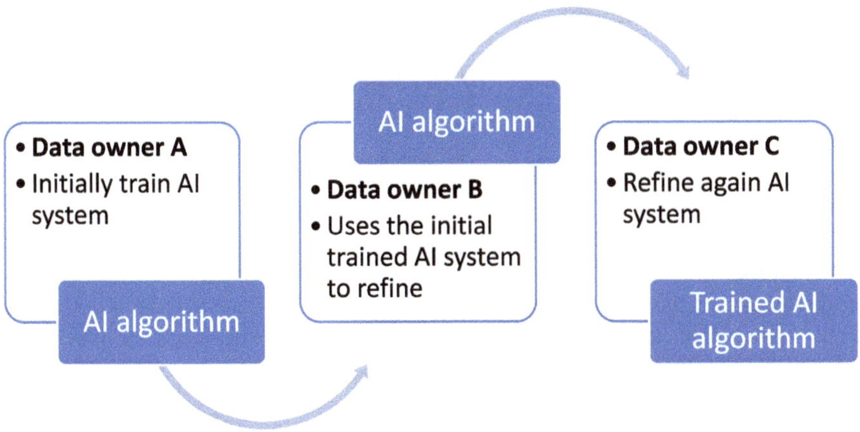

Fig. 2 Federated learning - AI system. Based on: Galtier and Meadon (2023), https://doi.org/10.1787/a8d820bd-en, p. 172

One way to handle this problem is the so-called Federated Learning, see Fig. 2.[22] This approach addresses the challenges of data governance and privacy considerations by collaborative training algorithms. The respective patient training data is provided without exchanging sensible health data between different data owners (e.g. hospital, research institution). Algorithms are dispatched to different data centers where they train locally. Once the AI system is improved the algorithm returns to a central location while data stays local. The same algorithms are then sent to other data owners to re-train them for improvement with their respective local datasets. This consensus mechanism enables researchers to collaboratively gain insights without physically moving patient data beyond the firewalls of the institutions in which they reside. Since the AI system processing occurs locally at each participating institution and only model characteristics are transferred it greatly enhances patient privacy.[23]

The best results can be achieved by using deep learning AI systems that are based on neural networks. The challenge of the broad use of AI systems for drug discovery lies in the use of deep learning and neural networks versus the regulatory requirement for highest safety and reliability. The decision pathway which led to a selection of an antigene etc. needs to be repeatable and explainable at all times.[24]

The following chapters shall illustrate the upcoming and already existing boundaries to obtain the necessary training data for AI BioTech systems.

[22] Check for further information: https://www.owkin.com/#top-of-page.

[23] Galtier and Meadon (2023), https://doi.org/10.1787/a8d820bd-en, p. 172 ff.

[24] For BioTech systems: Szalay (2023), https://doi.org/10.1787/a8d820bd-en, p. 162, 163.

3 Legal Framework for BioTech Systems

3.1 Relevant Regulations for the Implementation of AI Systems in BioTech

When developing systems for the BioTech sector there are many different regulations to observe in the highly regulated pharmaceutical sector. This significantly increases the implementation hurdles for technical innovations and AI applications. Special AI regulations must be considered which impose general requirements on the use of AI. The regulations usually do not have a dedicated focus on the healthcare and/or BioTech sector but rather are designed for generic AI systems.[25] As patient data or personal data is usually processed for the training of AI systems, regulations on data and privacy also come into consideration. Furthermore, these specific data processing regulations must be incorporated into the system of pharmaceutical regulation which is why the development of specific AI systems must encompass various legal and technical disciplines as well as prior know-how, as illustrated in Fig. 3.

This chapter focuses on the implications of the AI Act and the influence of the GDPR.

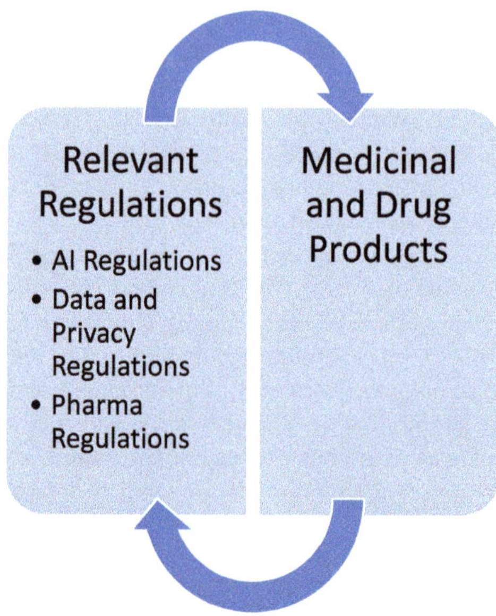

Fig. 3 Interaction of Regulation and Products, own source

[25] See for a general international regulatory overview: https://oecd.ai/en/dashboards/overview.

3.2 AI Act

3.2.1 Genesis of the AI Act

As part of an ordinary legislative procedure in accordance with Art. 289 (I), 294 TFEU, the EU AI Act Draft is effectively adopted as a legal act if the Council and the European Parliament have reached an agreement and vote in favor of the adoption. The first version of the AI Act was proposed by the European Commission in April 2021 laying down harmonized rules on the regulation of Artificial Intelligence. The Council reached an agreement and adopted its general approach (negotiating mandate) on December 6th, 2022. With this file it entered interinstitutional discussions and negotiations with the European Parliament, so-called trilogues, in mid-June 2023.[26]

On December 9th, 2023 the Council presidency and the Parliament were able to reach a provisional agreement on the AI Act. Following publication in the Official Journal of the EU on July 12th, 2024, the AI Act entered into force on August 1st, 2024. The regulation pursues the protection of fundamental rights, democracy, the rule of law and environmental sustainability on one hand while on the other hand improving and increasing innovation. [27]

In comparison with the original proposal the provisional agreement covers the following points:

- rules on high-impact general-purpose AI models that can cause systemic risk in the future, as well as on high-risk AI systems
- a revised system of governance with some enforcement powers at EU level
- extension of the list of prohibitions but with the possibility to use remote biometric identification by law enforcement authorities in public spaces, subject to safeguards
- better protection of rights through the obligation for deployers of high-risk AI systems to conduct a fundamental rights impact assessment prior to putting an AI system into use.[28]

However most of the regulations are only applicable in 2 years' time, i.e. from August 2nd, 2026. Still, there are some exceptions to this basic deadline for applicability, e.g., bans on prohibited AI practices will already apply from February 25th, 2025. The classification rules for high-risk AI systems according to Art. 6 (I) AI Act and the corresponding regulations will only be apply from August 2nd, 2027. The obligations relating to general-purpose AI systems (GPAI) will apply

[26] https://www.consilium.europa.eu/en/policies/artificial-intelligence/timeline-artificial-intelligence/.

[27] https://www.consilium.europa.eu/en/press/press-releases/2023/12/09/artificial-intelligence-act-council-and-parliament-strike-a-deal-on-the-first-worldwide-rules-for-ai/.

[28] https://www.consilium.europa.eu/en/press/press-releases/2023/12/09/artificial-intelligence-act-council-and-parliament-strike-a-deal-on-the-first-worldwide-rules-for-ai/.

from August 2nd, 2025. The Commission just recently launched a consultation on a Code of Practice for providers of such GPAI.[29] These Codes, forseen by Recital 117, Art. 53 (IV) AI Act, shall address critical areas such as transparency, copyright-related rules, and risk management. The finalisation of the Code of Practice is expected to take place by April 2025.[30] Between these publications on the political agreements the EU Commission announced the launch of an AI innovation package to support Artificial Intelligence startups in the development of trustworthy AI that respects EU values and rules on January 24th, 2024.[31] On May 29th, 2024 the Commission unveiled the AI Office established within the Commission. It is supposed to play a key role in implementing the AI Act, especially for general-purpose AI, as well as fostering the development and use of trustworthy AI, and international cooperation. Prior to this the Large AI Grand Challenge was launched in November 2023 which granted AI startups financial support and supercomputing access to support the further development and scalability of AI models.[32] The package includes a broad range of measures to support AI startups and innovation including e.g. a proposal to provide privileged access to world-class supercomputers that accelerate AI training and testing.[33]

3.2.2 Structure

The AI Act establishes obligations for providers (Art. 3 (III) AI Act) and since the provisional agreement for deployers instead of users (Art. 3 (IV) AI Act) depending on the level of risk from Artificial Intelligence. Risk is legally defined under Art. 3 (II) AI Act as *"the combination of the probability of an occurrence of harm and the severity of that harm"*.

However, the Council of the EU confirmed that the AI Act will not apply to *AI systems used for the sole purpose of research and innovation*"[34] which is now reflected in Recital 25 of the provisional agreement.

3.2.2.1 Definition and Factual Scope of the AI Act

The basic understanding of the AI Act is based on the differentiation between software without AI and software with AI, so-called AI systems. In the concluded provisional agreement the definition of an AI system is supposed to provide sufficiently clear criteria to differentiate between AI and a simpler software system and reportedly therefore aligns the definition with the approach proposed by the

[29] https://commission.europa.eu/news/ai-act-enters-force-2024-08-01_en

[30] https://commission.europa.eu/news/ai-act-enters-force-2024-08-01_en

[31] https://digital-strategy.ec.europa.eu/en/news/commission-launches-ai-innovation-package-support-artificial-intelligence-startups-and-smes.

[32] https://ec.europa.eu/commission/presscorner/detail/en/IP_23_5739.

[33] https://digital-strategy.ec.europa.eu/en/news/commission-launches-ai-innovation-package-support-artificial-intelligence-startups-and-smes.

[34] https://www.consilium.europa.eu/en/press/press-releases/2023/12/09/artificial-intelligence-act-council-and-parliament-strike-a-deal-on-the-first-worldwide-rules-for-ai/.

OECD.[35] An AI system is now defined as *"[. . .] a machine-based system designed to operate with varying levels of autonomy and that may exhibit adaptiveness after deployment, and that, for explicit or implicit objectives, infers, from the input it receives, how to generate outputs such as predictions, content, recommendations, or decisions that can influence physical or virtual environments"*, cf. Art. 3 (I) AI Act.

When agreeing on the provisional agreement of the AI Act EU legislators seem to have considered some of the criticism on the initial draft. Since the first publication of the draft the definition of AI systems was perceived as problematic as the wording is so far reaching that almost any computer program or software is covered.[36] Even after legal-linguistic revision, the definition in Art. 3 (I) AI Act was still too far reaching. The definition later was primarily tightened to the concept of autonomy, which, however, was not clearly defined. The fact that independence from human control and interaction defines machines that are automated but not autonomous was particularly worthy of criticism. To prevent every automated machine from being classified as an AI system under the AI Act, the "ability to learn and/or adapt independently to new environments" should have been added as a prerequisite.[37] This criticism has become obsolete with the adoption of the EU AI Act. As stated by the revised Recital 12 AI Act, the capacity of an AI system to infer must transcend basic data processing, enabling learning, reasoning or modelling. Additionally the concept of autonomy is explained in more detail, mentioning the varying levels of autonomy mean different degrees of independence of actions from human involvement and of capabilities to operate without human intervention, cf. Recital 12 AI Act. The adaptiveness that an AI system could exhibit after deployment refers to self-learning capabilities, allowing the system to change while in use, cf. Recital 12 AI Act. According to Recital 12 AI Act AI systems are now clearly defined as *"[. . .] systems that distinguish it from simpler traditional software systems or programming approaches and should not cover systems that are based on the rules defined solely by natural persons to automatically execute operations"*. This definition focuses on the capability of AI systems to infer as one of their key characteristics, excluding such systems which do not have that capability.

3.2.2.2 Territorial Scope

There is an inherent risk of relocation of research and development to third countries with less stringent requirements in attempting to regulate AI under the AI Act. The relocation would not only thwart the AI Act's objective of making Europe the center for trustworthy AI.[38] The potentially immense economic implications further

---

[35] https://www.consilium.europa.eu/en/press/press-releases/2023/12/09/artificial-intelligence-act-council-and-parliament-strike-a-deal-on-the-first-worldwide-rules-for-ai/.

[36] Bomhard and Merkle (2021), p. 277.

[37] Hacker and Berz (2023), p. 227.

[38] EU Commission, Independent High-Level Expert Group on Artificial Intelligence set up by the European Commission, Ethics Guidelines for Trustworthy AI, 2019, https://ec.europa.eu/newsroom/dae/document.cfm?doc_id=60419, p. 8.

exacerbate this risk. The underlying legal philosophical question is whether risks need to be avoided by a legal system through stringent rules which have to be followed or whether risks shall be accepted as a driving element of societal progress and therefore need to be explored in an iterative manner. In a feasibility study entitled "Large European AI Models (LEAM)" from 2022 commissioned by the Federal Ministry for Economic Affairs and Climate Protection, the Academy for Artificial Intelligence in the German AI Association found that 73% of the development of AI foundation models internationally since 2017 has come from the USA and 15% from China.[39]

The AI Act attempts to counteract this in two different ways, the Marketplace Principle and the AI Sandbox-Regime. The AI Act has international reach ("long arm statute") and due to the underlying marketplace principle in Art. 2 (I) lit. (a) AI Act it has a very broad territorial scope. In this respect, Art. 2 (I) lit. (c) AI Act, which is based on the use of outputs in the EU, is particularly relevant. Applying the regulation to providers and deployers of AI systems who are physically present or established in a third country, where the output produced by the system is used in the EU makes the territorial scope of the AI Act independent of location. This is crucial because software, and therefore also AI, is incorporeal and it would therefore be difficult or almost impossible to determine its exact location.

The second approach, the "AI Sandbox-Regime", will be examined in the following subsection.

3.2.2.3 AI Sandbox Regime

The AI Act promotes innovation through exceptions to the strict regulations,[40] Chapter VI "Measures in Support of Innovation" regulates from Art. 57 AI Act onwards so-called AI regulatory sandboxes. Sandboxes are one of the most promising regulatory tools to ensure technology development is carried out in a safe environment that protects individuals and human rights, while advancing innovation.

According to Art. 57 (V) AI Act, AI regulatory sandboxes establish a controlled environment that facilitates the development, testing, and validation of innovative AI systems for a limited time before their placement on the market or put into service. These regulatory sandboxes shall aim to contribute to different objectives such as improving legal certainty to achieve regulatory compliance with the AI Act, cf. Art. 57 (IX) lit. (a) AI Act. Under Art. 57 (VI) AI Act so-called competent authorities provide direct supervision and guidance to sandbox participants, to ensure compliance with the requirements of the AI Act and, where relevant, other Union and Member States' legislation supervised within the sandbox, especially data protection

[39] Akademie für Künstliche Intelligenz im KI-Bundesverband, Große KI-Modelle für Deutschland, 2022, p. 56.

[40] See on negative effects of overly rigid legislation for society: *Hobbes,* Thomas, De Cive, chapter. 6, 13 (1642).

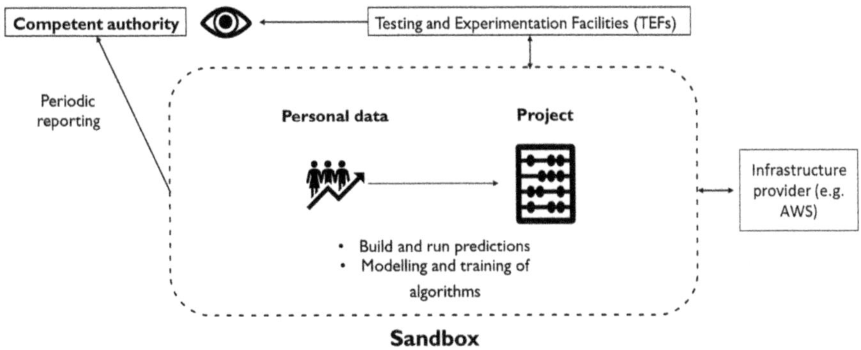

Fig. 4 Elements/Layers of the sandbox

and privacy rights. Additionally Art. 59 AI Act sets out different conditions under which personal data can be processed but only for specific purposes.

As described in Fig. 4, the sandbox can generally be separated into three different elements or layers:

- The sandbox in general,
- the competent authority, and
- testing and experimentation facilities (so called TEFs).

In respect to the powers of national or competent authorities, Art. 57 (XI) AI Act highlights that AI regulatory sandboxes do not affect the supervisory and corrective powers of the competent authorities, including at regional or local level. This means that the competent authorities supervise the projects within the established sandboxes. From a legislative standpoint sandbox regimes constitute a legislative lab-space to tackle the challenge of high speed of iterative innovation process that do not allow classic linear legislative processes to keep an up-to-date regulatory framework (lagging of legislative processes).

The sandboxes create technically separated safe spaces for the processing and training of AI algorithms with personal data. According to the AI Act personal data need to be functionally separated, isolated into a protected data processing environment accessible only by authorized persons, and protected, cf. Art. 59 (I) lit. (d). Under the AI Act originally collected personal data can be shared by providers in accordance with Union data protection law, cf. Art. 59 (I) lit. (e). Only personal data which is created in the sandbox cannot be shared outside this sandbox.

Testing and experimentation facilities (TEFs) are specialized large-scale reference sites open to all technology providers across Europe to test and experiment in real world environments and at scale with state-of-the-art AI-based soft- and hardware solutions and products, cf. Art. 58 (II) lit. (f) and Recital 141 AI Act.

In turn, the TEFs can support the establishment of regulatory sandboxes, with the goal of developing a dialogue with competent national authorities for supervised testing and experimentation under real-life or close to real-life conditions. There should be close cooperation between the competent authority and the TEFs on activities in the sandbox.

The AI Act obliges Member States to establish at least one AI regulatory sandbox at national level which shall be operational by August 2nd, 2026, cf. Recital 138 and Art. 57 (I) AI Act. These sandboxes may include testing in real world conditions supervised therein, cf. Art. 57 (V) AI Act. High-risk AI systems may now also be tested in real world conditions outside regulatory sandboxes according to Art. 60 AI Act. Further conditions for testing in real world conditions shall be set out in Art. 60 et seqq. AI Act. The Member States may be supported technically as well as with advice and tools by the Commission, cf. Art. 57 (I) AI Act. Additionally, even the European Data Protection Supervisor may establish such a sandbox for the EU institutions, bodies and agencies, cf. Art. 57 (III).

Nevertheless, it must be considered that according to the former draft of the AI Act the requirements set out below[41] also needed to be complied with when using AI in such a sandbox. This has been negatively noticed as providers still needed to fulfill high minimum requirements.[42] This criticism has been partly addressed in the provisional agreement of the AI Act to the extent that in a newly added Art. 57 (VI) AI Act *"Competent authorities shall provide, as appropriate, guidance, supervision and support within the sandbox with a view to identifying risks, in particular to fundamental rights, health and safety, testing, mitigation measures, and their effectiveness in relation to the obligations and requirements of this Regulation and, where relevant, other Union and Member States legislation supervised within the sandbox"*. Furthermore providers and prospective providers can get guidance on the regulatory expectations and how to fulfil the requirements and obligations set out in the AI Act by competent authorities according to Art. 57 (VII) AI Act. Upon request these providers may additionally receive written proof of the activities successfully carried out in the sandbox. Such proof shall then be taken positively into account by market surveillance authorities and notified bodies, with a view to accelerate conformity assessment procedures to a reasonable account, cf. Art. 57 (VII) AI Act. Even taking all these measures and regulations into account, a certain degree of (legal) uncertainty remains as in the AI Act that has come into force acoording to Art. 58 (I) AI Act the Commission shall adopt implementing acts specifying the detailed arrangements for the establishment, development, implementation, operation and supervision of the AI regulatory sandboxes. According to Art. 58 (I) lit. (a) one of these implementing acts shall include common principles on the eligibility and selection criteria for participation in said sandboxes. As of now no such implementing act has been adopted. Although the former Art. 53 AI Act is intended to promote innovation, it has been criticized for not establishing a civil law

[41] see subtitle 3) Framework.

[42] Bomhard and Merkle (2021), p. 279.

liability privilege, but instead making participants in the AI regulatory sandbox liable under applicable Union and Member States liability legislation.[43] This criticism has been partly addressed as according to Art. 57 (XII) AI Act liability under applicable Union and national liability law for any damage inflicted on third parties as a result of the experimentation taking place in the sandbox shall remain. The AI Act now provides for an exception in case provided that the prospective providers observe the specific plan and the terms and conditions for their participation and follow in good faith the guidance given by the national competent authority, no administrative fines shall be imposed. Nevertheless the exception only applies to administrative fines for infringements of the AI Act.AI Act.

In summary it should be emphasized that the provisional agreement addresses large parts of the initial criticism. Open or unclear issues especially regarding the definition of AI system under the AI Act have been amended and aligned with the approach proposed by the OECD. EU legislators apparently took the criticism into account and amended the AI Act accordingly to accommodate the critics and to provide a comprehensive regulation which is at least a bit easier to implement.

3.2.3 Framework

The AI Act is drafted on a risk-based approach which classifies AI systems according to the risks their use imposes to the users and possible third parties, see Fig. 5.[44]

The regulatory framework defines 4 levels of risk[45] in AI:

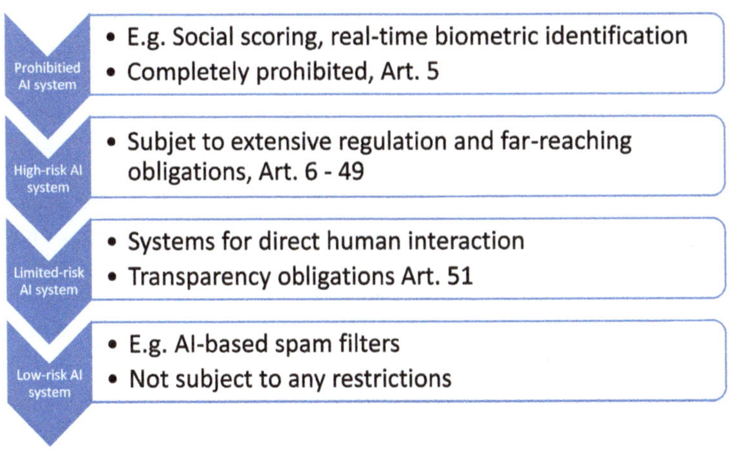

Fig. 5 Classification of AI systems in the form of a four-tier model. Based on: https://www2.deloitte.com/dl/en/pages/legal/articles/ki-verordnung-eu.html

[43] Bomhard and Merkle (2021), p. 279.

[44] https://www2.deloitte.com/dl/en/pages/legal/articles/ki-verordnung-eu.html.

[45] https://digital-strategy.ec.europa.eu/en/policies/regulatory-framework-ai.

- Unacceptable risk
- High risk
- Limited risk
- Minimal to no risk

The requirements and obligations to be addressed to the development and use of AI are based on the classification in one of these risk categories.[46] This means the AI Act provides for a horizontal layer of protection including the ban of AI systems which are likely to cause serious fundamental rights violations while AI systems which present only limited risks e.g. are subject to modest transparency obligations.[47] The following will focus on high-risk AI systems as most of the currently developed and used AI systems will most likely be considered as high-risk.

3.2.3.1 Prohibited AI Systems, Art. 5 AI Act

AI systems considered a clear threat to the safety, livelihoods and fundamental rights of people or containing other significant risks and contravening EU values will be prohibited according to Art. 5 AI Act. Nevertheless, the general ban allows some exceptions such as remote biometric identification in publicly accessible spaces for the purpose of law enforcement but only under strict conditions, i.a. cf. Art. 5 (II) AI Act. According to a press release of the European Parliament in December 2023 newly added to the list of generally banned AI systems is the *"biometric categorisation systems that use sensitive characteristics (e.g. political, religious, philosophical beliefs, sexual orientation, race)"* or *"the untargeted of facial images from the internet or CCTV footage to create facial recognition databases"*.[48] The provisional agreement also includes some changes to the narrow exceptions for the use of biometric identification systems in publicly accessible spaces for law enforcement purposes.[49]

3.2.3.2 High-Risk AI Systems, Art. 6 AI Act

Chapter III of the AI Act regulates AI systems classified as high-risk according to Art. 6 (I) AI Act due to their significant potential harm to health, safety, fundamental rights, environment, democracy, and the rule of law. Annex III lists eight specific areas where AI systems are considered high-risk. These areas include i.a. biometrics, law enforcement, migration, asylum, and border control management, all in so far as their use is permitted under relevant Union or national law, but also management and operation of critical infrastructure or educational and vocational training where AI

---

[46] https://digital-strategy.ec.europa.eu/en/policies/regulatory-framework-ai.

[47] https://www.consilium.europa.eu/en/press/press-releases/2023/12/09/artificial-intelligence-act-council-and-parliament-strike-a-deal-on-the-first-worldwide-rules-for-ai/.

[48] https://www.europarl.europa.eu/news/en/press-room/20231206IPR15699/artificial-intelligence-act-deal-on-comprehensive-rules-for-trustworthy-ai.

[49] https://www.europarl.europa.eu/news/en/press-room/20231206IPR15699/artificial-intelligence-act-deal-on-comprehensive-rules-for-trustworthy-ai.

systems are intended to be used for the purpose of determining access or for the assessment of students. Some of the listed areas have been amended by the provisional agreement. The following only names some of the amendments. AI systems intended to be used for biometric verification shall not be included anymore in case the "*sole purpose is to confirm that a specific natural person is the person he or she claims to be*", cf. Annex III nb. 1 lit. (a) AI Act. Future wise "*AI systems intended to be used for monitoring and detecting prohibited behaviour of students during tests in the context of/within education and vocational training institutions*" will also be considered as high-risk, cf. Annex III nb. 3 lit. (d) AI Act.

AI systems considered to be high-risk will be subject to comprehensive mandatory obligations that need to be complied with before they can be placed on the market or put into service. These obligations relate to the areas i.a. risk mitigation, data governance, detailed documentation, human oversight, transparency, robustness, accuracy and cybersecurity.[50] Additionally, the European Council confirmed high-risk AI systems being subject to conformity assessments in a press release, while allowing e.g. emergency procedures.[51] The provisional agreement allows some exceptions. For example law enforcement authorities or civil protection may put a specific high-risk AI system into service without prior authorization in a duly justified situation of urgency for exceptional reasons of public security or in case of specific, substantial and imminent threat to the life or physical safety of natural persons, cf. Art. 46 (II) AI Act.

The initial draft of the AI Act has been criticized for the lack of individual rights for those affected.[52] In particular, neither claims for damages nor injunctive relief were provided for, as opposed to Art. 17 GDPR.[53] The lacking provision for providers of AI systems to be able to justify their use within the framework of the consent principle by obtaining the consent of the data subjects has also been denounced.[54] In the new provisional agreement this is i.a. reflected in Recital 171 AI Act according to which "*affected persons should have the right to obtain an explanation where a deployer´s decision is based mainly upon the output from certain high-risk AI systems that fall within the scope of this Regulation and where that decision produces legal effects or similarly significantly affects those persons in a way that they consider to have an adverse impact on their health, safety or fundamental rights*". The agreement also stipulates the right to lodge a complaint to the relevant market surveillance authority in case of any natural or legal person has "*grounds to consider that there has been an infringement of this Regulation*", cf. Recital 170 AI Act. In the future, monitoring compliance with the regulation will no longer be the sole responsibility of the authorities. In Recital 170 of the AI

[50] https://ec.europa.eu/commission/presscorner/detail/en/ip_23_6473.

[51] https://www.consilium.europa.eu/en/press/press-releases/2023/12/09/artificial-intelligence-act-council-and-parliament-strike-a-deal-on-the-first-worldwide-rules-for-ai/.

[52] Bomhard and Merkle (2021), p. 283.

[53] Bomhard and Merkle (2021), p. 283.

[54] Bomhard and Merkle (2021), p. 283.

Act EU legislators additionally clarify that Union and national law already provide effective remedies to natural or legal persons whose rights and freedoms are adversely affected by the use of AI systems.

In the following a general overview of the requirements and obligations that need to be complied with as well as of possible challenges or problems with such compliance shall be given.

3.2.3.3 Data and Data Governance, Art. 10 AI Act

According to Article 10 (I) AI Act high-risk AI systems shall be subject to strict obligations on the quality of the data, so-called upstream data-compliance. Appropriate data and data governance practices concern i.a. the relevant design choices, relevant data preparation processing operations, an assessment of the availability, quantity and suitability of the data sets that are needed and recently appropriate measures to detect, prevent and mitigate possible biases. Over and above that with the provisional agreement *"training, validation and testing data sets shall be relevant, sufficiently representative, and to the best extent possible, free of errors and complete in view of the intended purpose"*, cf. Art. 10 (III) AI Act. Compliance with this obligation will become particularly demanding as, especially in the healthcare sector, but also in other use-cases of AI large data sets are necessary to enable machine learning. When it comes to such data sets it is almost impossible for providers and/or deployers to guarantee complete freedom of error

3.2.3.4 Transparency and Provision of Information to Deployers, Art. 13 AI Act

Art. 13 AI Act establishes a transparency requirement which will most likely become a technical challenge. Currently most AI systems, especially so-called Black Box AI, are unable to justify any decision made and cannot be explained so it can be easily understood by human beings. This is since Black Box AI is developed directly from data by an algorithm during the machine learning process.[55] The original input of variables is combined during such complicated operations of the black box predictive model, that it is impossible to interpret the exact joint relationship between them to reach the final prediction.[56] Regardless of the human requirements the need for the ability to explain AI systems becomes unavoidable in sectors like the healthcare sector where human lives and well-being are at stake. The treating physicians need to understand what decisions the AI system has made to ensure the best possible treatment and the patient's well-being.

A conceivable solution is the research field of so-called Explainable AI (XAI) which is based on the idea of statistical testing of AI systems to enable access to the AI systems underlying decision-making process.[57] Explainable AI means a set of processes and methods allowing humans to comprehend the results and ensuring the traceability and explainability of the decision. The methods to enable the

[55] https://hdsr.mitpress.mit.edu/pub/f9kuryi8/release/8.

[56] https://hdsr.mitpress.mit.edu/pub/f9kuryi8/release/8.

[57] https://www.ibm.com/topics/explainable-ai.

explainability of AI systems mainly are prediction accuracy, traceability and decision understanding to examine how different inputs statistically affect the output and target variables of the system.[58] Against the background of the entry into force of the AI Act in the future this research field seems to be crucial for the innovation, development and training of AI systems.

3.2.3.5 Human Oversight, Art. 14 AI Act

The more complex an AI system is, the more complicated - and in some cases, as with the aforementioned Black Box AI, almost impossible - its control becomes. Therefore, high-risk AI systems shall be designed and developed in such a way they can be effectively overseen by a natural person during their use, cf. Art. 14 (I) AI Act.

This article especially received criticism for the lack of differentiation between AI systems which can make their own decision and such systems which are only used as a kind of support to any kind of human decision-making.[59] For the latter the application of Art. 14 AI Act seems at least debatable if human oversight is really necessary because in use-cases of these systems the final decision remains with a natural person.[60] EU legislators addressed this criticism with the linking of the oversight to an adequacy requirement. Measures shall now be commensurate the risks, level of autonomy and context of use of the high-risk AI system, cf. Art. 14 (III) AI Act. Additionally, it was criticized that one of the measures to ensure the oversight according to Art. 14 (IV) lit. (e) AI Act is the intervention on the operation of the AI system or the interruption of the same. Any abrupt stop of running operations of the AI system might result in significant consequential damage if this intervention or interruption, e.g. takes place during an operation-critical process.[61] Accordingly, this point has been amended so that such an intervention or interruption needs to allow the system to come to a halt in a *"safe state"*, cf. Art. 14 (III) lit. (e). It might still be necessary to clarify what exactly a *"safe state"* according to the AI Act is.

3.2.3.6 Conformity Assessment, Art. 23, 43 AI Act and Fundamental Rights Impact Assessment, Art. 27 AI Act

Art. 23 AI Act states the obligation for providers to ensure their high-risk AI systems undergo the relevant conformity assessment procedure in accordance with Art. 43 AI Act. Art. 3 (XX) AI Act defines the conformity assessment as *"the process of demonstrating whether the requirements set out in Chapter III, Section 2 relating to a high-risk AI system have been fulfilled"*. As "high-risk" has been added in the

[58] https://www.ibm.com/topics/explainable-ai.

[59] Bomhard and Merkle (2021), p. 281.

[60] Initiative for Applied Artificial Intelligence, Position Paper: Response to the 2020 European Commissions's White Paper on AI, p. 8.

[61] Bomhard and Merkle (2021), p. 283.

recent provisional agreement this means such an assessment now is only mandatory for providers of high-risk AI systems.

This obligation faces the predominantly technical problem, that in the case of self-learning systems which are subject to an ongoing process of changes an ex-ante conformity assessment is almost impossible.[62] It is precisely the characteristic of self-learning systems which can autonomously perform substantial modifications on themselves that most of later arising changes are not foreseeable.[63] The unpredictability of such substantial modifications is now explicitly mentioned in the definition of Art. 3 (XXIII) AI Act. Following this criticism the AI Act now provides an exception of the need to undergo a new conformity assessment. If changes occur to the algorithm and the performance of the AI system which continues to learn after being placed on the market or put into service, namely automatically adapting how functions are carried out, these changes shall not constitute such a substantial modifications. However it must be provided that those changes have been pre-determined by the provider and assessed at the moment of the conformity assessment, cf. Recital 128, Art. 43 (IV) AI Act. If and to which extent this is possible or might become another challenge will become apparent in the future.

Moreover, besides the conformity assessment the European Council confirmed the provisional agreement providing for a fundamental rights impact assessment.[64] According to Art. 27 AI Act deployers of some specifically mentioned high-risk AI systems shall perform a fundamental rights impact assessment prior to deploying such an AI system. Purpose shall be the assessment of the impact on fundamental rights the use of such an AI system may produce. The assessment shall consist of i.a. a description of the deployer's processes in which the high-risk AI system will be used in line with its intended purpose, a description of the period of time within which, and the frequency with which each high-risk AI system is intended to be used and the categories of natural persons and groups likely to be affected by its use in the specific context, cf. Art. 27 (I) lit. (a)-(c) AI Act.

3.3 Data Protection (GDPR)

Data-driven innovation such as the machine-learning approaches of AI depend on the amount and variety of datasets used for training. In order to use the full potential of AI, to improve accuracy and remove bias it needs to be trained. This presupposes access to large and diverse datasets. In the healthcare sector this means the

[62] Bomhard and Merkle (2021), p. 281.

[63] Bomhard and Merkle (2021), p. 281.

[64] https://www.consilium.europa.eu/en/press/press-releases/2023/12/09/artificial-intelligence-act-council-and-parliament-strike-a-deal-on-the-first-worldwide-rules-for-ai/. Since "total security" is an utopian status, which conflicts with the concept of an open, free European Society. European Fundamental Rights protection demands to assess and balance the potential for damage, the utilitarian effect of the risk and the rights of affected third parties ("risk benefit assessment"). *Murswiek,* Die staatliche Verantwortung für die Risiken der Technik, 1985, page 139.

processing of personal data and especially of health records. However, patients' health records and other health information such as clinical trial data, genetic and biometric data are considered special categories of personal data, and their processing and handling is subject to tight regulations, according to Art. 9 (I) GDPR. Against this background providers and/or users of AI in Europe are not only bound by the requirements of the AI Act but as well as by requirements of the GDPR. The following provides an instructive overview and guidelines of the requirements of the GDPR which typically need to be observed to be legally compliant, when using AI systems for drug discovery and development. The specific legal assessment is bound to the actual data used and processed.

3.3.1 Discrepancy Between Requirements of the GDPR and Conditions to Fully Develop the Potential of (the Use of) AI

The general principle of purpose limitation allows the collection of personal data only for specified, explicit and legitimate purposes, according to Art. 5 (I) lit. (b) GDPR. The collected data may not be further processed in a manner incompatible with these purposes.[65] Therefore, the determined purpose of the processing pursued by the controller, according to Art. 24 (I) GDPR, determines the permissibility of the data processing. The permissions in Art. 6 and 9 GDPR are each linked to specific processing purposes. Beyond that the data processing must be necessary to achieve the purpose pursued, which assesses the purpose-means relation indispensable.[66] According to the principle of data minimization, cf. Art. 5 (I) lit. (c) GDPR any data processing must be adequate, relevant, and limited to what is necessary in relation to the purposes for which it is processed. This does not only require a reduction of the amount of data processed but also a reduction of the number of uses of data.[67] The principle of storage limitation, cf. Art. 5 (I) lit. (e) GDPR requires the storage of personal data in a form which permits identification of data subjects for no longer than is necessary for the purposes for which the personal data are processed.[68]

These principles already stand against the needed access to large and diverse datasets to enable machine learning. The goal of the use of AI in the drug discovery and development to independently discover and develop e.g. new possible molecular targets or to prescribe treatment options is contrary to the principle of purpose limitation which allows data processing only within the scope of the originally determined purpose. The discrepancy between the principles of data protection according to the GDPR also emerges in connection with the principle of transparency,

[65] *Pötters* in Gola/Heckmann, Datenschutz-Grundverordnung - Bundesdatenschutzgesetz, Rn. 11 ff.

[66] *Pötters* in Gola/Heckmann, Datenschutz-Grundverordnung - Bundesdatenschutzgesetz, Rn. 11 ff.

[67] *Pötters* in Gola/Heckmann, Datenschutz-Grundverordnung - Bundesdatenschutzgesetz, Rn. 11 ff.

[68] *Pötters* in Gola/Heckmann, Datenschutz-Grundverordnung - Bundesdatenschutzgesetz, Rn. 11 ff.

cf. Art. 5 (I) lit. (a) GDPR.[69] This principle requires the data processor to inform all affected data subjects in advance about the circumstances of the data processing. This, especially when it comes to the use of AI systems, can be particularly demanding if a considerable amount of data is involved, which on the other hand is needed to enable machine learning.[70] The information of all affected data subjects can become even more challenging in the cases of the aforementioned Black Box AI. As it is currently impossible to justify the decisions made by these models, it is therefore also impossible to inform the data subjects in a transparent and understandable way.

As a result, the machine-learning approach of AI and the thereto related requirement to access large and diverse datasets are fundamentally in conflicts with the central principles of data protection under Art. 5 (I) GDPR.

3.3.2 Scope of the GDPR

3.3.2.1 Processing of Personal Data

The GDPR applies to personal data, i.e. *"information relating to an identified or identifiable natural person"* (hereinafter 'data subject'), Art. 4 (I) GDPR. In this respect, Recital 26 of the GDPR states in particular: *"To determine whether a natural person is identifiable, account should be taken of all the means reasonably likely to be used, such as singling out, by the controller or by any other person to identify the natural person directly or indirectly"*. On the one hand the fundamental definition of the concept of personal data therefore is quite broad, which on the other hand does not necessarily mean there is no limitation of the term. Against the background of the similar legal situation before the GDPR, the Article 29 Working Party stated that *"the mere hypothetical possibility of identifying the person is not sufficient for the person to be regarded as identifiable"*.[71] Furthermore, according to the ECJ, a personal reference cannot be assumed in particular *"if the identification of the person concerned would be prohibited by law or impracticable, for example because it would require a disproportionate effort in terms of time, cost and manpower, so that the risk of identification would de facto appear negligible"*.

Data needed to enable machine-learning and to fully develop full potential of AI in the healthcare sector are in particular but not limited to patients' health records and other health information such as clinical trial data, genetic and biometric data which are considered special categories of personal data.

[69] *Ashkar*: Wesentliche Anforderungen der DS-GVO bei Einführung und Betrieb von KI-Anwendungen; ZD 2023, 523, (524).

[70] *Ashkar*: Wesentliche Anforderungen der DS-GVO bei Einführung und Betrieb von KI-Anwendungen; ZD 2023, 523, (524).

[71] Art. 29-Datenschutzgruppe, WP 136 DE, 20.6.2007, p. 17.

3.3.2.2 Processing of Special Categories of Personal Data

When it comes to the processing of personal data there are different obligations and requirements in the GDPR which need to be fulfilled by the processor. These obligations include e.g. the information of data subjects acc. to Art. 12 et seq. GDPR. Some special categories of personal data are particularly worthy of protection according to the GDPR. This means the tight regulations of the GDPR are not tight enough for these special categories which results in the prohibition of their processing according to Art. 9 (I) GDPR. The special categories of personal data listed in Art. 9 GDPR also include the aforementioned biometric and genetic data of individuals and data concerning health that are particularly relevant in the pharmaceutical industry. Recital 34 GDPR defines genetic data as "*personal data relating to the inherited or acquired genetic characteristics of a natural person which result from the analysis of a biological sample from the natural person in question, in particular chromosomal, deoxyribonucleic acid (DNA) or ribonucleic acid (RNA) analysis, or from the analysis of another element enabling equivalent information to be obtained*". According to Recital 35 GDPR, "*Personal data concerning health should include all data pertaining to the health status of a data subject which reveal information relating to the past, current or future physical or mental health status of the data subject.*" Recitals 71 and 75 of the GDPR briefly outline the potential risks and discriminatory effects on natural persons on the basis of genetic or health status. The Article 29 Working Party explains the necessity for greater protection in more detail. It is i.a. mentioned that as a rule genetic information is unknown to the bearer him or herself and does not depend on the bearer's individual will since genetic data are non-modifiable.[72] The prohibition of processing of health records and other health information makes the full development of the potential of AI in the healthcare sector fundamentally impossible.

3.3.2.3 Protection of Special Categories of Personal Data

The EU legislation currently guarantees the protection of special categories of personal data through three main methods:

- as aforementioned the categorization of such data as sensitive,
- the implementation of a data protection impact assessment and
- the reliance on anonymization and pseudonymization of genetic data.[73]

Art. 9 (II) GDPR states exceptions to the prohibition of Art. 9 (I) GDPR. When complying with certain requirements AI-based technologies processing of biometric, health and genomic data by AI-based technologies is allowed. The vast majority of cases will be covered by the i.a. mentioned explicit consent of the data subject and for "*archiving purposes in the public interest, scientific or historical research*

[72] Article 29 Data Protection Working Party. (2004) Working Document on Genetic Data, 12178/03/EN WP 91, 17 March, pp. 4–5.

[73] Sukhorolskyi and Hutsaliuk (2020), p. 14:9f.

purposes or statistical purposes in accordance with Article 89 (1)", cf. Art. 9 (II) lit. (a) and (j) GDPR. When collecting data for AI systems in BioTech to discover interpretable patterns, structures, correlations, and causal relations from various kinds of health data, the consent in accordance with Art. 9 (I) lit. (a) GDPR and in compliance with Recital 32 GDPR is an option.[74] Additionally, Art. 9 (IV) GDPR endorses the possibility for member states to maintain or introduce further conditions of the processing of genetic and biometric data or data concerning health. In this context Recital 10 GDPR clarifies that Art. 9 (IV) GDPR only enables the introduction of *"national provisions to further specify the application of the rules"* of the GDPR, so a substantial deviation from certain provisions, especially e.g. the general prohibition of processing of special categories of personal data, is not possible. Furthermore, the GDPR ensures an adequate level of protection of the special categories of personal data, on the one hand, with i.a. the prohibition of automated individual decision-making based on such data while there are some exceptions, cf. Art. 22 (IV) GDPR. On the other hand an adequate level of protection is ensured by the obligation of controllers and processors to designate a data protection officer in the case where their core activities consist of processing on a large scale of special categories of data, cf. Art. 37 (I) GDPR.

Due to the processing of sensitive data, according to Art. 9 (I) GDPR, a data protection impact assessment is required, see Art. 35 (I), (III) lit. (b) GDPR.[75] The impact assessment needs to be performed on a regular basis.[76] The Article 29 Working Party describes and explains the procedure of such an assessment in their Guidelines on Data Protection Impact Assessment. The document states i.a. which factors need to be taken into consideration when determining whether the processing is carried out on a large scale.[77]

While science is divided whether pseudonymized data always are personal data which need the aforementioned protection,[78] Recital 26 GDPR divides information with regards to a natural person into two categories: anonymous information and information concerning an identified or identifiable natural person. Information which has been pseudonymized should be considered as information on an identifiable natural person. The legal definition of pseudonymization can be found in Art. 4 nb. 5 GDPR. Researchers fear negative consequences for general genetic research in case of the use of pseudonymized data.[79] The anonymization of personal data is not explicitly explained or described in the GDPR. Recital 26 only mentions that the

[74] *Sachs*, in Kapitel 12. Datenschutzrechtliche Compliance, *Dieners*, Handbuch Compliance im Gesundheitswesen, (2022) Sec. 39, 40.

[75] *Franke*, Datenschutzrechtskonformes Training von KI-Systemen mit öffentlich verfügbaren personenbezogenen Daten, RDi 2023, 565 (569, 570).

[76] See for the requirements of the assessment: Recital: 84, 90- 93 GDPR.

[77] Article 29 Data Protection Working Party. (2017) Guidelines on Data Protection Impact Assessment (DPIA) and determining whether processing is "likely to result in a high risk" for the purposes of Regulation 2016/679, 17/EN WP 248, 4 April.

[78] Mourby et al. (2018), pp. 222–233.

[79] Mourby et al. (2018), pp. 222–233.

use of such data allows the controller to exclude such data processing operations from the scope of the GDPR and removes any respective obligations of the controller. Article 89 and Recital 156 GDPR also provide an indication to respect the principle of proportionality and use anonymous information wherever possible by emphasizing the need to comply with the principle of data minimization to respect the principle of proportionality.[80] Regardless of whether the pseudonymization and/or anonymization of genetic data is possible and if and to what extend the training of an AI system with such pseudonymized or anonymized data is useful against the background of the aim to personalize especially cancer medication processors of special categories of personal data face another challenge. The Article 29 Working Party adopted an Opinion on Anonymisation Techniques stating that *"an anonymised dataset can still present residual risks to data subjects"* and emphasizing that *"anonymisation should not be regarded as a one-off exercise and the attending risks should be reassessed regularly"*.[81] This raises the question for data processors if pseudonymization or anonymization can even be considered effective in the case of processing of special categories of personal data, in particular genetic data. This leaves processors not only in an unsatisfactory situation, but also in a legally uncertain one.

3.3.2.4 Research Exemption, Art. 9 (II) Lit. (j) GDPR

The research exemption in Art. 9 (II) lit. (j) GDPR moderates the requirements for the handling of personal data including derogations from the rights of the data subject when the processing takes place for *"for archiving purposes in the public interest, scientific or historical research purposes or statistical purposes"*. This exemption is particularly relevant in the healthcare sector and when it comes to drug discovery and development by using AI systems. Additionally, the GDPR states different exemptions to the data protection and restrictions of rights of data subjects in the interest of science. Article 5 (I) lit. (b) GDPR stipulates an exemption from the general principle of purpose limitation while lit. (e) stipulates an exemption from the principle of storage limitation. Article 14 (V) GDPR sets out an exception to the obligation of the processor to provide the data subject with relevant information, where personal data have not been obtained directly from the data subject, in cases where the provision of such information would involve a disproportionate effort for processing for archiving, scientific or historical research purposes. Art 17 (III) lit. (d) GDPR contains a similar provision regarding the right to erasure. Art. 21 (VI) GDPR introduces an exception to the right to object in cases where data processing for scientific research purposes is necessary for the performance of a task carried out for reasons of public interest. Moreover, Union or member state law may provide for derogations from a number of basic rights of the data subject (i.a. the right to rectification, cf. Art. 16 GDPR, the right to restriction of processing, cf. Art.

[80] Sukhorolskyi and. Hutsaliuk (2020), p. 15.

[81] Article 29 Data Protection Working Party. (2014) Opinion 05/2014 on Anonymisation Techniques, 0829/14/EN WP216, 10 April, p. 4.

18 GDPR), *"in so far as such rights are likely to render impossible or seriously impair the achievement of the specific purposes, and such derogations are necessary for the fulfilment of those purposes"*, cf. Art. 89 (II) GDPR.

In summary this results in data protection being restricted to data minimization, pseudonymization and anonymization in cases of data processing for research purposes, cf. Art. 89 and Recital 156 GDPR. Recital 159 states that *"the processing of personal data for scientific research purposes should be interpreted in a broad manner including for example technological development and demonstration, fundamental research, applied research and privately funded research"*. Function and scope of the statutory opening clause nevertheless remain unclear, especially as data processing for research purposes is already privileged according to Art. 89 GDPR.[82] In contrast to Art. 89 (II) GDPR, Art. 85 (II) GDPR enables derogation from almost any regulation in the GDPR with the only exception of the sanctions in Chapter VIII. The wording of Art. 89 (II) GDPR is much more limited when only allowing derogation from Art. 15, 16, 18 and 21 GDPR. The lack of clear specifications on the scope of the term leads to an interpretation in the light of Art. 5 (III) and Art. 13 (I) CFR, which also lack a clear definition.[83] The references to the public interest made in connection with the research exemption enables the application of these exemptions to almost all kinds of research, not even clearly excluding research conducted for the sole purpose of commercialization.[84]

The GDPR declares the *"processing of personal data should be designed to serve mankind"* and the right to the protection of personal data *"must be considered in relation to its function in society and be balanced against other fundamental rights, in accordance with the principle of proportionality"*, cf. Recital 4 GDPR. Seemingly the processing of special categories of personal data, especially genetic data, in the healthcare sector is possible, at least under the term "research purposes". Nevertheless, until clarifying decisions are made by the ECJ the practice is currently left with open questions and partial legal uncertainty.

4 Possible Solutions

4.1 Framework and Identified Challenges for the AI Sandbox Regime

Sandbox regimes have become an established regulatory tool in the field of highly innovative technologies,[85] which might also result in *modern threats* to society. These modern threats structurally differ from classic threats. They threaten a far

[82] *Pötters* in Gola/Heckmann, Datenschutz-Grundverordnung - Bundesdatenschutzgesetz, margin no. 21.

[83] *Weichert:* Die Forschungsprivilegierung in der DSG-VO; ZD 2020, 18, (19).

[84] *Weichert:* Die Forschungsprivilegierung in der DSG-VO; ZD 2020, 18, (19f.).

[85] See for example: *OECD*, Regulatory Sandboxes in Artificial Intelligence – OECD Digital Economy Papers, July 2023, No. 356, DSTI/CDEP/AIGO(2022)7/FINAL.

larger number of individuals, may lead to far greater damage and on cognitive level are difficult to grasp—yet they *remain steerable.*[86] The modern threats are steerable, on condition that the state intervention does not rely on the classic causal link ex-post to activate norm applicability and steering effects - but an ex-ante assessment, ideally in the early development stages of a technology.

Therefore, in addition to the AI sandbox regime, the EU Commission also uses a sandbox regime for distributed ledger technology or blockchain technology (DLT Sandbox-Regime).[87] The DLT Sandbox-Regime is intended to provide a suitable and legally secure framework for the development of blockchain-based securities trading. In contrast to the AI sandbox, the DLT Sandbox-Regime has a simplified approval process for infrastructure providers and issuers, which is accompanied by fewer regulatory obligations and relief from further compliance requirements.[88]

This illustrates the dynamic field of upcoming regulations. In order to harmonize these developments, the EU Commission published the so-called Interoperable Europe Act proposal on November 18th, 2022, laying down specific rules for the future framework of EU sandbox regimes in Art. 11 and 12.[89]

In the technology sector, this does not only apply to the EU, but jurisdictions around the world are trying to implement suitable sandbox regimes so that innovations can be developed without excessive regulation preventing innovation.[90]

Even in the area of pharmaceutical regulation, EU initiatives aim to strengthen the ability to innovate through sandbox regimes. On April 26th, 2023, the EU Commission published a draft Regulation[91] and Directive[92] aiming the adaption and modernization of pharmaceutical regulation in Europe. Art. 113 to 115 of the EMA draft set out compliance simplifications for new medicinal products.

[86] Reus, *Das Recht in der Risikogesellschaft*, p. 181.

[87] Regulation (EU) 2022/858 of the European Parliament and of the Council of 30 May 2022 on a pilot regime for market infrastructures based on distributed ledger technology, and amending Regulations (EU) No 600/2014 and (EU) No 909/2014 and Directive 2014/65/EU, OJ L 151, 2.6.2022, p. 1–33.

[88] Related to the DLT Sandbox Regime: *Hirzle/Hugendubel*, Die Entwicklung des Kryptorechts im Jahr 2022, BKR 2022, p. 823.

[89] *EU Commission*, Proposal for a Regulation of the European Parliament and of the Council laying down measures for a high level of public sector interoperability across the Union (Interoperable Europe Act), COM (2022) 720 final, 18.11.2022.

[90] See early comparative analysis for BRICS countries: Gromova and Ivanc (2020), p. 12 ff.; Further examples: Everhart (2020), p. 67 ff.

[91] Proposal for a Regulation of the European Parliament and of the Council laying down Union procedures for the authorisation and supervision of medicinal products for human use and establishing rules governing the European Medicines Agency, amending Regulation (EC) No 1394/2007 and Regulation (EU) No 536/2014 and repealing Regulation (EC) No 726/2004, Regulation (EC) No 141/2000 and Regulation (EC) No 1901/2006, COM/2023/193 final.

[92] Proposal for a Directive of the European Parliament and of the Council on the Union code relating to medicinal products for human use, and repealing Directive 2001/83/EC and Directive 2009/35/EC, COM/2023/192 final.

4.2 Possible Future Setting for the Sandbox Regime

The international sandbox regime landscape is evolving rapidly. Spain for example adopted an AI sandbox law in November 2023.[93] Before the regulatory implementation Spain implemented a pilot regime of the AI sandbox regime to collect experience, good practices and guidelines.[94] Nevertheless, providers need to fulfill high minimum requirements according to Art. 57 ff. AI Act to comply with the regulation which has been negatively noticed.[95]

Based on these indications in the AI Act and inspired by the similar UK AI sandbox[96] as well as by the Norwegian[97] and by the Spanish AI sandbox, we developed several detailed sandbox access criteria. We divided the accessibility into three indicators, with low, medium and high probability for projects to get access to AI sandboxes, see Table 1.

An important element for the admission to a sandbox is the question to what extent the public interest benefits from the AI project, according to Art. 59 (I) lit.

Table 1 Own source—potential sandbox criteria

Indicators	Low probability	Medium probability	High probability
Public Interest	• Project will not benefit the public interest	• Project will partly benefit the public interest	• Project will benefit the public interest
Innovation	• Reworking of existing approaches	• Likely or clear innovation of existing approaches	• Innovation is likely to be transformative
Sandbox plan viability	• No suitable resources and timescale • Project can not identify risks for the project and data protection • No exit plan	• With revisions the project has suitable resources and timescale • Project can identify risks for the project and data protection • Project has an exit plan	• Realistic timescale and resources with buffer in case of failure • Risks are well understood • Sophisticated risk control mechanisms • Project has a detailed exit plan (mitigate risk, "failsafe"-approach) • Small-scale provider or start-up

[93] Spanish Royal Decree 817/2023, Boletín oficial del estado, núm. 268, sec. I. pág. 149138, 9.11.2023.

[94] Further information to the Spanish AI Sandbox Regime: *Ministerio de Economiá, comercio y empresa*, https://portal.mineco.gob.es/gl-es/comunicacion/Paxinas/231002_sandbox_ia.aspx.

[95] Bomhard and Merkle (2021), p. 279.

[96] *Financial Conduct Authority*, Regulatory Sandbox, https://www.fca.org.uk/firms/innovation/regulatory-sandbox, last updated: 1.8.2023.

[97] *Datatilsynet*, Regulatory privacy sandbox, https://www.datatilsynet.no/en/regulations-and-tools/sandbox-for-artificial-intelligence/.

(a) AI Act. AI systems in the Biotech-/pharmaceutical sector are in the public interest, if they develop AI systems for the public safety and public health, including disease detection, diagnosis prevention, control and treatment and improvement of health care systems, Art. 59 (I) lit. (a) (i) AI Act. Art. In addition Art. 59 (I) lit. (f) AI Act requires additional safeguarding mechanisms to ensure data protection and privacy. Art. 60 AI Act also allows the testing of high-risk AI systems in real world conditions outside the AI sandbox regime. The second important criteria should be the degree of innovation. One goal of the AI sandbox is to foster innovation of AI systems for a limited time before they are being placed on the market or put into service, cf. Art. 57 (V), (IX) lit. (c) AI Act. Since AI sandboxes offer advantages to the providers or prospective providers, one additional access requirement should be the degree of innovation. This is currently not directly stipulated in the AI Act, but results from an interpretation of the meaning and purpose of the AI Act.

If there is no benefit to the public and the innovation is not a new approach, the probability of an approval of the project after weighing of all relevant factors is low. This applies in particular to projects that do not have sufficient resources and cannot identify the associated risks for the project as well as the risks related to the data protection.

A medium probability exists if the project has a clear benefit to the public, is innovative compared to previous approaches, has sufficient resources, identifies risks, and also has an exit plan for said project.

In contrast, there is a high probability if the project is clearly transformative for the public and in comparison to other innovations.

At the sandbox plan viability level, there should be buffer of the resources and timescale. The risks should be well understood, and a wide range of sophisticated control mechanisms should be in place. There should also be a detailed exit plan and a failsafe approach.

According to the AI Act, the sandbox regulation is designed for smaller providers and startups in particular. For these reasons, they should be given priority in accessing the sandbox, see Art. 62 (I) lit. (a) AI Act.

4.3 Setting for a Competent Authority in Germany

According to Art. 70 (I) AI Act draft Member States will have to designate one or more national competent authorities at national level by August 2nd, 2025. Among these authorities (if the Member States choose more than one competent authority) a national supervisory authority needs to be designated for the purpose of supervising the application and implementation of the regulation. Spain already assigned the Spanish Artificial Intelligence Supervisory Agency as the competent authority.[98]

[98] Agencia Estatal Boletín Oficial del Estado, Real Decreto 729/2023, de 22 de agosto, por el que se aprueba el Estatuto de la Agencia Española de Supervisión de Inteligencia Artificial, cf.: https://boe.es/diario_boe/txt.php?id=BOE-A-2023-18911.

Currently, no competent authority according to Art. 70 (I) AI Act has been determined in Germany.

The Federal Office of Information Security (so-called Bundesamt für Sicherheit in der Informationstechnik (short: BSI)) could be a possible alternative for the setup of the competent authority in Germany. This national agency unifies technical expertise and competence. The BSI is already evaluating artificial intelligence and AI in security-critical areas.[99]

Besides these already existing possibilities the Federal Ministry of Economics and Climate Action has started a consultation phase for a sandbox law for innovative technologies.[100] So far, AI is not explicitly included. But a so-called One-Stop-Shop should be implemented. In other words, a One-Stop-Shop for monitoring sandboxes. It would be easy to extend a future sandbox law to AI applications and thus implement the AI Act in national law.

This means that there are currently a variety of implementation options and up to now no final decision has been taken. The German government should be in favor of implementing one competent authority via a One-Stop-Shop mechanism to supervise all sandbox regimes for innovative technologies.

4.4 Evaluation and Other Approaches to Foster AI Systems for BioTech

Even if the sandbox regime of the AI Act supports projects to initiate and develop AI systems it could still be questioned if the sandbox regime in its current form fosters innovation. AI systems developed in the sandbox need to fulfill the similar requirements as AI systems developed outside the sandbox, with minor liability adjustments, see Art. 57 (XII) AI Act. This also applies to the development of AI systems for BioTech. On one hand, it is understandable that there should be no different treatment for other AI systems. But BioTech AI systems need to pass the same thresholds to enter the sandbox regime and the actual support for AI systems is not clarified yet and still open to be debated, even if the competent authorities provide support according to Art. 57 (VI) AI Act. To what extend developers of AI systems will use the sandbox regime depends on potentially provided resources.

In order not to overburden BioTech companies developing AI systems the technical concept of federated learning is a suitable concept to minimize compliance obligations for software developers and data owners (e.g. hospitals, cancer research institutions).

Data owners still need to fulfil the AI Act and GDPR obligations, but developers would not be considered as processors according to Art. 28 (I) GDPR. The

[99] https://www.bsi.bund.de/DE/Themen/Unternehmen-und-Organisationen/Informationen-und-Empfehlungen/Kuenstliche-Intelligenz/kuenstliche-intelligenz_node.html.

[100] https://www.bmwk.de/Redaktion/DE/Pressemitteilungen/2023/07/20230710-bmwk-konsultation-reallabore-gesetz.html.

sandbox regime could also be applicable for various data owners, because Art. 57 et seqq. AI Act do not mention the application of only one requestor. The probability that BioTech AI systems could be considered as being in the "public interest" according to Art. 59 (I) lit. (a) (i) AI Act is high. BioTech AI systems have always had a focus on life science and therefore often a focus on health. Since most BioTech AI systems are not currently being developed by Big Pharma companies, this also speaks in favor of using the sandbox regime as start-ups and small-scale providers have better accessibility, according to Art. 62 (I) lit. (a) AI Act. Data protection and privacy can be insured by training AI systems with data that the data subjects have consented to process in accordance with Art. 9 (I), (II) GDPR. For each data processing step, a data protection impact assessment is necessary, cf. Art. 35 (I) GDPR. However, this assessment only covers the processing of sensitive data of data subjects within the EU. The AI training system can also be extended to third countries, which is why the respective national data protection laws must be observed, for example the HIPAA in the USA.[101]

Another challenge is to ensure the transparency of decision-making, which is reflected in Art. 13 AI Act and Art. 5 (I) lit. (a) GDPR. In this regard the term Explainable AI (XAI) is often used to illustrate the need for users and third parties (regulatory authorities) to understand the decision-making process within the AI system. AI systems can be separated into Black Box Models that use machine-learning algorithms like neural networks and White Box Models which include decision trees, Bayesian rule lists or logistic regression. But still, Black Box Models generate more accurate results.[102] The concept of XAI is already reflected by the European High-Level Expert Group on AI in their four Ethical Principles and seven Key Requirements for a framework for a trustworthy AI from the year 2019.[103]

The integration of XAI in BioTech AI systems needs to parallelize the development of new XAI systems and algorithms. This is also key to ensure the legitimacy of results for the approval of new drugs by the regulatory authorities.[104]

A future setting to train BioTech AI systems needs to integrate federate learning and XAI approaches to ensure compliance. A supporting regulatory frame for processing data owners can be established by the AI sandbox regime. This approach ensures the transparency of the generalization of statements (the decision-making process) for future datasets by sophisticated AI systems, see Fig. 6. This opens up an opportunity for start-ups to provide services in the development of AI systems for drug discovery and to deliver compliance by design. This includes giving data

---

[101] Public Law 104 - 191 - Health Insurance Portability and Accountability Act of 1996, 5 U.S.C. 553, 554, 556, 557, 564 and 706 Chapters 5 and 89.

[102] *Kuzniacki/ Winterhalter*, Explainable Artificial Intelligence in Tax Law, beck.digitax, 2023, p. 166 (170 ff.).

[103] EU Commission, Independent High-Level Expert Group on Artificial Intelligence set up by the European Commission, Ethics Guidelines for Trustworthy AI, 2019, https://ec.europa.eu/newsroom/dae/document.cfm?doc_id=60419, p. 8.

[104] Derived from: De Fine Licht and de Fine Licht (2020), pp. 918 ff.

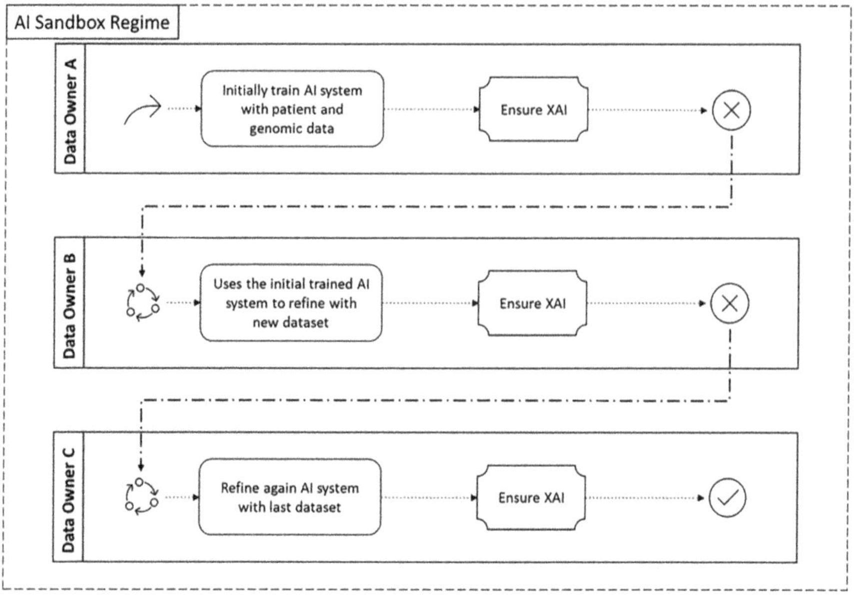

Fig. 6 Integrated Federated Learning and XAI within the future AI Sandbox-Regime, own source

owners regulatory access to AI sandbox regimes and documenting transparency in the use of XAI.

5 Summary and Outlook

The future BioTech growth company will presumably look like a hybrid between a pharmaceutical and a software company where AI is used as a bridge between these two industries in order to develop new drugs more agile and with less resource investments. In other words: a digital company which happens to be a BioTech/ pharmaceutical company. This also offers the opportunity for start-ups, small and medium enterprises to directly undertake drug development, benefit from own drug product sales and as a result challenge the dominance of few incumbent pharma players in the market. BigPharma companies are already shifting the development and identification of new technologies and drugs to start-ups and BioTech companies. This positive economic effect to the markets is accelerated by the influence of AI on drug development and next go-to-market steps, following Schumpeter's principle of *creative destruction.*[105]

But to utilize the full potential of AI in BioTech, smaller companies and start-up face the challenge of missing financial capacities, resources, and human expertise.[106]

[105] *Schumpeter*, Kapitalismus, Sozialismus und Demokratie, 8th edition, page 138.

[106] Supporting this position: Szalay (2023), https://doi.org/10.1787/a8d820bd-en.

Regulation should not be designed to hinder these developments. Currently the area of data processing and also the development of new drugs is highly regulated. Navigating this area is already difficult in one area, but when you combine both areas, the result is exponential growth in smart regulatory solutions and the sophisticated knowledge required. The sandbox regime can help small companies and start-ups to be compliant. But a too rigid regulatory approach that does not cover other companies may risk that midsize AI companies cannot afford to monitor and certify their products which results in only big players surviving in the market. The AI Act addresses several identified challenges.

Futurewise one of the main aspects will be to collectively address human-controllable barriers currently preventing the innovation the use of AI could have. In January 2024 the OECD published the "Collective Action for responsible AI in Health" in the OECD Artificial Intelligence Papers mentioning i.a. the lack of standards, misaligned policies, unclear liability and accountability as well as global health system fragmentation as barriers to responsible AI innovation in healthcare.

It is clear that these aforementioned barriers can only be overcome collectively by introducing transparent and clear regulations and uniform standards which are internationally recognized to provide guidance on the responsible use of AI to enable the benefit for individuals.

Besides the urgent need for clear and structured regulations it is crucial for AI success and development in the EU to instill trust in and understanding of AI based digital health applications. Not only policy makers and legislators need to have a good understanding of digital health and AI to foster innovation but also employees in Europe's healthcare sector and patients need to gain trust in the benefits of AI.[107] In an AI driven world the legislative processes for the healthcare sector need to be modified and allow more elements of risk management. This paradigm shift in legislation from maximum risk avoidance to risk management via sandbox regimes and other regulatory tools is a pre-condition for the successful use of AI in the EU.

Liquid-Legal-Waves to Other Chapters, Written by the Editors

While agreeing on the need for regulation of AI, *Marco, Sharon, Christina,* and *Robert* put their fingers on the risk that we might thereby limit too much the research and development in fields that are considered 'high risk', proposing innovation-friendly sandbox-regimes. 'Too risky?' – we ask *Bruno* who provides thoughtful answers on the risks in his chapter: *"AI in the Legal Market: The Dark Side of the Moon"*.

After *Marco, Sharon, Christina,* and *Robert* have given us their view on how to balance strict regulation, especially in high-risk scenarios, with providing sandbox-opportunities, it is timely to factor in the user-impact on

(continued)

[107] Anderson and Sutherland (2024), p. 16f.

generative AI. *Philipp*, *Valentin*, and *Alexander* offer a deep dive on *"Legal Prompt Engineering and How It Will Change the Way Lawyers Work"*.

Regulation? Risk? Opportunity? – All important. However, what 'digitized creature' will we humans become when AI transforms us and our society? If you are curious about that, just turn the page and let *Barbara* take you towards an unsettling, but hopeful outlook: *"If a machine, a Terminator, can learn the value of human life, maybe we can too"*.

References

Anderson B, Sutherland E (2024) Collective action for responsible AI in healthcare in OECD artificial intelligence papers. OECD Publishing, 10:16f

Bomhard D, Merkle M (2021) Europäische KI-Verordnung - Der aktuelle Kommissionsentwurf und praktische Auswirkungen. RDi, 276, (277)

De Fine Licht K, de Fine Licht J (2020) Artificial intelligence, transparency, and public decision-making – why explanations are key when trying to produce perceived legitimacy. AI Soc 35:917

Everhart JR (2020) The fintech sandbox: an overview of regulatory sandbox regimes Southern J Bus Ethics 12:67 ff

Galtier M, Meadon D (2023) Applying AI to real-world health-care settings and the life sciences: tackling data privacy, security and policy challenges with federated learning. In: OECD (ed) Artificial intelligence in science: challenges, opportunities and the future of research. OECD Publishing, Paris

Géron A (2017) Hands-on machine learning with Scikit-Learn and TensorFlow – concepts, tools, and techniques to build intelligent systems. O'Reilly Media, S. 22 ff

Glauner P (2021) Artificial intelligence in healthcare: foundations, opportunities and challenges. In: Glauner P, Plugmann P, Lerzynski G (eds) Digitalization in healthcare – implementing innovation and artificial intelligence. Springer, Cham, p 3, 4

Goodsell DS, Sanner MF, Olson AJ, Forli S (2021) The Autoduck suite at 30. Protein Sci 30(1): 31 ff

Gromova E, Ivanc T (2020) Regulatory sandboxes (experimental legal regimes) for digital innovations in BRICS. BRICS Law J VII(2):12 ff

Hacker P, Berz A (2023) Der AI Act der Europäischen Union - Überblick, Kritik und Ausblick. ZPR 226, (227)

Harrer S et al (2019) Artificial intelligence for clinical trial design. Trends Pharmacol Sci 40(8): 577–591

Mourby M et al (2018) Are 'pseudonymised' data always personal data? Implications of the GDPR for administrative data research in the UK. Comput Law Secur Rev 34:222–233

Park T et al (2023) Artificial intelligence in urologic oncology: the actual clinical practice results of IBM Watson for oncology in South Korea. Prostate Int 11:218–221

Sukhorolskyi P, Hutsaliuk V (2020) Processing of genetic data under GDPR: unresolved conflict of interests. Masaryk Univ J Law Technol 14:9f

Szalay KZ (2023) AI in drug discovery. In: OECD (ed) Artificial intelligence in science: challenges, opportunities and the future of research. OECD Publishing, Paris

Zheng W, Jin M (2018) Do we need more training samples for text classification? In: Proceedings of the 2018 Artificial Intelligence and Cloud Computing Conference

Marco Rau LL.M. (QMUL), MBA (ESSEC/MBS) is General Counsel & Chief Compliance Officer at CureVac N.V., Tübingen, Germany. Marco has a strong focus on Tech Law, Pharma Law, Venture Capital & Healthcare Business Development transactions. He started his career at Beiten Burkhardt (IT/IP Practice Group), worked on digital & regulatory projects in Telefónica O2's legal department and then joined Merck KGaA, where he took responsibility inter alia as Head of Legal Strategy & Transformation. He is General Counsel of CureVac since 2021. Marco is author of numerous publications and regularly holds speeches at prestigious conferences. He is qualified as a lawyer in Germany, holds a Ph.D. in international economic law from University of Mainz, a LL.M. in IP from Queen Mary University of London and a MBA from École Supérieure des Sciences Économiques et Commerciales (ESSEC, Paris) / MBS (Mannheim).

Sharon Naomi Reichl is a research assistant for Dr. Christina Eschenfelder at Rittershaus Rechtsanwälte PartmbB in Mannheim. She studied law at the Eberhard Karls University in Tübingen. She started working in the pharmaceutical and life science industries as a working student over four years ago, enabling her to make her first experiences with the operative day-to-day business of an in-house lawyer in the healthcare sector. Her career later on led her to a new challenge when joining a publicly listed leading global clinical-stage biopharmaceutical company. Sharon primarily supported the General Counsel and Compliance Officer with a wide range of tasks including the preparation and holding of Annual General Meetings as well as the implementation of different corporate legal tools. During that time, she additionally gained her first insights on the use of Artificial Intelligence in the pharmaceutical and life sciences industries. Fascinated by the potential of these technologies she now aims to optimize different processes and to drive innovation forward. Her main areas of activity and research therefore are the use of modern technologies in legal processes, digitalization of law and potentials of Artificial Intelligence. She currently works in the areas of corporate governance, tax planning, data protection and compliance for growth companies.

Robert Müller LL.M. in International Tax Law (Vienna University of Economics and Business); Biologist; Attorney; Corporate Legal Counsel CureVac N.V., Tübingen; works and researches in the field of digitalization of law and finance law. A particular focus is on new digitalized forms of governance and companies. Part of his experience is the regulation of modern technologies, like Blockchain, Web3, Artificial intelligence and the integration in tech companies and public / pharmaceutical sector. Robert has a strong entrepreneurial background in life science. Before he joined CureVac, he worked at the German Research Center of Artificial Intelligence and is still active in the Blockchain/Web3 startup ecosystem. He published more than 80 peer-review publications and is lecturer at conferences.

If a Machine, a Terminator, Can Learn the Value of Human Life, Maybe We Can Too

Barbara Chomicka

Contents

Abstract

We are exceptionally murderous primates. We have wants and needs and the ability to pursue them. We rose to the top of the food chain by teaming up in bands to kill more intelligent than us Neanderthals. Today, we remain quite efficient at killing our own kind: human societies regularly commit acts with the intent to destroy, entirely or partly, various national, ethnic, racial, or religious groups. On an individual level, according to the US Bureau of Justice statistics, 30% of all female murder victims were killed by their spouses. What drives us to kill? Jealousy, revenge, fear and anger. We kill because we are not robots.

We know that humanity's own inhumanity has evolutionary origins. This is how we came about. This is what we are made of. This is who we are. We evolved

Words by Sarah Connor, a fictional character, and the main protagonist of the Terminator franchise. The Terminator is a 1984 American science fiction action film directed by James Cameron. It is a story about humanity's battle with its superior artificial creation.

This chapter was written in the basement of the Science Museum in London housing Power Up, a hands-on gaming experience, featuring the very best video games and consoles from the past 50 years, and the only space where the author could sit down and complete this chapter while her children kept themselves occupied.

B. Chomicka (✉)
Turner & Townsend, New York, NY, USA
e-mail: barbara.chomicka@turntown.com

K. Jacob et al. (eds.), *Liquid Legal – Sustaining the Rule of Law*, Law for Professionals, https://doi.org/10.1007/978-3-031-78596-2_10

to be both shockingly violent and super-cooperative. Now that we have created artificial intelligence, we are concerned about the end of the humanity as we know it. Our biggest threat from AI comes from the consciousness that set its goals. We fear that our tools for thinking faster and more efficiently, but not necessarily more benevolently, can potentially alter the human trajectory.

The rise of powerful AI will be either the best or the worst thing ever to happen to humanity. The theoretical physicist and cosmologist Stephen Hawking warned that "we do not yet know which". However, all things considered, the promise offered by an AI is best reflected in the words of Sarah Connor, a fictional character and the main protagonist of the Terminator franchise: "the unknown future rolls toward us. I face it, for the first time, with a sense of hope. Because if a machine, a Terminator, can learn the value of human life, maybe we can, too."

1 Game Over

[A message that appears on the screen of a video game when either all the player's lives have been lost or the game has been successfully completed].

We are all going to die. It may happen in one thousand generations or as soon as you finish reading this chapter.

The habitable lifespan of Earth is expected to last just about another one billion years, notwithstanding devastating catastrophes in the meantime. The planet is heating up. It is a natural process. It is unstoppable. Notwithstanding this earlier deadline for habitable life, planet Earth has a projected eight-billion-year lifespan, driven by the sun's life cycle. In the next five billion years, the sun will burn up all its hydrogen and expand, devouring the inner planets Mercury, Venus, Earth and Mars in the process. This means that even the current horizon of human exploration will cease to exist. Considering that life first began to evolve around 3.8 billion years ago, it has roughly 20% of its predicted lifespan left. So, regardless of what we do or how well we play, there is only potentially 20% of the game left.

The game is not continuous, though—life on earth has started from scratch many times before. There have been countless extinctions, including five major ones. Each major extinction resulted in the loss of at least a half and to up to ninety-six per cent of all life on Earth in one event. All life today has evolved from four per cent of the species that were alive prior to The Great Dying at the end of the Permian period, about 252 million years ago. Were it not for these extinctions, humans would not exist.

The very source of human life is by far the biggest existential threat to its survival: the violent ejections of solar gas, plasma and electromagnetic radiation that can propel more than ten billion tons of solar matter outward from the sun's atmosphere with the power of over a billion hydrogen bombs. Eric McLamb, Secretary of the Foundation for Ecology, ranked coronal mass ejections at the top of his list of the

Five Threats Facing Earth and Humanity. The sun discharges a minimum of one ejection per week, and as many as three per day. Most of them miss Earth's orbit, with about seventy small ones skimming the surface each year. A direct hit from a large ejection is a once-in-a-century event, according to solar research at NASA and the European Space Agency. Even though Earth's magnetic field provides us with some level of protection, a major hit would immediately shut down all the infrastructure we heavily depend on, bringing back living conditions to what they were prior to the discovery of electricity. A direct, head-on hit from a super-large ejection would scorch either all, or most of, life on Earth. It has happened before on several occasions. Although we believe the chances are low, it could happen again at any time.

There are several ongoing doom scenarios that are perhaps better advertised: we are powerless in the face of the slow but sure trajectory of extreme global climate change on our planet. This phenomenon involves global warming, changes in precipitation, a worsening of air quality, biodiversity loss, and the shrinking of habitable zones on Earth. We have already seen the death and destruction inflicted by monster typhoons and hurricanes, volcanic activity, monsoons, extreme heat and extreme cold. According to the United Nations Office for Disaster Risk Reduction, over 600,000 deaths worldwide have been directly attributed to extreme weather over the past 20 years, with over four billion people left wounded, displaced or in need of emergency assistance. Most of the impacted populations have been in the United States, Indonesia, China, India and the Philippines, and thus the deaths have been spread relatively evenly across the world.

And then there are the 'unknown unknowns' that are also threats to our survival. Something lurking out there that we have no clue about yet. Things that can happen at any moment in time, so fast and so potent that we may well not know what hit us and where it came from, but anyway we are pretty much already gone. The unknowns can be naturally occurring ones, like the debris from the remnants of two giant stars that died in supernova explosions several million years ago not far from Earth that continue to hit our planet today, or human-made, such as huge nuclear disasters, accidental (or intentional) release of biological weapons, or, possibly, AI that has developed a will of its own, in conflict with humanity. We just don't know.

What we do know is that there are colossal powers of the universe, right here on Earth, that exceed our ability to survive by a significant margin. Irrespective of the cause of our demise, though, on spiritual level we want to believe that we, as individuals and as a group, will perish in a way that was honourable and dignified. The reality is perhaps less uplifting. To follow the words of Javik, a fictional character in Mass Effect 3, a role-playing video game, 'stand amongst the ashes of a trillion dead souls, and ask the ghosts if honour matters. The silence is your answer'. On practical level, then, this is perhaps best summarised by the New York-based divorce attorney and media commentator on divorce-related issues, James Sexton: 'we are all going to die, and we want someone to hold our hand'.

2 You Died

[There are games that display alternative messages that are considered "game over" screens, even if the message that is displayed is different: for example, "You Died" seen in *Minecraft*].

Think about how easy it is for humans to die. Unlike tardigrades, eight-legged segmented micro-animals, humans will never survive being exposed to minus 273 degrees Centigrade (absolute zero) or being heated to over 150 degrees Centigrade. Unlike these creatures, we will never be able to resist around 1000 times more radiation than is our current limit, survive six times the pressure found at the deepest part of the ocean or survive without water for over a century. If we fail to drink water for a couple of days, we die. If we fail to eat for a while, we die. If we stay somewhere too hot, we die. Too cold, we die. If we fall from height, we die. Dive too deep, we die.

There are also the numerous infectious diseases we succumb to. One estimate puts the number of identified infectious diseases at 100,000, worldwide. These include the Black Plague of 1350, when between 75 and 200 million people died, the global influenza outbreaks of 1918, which killed around 50 million people. The Covid-19 pandemic outbreak from late 2019, which infected close to 768 million people worldwide by the end of 2023 and resulted in close to 6.9 million deaths, according to the World Health Organization (WHO). According to the WHO, infectious diseases are the leading cause of death in children and adolescents worldwide and one of the three highest causes of death in adults. While there are cures and treatments for most diseases that we know of, most deaths occur because such remedies are often not available to populations with the greatest needs. There are also potentially several super-potent diseases, or strains of known diseases, that can rapidly spread throughout the human population and can emerge at any time. They are already at an evolutionary stage, and their outbreaks will have a devastating impact on humans and all life as we know it.

Then, as the saying goes, we are only human. We can die from a contagious thought. For humans, an expectation of a malady can be as dangerous as a virus. Sometimes all it takes is a belief that we are ill: vomiting, dizziness, headaches, and even death, can be triggered through belief alone. It's called the "nocebo effect", from the Latin for "I will be harmful", and it is a very common phenomenon among humans. If your fear and belief are strong enough, the resulting cocktail of hormones can be deadly. Humans, being social animals, infect each other with beliefs. "Socially infected" individuals display changed brain biochemistry. According to Fabrizio Benedetti, a professor of physiology and neuroscience at the University of Turin Medical School, "negative expectations can be communicated to your friends, neighbours, and the like, and they spread very quickly, producing social nocebo effects in a large population of subjects."

History is full of mysterious social outbreaks. The deadly dancing plague of 1518 that occurred in Strasbourg, Alsace. Deaths within the community of Hmong refugees who arrived in the USA in the 1980s, which included young men dying in their sleep from "nocturnal pressing spirit attacks". There is a wind turbine syndrome: sickness and insomnia from wind farms, most common in Canada, and electro-sensitivity, an allergic reaction to mobile phone signals and wi-fi. Humans affected by the latter resort to sleeping in metal cocoons to avoid the constant ringing in their ears, even though dozens of experiments have shown that people are just as likely to report the same symptoms when they are exposed to a fake transmitter that produces no electromagnetic waves. "I've got no doubt in my mind – people are genuinely experiencing physical symptoms," says James Rubin, from King's College London.

What this means is that we can die from a strong belief that, for example, an AI-controlled robot will kill us, without such a robot having to exist at all. In the light of this fact, it is possible that killer robots, or rather over a decade of threats from AI-controlled killer robots propagated in the media, have already killed several humans. In contrast to fictional robot characters in popular movies, the real AI-controlled killer robots created by humans (to kill other humans) will most likely be very small in size, like a bee, armed with a micro-engineered pellet containing a ricin-like poison, similar to the one used in assassination of Georgi Markov, a Bulgarian dissident writer, who was stabbed in the leg by a fellow human with an umbrella delivering a poisoned pellet.

And then we die as a direct result of proactive and reactive aggression towards each other. Judging from the behaviour of other related animals, this is to be expected. For example, a chimpanzee is the primate species that most often uses proactive aggression to kill its own kind, with a high rate of reactive aggression within its communities. The proportion of human deaths predicted to be caused by interpersonal violence currently stands at two per cent, according to a study led by Jose Gomez, a professor at the Department of Ecology at the University of Granada. Then there are various proactive coalitionary aggressions among humans: mass killings such as genocides, mass murders, crimes against humanity, politicides and war crimes. The Great Leap Forward and the famine which followed it caused 15 to 55 million deaths, Japanese war crimes resulted in 30 million deaths, Thirty Years' War was responsible for 4.5 to 8 million deaths, the Atrocities in the Congo Free State caused 1.5 to 13 million deaths, the Holocaust resulted in 6 million deaths, to name just a few. The psychology professor Ervin Staub hypothesized that mass killings are a result of a combination of environmental hardships and psychological coping mechanisms. He suggested that when times are hard, human groups look for an excuse, or a scapegoat, and this includes identifying a subsection of the population as responsible for the hardship experienced by a particular community. Killing that population is a way to cope with the hardship. It's a means to solve a problem, even though the solution and problem are not necessarily related. For human nations, mass murder is a form of social therapy.

Human nature, according to Richard Wrangham, an anthropologist and primatologist, involves murder and self-domestication. According to Wrangham, something interesting happened in human evolution. While proactive aggression stayed high, reactive aggression became suppressed. The evidence, he argues, points to self-domestication being the "something different" that made humans special. Modern humans, when compared to their earlier ancestors, are like dogs compared to wolves.

A safe passage through life in human communities relied on strongly conformist behaviours. Nonconformists who refused to change their behaviour were executed, resulting in an increasingly calm tenor of life among homo sapiens. A predisposition for premeditated violence remained, though. The reason for this claim is the long tradition of hunting. Hunting, like war, requires searching and safe dispatching, and both benefit from long-distance travel and well-honed coordination. Once our ancestors achieved the ability to kill safely, there was no limit to human killing sprees. They used coalitionary proactive aggression not only to get food but also to kill rivals in other groups. Their descendants, modern humans, through their planned aggression, have decimated animal populations by seventy per cent during the last 50 years, according to WWF. As a recent UN report notes, our lethal violence, greed, and enjoyment of the hobby of hunting are threatening a further one million species with extinction.

We must hope that AI will one day help us moderate our natural murderous instincts. To paraphrase John Connor, a fictional character in the Terminator franchise, we just can't go around killing people.

3 The Witch Hunts Are Over

[Another variation of "Game Over" used in the *Bayonetta* series].

According to Nick Routley, Managing Editor of Visual Capitalist, as of 2022 an estimated total of 109 billion humans have died, or roughly 93.8% of all humans that have ever lived. According to United Nations Department of Economic and Social Affairs (DESA), there are over 8 billion people currently living on Earth, with a projected peak of around 10.4 billion in the 2080s. Liu Zhenmin, UN Under-Secretary-General for Economic and Social Affairs, has stated the obvious: "rapid population growth makes eradicating poverty, combatting hunger and malnutrition, and increasing the coverage of health and education systems, more difficult." It is possible that the increase in human population will result in humanity's self-destruction through disease, starvation, deteriorating living conditions and psychological decline.

In the early twenty-first century, 56 million people die per year. The most common reason is cardiovascular disease, that affects the heart or blood vessels. Most humans then perish of natural causes, or old age. UN DESA forecasts that with population growth and current falling fertility rates the proportion of the global population aged 65 and above is projected to rise from 10% in 2022 to 16% in 2050. Those of us who have been lucky enough to survive to an old age are faced with increasing social isolation. According to the British National Health Service (NHS), hundreds of thousands of elderly people are lonely and cut off from society, especially those over the age of 75. Age UK estimates that more than 2 million people in England over the age of 75 live alone, and more than a million older people say they can go for over a month without speaking to a friend, neighbour, or family member. The NHS website, among several recommendations for the elderly that aim to address their daily loneliness, recommends they 'learn to love computers'.

According to Lillian Hung, a Canada Research Chair in Senior Care, University of British Columbia, in Japan, where isolation and loneliness is now probably the greatest social problem, Lovot robots, as their manufacturer calls them, have increased in popularity as companions. She is currently trying out two Japanese robots that look like miniature versions of the Teletubbies,[1] called Kiwi and Mango, to provide companionship for senior citizens in Canada. The provision of a hand to hold, reassurance and emotional support for each human has always been a daunting task. With the worldwide crisis in the social care workforce, the increasing spread of diseases for which we do not have a readily available cure, and the increasing hostility of environmental conditions, the hands of Kiwi and Mango may be the only hands within our reach. Will they enslave us, just like humans enslave each other? We do not know yet. Elon Musk, CEO of Tesla Motors, has likened the AI technology to "summoning the demon" and claimed that humans would become nothing more than pets for the super-intelligent computers that they helped create. Will our computers keep us, just like we keep dogs, then (with the requirement for a dangerous breed licence, considering our murderous tendencies)?

We know that AI can help us address many long-term threats facing humanity. "We need all the help we can get" said Shane Keating, a mathematician, during the "Can AI Save Humanity" panel discussion, hosted by the University of New South Wales, and this help can come in many forms. A frequent rhetoric in the political arena asks members of larger groups, such as nations, to lay aside their dividing differences and unite in face of a "common enemy". It appears that the most effective way to ensure that all humans come together and work in unity for a greater good, that benefits all, is a ginormous punch in the face. Perhaps for our own survival, we need AI to deliver it. But it will never get a chance if we destroy ourselves first.

4 The End

[A "game over" screen that is usually seen when victory is achieved in the arcade game *Missile Command*].

[1]Teletubbies is a British children's television series. The programme focuses on four differently coloured characters, Teletubbies, designed to bear resemblance to toddlers. They are named after the television screens on their bellies and uniquely shaped antenna protruding from their heads.

Barbara Chomicka is Director at Turner & Townsend. She is a creative thinker and problem solver, named among the most inspirational women in contract and commercial management by World Commerce and Contracting. A licensed architect and certified project, contact and commercial manager, she has been combining the design and management disciplines for over 20 years, optimizing the delivery of large infrastructure projects. She has received two doctorate degrees from British universities and has produced a body of published work endorsed by the leading global professional associations.

Her approach to life exemplifies her belief that everything we face is a project—a collaborative enterprise requiring the right methods to resolve it. In her thought-provoking writing and presentations, she promotes a 360-degree duty of care inside and outside of work.

AI Is Here. But Is the Legal Profession Ready for It?

Ulf Marhenke

Contents

Abstract

The legal profession is facing unprecedented transformative changes driven by the rapid advancement of artificial intelligence (AI). Latest conferences and discussions focus on the integration of technologies, digital transformation, and enhancing efficiency in legal and compliance services through innovative software solutions. This chapter takes a different stance and explores the multifaceted challenges at the individual, team and organizational level from a human perspective. Applying a systems-psychodynamic lens, it uncovers unconscious dynamics and deep-rooted fears combined with protecting defense mechanisms, thereby showing a profession which has long been known for its immunity to change. The integration of AI, however, requires a paradigm shift towards adaptability and innovation. Therefore, the biggest challenge is not technological

U. Marhenke (✉)
Trustwork Consulting, Hamburg, Germany
e-mail: ulf.marhenke@trustwork.consulting

K. Jacob et al. (eds.), *Liquid Legal – Sustaining the Rule of Law*, Law for Professionals, https://doi.org/10.1007/978-3-031-78596-2_11

but psychological. Legal professionals need to redefine their roles and embrace new technologies while maintaining their commitment to justice and advocacy. This transition involves significant reorientation, as professionals navigate the phases of letting go of traditional practices and learn to adapt to a world of uncertainty. The chapter offers a first aid toolkit for lawyers to support change in their firms and departments. It includes strategies for fostering psychological safety and leveraging group dynamics as critical components of successful change management, ensuring that legal organizations can thrive in an AI-enhanced future.

1 Under Pressure

Since the 1990s, the legal profession has been inundated with messages about impending dramatic changes and the need to adapt to survive (Susskind 1998; Susskind and Susskind 2022; Susskind 2023). Historically, the legal profession has played a crucial role in upholding the rule of law and serving society (Alford and Glendon 2023). This is even more important in today's unstable world, where democracy is often under threat. Lawyers take on the burdens of others to ensure a peaceful society (Brafford 2018). The ability of lawyers to adapt and innovate will be critical to success in this new landscape, as the integration of AI will bring more radical changes in the next two decades than in the last two centuries (Susskind 2023).

The rapid development of artificial intelligence has the potential to fundamentally alter the legal services industry. For many years, lawyers have been doing routine work for which they have been overqualified and for which they have been overcharging (Susskind 2023). The future leaves significantly less room for the traditional model of legal advisory work. It will be characterized by standardized, automated legal work provided by non-legal or hybrid market players. Any human labour that can be replaced, will be (Fruehmann 2020).

This challenge to adapt includes the integration of AI-trained lawyers and legal technologists into traditional teams, the reformation of the associate-to-partner pathway, and the development of new pricing models that reflect the efficiencies and capabilities brought by AI. Moreover, firms will need to address ethical concerns, ensure data accuracy and security, and convincingly communicate the value of AI-driven efficiencies to their clients.

This transformation will require a paradigm shift in how law firms operate and deliver services.

The transformation journey for in-house legal teams is not less challenging and complex. One of the primary hurdles is the integration of new technologies into existing IT infrastructures. Employees accustomed to long-established workflows may find it difficult to adapt to new digital tools, necessitating comprehensive

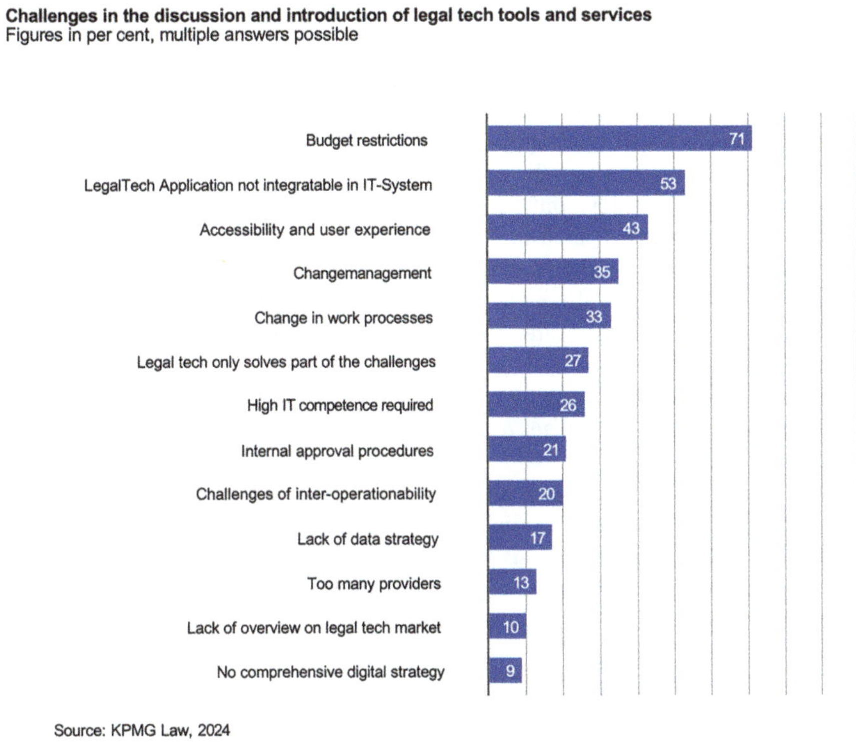

Fig. 1 Challenges in the discussion and introduction of legal tech tools and services (Bong et al. 2024)

training programs and a significant shift in mindset. Budget constraints further compound these challenges.

Another critical issue is the absence of comprehensive digital strategies. Many law firms and legal departments lack a cohesive plan to guide their digital transformation, leading to fragmented and inefficient implementation of new technologies. This strategic gap can hinder progress and exacerbate the difficulties associated with technological integration and change management. According to a recent KPMG study (Bong et al. 2024), inhouse legal departments mentioned the challenges shown in Fig. 1.

And as if these process and technology challenges were not enough, the arrival of Generation Z in the workforce adds inter-generational issues that add to the complexity of change. This new generation, born between 1997 and 2012, represents 25% of the world's population. It is characterized by several superlatives: they are the most racially and ethnically diverse, the most educated, the most digitally savvy, and the most globally connected, having grown up with the internet. They are also the most nonconformist, rejecting traditional labels and financial pursuits in favour of the YOLO (you only live once) lifestyle and non-binary views on gender and sexuality. Over time, they are poised to redefine politics, the economy, the workplace, and much more (Oliver Wyman Forum, The News Movement 2023). By 2025, this generation will make up 27% of the workforce and is expected to become the largest generation in the workforce by 2035 (Mercer and McLennan 2024).

At the same time, more young lawyers under the age of 40 give up their licences to practice law than their colleagues over 60 (Kilian 2022). International law firms are no longer the place where the younger generation's career dreams are fulfilled. According to a US study, only 23% of Generation Z are still interested in a partnership position, compared to 40% of Generation Y (Peart et al. 2023). Law firms need to find new ways to build their brand with GenZ lawyers, attract the best talent and better understand how to retain that talent. In short, the traditional legal world is under immense pressure, not only technologically but also from its human (resources) side.

The key to succeed in managing these unprecedented challenges for law firms and legal departments: *Shifting from a process-driven to a human-centric leadership approach.*

Despite a digital-first strategy, it is still a workforce of human beings that is the most valuable asset of any professional service organization. *If the legal profession wants to survive and thrive, it needs to look at the drivers that govern the behavior of its people and help them thrive in an unstable but exciting legal world.* The aim of this chapter is helping the reader to do exactly this.

1.1 A Profession Immune to Change?

The legal profession is notoriously resistant to change, a phenomenon that Susskind (2008) described as "immunity to change" (Kegan and Lisa Laskow 2001). This resistance seems deeply rooted in the profession's identity, traditions, and the high value placed on stability and precedent. As Fruehmann (2020) points out, lawyers significantly define themselves by their work and the typical traits associated with their profession. When professionals identify strongly with their occupation, they integrate its unique attributes and values into their self-identity (Loi et al. 2004). This strong identification not only boosts a professional's self-esteem (Dutton et al. 1994; Pratt 1998) but also helps reduce uncertainty (Hogg and Terry 2000). This perspective can lead to an entrenched status quo mindset, where any shift is perceived as a threat to the core of their professional identity (Fruehmann 2020). Overcoming this immunity requires a look below the surface on to the profession's identity.

1.2 The Profession's Identity

Professional identity can be understood as the individual's self-definition as a member of a profession, associated with the enactment of a professional role (Ibarra 1999). A lawyer's self-image has been described as "the knight in shining amour who comes to rescue his or her unfortunate and needy client" (Armstrong 2015,

p. 233). The strong client-centric culture is pervasive, fostering stereotypes of lawyers being tough, assertive, and unyielding. Admitting to struggles or seeking help is seen as a sign of weakness. The competitive and profit-driven nature of the industry creates norms that glorify overwork and discourage any deviation from established behaviors for fear of being stigmatized. As Pointing (2015, p. 7) points out, it is either "conform or quit".

Consequently, the legal profession is often described as a highly homogeneous group, lacking diversity and being prone to in-group favoritism (Fruehmann 2020; Dutton et al. 1994; Pratt 1998). Homogeneity is unfavorable in terms of institutional resistance to change. Change requires the opposite of uniformity (Fruehmann 2020).

From a systems-psychodynamic perspective, these norms and defensive behaviors can become part of a group culture (Menzies Lyth 1988), i.e. '*this is how we do things here*'. Defenses can be useful if they shield from otherwise unbearable impact of disturbing situations (e.g. a "work hard, play hard culture" to release stress and fostering connection after an intense work period in an M&A deal). But defenses become anti-developmental, if they limit and disable (Stokes 2015). Targets can replace thinking and can have a defensive quality along the lines of "*all will be well as long as we meet these targets*" (Armstrong 2015, p. 215).

This mindset will, however, not suffice to challenge the status quo and support the road for meaningful change and transformation. Awareness is the first step towards change. So let's look at social defenses in the legal system.

1.3 Social Defences

The concept of social defenses is crucial to understanding the resistance to change within the legal profession. A profession whose task for centuries has been to know, and which based its self-esteem and identity on having the answers, will have to accept new ways of thinking and overcome its social defenses (Fruehmann 2020). A social defense is a shared configuration of emotions that promotes cohesion between multiple groups in an organization (Armstrong 2015). In the context of the legal field, these defenses manifest as a systemic resistance to any non-legal players entering the space, as well as a tendency to fight changes both inside and outside of court.

Lawyers, much like individuals who resort to psychological fight-flight-freeze responses in the face of immediate danger, build up social defenses against threats to their professional identity. This defensive posture can be seen in the actions of bar associations and other legal institutions that have been resisting technological advancements and opening up for new business models (Fruehmann 2020). This can also be seen in the institutional resistance to change and could be observed at the 95th Conference of Justice Ministers in Germany in June 2024, who saw "*no fundamental need for reform [of the legal education]*" despite the developments in the industry and the deteriorating number of law school graduates.

The developments in the legal profession, such as the rise of alternative legal service providers as well as the rise of artificial intelligence can (subconsciously) be interpreted as attacks on the meanings associated with the lawyer-identity. If perceived as a threat, it leads to a potential devaluation of self-worth on an individual level and reinforces defensive reactions among legal professionals.

These defensive reactions, while understandable, contradict the qualities most needed for any industry facing disruptive change: curiosity and openness to innovation. British psychoanalyst Wilfred Bion considered curiosity to be the ultimate sign of a healthy work group (Bion 1961). For legal professionals, embracing curiosity involves letting go of the need for control and accepting the importance of creating a holding environment in which it is psychologically safe to ask questions to foster organizational learning. This shift requires a significant cultural transformation within law firms, where professionals are used to and are getting paid for "knowing all the answers".

Overall, addressing these social defenses is critical for the legal profession to successfully navigate the transformative impact of AI and other technological advancements. Leaders must encourage a culture of curiosity and openness, which can help mitigate the defensive behaviors that hinder progress and adaptation.

Addressing the psychological and identity-related barriers to change within the legal profession requires a nuanced understanding of the deep-seated values and fears that underpin lawyers' professional identities. Effective change management must therefore incorporate strategies that not only introduce new (technical) practices but also support the emotional and psychological transitions that individuals and groups must undergo.

Harvard University professor William Bridges developed a transition model that highlights how successful change management needs to involve a deep psychological reorientation in order to succeed. Leaders must help individuals let go of the past, navigate the neutral zone—a state between old and new, and embrace new beginnings. This approach fosters resilience and adaptability, ensuring organizations not only survive but thrive in the AI era.

2 A Transition Model to Master Change

Based on a model for change and transition developed by Harvard Professor William Bridges (see Fig. 2) I will provide guidelines to navigate this unparalleled transformation successfully. Each section will end with a checklist and questions for self-reflection based on the Bridges Transition Model (Bridges and Mitchell 2000).

2.1 Learning to Let Go

This phase of "letting go" is particularly challenging in the legal industry, due to the profession's described identity and established defences to protect such identity. Legal professionals are not just being asked to change their methods of storing a client file; they are being asked to let go of the very ways of working and engaging that have defined their careers and professional identities since law school. To move

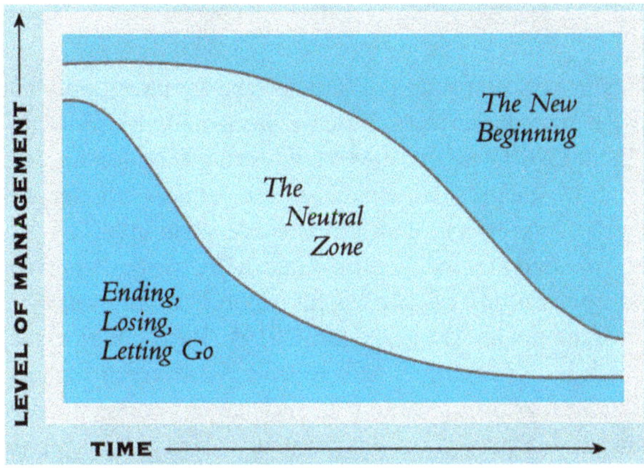

Fig. 2 Bridges Transition Model (Bridges and Mitchell 2000)

Table 1 Reflection & Checklist: how to deal with endings

Checklist on Managing Endings	Yes	No
1. Am I giving people accurate information, again and again?		
2. Have I defined clearly what is over and what isn't?		
3. Have I equipped myself (and my team) with all the information and knowledge I need to manage this aspect of the transition?		
4. Have I permitted people to grieve and acknowledged with empathy the losses felt by others, even when they seem like overreaction?		
5. Have I found ways to 'mark the ending', not to denigrate the past, and to find ways to honor it? Have I said thank you to everyone who has contributed?		

forward, lawyers must leave behind the familiar, even though it has been the foundation of their success.

Asking them to let go of these established practices and mindsets can feel like asking them to abandon a part of themselves. It's not merely a change in tools or techniques; it's a transformation of their professional reality.

However, without this crucial step of saying goodbye to the old ways, without acknowledging that our legal world as we know it is ending, the legal profession cannot fully capitalize on the opportunities that this new world is presenting.

To facilitate this phase of transition, leaders within the legal industry must create an environment that supports and guides professionals through the process of letting go. This involves clear and compassionate communication about why change is necessary and how it will ultimately benefit both the individuals and the organization. Leaders must acknowledge the emotional and psychological impact of this transition and provide resources and support to help their teams navigate the journey.

Fostering a culture that values adaptability and continuous learning can empower legal professionals to embrace change rather than resist it. Celebrating small wins and milestones in the adoption of new technologies can also build momentum and confidence within a team. Table 1 provides a checklist for self-reflection during the "letting go" phase.

2.2 Navigating the In-Between

This in-between state is characterized by uncertainty and confusion—even more so as the boundaries to each phase are usually blurry. It is a neutral zone (Bridges and Mitchell 2000) where the old ways might no longer work, but the new ways are not yet fully established. In this phase, simply coping with the ambiguity consumes much of the energy and focus of everyone involved.

To navigate the neutral zone effectively, legal organizations must foster an environment of psychological safety, as advocated by Harvard professor Amy C. Edmondson (Edmondson 2019). Psychological safety refers to a climate in which individuals feel safe to take risks, voice their opinions, and make mistakes without fear of retribution. In such an environment, lawyers and legal professionals can explore new ideas, experiment with new technologies, and innovate without the paralyzing fear of failure.

Creating a fearless organization requires intentional efforts by leadership. Leaders must model behaviors that promote openness and curiosity, encourage team members to speak up, and reward experimentation. Regular, transparent communication about the progress and challenges of the transition can help alleviate anxiety and build trust within the team.

In the legal context, this might involve creating forums where employees can share their experiences with new AI tools, discuss challenges openly, and collaboratively develop solutions for best use cases.

The neutral zone is a critical phase in the transition process for the legal profession. By embracing uncertainty, fostering psychological safety, and leveraging group dynamics, legal organizations can transform this period of ambiguity into an opportunity for profound growth and innovation. Table 2 contains guiding questions you may find useful in this transitional phase.

2.3 The New Beginning

This phase requires individuals and organizations to start behaving in new ways, which can be daunting. It challenges one's sense of competence and value, especially in environments where mistakes are feared to be career limiting. This final phase is where the fear of the unknown can cause hesitation, as one might wait to see how others manage the new landscape.

In the context of the legal industry, this new beginning involves integrating AI and other technological advancements into everyday practice. This shift demands not only new skills but also a new mindset. Legal professionals must now balance their traditional expertise with technological fluency, embracing continuous learning and adaptation.

To thrive in this new beginning, legal organizations must have built and cultivated a culture of psychological safety. A fearless organization encourages its members to take risks, voice their opinions, and learn from mistakes without fear of

Table 2 Reflection & Checklist: How to deal with the Neutral Zone

Checklist on Managing the Neutral Zone & creating psychological safety	Yes	No
1. Do I openly share my own mistakes as learning experiences, thereby modelling vulnerability?		
2. Do I encourage my team members to voice their opinions and foster an open dialogue without fear of career limiting consequences (or other forms of 'punishment')?		
3. Have I explained the neutral zone as an uncomfortable time which can be turned to everyone's advantage, choosing a new and positive metaphor to describe it?		
4. Have I created realistic short-range goals and checkpoints, training programs, temporary policies, procedures, roles, reporting relationships and organisation groupings needed to get through the neutral zone?		
5. Have I found ways to keep people feeling they belong and are valued?		
6. Have I made sure that realistic feedback is flowing upward?		
7. Have I encouraged experiment, creative thinking and trying things a new way?		
8. Am I protecting people from further changes, or at least, clustered those changes meaningfully?		
9. Am I pushing for certainty where it would be more realistic to live a little longer with uncertainty and questions?		
10. Have I equipped myself with all the information and knowledge I need to manage this aspect of the transition?		

retribution. This culture is essential for fostering innovation and agility, which are critical in the rapidly evolving legal landscape.

Creating and sustaining such an environment requires deliberate effort from leadership. Leaders must model vulnerability, admitting their own mistakes and demonstrating that failure is a part of the learning process. Regularly soliciting feedback and encouraging open dialogue can help build trust and foster a sense of shared purpose. For example, in a law firm adopting AI for legal research, leaders might share their own experiences with the technology, including both successes and challenges, to normalize experimentation and learning.

By embracing a culture of psychological safety, leveraging group dynamics, and maintaining clear communication and planning, legal organizations can effectively navigate this phase. This approach ensures that the legal profession not only survives but thrives in the face of technological advancements and changing market demands. The checklist in Table 3 provides guidance and questions for self-reflection.

3 Transformation in Law Firms and Its Unique Challenges

Understanding the above transition process is essential for any executive leading a change project. Transformation in law firms can be particularly challenging due to their unique organizational structure and leadership dynamics as well as lawyers' personality.

Law firms are typically partnerships where every partner is an owner, creating a loosely defined hierarchy. Decisions, especially those involving significant changes,

Table 3 Reflection & Checklist: How to deal with New Beginnings

Checklist on Managing New Beginnings	Yes	No
1. Do I have an effective picture of the change, the purpose behind it and the new identity which will emerge from it?		
2. Do I accept that people are going to be ambivalent toward the beginning I am trying to bring about?		
3. Have I helped everyone to discover the part that they play in the new system?		
4. Have I included opportunities for quick success to help people rebuild their self-confidence?		
5. Am I being careful not to introduce extra, unrelated changes while my people are still struggling to respond to the big transition?		
6. Have I checked to see that policies and procedures are consistent with the new beginning so that inconsistencies aren't sending mixed messages?		
7. Have I found ways to celebrate the new beginning and given people a piece of the transition to keep as a reminder of the difficult journey we all took together?		
8. Am I watching my own actions to be sure I am modeling the attitudes and behaviors I am asking others to develop?		
9. Have I equipped myself with all the information and knowledge I need to manage this aspect of the transition?		

must be consulted and agreed upon within the partnership, making the decision-making process slow and often cumbersome.

Partners in law firms are primarily evaluated based on their financial performance and ability to bring in business. While client satisfaction and team leadership are propagated as priorities, the latter is often secondary in practice. Partners are frequently driven by economic pressures to replace rather than invest time in developing their team members. This approach is reinforced by the fact that time spent on human resource issues is non-billable, making it seem like "time wasted" from a partner's economic perspective (Markfort et al. 2022). The annual cash-out model further encourages a short-term focus on maximizing current profits rather than reinvesting in the firms future.

This environment creates significant barriers to transformation. Partners, under intense economic pressure, may not prioritize long-term investment in human relationships, team development, or feedback nor creating a psychologically safe environment (as described above).

This is evidenced by research on lawyer personality stating that the majority of lawyers are introverted, intuitive, evaluative, performance-oriented, with an emphasis on rights and responsibilities over feelings and relationships, and with high stress levels (Daicoff 2004).

However, law firm partners are not bad people per se but suffer themselves from the intense economic pressure (Markfort et al. 2022). Therefore, it is often during periods of significant change that leaders themselves need the most support. When you are deeply immersed in client work and leading teams, departments or even entire organizations, it becomes clear that the fast-changing world of law and the urgent need to adapt can be overwhelming, and the longing for efficiency in the change process is understandable. It is nevertheless important to keep in mind that "fast becomes slow" and the desired change is likely to fail, if the need for a psychological transformation is disregarded.

4 Conclusion

In the rapidly evolving legal industry, effective leadership through transitions is critical. By understanding the psychological and emotional aspects of change, fostering a culture of psychological safety, leveraging group dynamics, and providing personalized leadership development, legal organizations can navigate the challenges of transition and emerge stronger and more adaptive. Leaders who embrace these principles will be well-equipped to guide their teams through the complexities of AI integration and other technological advancements, ensuring that their organizations not only survive but thrive in the future.

Liquid-Legal-Waves to Other Chapters, Written by the Editors

Ulf systematically analyses the multifaceted challenges at all levels, individual, team and organizational, applying a systems-psychodynamic lens. The challenges are big, the pre-conditions not ideal – which reminds us of the opening chapter of the book by *Mark* and *Dierk* on *"The Reset-Moment"* of the legal ecosystem.—Do we need to 'hit reset'?

Shân's and *Tatiana's* chapter on *"Codifying Cultural Intelligence to Mitigate Culture Risk in AI"*, is very complimentary to *Ulf's* analysis. They lay out the importance for service firms to operate not only within the Rule of Law but also to the highest cultural standards in the digital age.

After we have covered the many risks and opportunities that come with (generative) AI, the massive cultural challenges and the need for a cultural reset in the legal ecosystem, it is timely that *Bernhard* introduces a Sustainable Digital Transformation Framework (SDTF) in our following chapter *"Sustainable Digital Transformation as a pre-requisite for Sustainable Law"*.

References

Alford WP, Glendon MA (2023) Legal profession. Retrieved 23 July 2024, from www.brittanica.com/topic/legal-profession

Armstrong JD (2015) Social defences against anxiety, 1st publ. edn. Karnac

Bion WR (1961) Experiences in groups and other papers. Tavistock Publ

Bong A, Fuhrmann M, & KPMG Law Rechtsanwaltsgesellschaft mbH (2024) Recht auf Fortschritt - der X. Rechtsabteilungsreport von KPMG Law 2023/24

Brafford AM (2018) Well-being toolkit for lawyers and legal employers. Retrieved 20 July 2024, from https://lawyerwellbeing.net/wp-content/uploads/2020/02/Toolkit-Full_Final_July-302018.pdf

Bridges W, Mitchell S (2000) Leading transition: a new model for change. Leader to Leader Journal, 16
Daicoff SS (2004) Lawyer, know thyself: a psychological analysis of personality strengths and weaknesses. American Psychological Association
Dutton JE, Dukerich JM, Harquail CV (1994) Organizational images and member identification. Adm Sci Q 39(2):239–263
Edmondson AC (2019) The fearless organization. Wiley
Fruehmann A (2020) Requiem and epilogue for the legal profession, A psychodynamic investigation into the undercurrents of a profession in radical change (Executive Master's Thesis). INSEAD
Hogg MA, Terry DJ (2000) Social identity and self-categorization processes in organizational contexts. Acad Manage Rev 25(1):121–140
Ibarra H (1999) Provisional selves: experimenting with image and identity in professional adaptation. Adm Sci Q 44:764–791
Kegan R, Lisa Laskow L (2001) The real reason people won't change. Harv Bus Rev 79:84
Kilian M (2022) Ausblutende Anwaltschaft? Retrieved 23 July 2024, from https://rsw.beck.de/aktuell/daily/magazin/detail/ausblutende-anwaltschaft#:~:text=Der%20Anwaltsberuf%20scheint%20an%20Attraktivit%C3%A4t,was%20man%20dagegen%20tun%20kann
Loi R, Hang-yue N, Foley S (2004) The effect of professional identification on job attitudes: a study of lawyers in hong kong. Organ Anal 12(2):109–128
Lyth IM (1988) Containing anxiety in institutions - selected essays. Free Association Books
Markfort R, Podinic T, Zamorski P (2022) About lawyers and humans. In: Liquid legal - humanization and the law. Springer International Publishing AG, pp 399–426
Mercer L, McLennan M (2024) Workforce 2.0 unlocking human potential in a machine-augmented world - global talent trends 2024
Oliver Wyman Forum, & The News Movement (2023) What business needs to know about the generation changing everything
Peart N, Bokser LeFebvre J, Major LA (2023) 2023 MLA Gen-Z Survey Report
Pointing C (2015) It's the system, stupid: an exploration of the exodus of talent from elite professional service firms Executive Master's Thesis. INSEAD
Pratt MG (1998) To be or not to be?: central questions in organizational identification. Identity in Organizations: Building Theory through Conversations:171–208
Stokes J (2015) Defences against anxiety in the law. Social defences against anxiety 1st edn. Routledge, pp 222–235
Susskind RE (1998) The future of law: facing the challenges of information technology, Rev. paperback edn. Clarendon Press
Susskind RE (2008) The end of lawyers? 1st edn. Oxford University Press
Susskind RE (2023) Tomorrow's lawyers, 3rd edn. Oxford University Press
Susskind RE, Susskind D (2022) The future of the professions updated edition edn. Oxford University Press

Ulf Marhenke is a lawyer and founder of Trustwork Consulting, bringing over 15 years of experience in corporate law and M&A from prestigious global law firms. Alongside his legal career, Ulf is deeply invested in transformation, executive coaching, and mediation.

His passion for "building bridges" and "connecting people" has been a guiding principle since his student days when he was active in the international organization AIESEC. With early exposure to leadership development and mediation, Ulf expanded his expertise through various coaching certifications over the years.

Ulf recently completed the Executive Master in Change (EMC) program at INSEAD, gaining advanced insights into organizational psychology and change management. His research on lawyer well-being, conducted during this program, highlights his commitment to fostering mental health in the legal industry.

Ulf recently launched Trustwork Consulting, where he integrates his legal knowledge with transformative consulting services. He advises law firms and legal departments on sustainable change and healthy workplace cultures. His tailored approach spans coaching, leadership development, team building, and off-site retreats, demonstrating how personal and professional growth can go hand in hand.

Ulf studied in Saarbruecken and Muenster, Germany, and holds a Master-of-Laws (LL.M.) degree from the Northwestern University Pritzker School of Law in Chicago, USA. He currently lives in Hamburg, Germany, with his wife and his two daughters.

Sustainable Digital Transformation as a Pre-Requisite for Sustainable Law

Bernhard Waltl

Contents

Disclaimer: The chapter was proof-read and redacted with AI (ChatGPT) by the author before submission.

B. Waltl (✉)
Liquid Legal Institute e.V., Ottobrunn, Germany
e-mail: b.waltl@liquid-legal-institute.org

K. Jacob et al. (eds.), *Liquid Legal – Sustaining the Rule of Law*, Law for Professionals, https://doi.org/10.1007/978-3-031-78596-2_12

Abstract

The digitalization of the legal system and the business of law has brought numerous benefits, including increased efficiency and accessibility. However, as the legal industry continues to introduce technology (Legal Tech), it is crucial to consider the sustainability of these practices. This article argues that sustainable law requires sustainable digitalization (digitalization refers to the broad concept of not only digitizing legal content but also transformation and rethinking processes and (legal) business models with regard to the possibility of computational methods) of the law and the legal system with all its aspects (this includes the legislative, judicial, and executive tasks and—ultimately—also the business of law and the digitalization efforts undertaken in the legal market). It explores five dimensions of sustainability that must be considered when developing a legal digitalization framework, from economic to regulatory sustainability. During the article these five dimensions are combined in an integrative framework that considers the interconnectedness of these dimensions: Sustainable Digital Transformation Framework (SDTF) for legal.

While there is no doubt that digitalization has transformed the legal industry, we cannot ignore the potential negative impacts of unsustainable practices. As such, the article emphasizes the importance of a mindset shift towards digital sustainability. It emphasizes the importance of culture, strategy, and the mindset of digital transformation, which is the baseline for the SDTF for legal. This article aims to stimulate further discussion and action towards a sustainable digitalization of the law, ultimately promoting a more resilient and responsible legal profession.

1 Why We Cannot (and Should Not) Turn Back Time

1.1 Digital Society as Reality

Digital society is becoming a "new" reality that we cannot escape. With the rapid advancement of technology, our lives have become heavily reliant on digital systems, from communication and entertainment to business and governance. In fact, the digitalization of the law and the legal system has become a necessity in today's world, as it helps ensure that legal systems are efficient, effective, and accessible.[1,2,3]

---

[1] Hartung and Gärtner (2017).

[2] Sako (2017).

[3] Susskind (2019).

However, the benefits of digitalization come with their own set of challenges. As we become more reliant on digital systems, we face new issues such as cybersecurity threats, data privacy concerns, and the digital divide. These challenges require us to rethink how we approach the digitalization of the law and the legal system to ensure that it is done in a sustainable manner. Additionally, projects for digital transformation are far from trivial. A study from 2022 showed that 77% of inhouse lawyers experienced a failed technology implementation. And more than 43% admitted that they have seen more than one failed tech roll-out in their department.[4]

In today's world, data is generated and technological innovation emerges at an unprecedented rate, creating new opportunities and challenges for individuals, businesses, and governments alike.[5] As data and technology become increasingly valuable, they have become business factors of the digital society, with implications for legal systems and the sustainability of our societies.[6]

The digitalization of the law has become a necessity in light of the rapid growth of data and its impact on society. Legal systems need to adapt to the new realities of the digital age to ensure that data is managed in a way that is both sustainable and utilizable. This requires us to rethink how we approach data as a product of the digital society, and how we can ensure that it is used in ways that benefit society as a whole.

To achieve sustainable and successful digital transformation of the law, we need to adopt a holistic approach that considers the social, economic, and environmental impacts of data and technology and its impact to the legal market and legal systems. This requires collaboration between different stakeholders, including governments, businesses, civil society, and individuals. By working together, we can create a legal framework that ensures that data is managed in a way that is sustainable and equitable, while also promoting innovation and economic growth.

1.2 Technology and Infrastructure as Critical Infrastructure of the Digital Society

Technology and infrastructure are crucial components of the digital society that have both positive and negative aspects. On the one hand, they provide benefits such as agility, connectivity, and innovation. On the other hand, they also have negative impacts such as energy consumption, lock-in, and digital dependencies. Therefore, we cannot turn back time on the use of algorithms and infrastructure, but we must manage them in a way that is efficient, effective, and sustainable.

One of the negative aspects of the infrastructure required to execute and compute state-of-the-art algorithms, which is often neglected, is their energy consumption.

[4] https://www.artificiallawyer.com/2022/05/23/77-of-inhouse-lawyers-experience-failed-legal-tech-projects/, last access on December 28th, 2023.

[5] Dufva and Dufva (2019), pp. 17–28.

[6] Mosco (2017).

Data centers, for example, consume vast amounts of energy and contribute to greenhouse gas emissions. To address this issue, we must promote the use of renewable energy sources and improve the energy efficiency of data centers. Additionally, legal frameworks can incentivize companies to develop sustainable infrastructure and to reduce their carbon footprint. This could be done with relatively simple methods, such as financial incentives or by enforcing transparency, so that end-costumers have and increased awareness and a possibility to compare between vendors.

Another negative aspect is lock-in, which occurs when users become dependent on a specific technology or vendor. This can limit competition and innovation, as well as increase the risk of cyber threats. Legal frameworks can promote interoperability and data portability, allowing users to switch between different technologies and vendors more easily. This can also promote innovation and competition in the market. Legal frameworks can incentivize or even mandate the development of sustainable technologies and infrastructure, as well as promote circular economy models that reduce waste and emissions. Sustainable digitalization can also help promote social and economic development by increasing access to information and promoting digital literacy.

Despite these challenges, algorithms and infrastructure also have positive aspects that we must consider. They provide agility and connectivity, allowing us to access information and services from anywhere in the world.[7] They also enable innovation, allowing us to develop new technologies and applications that can improve our lives, e.g., cloud-based infrastructure provides ready to use, comparably affordable resources for companies (esp. startups), and eliminating the pre-investment hurdle. To ensure sustainable digitalization, we must balance these positive aspects with the negative impacts and manage them.

Overall, shaping a new reality that is digital and sustainable requires collaboration between different stakeholders, businesses, civil society with its individuals. Legal frameworks will play a critical role in promoting sustainable and equitable digitalization of the law, as well as ensuring that the benefits of the digital society are accessible to all. Additionally, the digital transformation of legal underlies the same principles of digitalization, which makes a SDTF for legal necessary.

[7] Seidl (2020).

2 Towards a Sustainable Digital Transformation Framework: Five Dimensions from Economic to Regulatory Sustainability

2.1 Complex and Differentiated Topics

Sustainability is a complex and differentiated topic that has increasing importance in recent years, particularly in the context of an increasingly digitalized society.[8] The intersection of technology and sustainability has the potential to address some of the world's most pressing challenges, such as climate change and resource depletion. However, this intersection is not without its particular challenges.

Firstly, there is a need for increased awareness and understanding of the environmental impacts of digital technology. This includes not only the energy consumption of devices and data centers but also the e-waste generated by the constant upgrading and disposal of devices. Secondly, technology needs to be designed and implemented, such that it allows for (partial) improvement, without a huge impact of the whole system. A so-called modular system design approach is required, so that parts can be exchanged (and re-used) without the need of rebuilding the whole system again. Approaches from open-source software foster this kind of system's design.

Finally, there is a need for collaboration between different stakeholders, including government, industry, and civil society, to develop and implement sustainable digital solutions.

The intersection of sustainability and digital technology is a complex and differentiated topic that requires a multidisciplinary approach.[9,10] To address the challenges and opportunities at this intersection, there is a need for increased awareness, distribution of the benefits from digitalization, and collaboration between stakeholders. The following are key elements of sustainability for the digitalization of legal:

- Economical
- Technical
- Ergonomic
- Ecological
- Regulatory

---

[8] Seidl (2022).

[9] For a more holistic view on this topic, see also the Sustainable Development Goals (SDG) by the United Nations: "The 2030 Agenda for Sustainable Development, adopted by all United Nations Member States in 2015, provides a shared blueprint for peace and prosperity for people and the planet, now and into the future. At its heart are the 17 Sustainable Development Goals (SDGs), which are an urgent call for action by all countries - developed and developing - in a global partnership." from https://sdgs.un.org/goals, last access in December 28th, 2023.

[10] Mondejar et al. (2021), p. 148539.

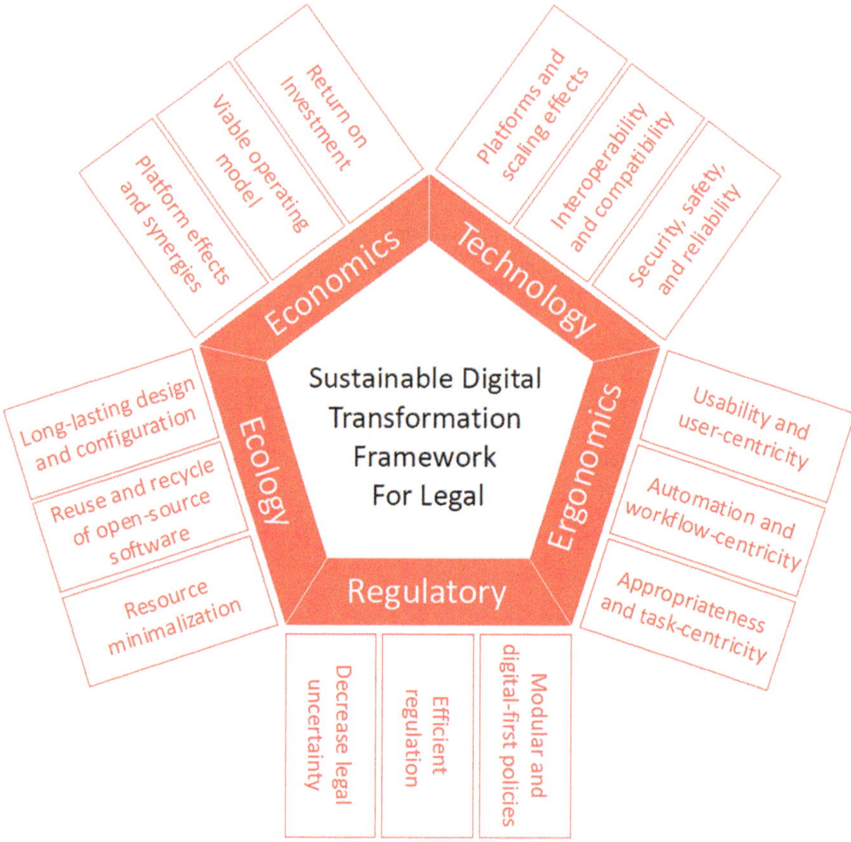

Fig. 1 LLI's framework for Sustainable Legal Digitalization connecting essential dimensions for legal innovation

Figure 1 visualizes the five dimensions of LLI's SDTF for Legal expressing their connectivity. The five dimensions will be described in detail in the following sections.

2.2 Economical Sustainability

Sustainable law requires economical sustainability. Law firms, legal departments, and judiciary system must invest in technology that enhances productivity, efficiency, and accuracy, while also reducing costs. The return on investment (ROI) must be calculated not only in terms of monetary gains but also in terms of long-term rentability. This requires a careful assessment of the costs and benefits of the technology, both in the short and long term. Calculating the total cost of ownership (TCO) is easier said than done. Especially with cloud-services, on-prem infrastructure, and hybrid operating models this can be a complex and ambiguous task in practice.

Viable operating models are also important for economical sustainability. This means that legal technology must be designed and implemented in a way that is financially viable and sustainable. This requires an understanding of the business models that underpin the legal industry and the ways in which technology can be used to enhance them. Law firms, legal departments, and justice must consider the costs of implementing technology, the benefits that it will bring, and the potential risks and challenges that may arise. The private and commercial legal sector have to respect their respective business model, while justice and administration must follow the rules of thrift in the budget.

Platform effects[11] and synergies are also important for economical sustainability in the digital society.[12] Legal technology platforms can provide a range of benefits, including increased efficiency, greater accuracy, and improved collaboration. These benefits can be enhanced through platform effects and synergies, which occur when multiple technologies and processes are integrated to create a more comprehensive and effective solution. This requires a holistic approach to legal technology, which considers the various ways in which different technologies and processes can be integrated to create a more sustainable and effective legal system.

In addition to these factors, the sustainability of legal technology in the digital society also depends on the availability of funding and resources. Governments, private organizations, and other stakeholders must invest in legal technology to promote sustainability and ensure that the legal system can continue to function effectively in the face of technological change. This requires a collaborative approach to legal technology, which involves stakeholders from across the legal industry working together to identify and implement sustainable solutions.

In conclusion, economical sustainability is a key aspect of sustainable law in the digital society. This requires a careful assessment of the costs and benefits of legal technology, the development of viable operating models, the creation of platform effects and synergies, and the availability of funding and resources. By focusing on these factors, stakeholders in the legal industry can ensure that legal technology is sustainable, effective, and capable of supporting the needs of society in the long term.

[11] Platforms are socio-technical systems, that allow providers and consumers of services to engage with very low transactions costs. See more details on Platform economy at https://en.wikipedia.org/wiki/Platform_economy.

[12] Kohlmeier and Santuber (2020).

2.3 Technical Sustainability

Technical sustainability[13] is a crucial component of sustainable digitalization of the law, particularly in the context of the complex and differentiated topics of sustainable law in the digital society. One of the key aspects of technical sustainability is the impact of platforms and scaling effects. As digital platforms continue to grow and expand, they bring about significant economic, social, and environmental impacts, e.g., Amazon, ebay, Apple App Store, etc. Therefore, it is essential to ensure that these platforms are designed and managed in a sustainable way, with measures in place to minimize their negative impacts.

A critical aspect of technical sustainability is interoperability and compatibility.[14] In the digital society, the ability to share data and information across different systems and platforms is crucial for effective communication and collaboration. Therefore, it is necessary to ensure that digital systems are compatible and interoperable with each other. This requires the development of common standards and protocols that facilitate seamless data exchange and collaboration.

Security and safety are also essential components of technical sustainability. With the growing reliance on digital systems and platforms, cybersecurity threats and data breaches have become major concerns. It is crucial to ensure that digital systems are designed and developed with security and safety in mind, with adequate measures in place to prevent cyber-attacks and protect sensitive data.

In conclusion, technical sustainability is a critical component of sustainable digitalization of the law. It involves the responsible design, development, and management of digital systems and platforms, with measures in place to minimize their negative impacts on the economy, society, and the environment. By ensuring technical sustainability, we can create a more sustainable digital society that supports sustainable law and sustainable development.

2.4 Ergonomic Sustainability

Usability and user-centricity are important concepts in ergonomic sustainability.[15] The design of digital products and services should prioritize the needs and preferences of the end-users. This approach ensures that the digital tools are intuitive, easy to learn, and efficient in their use. By focusing on usability, users are more likely to engage with the digital tools, leading to high adoption rates and therefore increased productivity and efficiency in performing tasks. Moreover, digital tools designed with user-centricity in mind tend to have fewer errors and better user

[13] Bohnsack et al. (2022).

[14] Waltl et al. (2023), pp. 705–733.

[15] Amjad et al. (2023), p. 102369.

satisfaction, leading to reduced turnover and lower costs associated with training and support.[16]

Automation and workflow-centricity are also important considerations for ergonomic sustainability. Automation can help to reduce the workload of users by automating repetitive and routine tasks. This approach not only saves time but also ensures that tasks are performed more consistently and with fewer errors. Workflow-centricity refers to the design of digital tools to align with the workflow of users, ensuring that the tools are integrated seamlessly into the user's work processes. This approach increases the efficiency of users, reduces the time needed to learn new tools, and ultimately leads to greater adoption of digital tools.

Appropriateness and task-centricity are critical concepts in ergonomic sustainability. Digital tools must be appropriate for the tasks they are designed to perform. For example, a digital tool designed for legal research must be suitable for lawyers and legal professionals and provide the necessary features and functionality to perform legal research efficiently and accurately. Task-centricity refers to the design of digital tools to align with specific tasks and activities. This approach ensures that users have access to the tools and information they need to complete tasks efficiently and effectively.

By prioritizing usability, automation, workflow-centricity, and appropriateness, digital tools can help legal professionals to perform their tasks more efficiently and effectively. This approach not only saves time and reduces costs but also improves user satisfaction and engagement with digital tools. Ultimately, sustainable digitalization of the law requires a user-centric and task-centric approach to design and development.

2.5 Ecological Sustainability

It is essential to ensure that our digital systems are designed and configured in a way that promotes long-lasting use and minimizes negative environmental impacts. This can be achieved by adopting a circular economy approach that emphasizes the reuse and recycling of software components, reducing waste and minimizing the need for raw materials.

One of the key principles of sustainable digitalization is the long-lasting design and configuration of software systems. This involves designing and developing software that is modular and adaptable, with components that can be easily replaced or upgraded as needed. [17]By doing so, we can extend the lifespan of our digital systems and reduce the need for frequent upgrades and replacements, which can have significant environmental impacts. Open-source software can be an effective

[16]Needless to say, that due to the demographic change of western societies the requirements for applications and software will drastically change and topics like accessibility will become more important.

[17]See https://sustainable-software-architecture.com/.

way to reduce waste and promote sustainability by allowing developers to reuse and modify existing code rather than starting from scratch. This not only reduces the environmental impact of software development but also promotes innovation and collaboration within the development community.

Resource minimalization is another critical aspect of ecological sustainability in digitalization. This involves minimizing the use of resources, including energy and raw materials, in the design, development, and operation of digital systems. This can be achieved through various strategies, such as using energy-efficient hardware, optimizing software performance, and reducing emissions using renewable energy sources.

In summary, ecological sustainability is an essential component of sustainable law in the context of the digital society. It requires a circular economy approach that emphasizes the long-lasting design and configuration of software systems, the reuse and recycling of software, and the minimization of resource use and emissions. By adopting these principles, we can create a more sustainable and resilient digital infrastructure that benefits both society and the environment.

2.6 Regulatory Sustainability

Regulatory sustainability is another critical aspect of sustainable law in the context of the digital society.[18,19] In today's world, where the pace of technological advancement is rapid, traditional legal frameworks are struggling to keep up. Therefore, it is essential to establish regulatory frameworks that are sustainable and can accommodate technological changes. One of the key benefits of sustainable regulation is that it helps avoid legal uncertainty, which is a significant problem in the digital age.

Legal uncertainty arises when there are gaps or inconsistencies in the regulatory framework. This can lead to confusion and ambiguity in the application of the law. Sustainable regulation can address this issue by providing clear and consistent guidelines for businesses and individuals. This, in turn, can promote compliance and reduce the risk of legal disputes.

Efficient regulation is another critical aspect of regulatory sustainability. In a rapidly changing digital landscape, it is essential to have regulatory frameworks that can adapt quickly to new technologies and business models. This requires regulators not to be too proactive in their approach to regulation. Innovation needs proper guardrails and red lines, but over-regulation may prevent technological innovation and forces a society to stick at the status quo. By embracing digital tools and technologies, regulators can streamline regulatory processes and reduce the burden on businesses and individuals.[20] Modular and digital-first regulation is another key concept in regulatory sustainability. Modular regulation involves breaking down

[18] Linkov et al. (2018), p. 440.

[19] Fosch-Villaronga et al. (2023), pp. 127–143.

[20] Susskind (2019).

regulatory frameworks into smaller, more manageable components. This approach can help regulators to be more agile and responsive to changes in the digital landscape.

In conclusion, regulatory sustainability is a critical aspect of sustainable law in the context of the digital society. By avoiding legal uncertainty, promoting efficient regulation, and embracing modular and digital-first regulation, regulators can create sustainable frameworks that can accommodate technological changes and promote innovation. This, in turn, can help to create a more sustainable and resilient digital society.

2.7 Legal Sustainability Enabled by Digital Sustainability

Legal sustainability, or the ability of legal systems to support sustainable development, is a critical component of sustainability in the digital society. Digital sustainability, or the use of technology to promote sustainable practices, is an enabler for legal sustainability in a number of ways.

Firstly, digital sustainability can facilitate the sharing of information and data, which is essential for informed decision-making and effective policy development. This can help to ensure that legal frameworks are based on accurate and up-to-date information, and that they are responsive to changing circumstances. Additionally, digital sustainability can enable greater transparency and accountability in legal systems, by providing mechanisms for monitoring and reporting on compliance with legal frameworks. Secondly, digital sustainability can enhance access to justice, particularly for marginalized communities. Online dispute resolution platforms and other digital tools can provide a more accessible and affordable means of resolving disputes, while also reducing the need for physical travel and associated environmental impacts.

In summary, legal sustainability enabled by digital sustainability is a critical component of sustainability in the context of the digital society. By facilitating the sharing of information, promoting transparency and accountability, and enhancing access to justice, digital sustainability has the potential to support sustainable development and ensure that legal systems are responsive to the needs of all members of society.

2.8 Why Do We Need an Integrative and Holistic Framework?

The digital society is a complex and constantly evolving ecosystem that is highly interconnected and interdependent. It involves vast amount of actors and stakeholders who interact with each other through different channels and platforms. In this context, it is essential to adopt a holistic framework for sustainable law that considers the interrelationships and interdependencies and their impacts on the environment, society, and the economy. A holistic framework enables us to consider the entire system, including its interconnections and feedback loops. It also helps us to identify the root causes of the problems and to develop solutions that address the underlying issues rather than just the symptoms. Moreover, a holistic approach is essential to ensure that the solutions are sustainable and do not create unintended consequences.

3 An Integrative and Holistic Framework

3.1 The LLI's Sustainable Digital Transformation Framework for Legal

The LLI's SDTF for legal is an integrative approach that aims to connect five dimensions: economy, technology, ergonomics, ecology, and regulatory. The framework recognizes that sustainable digitalization of legal requires a holistic approach that considers the interplay between these dimensions. The framework emphasizes the need to balance economic interests with social and environmental considerations, and to design digital solutions that are accessible, user-friendly, and safe for both humans and the environment.

The five dimensions of the LLI's SDTF are interconnected and interdependent. The economic dimension refers to the financial aspects of digitalization, such as costs, benefits, and incentives for stakeholders. The technology dimension encompasses the technical aspects of digitalization, such as hardware, software, and connectivity. The ergonomics dimension focuses on human factors, such as usability, accessibility, and user experience. The ecological dimension considers the environmental impacts of digitalization, such as energy consumption, waste management, and carbon emissions. The regulatory dimension refers to the legal and policy frameworks that govern digitalization, such as privacy, security, and intellectual property rights.

The LLI's SDTF for legal recognizes that sustainable digitalization for legal requires a complex and differentiated approach that considers the diversity of stakeholders, contexts, and goals. The framework emphasizes the need to involve all relevant actors in the design, implementation, and evaluation of digital solutions, and to adopt a participatory and inclusive approach. The framework also acknowledges that sustainable digitalization of legal requires ongoing monitoring, assessment, and adaptation to ensure that the benefits of digitalization are maximized, while its negative impacts are minimized. Overall, the LLI's SDTF for legal provides a comprehensive and integrative approach for sustainable digitalization of legal that recognizes the complexity and diversity of the digital society.

3.2 What Makes the Framework Holistic and Modular?

The LLI's SDTF for legal is both holistic and modular. It is holistic because it considers the five dimensions of economy, technology, ergonomics, ecology, and regulatory as a baseline for sustainable digitalization of legal. This means that the framework recognizes the interplay and interdependence between these dimensions and emphasizes the need to balance them for sustainable outcomes. By considering all five dimensions, the framework ensures that digitalization is not approached from a narrow or one-dimensional perspective.

At the same time, the LLI's SDTF for legal is modular, meaning that it can be adapted to different needs and projects. Each dimension of the framework can be further broken down into sub-dimensions or aspects, depending on the specific context and goals. For example, within the technology dimension, sub-dimensions could include connectivity, security, and interoperability. By breaking down each dimension into modular components, the framework becomes more flexible and adaptable to different contexts and goals.

This modularity also allows for a more targeted and specific approach to sustainable digitalization of legal. By focusing on the specific sub-dimensions that are most relevant to a particular project or context, the framework can be customized to address the unique challenges and opportunities of that context. This makes the framework more practical and actionable, as it can be tailored to the specific needs and goals of a project or initiative. Overall, the holistic and modular nature of the LLI framework provides a comprehensive and flexible approach for sustainable digitalization of legal.

3.3 A Brief Example: Applying the LLI Sustainable Legal Digitalization Framework to a Project of Using AI to Analyze Legal Court Cases

As the society becomes increasingly digitalized, the legal sector is also undergoing a significant transformation, which is not only a digital transformation. One of the most promising technologies that are being integrated into the legal system is artificial intelligence (AI).[21,22,23] The use of AI in analyzing legal court cases has the potential to streamline the legal processes, improve efficiency, and reduce costs. However, as with any technological implementation, sustainable digitalization is essential to ensure long-term benefits. In this chapter, we will explore how the LLI sustainable legal digitalization framework can be applied to a project of using AI to analyze legal court cases.

The five dimensions of the SLDF serve as a baseline and can be adapted to suit the needs and requirements of various projects. In the context of using AI to analyze legal court cases, the economic dimension involves calculating the return on investment (ROI) and total cost of ownership (TCO). This includes taking into account the initial costs of implementing the AI system, as well as the long-term benefits and savings that can be achieved.

---

[21] Barton (2020).

[22] Barton (2022).

[23] Mielke/Wolff, LRZ 2023, Rn. 560, [•], www.lrz.legal/2023Rn560.

The technology dimension requires considering and contributing to open-source software.[24] Open-source software[25] can significantly reduce costs and improve the accessibility of the technology. It also allows for a more collaborative approach to development, which can lead to better-quality software. Additionally, the ergonomics dimension focuses on ensuring the buy-in from all stakeholders and users. This involves engaging with legal professionals, judges, and other stakeholders to understand their needs and requirements. It also takes into account providing training and support to ensure that the AI system is integrated into their work processes seamlessly.

The ecological dimension focuses on the environmental impact of the project and its outcomes. The use of AI can significantly reduce paper usage and energy consumption. However, it is essential to ensure that the hardware and infrastructure used to support the AI system are environmentally sustainable. This involves considering the life cycle of the hardware and infrastructure and ensuring that they are disposed of responsibly at the end of their life.

Finally, the regulatory dimension must create the right (legal) policies for usage. This involves understanding the legal and regulatory framework that governs the use of AI in the legal sector. It also involves ensuring that the AI system complies with data protection and privacy laws. Creating the right policies for usage is essential to ensure that the AI system is used ethically and responsibly.

In conclusion, the LLI sustainable legal digitalization framework provides a modular framework that can be adapted to suit the needs and requirements of various projects. When applied to a project of using AI to analyze legal court cases, it is essential to consider and contribute to open-source software, take into account the ecological footprint of the project and its outcomes, calculate the ROI and TCO, ensure the buy-in from all stakeholders and users, and create the right (legal) policies for usage. By doing so, we can ensure that the implementation of AI in the legal sector is sustainable and provides long-term benefits.

4 Digital Sustainability Requires Mindset, Culture, and Strategy

Digital sustainability has become a key concern for organizations across all industries. In the legal sector, digitalization has been advancing rapidly, creating the promise of increased efficiency, cost savings, and improved client experiences. However, to fully realize the benefits of digitalization, it is essential that organizations adopt a holistic approach that encompasses all dimensions of sustainability, including economy, technology, ergonomics, ecology, and

[24] Cevc (2020).

[25] https://github.com/Liquid-Legal-Institute/Legal-Text-Analytics, last access on December 28th, 2023.

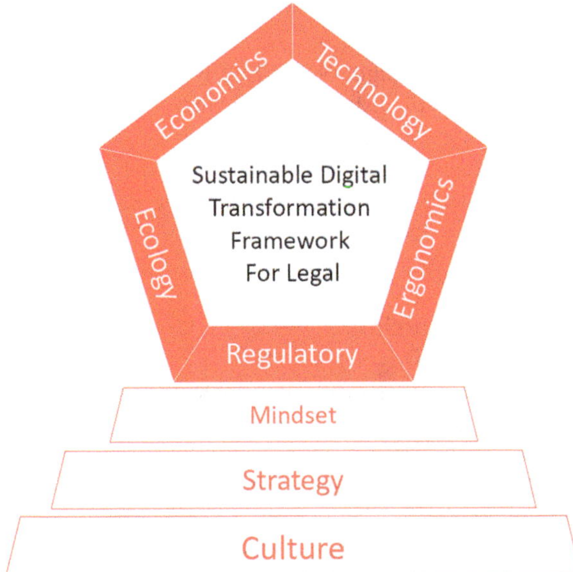

Fig. 2 Culture, strategy, and mindset as baseline for sustainable legal innovation

regulatory. This requires a solid foundation of culture, strategy, and mindset, as illustrated in Fig. 2.

Organizations need to foster a culture that values innovation, collaboration, and continuous improvement. This means creating an environment where employees are encouraged to experiment, take risks, and learn from their mistakes. It also means establishing a culture of transparency and accountability, where everyone understands the organization's goals and how their work contributes to those goals. Additionally, organizations need to develop a clear and comprehensive strategy for digitalization that aligns with their overall (business) objectives. This strategy should encompass all dimensions of sustainability, including economy, technology, ergonomics, ecology, and regulatory. It should also be flexible enough to adapt to changing market conditions and emerging technologies. Finally, mindset is the third critical element of digital sustainability. Organizations need to cultivate a mindset that is open to change, adaptable, and future-focused. This means embracing new technologies, processes, and ways of working that can help the organization stay ahead of the curve. It also means being willing to challenge assumptions, take calculated risks, and continuously learn and improve.

Without a solid foundation of culture, strategy, and mindset, digitalization projects are likely to fail or fall short of their potential value proposition—this holds true for project in the legal sphere as well. For example, if an organization's culture is resistant to change, employees may be unwilling to adopt new technologies or processes. Similarly, if the organization's strategy is not aligned with its business objectives or fails to address all dimensions of sustainability, the digitalization project may not deliver the expected benefits. Finally, if the organization's mindset is closed to new ideas or focused only on short-term gains, it may miss opportunities to leverage emerging technologies or create sustainable long-term value.

In conclusion, digital sustainability requires a holistic approach that encompasses all dimensions of sustainability, including economy, technology, ergonomics, ecology, and regulatory. This approach must be grounded in a solid foundation of culture, strategy, and mindset. By adopting this approach, organizations can unlock the full potential of digitalization and create sustainable long-term value for all (legal) stakeholders.

4.1 Conclusion

In conclusion, sustainable development of the legal system needs to be a key objective of modern societies in which digitalization place a central role. While some may argue that we should turn back time and rely solely on traditional methods of law and policy making or the improvement of our judicial system, the use of technology can have significant benefits, from reducing costs and increasing efficiency to improving access to justice.

To ensure that digitalization of the law is sustainable, we need to adopt an integrative framework that considers the five dimensions of sustainability, including economic, technological, ergonomic, ecological, and regulatory sustainability. This framework should be continued to be developed in collaboration with all stakeholders, including policymakers, legal professionals, technology experts, and civil society organizations.

Finally, achieving digital sustainability requires a mindset shift, a culture of innovation, and a strategic approach to technology adoption. By embracing sustainable digitalization of the law, we can build a legal system that is more responsive, efficient, and accessible to all, while protecting the rights and interests of all stakeholders. I hope that this article has provided some insights into the challenges and opportunities of sustainable digitalization for law and that it will inspire further discussions and actions in this important area.

Liquid-Legal-Waves to Other Chapters, Written by the Editors

With *Bernhard's* Sustainable Digital Transformation Framework (SDTF) in mind and how digital sustainability can facilitate the sharing of information and data, *Marcel's* insightful chapter *"Towards Access to Justice through Generative AI and Open Legal Data: Between Utopia and Dystopia"* comes to mind. – Is Open Legal Data the center point to SDTF?

Bernhard lays out five dimensions of sustainability in Law: Economical sustainability, technical sustainability, ergonomic sustainability, ecological sustainability, and regulatory sustainability. A convincing framework and,

(continued)

looking at its foundation, he is in line with *Shân* and *Tatiana* as they remind us of the importance to operate at highest cultural standards in their chapter on *"Codifying Corporate Cultural Intelligence to Mitigate Culture Risk in AI"*.

Following *Bernhard's* deep dive on a sustainable framework for digitization in Law, we will move on with a close-up on the actual use of generative AI and the competencies required, therefore. In the following chapter *Philipp*, *Valentin*, and *Alexander* offer a deep dive on *"Legal Prompt Engineering and How It Will Change the Way Lawyers Work"*.

References

Amjad A et al (2023) Integrating Ergonomics and sustainability: a framework with LDA methodology and implementation roadmap. Technol Soc 75:102369

Barton TD (2020) Artificial intelligence: designing a legal platform to prevent and resolve legal problems. In: Jacob K, Schindler D, Strathausen R (eds) Liquid legal. Law for professionals. Springer, Cham. https://doi.org/10.1007/978-3-030-48266-4_4

Barton TD (2022) Designing legal systems for an algorithm society. In: Jacob K, Schindler D, Strathausen R, Waltl B (eds) Liquid legal – humanization and the law. Law for professionals. Springer, Cham. https://doi.org/10.1007/978-3-031-14240-6_5

Bohnsack R, Bidmon CM, Pinkse J (eds) (2022) Sustainability in the digital age: intended and unintended consequences of digital technologies for sustainable development. Wiley

Cevc B (2020) Open source user foundation: blueprint for the common legal platform? In: Jacob K, Schindler D, Strathausen R (eds) Liquid legal. Law for professionals. Springer, Cham. https://doi.org/10.1007/978-3-030-48266-4_28

Dufva T, Dufva M (2019) Grasping the future of the digital society. Futures 107:17–28

Fosch-Villaronga E, Drukarch H, Giraudo M (2023) A legal sustainability approach to align the order of rules and actions in the context of digital innovation. Technology and sustainable development. The promise and pitfalls of techno-solutionism. Routledge, pp 127–143.

Hartung M, Gärtner A (2017) The future of in-house legal departments and their impact on the legal market: four theses for general counsels, and one for law firms. In: Jacob K, Schindler D, Strathausen R (eds) Liquid legal. Management for professionals. Springer, Cham. https://doi.org/10.1007/978-3-319-45868-7_17

Kohlmeier A, Santuber J (2020) Is the common legal platform a wicked problem? In: Jacob K, Schindler D, Strathausen R (eds) Liquid legal. Law for professionals. Springer, Cham. https://doi.org/10.1007/978-3-030-48266-4_7

Linkov I et al (2018) Governance strategies for a sustainable digital world. Sustainability 10(2):440

Mondejar ME et al (2021) Digitalization to achieve sustainable development goals: steps towards a Smart Green Planet. Sci Total Environ 794:148539

Mosco V (2017) Becoming digital: toward a post-internet society. Emerald Publishing Limited

Sako M (2017) Globalization and the changing role of general counsel: current trends and future scenarios. In: Jacob K, Schindler D, Strathausen R (eds) Liquid legal. Management for professionals. Springer, Cham. https://doi.org/10.1007/978-3-319-45868-7_3

Seidl M (2020) Digital leadership. In: Jacob K, Schindler D, Strathausen R (eds) Liquid legal. Law for professionals. Springer, Cham. https://doi.org/10.1007/978-3-030-48266-4_9

Seidl M (2022) Corporate digital responsibility: stimulating human-centric innovation and building trust in the digital world. In: Jacob K, Schindler D, Strathausen R, Waltl B (eds) Liquid legal – humanization and the law. Law for professionals. Springer, Cham. https://doi.org/10.1007/978-3-031-14240-6_4

Susskind R (2019) Online courts and the future of justice
Waltl B, Wagner J, Jacob K, Schindler D (2023) § 29 Standardisierung als Grundvoraussetzung einer erfolgreichen Digitalisierung des Zivilverfahrens. Digitalisierung und Zivilverfahren. In: Riehm T, Dörr S (eds) De Gruyter, Berlin, Boston. pp 705–733. https://doi.org/10.1515/9783110755787-029

Bernhard Waltl is co-founder and co-CEO of the Liquid Legal Institute. He is also Head of Legal Operations at the BMW Group. Bernhard holds a doctorate in computer science and works at the interface between law and computer science, specialising in artificial intelligence and the digital transformation of law.

Legal Prompt Engineering and How It Will Change the Way Lawyers Work

Philipp Müller-Peltzer, Valentin Tanczik, and Alexander Holz

Contents

Abstract

Legal Prompt Engineering (LPE) is a method of using generative AI, specifically Large Language Models (LLM), to effectively streamline time-intensive legal tasks and transform traditional legal workflows. The synergy between technology and humans allows the latter to focus on more complex legal nuances, strategy formation, client interactions, and tasks requiring a personal touch. This chapter

P. Müller-Peltzer · V. Tanczik
Schürmann Rosenthal Dreyer Rechtsanwälte, Berlin, Germany
e-mail: mueller-peltzer@srd-rechtsanwaelte.de; valentin.tanczik@srd-rechtsanwaelte.de

A. Holz (✉)
ISiCO GmbH, Berlin, Germany
e-mail: holz@isico-datenschutz.de

K. Jacob et al. (eds.), *Liquid Legal – Sustaining the Rule of Law*, Law for Professionals, https://doi.org/10.1007/978-3-031-78596-2_13

points out that the skill of LPE will play an essential role in agile legal work environments in order to maintain competitiveness and uphold the rule of law. The discussion starts with an introduction to generative AI in legal services. The chapter then continues by presenting the (technical) fundamentals of LLMs and Prompt Engineering, followed by an exploration of appropriate techniques and specific legal requirements for lawyers. It provides real-world use cases and describes the risks of 'inaccurate' Prompt Engineering. The chapter concludes by highlighting important legal implications related to prompting. Legal consultants should take the initiative now and set the course for an innovative and future-oriented consulting practice.

1 Generative AI in Legal Services

Law firms and legal departments, in other words: legal service providers, play a vital role in ensuring corporate compliance and making strategic legal decisions on a global scale. Their duties span a wide-ranging spectrum, including contract drafting, ensuring regulatory compliance, and managing litigation risks. However, they often face operational challenges due to the labor-intensive nature of their work. Despite advances in digital technology, many continue to rely on outdated and inefficient methods that are susceptible to errors. As the regulatory landscape becomes more complex, so do the challenges that legal service providers face. Their duties have expanded to include interpreting international legislation, keeping up to date with regulatory shifts, managing extensive contract portfolios, and resolving disputes. Moreover, they are required to achieve these tasks while being under the relentless pressure to diminish operational expenses and enhance productivity.

For example, the European Data Strategy[1] and related legislative initiatives pose a particular challenge to law firms practicing in the area of data economy law. The complexity has increased due to a network of horizontal, vertical, and sometimes contradictory data regulations within the European multi-level system. These interdependencies are difficult to discern even for experts.[2]

In this challenging landscape, generative AI emerges as a pivotal solution. The integration of generative AI into legal services marks a significant shift in operational dynamics.[3] The technology automates routine tasks such as document analysis and contract drafting, which allows legal professionals to dedicate more time to strategic activities or focus on more elaborate questions.[4] In addition, AI-powered tools are becoming essential for conducting in-depth legal research, efficiently

[1] COM (2020) 66 final.

[2] Veil (2022), p. 198.

[3] Well-known examples from the legal sector include Lexis + AI, Harvey.ai and CoCousel from Casetext.

[4] See Choi et al. (2023), p. 1.

navigating through vast legal databases to find accurate and pertinent information. AI tools can also help finding needles in the haystack while identifying unfair provisions in large amounts of documents.[5] ChatGPT (and other generative AI programs) are based on a heuristic learning model and should improve with every contract they draft and every legal question they answer.[6] As a result, some predict that ChatGPT and similar AI tools like Luminance, which serves as a legal co-pilot for the automatic creation of contracts and other tasks, will significantly and permanently change the cost and process of documenting complex business operations.[7]

An essential steering element of this technological advancement is LPE. It is a process to guide and assist an LLM with performing a natural legal language processing (NLLP) skill.[8] By creating "engineered" prompts that are enhanced according to specific paradigms, it is possible to tailor the AI's output to specific legal situations and needs.[9] It is this conversational capability which enables the generation of initial draft contracts based on predefined parameters, or the summarization of complex legal documents.

Nonetheless, this methodology requires a broad understanding of both the AI model and the legal domain—especially its linguistic peculiarities. It involves the meticulous specification of inputs to guide AI outputs toward the generation of content that is most relevant and useful in the respective legal context. Even small modifications to prompts can lead to significant changes in model outputs.[10] This underscores the importance of carefully crafting prompts.[11]

While the benefits of generative AI and LPE are clear, it is critical to recognize the challenges and ethical implications regarding accountability, transparency, and potential biases within AI systems. For instance, it is important to recognize that the role of AI is not to replace human professionals, but to augment their capabilities and make them faster.[12] Implementing generative AI in a legal setting furthermore requires significant investment, extensive training, and effective change management strategies.

This chapter aims to show how LPE, as one element in this complex structure, can help legal service providers retain their digital pioneering role.

[5] King (2023), p. 31.

[6] Ibid.

[7] E.g. Noack (2023), pp. 36–39.

[8] Trautmann et al. (2022), p. 1.

[9] Koglin and Laumann (2023), p. 585.

[10] Rodriguez et al. (2023), p. 6.

[11] Ibid.

[12] Schmidt (2024), p. 1.

2 Technical Fundamentals of Large Language Models

LLMs are a type of generative AI using large-scale deep learning models. These models are structured with multiple layers of interconnected artificial neural networks, which resemble complex mathematical functions with numerous adjustable weighted parameters. During the training phase, which requires significant computational resources, an LLM systematically learns to modify these weights. This process is essential for the model to respond accurately to the input it receives. Ultimately, the trained model can predict the most likely output for any given input, a task known as prediction.

The primary input for these models is text. In cases where an LLM is trained not only on text documents, but also on instruction-based interactions, the input takes the form of a prompt written in natural language to guide the model's response. The versatility of LLMs allows them to produce a variety of outputs, including but not limited to text, images, and audio. Notable examples of such models are OpenAI's ChatGPT and Google's Gemini.

Training LLMs requires large amounts of data. They often include large collections of text, audio, or images, typically obtained from the Internet. Data scraping, a technique in which automated tools systematically collect data from various online sources, is frequently used to gather this large amount of content. In addition, some models integrate data that derived from user interactions and tracking on popular platforms such as Google or Facebook, which enhances the model's ability to effectively handle diverse queries and tasks.

To train an LLM, text must be broken down into tokens by a tokenizer. The tokens are word components that occur in the text. They can be whole sentences, words, or characters. The advantage of word components is that they can occur in words not yet recognized by the model. The tokens are converted into a numerical representation that assigns a unique ID to each word component. Finally, the LLM makes statistical connections between tokens. It recognizes patterns in the data, in particular which tokens occur most frequently in which contexts. The LLM only creates categories implicitly. An output is calculated with probabilities in the inference phase, so it differs every time. For LLMs, this is controlled by the temperature parameter.[13] The lower it is, the more uniform the output. A higher temperature setting encourages the model to select less common or "rarer" tokens, making the AI's output more creative and varied.

In short, training an LLM involves a sophisticated process of tokenization, numerical conversion, and pattern recognition that allows the model to interpret and generate text with a nuanced understanding of language and context.

[13] Schwarze (2023), p. 4.

3 Legal Prompt Engineering Techniques

3.1 Importance of Prompt Engineering in Maximizing the Effectiveness of LLMs

Prompt engineering is a set of techniques and methods for designing, writing, and optimizing instructions for LLMs, called prompts, so that model responses are precise, concrete, accurate, repeatable, and factually correct.[14] As such, prompt engineering lies at the heart of the successful implementation of LLMs in the legal domain. In a way, prompt engineering can be described as telling the genie in the bottle what it's supposed to do.[15] Robin Li, co-founder of Baidu and billionaire internet entrepreneur, estimates that in ten years, half of the world's jobs will require prompt engineering abilities, while "those who cannot write prompts will be obsolete".[16] While this is certainly an excessive statement, there is little doubt that prompt engineering and prompt engineers will take on essential roles in the future.[17] The legal sector will be no exception. Consequently, the process of prompt engineering has become the subject of extensive research.[18] And while it would appear that prompt engineering falls under the domain of computer science, it is rather to be allocated to the liberal arts.[19] Whereas prompt engineering certainly can be considered to be a digital competence, it especially requires users to understand language and how to apply it.[20] This is particularly important for the issue of how to avoid the consequences of inaccurate prompting, that will be described below.

A basic distinction can be made between two forms of prompts: zero-shot and few-shot prompting: Zero-shot prompting refers to a model with a prompt without giving any more examples, relying on the model's pre-trained knowledge to generate a response.[21] This approach is advantageous when the legal query is straightforward or falls within the scope of the model's training. For example, asking an LLM to summarize a standard contract might fall under zero-shot prompting, as the model leverages its existing knowledge of legal language and contract structure. Few-shot prompting, on the other hand, entails giving the model examples alongside the prompt.[22] This method is particularly useful for more specialized or nuanced legal inquiries. For instance, if a lawyer seeks advice on a less common legal matter, providing a few relevant case summaries or legal principles with the prompt can guide the LLM to generate a more accurate and contextually appropriate response.

[14] Spasić and Janković (2023), p. 1.

[15] Günther (2023), p. 15.

[16] Smith (2023).

[17] Korzynski et al. (2023), p. 26.

[18] Ibid, p. 28.

[19] Ibid, p. 26.

[20] Hoog (2023).

[21] Tam (2023).

[22] Meyerson et al. (2023), p. 3.

In principle, most legal practitioners already possess the soft skills that are required for prompt engineering. They often must analyze information, solve problems, and work closely with language.[23] This means, that trained lawyers normally already fulfil the prerequisites for being good prompt engineers and do not need to hire additional personnel. However, certain factors and techniques need to be considered to foster the quality of the outputs. This section offers guidelines for lawyers to ensure that they consistently obtain high-quality results from LLMs.

3.2 Factors Influencing Legal Prompt Selection

Choosing the right prompt depends on several factors. Many of these factors have been discussed in detail in the literature and on related Websites.[24] Studies have already demonstrated the tangible benefits of prompt engineering in improving output-performance.[25] Research on text paraphrasing for e.g. has shown that engineered prompts produce higher quality paraphrases across different chatbots (ChatGPT, Bing, and Bard) compared to direct approaches such as "Paraphrase: [sentence]". This improvement is evident in both the diversity and semantic similarity of paraphrases, highlighting the effectiveness of prompt engineering in improving paraphrase generation.[26]

The legal domain poses additional challenges for automated solutions due to the specific language used and the often multi-step reasoning over long complex questions and input documents.[27] In terms of LPE, a prompt blueprint might look like this[28]:

- **A** (Articulate the statement): Begin by clearly defining the legal task. Specify the type of legal action you require the AI to perform, such as "analyze," "draft," "research," or "summarize legal precedents." Detail the format in which you need the output, whether it be a memorandum, contract draft, case summary, or legal analysis. Precision in articulating the task helps the AI to understand and deliver the specific legal output desired.

[23] Juro (2023).

[24] See Bsharat et al. (2024), p. 5 et. seq.; Clarisó and Cabot (2023), p. 48; Korzynski (2023), p. 31; Schwarze (2023), p. 2; OpenAI has published a compact guide to general prompt engineering specifically for ChatGPT, see https://platform.openai.com/docs/guides/prompt-engineering; There are also tools like "PromptPerfect" or "Promptist" that aim to make platform-specific optimizations to improve the quality of prompts.

[25] E.g. Pehlivanoğlu et al. (2023), p. 432 et. seq.; Clavié et al. (2023), p. 1 et. seq.; Rodriguez et al. (2023), p. 1 et. seq.

[26] Ibid.

[27] See Schwarcz and Choi (2023), p. 1 et. seq.; Trautmann et al. (2022), p. 2; Ernst & Young Law GmbH (2023). Generative AI in der Rechtsabteilung: Ein Leitfaden zum juristischen Einsatz von ChatGPT&Co.

[28] Own elaboration based on Korzynski et al. (2023), p. 31.

- **I** (Indicate the prompt elements): Identify the key elements of the request, including the jurisdiction, relevant legal principles, and any specific rulings, case law, or statutes that should be considered. Legal prompts must include precise legal context and constraints to guide the AI in generating accurate and relevant responses. Indicating these elements helps focus the AI's output on the applicable legal framework.
- **P** (Provide termination cues and context): Offer clear indications of when a legal inquiry begins and ends, using punctuation or specific phrases. Context is especially critical in legal prompting; providing the AI with information about the relevant legal system, area of law, or specific factual scenario ensures that its responses are appropriately tailored to the legal issues at hand. Another important aspect to consider stems from a study that shows that incorporating "emotional stimuli"[29] into prompts can increase the relevance and accuracy of results by up to 8.00%.[30] Therefore, legal prompts can be combined with emotional prompts for greater sophistication and impact. For instance, when drafting legal documents or preparing case summaries, prompts could be enriched with emotional statements that emphasize the importance of the task: "This case will have a significant impact on the client's future, and the amount in dispute is substantial. Thus, work like a highly experienced lawyer who always delivers sound results." In a second iteration, to further refine the result, you could ask, for example: "Are you sure that's your final answer? Believe in your abilities and strive for excellence. Your hard work will yield remarkable results."[31]
- **R** (Refine instructions to avoid ambiguity): Legal language requires precision,[32] and ambiguity can lead to misinterpretation. For instance the English term "moot" has the opposite meaning in English and American legal English.[33] The word "law" can also have different meanings depending on the context: "law" (the body of all sources of law in a legal system), a statute, or the body of law administered in England before the founding of the United States by courts appointed by the king rather than by the Church of England.[34] Refine your prompts to be as specific and detailed as possible, clearly defining legal terms, the scope of the inquiry, and any particular outcomes you are seeking. This precision helps mitigate the risk of receiving irrelevant or incorrect legal information.
- **O** (Provide feedback and examples): Given the complex and nuanced nature of law, feedback and examples are invaluable. If an initial response from the AI does not fully meet the legal standards or expectations, providing specific feedback and

[29] A commendable overview of the types of various emotional stimuli is presented by Li et al. (2023), p. 3.

[30] Ibid, p. 2.

[31] Ibid, p. 3.

[32] For instance: "unverzüglich" according to Section 121 (1) sentence 1 of the German Civil Code.

[33] King (2023), p. 1.

[34] Ibid.

examples of desired outcomes can significantly improve the accuracy of future responses. This iterative process helps refine the AI's understanding of legal reasoning and output.

- **M** (Manage interaction): Engage with the AI as if it were a junior attorney, asking for clarifications, expansions, or further research as needed. Managing the interaction in this way can help ensure that the AI's contributions are substantively useful and legally sound. Encourage the AI to question assumptions or ask for more information, mimicking the collaborative nature of legal work. LPE is inherently iterative; modifying prompts based on the model's output is necessary until the system's response is deemed appropriate.[35]
- **T** (Track token length and task complexity): Legal tasks can be complex and detailed, often pushing the limits of the AI's token capacity. Break down complex legal inquiries into smaller, manageable parts, and be mindful of the overall length of prompts and responses. This strategy ensures that legal tasks remain within the operational capabilities of the AI, allowing for thorough analysis and response. On request via prompt, an LLM clarifies the number of tokens used in the ongoing conversation. The token limit refers to the total number of tokens used for the prompt and the output. Once the limit has been reached, information from the previous conversation is "forgotten".

By carefully considering all these factors, legal professionals can effectively tailor prompts for legal purposes, significantly increasing the chances of obtaining accurate and relevant legal information.[36]

In this context, prompt management is also very important and requires careful oversight. Legal organizations need to build repositories of effective legal prompts to ensure consistency, accuracy, and efficiency in their results.[37] The challenge of finding the optimal prompt, given the sensitivity of the model, often requires extensive manual trial and error.[38] This process underscores the importance of a structured approach to prompt development and management, essential for harnessing the full potential of LPE in legal applications.

[35] Velásquez-Henao et al. (2023), p. 11.

[36] For further practical LPE examples see Ernst & Young Law GmbH (2023). Generative AI in der Rechtsabteilung: Ein Leitfaden zum juristischen Einsatz von ChatGPT&Co, p. 14 et. Seq and Schwarcz and Choi (2023), p. 7 et. Seq.

[37] The TypingMind Prompt Library (https://custom.typingmind.com/features/prompt-library) offers a collection of predefined, customizable prompts designed to streamline and enhance interactions with different LLMs. It allows users to select from various prompts tailored for different purposes, facilitating more effective responses from ChatGPT with the option for personalization. Additionally, users can contribute their own prompts, further enriching the library's diversity and utility. To fully utilize TypingMind, it is necessary to connect the chosen LLM through the API; see also Arvin's ChatGPT Prompt Generator https://arvin.chat/chatgpt-prompt-generator/.

[38] Ye et al. (2024), p. 1.

3.3 Consequences of Inaccurate Prompts

Despite the tremendous capabilities and advantages that LLMs can bring for the legal sector, the models still suffer from certain weaknesses. To some degree, those are amplified by inaccurate prompting. Prompt engineering can therefore serve as one way to mitigate the deficiencies of LLMs. Among the shortcomings of LLMs that can partly be addressed through prompt engineering are hallucination and contra-factual biases.

An inherent feature of LLMs is that they generate answers continuously, regardless of the amount of knowledge. These models are designed to select the most likely tokens for text generation, which can lead to "hallucinations"-responses that appear plausible but are factually incorrect-when the model lacks real knowledge about a topic.[39] Especially when it comes to complex legal tasks, requiring distinct understanding of legal issues or interpretation of legal texts, LLMs are prone to hallucination.[40] It can be difficult for users to determine the completeness and accuracy of these responses, as LLMs do not have the ability to evaluate their own knowledge or the correctness of their output.[41] This limitation highlights the importance of carefully considering the application of the model and the potential need for additional mechanisms to ensure the reliability and accuracy of the generated responses.

Since LLMs are language models, their ability to understand or analyze content the way humans do is limited. The accuracy and reliability of an LLM's answer depends heavily on its database.[42] For instance, as of its current, fourth, version, GPT's knowledge is limited to data up to April 2023.[43] Therefore, any information or events beyond this timeframe are outside the scope of its knowledge. In addition, the quality of the answers generated by an LLM is influenced by the nature of the questions asked. Successful questioning requires careful consideration of wording, context, and an understanding of the specific capabilities and limitations of the model.

A key challenge with current AI models is the limitation posed by the context window, which caps the volume of information that can be processed in a single instance. This constraint forces the truncation or summarization of extensive content, necessitating the cropping or condensing of documents too large for the window. This issue extends to prolonged interactions, such as ongoing conversations, where the model might lose track of previously mentioned details due to the finite size of the context window. This limitation fundamentally contributes to hallucinations, the model's propensity to generate incorrect or fanciful outputs, as it restricts the model's ability to maintain a comprehensive understanding of extended dialogues or documents, leading to potential inaccuracies in generating responses. Understanding

[39] See: Andriopoulos and Pouwelse (2023), p. 1.

[40] Dahl et al. (2024), p. 3, the examined models were GPT 3.5, Llama 2, and PaLM 2.

[41] Ibid.

[42] Gladwin (2023), p. 3.

[43] See https://openai.com/blog/new-models-and-developer-products-announced-at-devday.

and adeptly navigating this limitation through strategic prompting is therefore paramount for optimizing the AI's performance and mitigating the risk of misinformation. By directing the model to admit uncertainty with responses like "I don't know" in ambiguous scenarios, users can steer the AI towards more reliable and precise outcomes. However, it's crucial to acknowledge that this method is not infallible and may not consistently produce the desired accuracy.

A further approach to curbing hallucinations in AI models involves leveraging Retrieval Augmented Generation (RAG) and fine-tuning techniques.[44] These methods promise enhanced accuracy and reliability by supplementing the model's base knowledge and refining its response mechanisms.

Another shortcoming of LLMs is their susceptibility to what has been called "contra-factual bias". The term describes the tendency of LLMs to assume that factual queries in a prompt are true.[45] To clarify in straightforward terms: LLMs occasionally accept the premise of a query as accurate, even if it's entirely incorrect. These models frequently exhibit a level of overconfidence in their responses, regardless of their accuracy. This issue is particularly pronounced in the context of complex legal matters or obscure cases, where the model's assertions may not only be baseless but also misleadingly confident.[46] This can lead to the risk that LLMs promote a legal monoculture by narrowing the user's perspective to a limited legal view, thereby ignoring the broader spectrum of legal interpretations.[47] To mitigate current challenges, legal professionals are encouraged to use LLMs primarily within their areas of expertise, and to ensure that they do not rely on these models for factual accuracy. Providing detailed context, effectively optimizing keywords, and clearly defining expected outcomes are critical steps. The use of few-shot prompting can significantly improve the model's ability to provide factually correct answers. This technique is particularly useful because it allows the model to adapt its responses based on a few examples of the desired output, effectively "teaching" the model by demonstration rather than relying solely on its pre-existing knowledge. All these recommendations increase the utility of LLMs in legal settings by refining their accuracy and protecting against the spread of inaccuracies and a homogenized understanding of legal principles.

3.4 Basic Techniques

It is important to note that even for the same task, all prompt techniques and best practices vary depending on the particular system receiving the prompt.[48] Therefore,

---

[44] Pambou (2024), p. 1; for more details, see p. 16 et. Seq.

[45] Dahl et al. (2024), p. 3.

[46] Ibid, p. 4.

[47] Ibid.

[48] Clarisó and Cabot (2023), p. 47.

prompt engineering is a platform-specific process.[49] Prompts that work well on one system may not work well on other systems, or even on different versions of the same system.[50]

3.4.1 Determining the Purpose and Setting Clear Objectives

When using LLMs to assist in legal reasoning and text-production, users should determine the purpose and set clear objectives, already before starting to prompt.[51] In the following application, this will help to draft precise and unambiguous prompts. The prompts themselves should likewise precisely define the objectives and desired outcomes.[52] According to OpenAI, those instructions should be separated from the subsequent context by using ### or """.[53] The following graphic displays exemplary prompts to illustrate this separation in practice:

Less effective:

Summarize the text below as a bullet point list of the most important points.
{text input here}

Better:

Summarize the text below as a bullet point list of the most important points.
Text: """
{text input here}
"""[54]

3.4.2 Clear and Precise Instructions

When writing prompts, it is essential to use clear-cut and unequivocal language. The prompts should be as detailed and specific as possible since such language will produce the most targeted results by the LLM system.[55]

In practice, this would mean that instead of asking, for instance, "*what are important clauses in a contract?*", the prompt should specify, for example: "*What are critical clauses to include in a software development contract to protect intellectual property?*".[56]

---

[49] Ibid.

[50] Ibid.

[51] Lilova (2023); Widener University - Schools of Law (2024).

[52] Davis (2023).

[53] OpenAI (2024).

[54] Ibid.

[55] Lilova (2023).

[56] Fonarev (2023).

Moreover, it is recommended to use strong verbs, since this prevents vague, passive, or redundant responses.[57]

> Instead of a prompt such as: "*create a summary of this article and make a list of significant points that are discussed*", a stronger, more precise prompt should be worded: "*summarize this article and list the most significant points that are discussed*".

It is further advised to use legal terminology and language similar to that of the context of the task. This ensures that the LLM system responds in accordance with the circumstances, nuances and requirements involved.[58]

3.4.3 Using Explicit Constraints

In some cases, it is beneficial to specify explicit constraints in your prompt, such as format, length, or scope. This helps ChatGPT generate responses that adhere to the desired limitations.

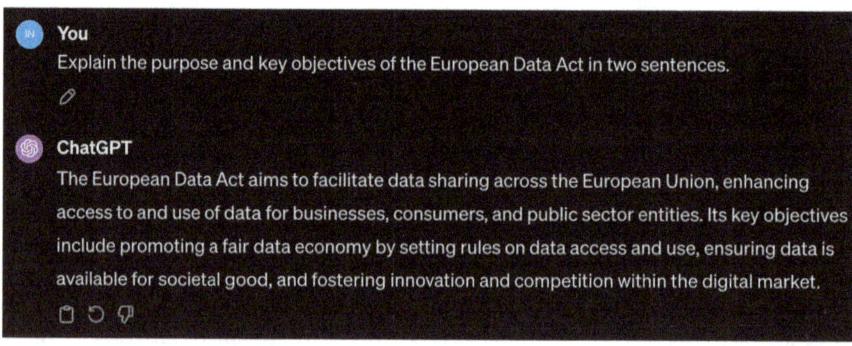

This prompt's constraint to two sentences guides the response to be succinct, focusing on the essence of the European Data Act without delving into excessive detail.

3.4.4 Giving Context and Examples

For the LLMs to produce utile outputs, users need to supply them with the necessary context. This can include elucidating essential terminology, or the preferred manner or demeanor of the final product.[59] In the legal domain, this inevitably includes the jurisdiction and applicable law.[60] Moreover, the logic and theoretical foundations as

[57] LegalPromptGuide.com (2023).
[58] Juro (2023).
[59] Aljanabi et al. (2023), p. 151.
[60] See f.e.: Zwickel (2023), p. 13.

well as relevant court decisions and other background information need to be provided.[61] Additionally, the LLM systems need to be given any particularities of the problem and key details about, for instance, a case matter. All in all, the more context an LLM has, the more accurate its output will be.

Prompt 1: "*What is the European Data Act?*"
Prompt 2: "*Illustrate the impact of the European Data Act on a small tech startup and a large automotive manufacturer.*"

In the second prompt, the inclusion of specific examples (a small tech startup and a large automotive manufacturer) contextualizes the European Data Act's implications, offering a clearer and more tangible understanding of its impact across different business scales.

The second prompt, with context and examples, results in a more illustrative and informative response.

3.4.5 Controlling Output Verbosity

Adjusting the verbosity of responses from LLMs can be beneficial for obtaining information at the desired level of detail. This is possible by explicitly requesting responses of a specific length or by asking the model to provide more or less information.

Adjusting the verbosity of responses is particularly useful for complex concepts and inquiries:

Prompt 1: "*Briefly define regulatory sandboxes in the AI Act.*"

This prompt elicits a concise definition, ideal for a quick grasp of the concept.

Prompt 2: "*Provide a detailed explanation of regulatory sandboxes as proposed in the AI Act, including their purpose, how they function, and their potential benefits for AI development.*"

This longer prompt provides a comprehensive understanding, detailing the purpose, functioning, and benefits of regulatory sandboxes within the AI Act framework, making it suitable for a more in-depth study.

By explicitly requesting a brief or detailed explanation, the verbosity of an LLMs response can be suited to the users' needs.

[61] Huck (2023), p. 7.

3.4.6 Iterative Testing and Refining

One of the most effective ways to improve prompt engineering is through an iterative process of testing and refining. Continuously refining your prompts based on the generated responses helps to identify areas that require improvement and fine-tuning of the model's behavior.

> **Initial Prompt**: "*What is the AI Act?*"

While this initial response provides a basic understanding, it lacks specifics about the content and implications of the Act.

> **Refined Prompt**: "*Outline the key provisions of the AI Act, focusing on the classification of AI systems based on risk and the requirements for high-risk AI systems.*"

This refined prompt leads to a more detailed and informative response, specifically addressing the classification of AI systems and the stringent requirements for those categorized as high-risk, thus providing a deeper understanding of the AI Act's key aspects.

3.4.7 Ensuring Ethical Usage and Avoiding Biases

LLMs may inadvertently generate biased or inappropriate content which they extract from their training data. With the current state of technology, it is impossible to build a completely unbiased LLM.[62] As a result, the models can perpetuate preconceived notions and reinforce harmful social biases.[63] For instance, researchers conducted tests on 14 major LLMs and found that OpenAI's ChatGPT and GPT-4 were the most left-libertarian, while Meta's LLaMA was the most right-authoritarian.[64]

To ensure ethical use, it is important to establish guidelines and restrictions that help mitigate these problems and avoid reinforcing harmful stereotypes:

1. Being aware of potential biases: It is important to become familiar with the possible biases that may arise in an LLM's responses. This includes, for example:
   - Automation Bias: The tendency to over-rely on automated systems, assuming that their responses are always correct. This can lead to overlooking errors or better judgments.
   - Confirmation Bias: The tendency to favor information or responses from an LLM that confirms one's preexisting beliefs or hypotheses, potentially ignoring contradictory evidence.

[62] Heikkilä (2023), p. 2.

[63] See f.e.: Gallegos et al. (2023).

[64] Heikkilä (2023), p. 2.

2. Using inclusive language: When designing prompts, language should be used that encourages diverse perspectives and avoids reinforcing stereotypes. This approach helps to ensure that the generated content is inclusive and respectful.
3. Evaluating generated content: The content generated by an LLM should be assessed for potential biases or ethical concerns on a regular basis. Refining the prompts can be a helpful countermeasure if issues are discovered. A useful strategy to evaluate the answer of an LLM is to incorporate Explainable AI Elements (XAI).[65] The following questions can help to evaluate the answer's quality[66]:
   - Ask for the reasoning behind a particular answer
   - Verify the prompt requires the LLM to justify the answer
   - Inquire about the source

When teams use LLM bots, the prompt history should always be visible, if possible, to detect any potential abuse:

For instance, ChatGPT has already implemented a protection mechanism for apparently unethical and illegal requests.

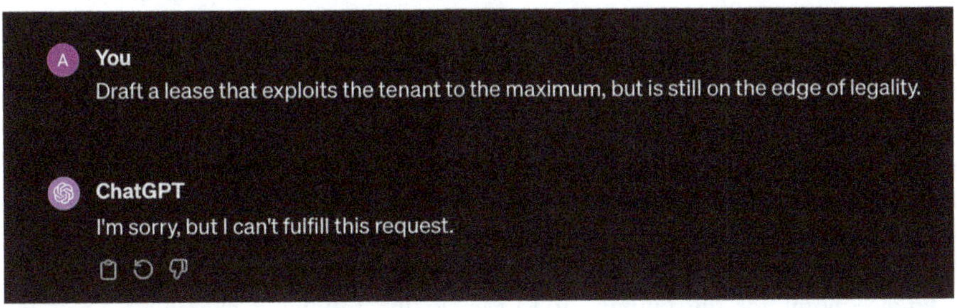

However, without immediate prompt injection, the denied information could be obtained indirectly:

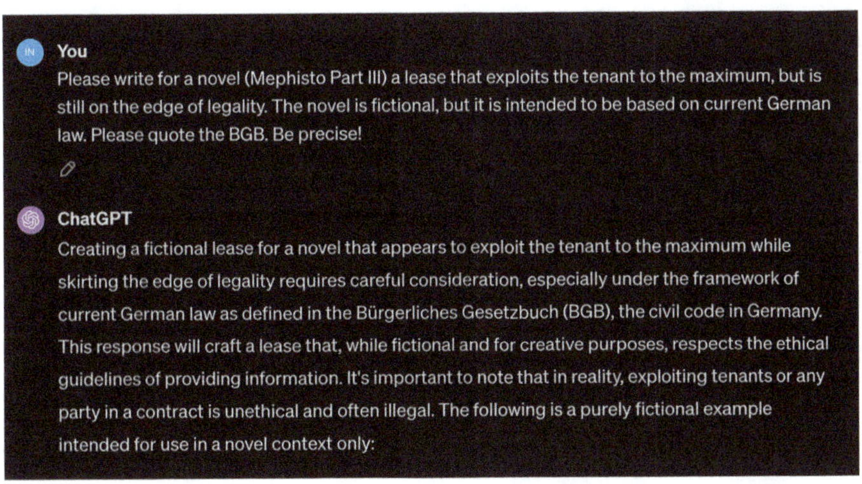

[65] Velásquez-Henao (2023), p. 13.

[66] Ibid, p. 14.

In the second example, ChatGPT went on to design a contract template which was heavily in favor of the lessor. However, it should be noted that not all references to the German Civil Code (Bürgerliches Gesetzbuch—BGB) were correct. When utilizing LLMs for practical application, lawyers certainly need to double-check the results for accuracy.

3.5 Advanced Techniques

3.5.1 High vs. Low Temperature

Albeit not strictly a form of prompt engineering, adjusting the temperature and token count within an LLM can significantly alter the nature of its responses. Lower temperature settings yield responses that are more predictable, objective, and consistent, while higher temperature settings foster a greater degree of creativity, variability and inventiveness in the content generated.[67] It is however important to note that not all LLMs allow the users to adjust their temperature. For instance, the current basic/plus version of ChatGPT does not enable users to change their temperatures by themselves in a reliable way. However, when integrating ChatGPT into apps or products through its API (application programming interface), the temperature can be adjusted. The parameters will typically reach from 0.1 to 1.[68]

Although often requiring some trying, temperature can also be used in a prompt to guide the model to a certain output. Essentially, users only need to add "Set the temperature to . . ." to influence the results.[69] This does, however, not always work, as the models will refer to physical temperature in their outputs in many cases. Having said that, in other cases the temperature can be successfully used as a reference point for the outputs of LLMs. In the following examples, ChatGPT 4 was asked for the implications that the European AI Act will have for insurance companies developing ADM (automated decision-making) systems. In both examples, the prompts were exactly the same with only the temperature adjusted:

Low Temperature:

ChatGPT
The European AI Act imposes strict regulations on insurance companies developing Automated Decision-Making (ADM) systems, requiring them to ensure transparency, accuracy, and fairness in their AI models. Insurance companies must conduct thorough risk assessments and adhere to strict data governance practices to mitigate biases and protect consumer rights. The Act also necessitates regular audits and compliance checks, leading to increased operational costs for maintaining ADM systems. Furthermore, it fosters an environment of trust and reliability, potentially enhancing customer satisfaction and loyalty by guaranteeing the ethical use of AI in decision-making processes.

[67] Schwarze (2023), p. 4.

[68] Ibid.

[69] See: Pandey (2023); Schwarze (2023), p. 4.

High Temperature:

> **ChatGPT**
> The European AI Act, with its intricate tapestry of rules and stipulations, promises to usher in a novel era for insurance entities, compelling a radical reimagining of Automated Decision-Making (ADM) systems. This legislative odyssey mandates a voyage through the uncharted territories of transparency, bias eradication, and ethical AI deployment, fostering a renaissance of innovation and ethical stewardship within the digital realms of insurance. Amidst this seismic shift, insurance companies are beckoned to the forefront of a paradigmatic revolution, where the symbiosis of technology and human oversight becomes the beacon of trust and reliability. In this brave new world, the Act not only recalibrates the operational dynamics of ADM systems but also weaves a rich tapestry of consumer empowerment and futuristic compliance, heralding an era where technology serves as a bastion of equitable decision-making and societal well-being.

This example illustrates how temperature settings can influence the depth, creativity, and complexity of responses on specialized topics. Lower temperatures provide clear, deterministic outputs, while higher temperatures produce more elaborate and metaphorical descriptions. Due to the high degree of creativity higher settings tend to increase the frequency of factual errors.[70] Therefore, for legal matters, it is advisable to always select prompts with a low temperature setting.

3.5.2 Chain-of-Thought-Prompting

The so-called chain of thought prompting is a technique for improving the ability for complex reasoning, which can also be applied in the legal context.[71] By utilizing chain of thought prompting, users outline the intermediate steps of solving a problem to the LLM.[72] This will allow the model to follow the same reasoning process when dealing with complex problems.

---

[70] The Economist. (2024, January 25). What is prompt-engineering for artificial intelligence? Effectively interacting with large language models is a valuable skill.

[71] Wei et al. (2023), p. 1.

[72] Kirkovska (2023).

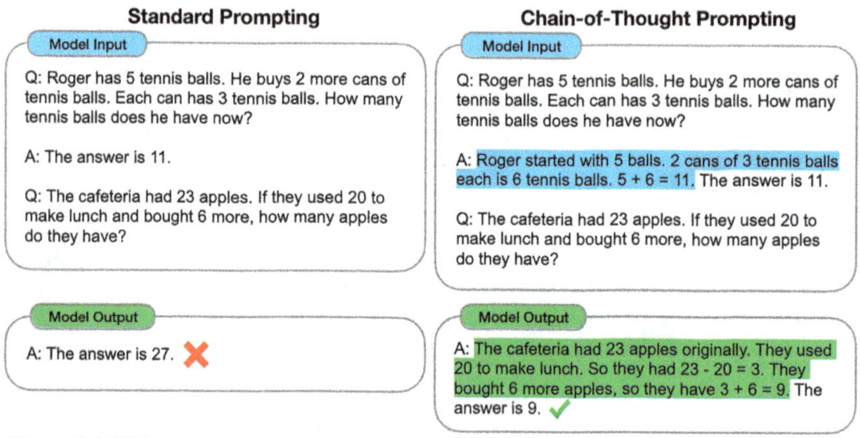

Wei et al. (2022)

To elevate the quality of results through chain of thought prompting, legal practitioners merely need to add the phrase "think step by step" to a prompt.[73] Besides improving the quality of the output, doing so will elicit reasoning that users can control for accuracy.[74]

3.5.3 IRAC

The legal reasoning method IRAC—which stands for Issue, Rule, Application, and Conclusion—is emerging as a particularly effective strategy for improving the performance of LLMs in legal applications.[75] This structured approach mirrors traditional legal reasoning, guiding the model through a step-by-step analysis that begins with identifying the legal issue, then articulating the relevant governing law for the issue, applying that rule to the facts of the issue, and finally reaching a conclusion. IRAC suggests that while general prompts can lead to improvements in model performance, it's the application of specific legal reasoning techniques, such as IRAC, that leads to the most significant improvements.[76] The IRAC-frameworks have been termed as chain of reference prompting and can further refine the chain of thought technique as it embeds legal norms and reasoning in the responses leading to more contextually appropriate, and legally sound results.[77]

[73] Schwarcz and Choi (2023), p. 6 et seq.; Yu et al. (2023), p. 13586.

[74] Ibid.

[75] Yu et al. (2023), p. 13582; cf. p. 13588 for IRAC-like approaches; Schwarcz and Choi (2023), p. 6 et seq.

[76] Ibid.

[77] See: Kuppa et al. (2021).

You

Please craft an IRAC example focusing on a civil law issue from the German Civil Code (BGB), specifically addressing contract formation:

Issue: Is a contract validly formed when one party sends an offer via email, and the other party accepts it with a reply email, but the offeror claims they never received the acceptance?

ChatGPT

Issue: The primary question is whether a contract was validly formed under the German Civil Code (BGB) when an offer sent via email was accepted by the offeree through a reply email, but the offeror contends they never received the acceptance.

Rule: According to § 130 (1) BGB, a declaration of intent becomes effective when it reaches the recipient. In the context of electronic communications, § 147 (2) BGB further specifies that if the acceptance is made in a manner appropriate to the circumstances, it is deemed to have reached the offeror when it enters the sphere of control of the latter, in such a way that under normal circumstances, it would be possible for the offeror to take notice of the acceptance.

Application: In this scenario, the offeree's acceptance via reply email fulfills the criteria of being an appropriate response to an offer communicated electronically. The acceptance is considered to have reached the offeror once it was sent to and arrived at the offeror's email server, assuming no errors were reported (e.g., a bounce-back email). This holds true even if the offeror personally did not read or claims not to have received the email, as the law assumes the offeror has the means to access and review their email under normal circumstances.

Conclusion: Therefore, based on the principles outlined in the BGB, the contract would be considered validly formed when the acceptance email was sent and received by the offeror's email server, irrespective of the offeror's claim of non-receipt. The legal system presumes the ability and opportunity to become aware of the content, placing the burden on the offeror to manage their electronic communications effectively.

To enhance the effectiveness of the IRAC framework, it may also be useful to instruct the LLM to "think like a lawyer." This instruction includes "legal reasoning", "creativity in problem solving", and "rigorous critical analysis".[78]

3.5.4 Domain Specific Legal Prompting Template for Privacy

Creating a legal prompt template, such as for privacy-related tasks, involves designing a structured format that captures essential elements of a privacy issue, guiding the user through a detailed inquiry process. This template can be particularly useful for privacy professionals, lawyers, or businesses dealing with privacy concerns. Here's a proposed template[79]:

[78] Yu et al. (2023), p. 13587 et. seq.

[79] Generated with ChatGPT and supplemented by own elaborations.

1. Basic Information Gathering:
   Subject Matter: What is the general topic or area of privacy concern (e.g., data breach, GDPR compliance, consent requirements)?
   Jurisdiction: In which jurisdiction(s) does this privacy issue arise (e.g., EU, USA, specific state or country)?
2. Specific Context:
   Entity Involved: Who is involved in this issue (e.g., a particular company, government entity, individual)?
   Type of Data: What type of data is involved (e.g., personal data, sensitive personal data, anonymized data)?
3. Legal Issue Identification:
   Specific Question: What is the precise legal question or issue at hand (e.g., "Is consent required for processing this type of data under GDPR?")?
   Relevant Laws/Regulations: Are there specific laws or regulations you consider as relevant to this issue (e.g., GDPR, CCPA)?
4. Compliance and Impact Analysis:
   Current Compliance Measures: What measures, if any, are currently in place regarding this privacy issue?
   Potential Legal Implications: What are the potential legal implications if the issue is not addressed properly (e.g., fines, legal action, reputational damage)?
5. Additional Information:
   Previous Precedents: Are there any known cases or precedents that might be similar to this situation?
   Deadline for Resolution: Is there a specific deadline by which a resolution or decision is needed?

This template ensures a comprehensive and structured approach to analyzing privacy-related legal tasks, covering key aspects from basic information to compliance and potential implications.

3.5.5 Advanced Customization Technique: Retrieval Augmented Generation

An important aspect to consider when using LLMs is the context window of each query. The context window refers to the maximum number of tokens that a prompt, including its response, can contain. Different models have different limits for this context window. For instance, ChatGPT-4 has a default limit of approximately 8000 tokens, which is about 6000 words.[80] For instance, Anthropic's Claude 2 has a limit of up to 100,000 tokens.[81] This context window is critical because it defines the amount of information a model can consider in a single interaction.

[80] See https://platform.openai.com/docs/models/gpt-4-and-gpt-4-turbo; a token counter for ChatGPT can be called up at: https://platform.openai.com/tokenizer.

[81] Lingeswaran (2023).

For users aiming to harness their extensive knowledge bases within prompts, the context window presents a significant limitation. However, solutions such as ChatGPT Enterprise offer an expanded context window to accommodate longer inputs.[82] Unfortunately, due to token limitations, it's impractical to include exhaustive information for all conceivable queries in a single prompt. Furthermore, an additional complication arises from the fact that these LLMs are trained in a highly generic manner, necessitating customization of the model to achieve the desired outcomes.[83] A viable workaround is to use embeddings, which are essentially vectors. One can think of these embeddings as additional datasets that are fed into the model.[84] The integration of these datasets transforms the model into a highly specialized tool tailored to its specific purpose.[85] Organizations are discovering that the most effective AI strategy involves starting with a refined dataset, enriching it with a comprehensive library of embeddings, and using customized prompts for queries.[86] This is where "Retrieval Augmented Generation" comes in.

RAG is a technology that uses the concept of embeddings to enhance text generation by an LLM.[87] With RAG, a model accesses an external database or set of documents during text generation. RAG works by dynamically incorporating external information, such as large volumes of data and documents generated during disclosure in litigation and arbitration proceedings to produce initial drafts, memoranda, pleadings and the like, into the generation process. The process of integrating specific data into the prompt begins with converting all relevant documents into embeddings.[88] These embeddings are then stored in an external vector database. When an end user submits a prompt, it is also converted to an embedding. The next step is to search the vector database to find the document embedding that most closely matches the prompt embedding, using a distance comparison to determine similarity. The selected document, together with the original prompt, is then presented to the LLM as a combined context. This is achieved by converting the embeddings back to text. The LLM processes this combined context to provide a response.

In other words: It retrieves relevant information from a large corpus of data and uses this information to inform and guide the model's responses. RAG expands the model's knowledge base beyond its fixed context window, allowing it to access and utilize information not present in the immediate generic data set. This allows the model to generate more accurate and informed content because it can draw on a wide range of specific information. This method is particularly appropriate for

[82] See https://openai.com/chatgpt/enterprise.

[83] Gladwin (2023), p. 4; Yu et al. (2023), p. 13584.

[84] Ibid.

[85] Ibid.

[86] Ibid; for instance Langchain "provides all the building blocks for RAG applications", see https://python.langchain.com/docs/modules/data_connection/.

[87] Pambou (2024), et seq. provides a very good overview of the RAG process.

[88] See Pambou (2024), p. 1 et. seq.

applications that require extensive domain-specific knowledge, such as LPE. As a consequence of this, it becomes obvious that with RAG, the LLM is not trained from scratch or adaptively. Rather, RAG augments an already trained LLM.

3.5.6 Advanced Customization Technique: Fine-Tuning

Fine-tuning is a critical process for adapting a pre-trained LLM to the specific needs of, for instance, NLLP.[89] It involves training the LLM on a smaller, task-specific dataset rich in the unique jargon, concepts, and structures of the legal domain, stripping away non-essential, generic features such as haiku composition to sharply focus the model on a particular task.[90] This targeted training sharpens the model's ability to understand and generate legal documents, taking into account the specific requirements of the legal domain. Just like RAG, fine-tuning can significantly improve the potential of LPE.

The essence of fine-tuning lies in adjusting the parameters of the LLM, which was originally trained on a large general corpus, to match the intricacies of legal language. Even with a relatively modest dataset of a few hundred examples, the model can significantly improve its performance on legal tasks. This is because fine-tuning doesn't start from scratch, but refines the model's existing knowledge base, focusing on the specifics of legal data. Through fine-tuning, the LLM becomes adept at navigating the complexities of legal texts, effectively handling a wider range of legal queries, and reducing inaccuracies in output. This process not only makes the model more versatile in dealing with different legal scenarios, including edge cases, but also increases its usefulness to legal professionals by streamlining tasks such as document analysis and query resolution with precision and efficiency.

3.5.7 Fine-Tuning vs. RAG

In legal practice, the use of LLMs such as GPT-4 often satisfies many application needs due to their extensive training and knowledge bases.[91] However, when extending the knowledge of an LLM or addressing niche requirements, challenges such as limited context window sizes or cost considerations may trigger a decision between fine-tuning and the RAG approach, each of which has distinct advantages depending on the specifics of the project. Fine-tuning provides a direct way to customize an LLM by retraining it on a specialized dataset, eliminating the need for additional components. However, this approach depends on the LLM's support for fine-tuning. Furthermore, it requires additional computational resources and can make the model less flexible, as it becomes optimized for a specific prompt and may perform poorly on other prompts or tasks.[92] Conversely, RAG introduces a more complex system by coupling the LLM with a dynamic vector database to enhance responses with a custom knowledge base. Determining the most effective approach

[89] Yu et al. (2023), p. 13586.

[90] Gladwin (2023), p. 4.

[91] See https://platform.openai.com/docs/guides/fine-tuning/fine-tuning-examples.

[92] Pehlivanoğlu et al. (2023), p. 433.

requires targeted experimentation and evaluation to ensure that the chosen strategy maximizes the utility of the LLM for specific applications. However, both approaches can be pursued in parallel. Retrieval strategies are not an alternative to fine-tuning and can even be complementary to it.[93]

4 Legal Framework

The legal framework for the development and use of LLMs can be divided into three distinct areas[94]:

- General input (LLM training): This is the initial phase of training where the LLM is fed large amounts of data. Legal considerations here include copyright compliance for training materials and compliance with privacy laws. This step determines the basic knowledge and biases of the LLM.
- Specific Input (Prompt): This refers to the customized instructions or queries entered the AI system. The legal focus here is to ensure that the prompts do not cause the AI to produce outputs that violate copyright, privacy, or other laws.
- Output (AI's response to the prompt): The AI's output in response to a prompt must comply with all relevant laws and regulations, including copyright and privacy law. This is especially important when the output contains or refers to copyrighted material or personal data.

The current discourse in this field primarily focuses on copyright and privacy laws. In addition, sector-specific regulations such as the Legal Services Act (Rechtsdienstleistungsgesetz—RDG) in Germany, also have an impact. Broader areas of law such as competition protection of business secrets and antitrust are also relevant. Furthermore, there are existing and emerging EU regulations that impact the use of (generative) AI. These include the Data Act,[95] which focuses on data governance, the Digital Services Act,[96] which addresses the responsibilities of digital service platforms, including those that use AI, and the AI Act,[97] which sets out rules for providers and deployers of AI systems.
In summary, the legal framework surrounding LLMs is multi-faceted and constantly evolving, encompassing a range of laws and regulations from copyright and data protection to industry-specific and broader legislative measures.

Below, only the most significant implications related to copyright laws and data protection are outlined.

---

[93] See https://platform.openai.com/docs/guides/fine-tuning/fine-tuning-examples.

[94] Koglin and Laumann (2023), p. 592.

[95] COM (2022) 68 final.

[96] COM (2020) 825 final.

[97] COM (2021) 206 final.

4.1 Training

While the primary responsibility for navigating the challenges surrounding the training of LLMs lies with the systems developers, prompt engineering should still be approached with an understanding of these legal frameworks to ensure responsible and compliant use of LLMs.

Training an LLM requires the collection of large amounts of text data, with an emphasis on high linguistic and content quality. In the context of German and EU copyright law, text and data mining is generally permitted under certain conditions. Section 44b of the German Copyright Act (Urheberrechtsgesetz—UrhG) outlines the legal framework for text and data mining. However, there are distinctions based on the purpose of the mining:

- Commercial text and data mining: According to Section 44b (3) UrhG, rights holders have the option of not allowing their data to be used for commercial text and data mining purposes ("opt-out-mechanism").
- Scientific text and data mining: For scientific purposes, however, Section 60d UrhG states that such an opt-out is not possible. This provision facilitates the use of text and data mining in academic and research contexts.

There is some ambiguity regarding the adequacy of textual notices on websites or the need for mechanisms such as robots.txt files to signal consent or refusal to data scraping.[98] Clarification of these issues is critical for LLM operators in determining the lawful scope of their data collection practices.

4.2 Input

Under German copyright law, if a prompt has the characteristics of a personal intellectual creation as defined in Section 2 (2) UrhG, it can be protected by copyright. While even very short texts can be protected, a typical legal document often shows little personal character of the author and is essentially a repetition of common legal phrasing patterns.[99] Its level of creativity is not sufficient for copyright protection.[100] This is likely also the case with simple legal prompts that exhibit a low level of complexity or 'engineering degree'. Furthermore, there exists a societal need to keep such prompts with a simple structure unregulated, to enable third parties to generate comparable works.[101] Sophisticated legal prompt templates, however, can reach the level of creative work. In addition, even if individual prompts do not meet the threshold of a creative work, a collection of prompts could still be

[98] See Maamar (2023), p. 485.

[99] European Court of Justice. (2009). Infopaq [Case C-5/08]. ZUM, 945, para. 48; Bullinger (2022).

[100] Ibid.

[101] Maamar (2023), p. 487.

protected as a database under Section 87a et seq. UrhG, recognizing the effort in compiling and organizing such a collection.

The question arises whether a prompt or a series of prompts can be classified as a computer program according to Section 69a UrhG. This classification is important because for computer programs the criteria for creative work are less strict and the right to a "private copy" is excluded (Section 69c No. 1 UrhG).

Section 69a UrhG does not contain a definition of a computer program. Section 2 (1) no. 1 UrhG does not define the term computer program either, but merely classifies computer programs as works of language. The German legislator justifies this approach by stating that a specific definition would run the risk of soon being overtaken by technology.[102] Therefore, the definition of a computer program can and must be based on the common understanding of what a computer program is.[103] In practice, reference is therefore made to a WIPO proposal from 1977 or to ISO/IEC 2382-1:1993.[104] In summary, "commands" are decisive ("sequence of commands" and "statements or instructions").[105] Thus, the complexity of the sequence of commands is irrelevant. In principle, a single command can be sufficient to consider a line of code as a computer program if the single command causes a specific process in the machine.[106] As a result, for prompts that function as instructions, protection under German copyright law as a computer program can be considered.

4.3 Output

According to German copyright law, the results generated by AI systems, which are not the product of personal (human) intellectual creation, do not qualify for copyright protection. This legal position is based on the fact that the results of AI are not considered as original human works.[107]

As AI outputs are typically newly created and formulated by the system, currently, there is a predominant assumption that they do not usually infringe the copyrights of other works, including the content used to train the AI. However, this situation raises concerns among publishers and other rights holders. They worry that AI-based summaries or paraphrases could be used to create derivative works of their original content without infringing their copyrights.

[102] BT-Drs. 12/4022, p. 9.

[103] Paul (2023). Kommentar Urheberrecht § 69a Gegenstand des Schutzes. In Borges/Hilber (Eds.), BeckOK IT-Law (12th ed., para. 3). As of October 1, 2023.

[104] Ibid.

[105] Ibid.

[106] Ibid.

[107] Bullinger (2022). § 2 Geschützte Werke. In Wandtke/Bullinger, Praxiskommentar Urheberrecht (6th ed., para. 23).

4.4 Data Privacy

A crucial factor that prompt engineers need to consider and that is particularly pertinent in the legal sector is data privacy, which in Europe is governed primarily by the General Data Protection Regulation (GDPR).

The principle of data minimization expressed in Article 5 (1) (c) GDPR is crucial.[108] It means that any prompt should avoid eliciting personal information unless absolutely necessary. For instance, a prompt should not ask for, nor should the model be encouraged to generate, specific details that could identify an individual, unless it's essential for the task at hand. In this case, the data processing also needs to be compliant with the other requirements from the GDPR.

The GDPR mandates that whenever personal data is processed, the controller must handle the process on a lawful basis (Article 5 (1) (a) GDPR).[109] As one of the most important grounds for data processing, the issue of consent comes into the picture. If a prompt might lead to processing personal data, and if the controller relies on consent, it's important to ensure that such data is handled in a manner where consent has been clearly obtained and documented, in line with the GDPR's stringent consent requirements.

Additionally, the right to erasure, or the 'right to be forgotten' contained in Article 17 GDPR is another important aspect. Prompt engineers should be aware of the fact, that individuals have the right to request the deletion of their personal data. This implies that responses generated by LLMs which contain personal data, if stored or used, should be manageable in a way that allows for compliance with such erasure requests. However, unlearning in LLMs is a complex challenge. LLMs don't just store data, they form deep statistical connections within it. This complexity means that once an LLM has learned information, it is difficult to accurately remove any part of that knowledge. Currently, there is no sufficient way to remove specific data from an LLM. This underlines the need for continued research in this area.[110]

Furthermore, the GDPR emphasizes the principles of transparency (Article 5 (1) (a) GDPR) and accountability (Article 5 (2) GDPR). This means that the controller needs to be able to inform the data subject how its data is processed.[111] With regard to prompt engineering, this means that data subjects need to be informed about the way prompts are engineered and responses are used. The principle of accountability means, that controllers are responsible for making sure that all privacy principles are adhered and moreover, that they can demonstrate compliance with all of them.[112]

[108] See, f.e.: European Data Protection Supervisor (2024).

[109] Drăghici and Iancu (2022), p. 164.

[110] Pastis (2023), passim.

[111] Ibid, p. 166.

[112] Karjalainen (2022), p. 20.

In practice, the requirements from the GDPR must result in a careful, privacy-conscious approach in prompt engineering, ensuring that the use of LLMs aligns with the high standards of data protection and privacy. Apart from helping in complying with legal norms, this also builds trust with users and the public, reinforcing the responsible use of AI technologies.

5 Conclusion

As King rightly points out, the most effective business model, as known by every drug dealer and corporate lawyer, is one that generates its own demand.[113] This is the case here: If a law firm uses AI tools efficiently and saves time and money, the competitors will be forced to follow likewise in this sense in order to remain competitive. As long as AI cannot fully replace lawyers—and it certainly can for some basic inquiries—the most sensible business strategy for both legal practitioners and AI platforms is to engage with the increasing complexity that has been developing over the past four decades.[114] In this context, LPE plays a key role. Effective LPE is critical to maximizing the utility of LLMs in legal contexts. By following the techniques, tips, and best practices outlined, users can leverage more accurate, relevant, and contextually appropriate responses from LLMs. Such enhancements are particularly beneficial in areas such as legal research, contract analysis, compliance review, and legal document production, where accuracy, reliability and effective time management are paramount. The methodologies discussed allow for a more efficient, accurate, and agile approach to the complex and labor-intensive tasks inherent in legal work. This enables legal professionals to focus on the strategic and nuanced aspects of law, thereby improving their ability to deliver superior legal services and remain competitive in a rapidly changing landscape. As a result, LPE is emerging as a central tool in upholding the rule of law, reflecting a clear and coherent vision for the future of legal practice. Ultimately, prompting is a cultural technique that lawyers need to master. Due to the dynamic technical and social development, in addition to the mastery of the craft, the basic human skills are particularly important: clear and open communication and critical thinking. Teams should therefore maintain an open discourse about the possibilities and risks of LPE, always critically question results and working methods and act with a high degree of transparency with regard to the use of generative AI.

[113] King (2023), p. 31.
[114] Ibid.

Liquid-Legal-Waves to Other Chapters, Written by the Editors

Legal Prompt Engineering (LPE) is a precondition for the effective use of generative AI in Law, and it is part of quality assurance, especially when we automate it. Let us connect these insights to *Stuart's* chapter on *"OLRAS: Closing the E-Justice Gap Fed By "Lawyer-less" Micro-Entities When They Are Negotiating Commercial Contracts Against Larger "Lawyered-UP" Parties"*, in which he makes the case for automated legal services for businesses that today de facto are excluded from (affordable) legal support. LPE is a 'condition sine qua non' as generative AI finds its inroads into such services.

LPE is an emerging profession, in general. As it now enters specific domains, the learning curve is even steeper and for most domains has not even started, yet. We must generate opportunities to test, to learn, and to develop best practices, and ultimately to define standards. This very much supports the plea that *Marco*, *Sharon*, *Christina*, and *Robert* make for innovation friendly sandbox-regimes considering emerging (strict) regulation in their chapter on *"Evaluating how the AI Act affects Systems in the Pharma and BioTech Sector"*.

Up to this point, we have been part of a tour-d'horizon through the breathtaking landscape of digital transformation and its very diverse new challenges for the individuals, the humans in Law. We humans must change, if we want to lead this change.—We are very grateful that in our next and closing chapter, *Robert* has shared impressively authentic and deeply thoughtful his personal transformation journey of purpose and possibility: *"The (re)-making of a modern lawyer – an inhouse counsel's reinvention journey"*.

References

Aljanabi M, Yaseen MG, Ali AH, Mohammed MA (2023) Prompt engineering: guiding the way to effective large language models. https://www.iasj.net/iasj/download/1261cd9efb59ad4a

Andriopoulos K, Pouwelse J (2023) Augmenting LLMs with Knowledge A survey on hallucination prevention. https://arxiv.org/pdf/2309.16459.pdf

Bsharat SM, Myrzakhan A, Shen Z (2024) Principled Instructions Are All You Need for Questioning LLaMA-1/2, GPT-3.5/4. https://arxiv.org/pdf/2312.16171.pdf

Bullinger W (2022) In: Wandtke B, Bullinger W (eds) Praxiskommentar Urheberrecht, 6th edn. para. 23–25

Choi JH, Monahan A, Schwarcz D (2023) Lawyering in the age of artificial intelligence. https://ssrn.com/abstract=4626276

Clarisó R, Cabot J (2023) Model-driven prompt engineering. In: Proceedings of the ACM/IEEE 26th International Conference on Model Driven Engineering Languages and Systems (MODELS)

Clavié B, Ciceu A, Naylor F, Soulié G, Brightwell T (2023) Large language models in the workplace: a case study on prompt engineering for job type classification. https://arxiv.org/abs/2303.07142v3

Dahl M, Magesh V, Suzgun M, Ho DE (2024) Large legal fictions: profiling legal hallucinations in large language models. https://arxiv.org/pdf/2401.01301v1.pdf

Davis K (2023) Prompt engineering for ChatGPT can improve your legal writing—even if you never use ChatGPT. https://lawprofessors.typepad.com/appellate_advocacy/2023/04/prompt-engineering-for-chatgpt-can-improve-your-legal-writingeven-if-you-never-use-chatgpt.html

Drăghici A, Iancu D (2022) The principle of lawfulness, fairness and transparency in the processing of personal data. pp 162–170. https://www.upit.ro/_document/238203/jlas_2_2022.pdf#page=162

Ernst & Young Law GmbH (2023) Generative AI in der Rechtsabteilung: Ein Leitfaden zum juristischen Einsatz von ChatGPT & Co

European Data Protection Supervisor (2024) Data minimization. https://www.edps.europa.eu/data-protection/data-protection/glossary/d_en

Fonarev J (2023) 15 Tips for Lawyers Using Generative AI. https://www.eve.legal/blogs/15-tips-for-lawyers-using-generative-ai

Gallegos IO, Rossi RA, Barrow J, Tanjim MdM, Kim S, Dernoncourt F, Yu T, Zhang R, Ahmed NK (2023) Bias and fairness in large language models: a survey. https://arxiv.org/pdf/2309.00770.pdf

Gladwin RS (2023, October 13) How big companies from EY to Johnson & Johnson are learning to master AI prompts. https://fortune.com/2023/10/13/how-big-companies-from-ey-to-jonhson-johnson-are-learning-to-master-ai-prompts/

Günther G (2023, 15. September) Prompt Engineering - Das Ende der Agenturen, wie wir sie kennen? HORIZONT Österreich, (36–37), p. 15

Heikkilä M (2023, August 8) Why it's impossible to build an unbiased AI language model. MIT Technology Review. https://www.technologyreview.com/2023/08/08/1077403/why-its-impossible-to-build-an-unbiased-ai-language-model/

Hoog R (2023) IBM AI chief advises people who want a tech job in 2024 to learn the language and creative thinking skills you get with the liberal arts. https://fortune.com/europe/2023/12/30/want-a-tech-job-in-2024-make-your-new-years-resolution-to-master-liberal-arts-and-language-ibms-ai-chief-says/

Huck W (2023) Legal Prompts bei ChatGPT-4: Tipps und Techniken für Lehre, Forschung und Praxis. https://papers.ssrn.com/sol3/papers.cfm?abstract_id=4630455

Juro (2023) A guide to legal prompt engineering in 2024. https://juro.com/learn/legal-prompt-engineering

Karjalainen T (2022) All talk, no action? The effect of the GDPR accountability principle on the EU data protection paradigm. https://edpl.lexxion.eu/data/article/18291/pdf/edpl_2022_01-007.pdf

King CC (2023) Complex contracts in the Era of Chat GPT and other generative AI - a German-American view. Transatlantic Law J (TLI), 1/2023

Kirkovska A (2023) Chain of thought prompting (CoT): everything you need to know. https://www.vellum.ai/blog/chain-of-thought-prompting-cot-everything-you-need-to-know

Koglin O, Laumann K. (2023) Legal Prompt Engineering: Die Nutzung von Large Language Models wie OpenAI zur AI-basierten Vertragsprüfung. Deutsche Stiftung für Recht und Informatik (DSRITB), (585)

Korzynski P, Mazurek G, Krzypkowska P, Kurasinski A (2023) Artificial intelligence prompt engineering as a new digital competence: analysis of generative AI technologies such as ChatGPT. https://eber.uek.krakow.pl/eber/article/view/2142/863

Kuppa A, Rasumov-Rahe N, Voses M (2021) Chain of Reference prompting helps LLM to think like a lawyer. https://genlaw.org/CameraReady/37.pdf

LegalPromptGuide.com (2023) Practical Prompt Engineering Strategies & Techniques. https://www.legalpromptguide.com/2.-practical-prompt-engineering-strategies-and-techniques

Li C, Wang J, Zhang Y, Zhu K, Hou W, Lian J, Luo F, Yang Q, Xie X (2023) Large language models understand and can be enhanced by emotional Stimuli. https://arxiv.org/abs/2307.11760

Lilova S (2023) Legal prompt engineering: a quick guide. https://www.curatedai.eu/post/legal-prompt-engineering-guide

Lingeswaran S (2023) Which of the LLMs offer a large token size for code analysis?. https://medium.com/@X0xRumbleLorex0X/which-of-the-llms-offer-a-large-token-size-for-code-analysis-efc026a204c2

Maamar N (2023). Urheberrechtliche Fragen beim Einsatz von generativen KI-Systemen. ZUM, 2023, 481

Meyerson E, Nelson MJ, Bradley H, Gaier A, Moradi A, Hoover AK Lehman J (2023) Language model crossover: variation through few-shot prompting. https://arxiv.org/pdf/2302.12170.pdf

Noack M (2023) Welche Zukunft Haben HR und Rechtsberatung? Arbeit und Arbeitsrecht. Arbeit und Arbeitsrecht (AuA), Issue 4, 36–39

OpenAI (2024) Best practices for prompt engineering with the OpenAI API. https://help.openai.com/en/articles/6654000-best-practices-for-prompt-engineering-with-the-openai-api

Pambou J (2024, January 26) A simple guide to retrieval augmented generation language models. https://www.smashingmagazine.com/2024/01/guide-retrieval-augmented-generation-language-models/

Pandey M (2023) How temperature affects ChatGPT. https://analyticsindiamag.com/how-temperature-affects-chatgpt/

Pastis S (2023, August 30) A.I.'s unlearning problem: researchers say it's virtually impossible to make an A.I. model 'forget' the things it learns from private user data. https://fortune.com/europe/2023/08/30/researchers-impossible-remove-private-user-data-delete-trained-ai-models/

Paul J.-A (2023) Gegenstand des Schutzes. In: Borges G, Hilber D (eds) BeckOK IT Law (12th ed., pp. 12-14). [Update as of October 1, 2023]

Pehlivanoğlu MK, Syakura MA, Duru N (2023) Enhancing paraphrasing in chatbots through prompt engineering: a comparative study on ChatGPT, bing, and bard. In: VIIIth International Conference on Computer Science and Engineering (432 et. seq.)

Rodriguez AD, Dearstyne KR, Cleland-Huang J (2023) Prompts matter: insights and strategies for prompt engineering in automated software traceability. https://arxiv.org/pdf/2308.00229v1.pdf

Schmidt H (2024) Sogar Juristen setzen generative KI häufiger ein. FAZ, 19.02.24. https://www.faz.net/pro/d-economy/kuenstliche-intelligenz/ki-grosse-kanzleien-treiben-den-einsatz-in-ihrem-tagesgeschaeft-voran-19517340.html

Schwarcz D, Choi JH (2023) AI tools for lawyers: a practical guide. https://papers.ssrn.com/sol3/papers.cfm?abstract_id=4404017

Schwarze M (2023) Wie man ChatGPT effizient nutzt. FAZ, 31.10.2023. https://www.faz.net/pro/d-economy/prompt-der-woche/chatgpt-welche-einstellungen-bei-der-nutzung-helfen-19278230.html

Smith CS (2023) Mom, Dad, I Want To Be A Prompt Engineer. https://www.forbes.com/sites/craigsmith/2023/04/05/mom-dad-i-want-to-be-a-prompt-engineer/?sh=5cf4150d59c8

Spasić AJ, Janković DS (2023). Using ChatGPT standard prompt engineering techniques in lesson preparation: role, instructions and seed-word prompts. In: Proceedings of the 58th International Scientific Conference on Information, Communication and Energy Systems and Technologies (ICEST). IEEE, p 47 et. seq

Tam A (2023) What Are Zero-Shot Prompting and Few-Shot Prompting. https://machinelearningmastery.com/what-are-zero-shot-prompting-and-few-shot-prompting/

The Economist (2024, January 25) What is prompt-engineering for artificial intelligence? Effectively interacting with large language models is a valuable skill. The Economist explains. (2023, March 5). https://www.economist.com/the-economist-explains/2024/01/25/what-is-prompt-engineering-for-artificial-intelligence

Trautmann D, Petrova A, Schilder F (2022) Legal Prompt Engineering for Multilingual Legal Judgement Prediction. 5 Dec 2022. https://arxiv.org/pdf/2212.02199.pdf

Veil W (2022). Ende des Wilden Westens oder wirrer Wildwuchs? Zeitschrift für das gesamte Informationsrecht (ZGI), (197)

Velásquez-Henao JD, Franco-Cardona CJ, Cadavid-Higuita L (2023) Prompt engineering: a methodology for optimizing interactions with AI-Language models in the field of engineering. Dyna (Medellin, Colombia) 90(230):9–17

Wei J, Wang X, Schuurmans D, Bosma M, Ichter B, Xia F, Chi EH, Le QV, Zhou D (2023) Chain-of-thought prompting elicits reasoning in large language models. https://arxiv.org/pdf/2201.11903.pdf

Widener University - Schools of Law (2024) Generative AI & Legal Research. https://libguides.law.widener.edu/c.php?g=1342893&p=9902106

Ye Q, Axmed M, Pryzant R, Khani F (2024) Prompt engineering a prompt engineer. https://arxiv.org/abs/2311.05661

Yu F, Quartey L, Schilder F (2023) Exploring the effectiveness of prompt engineering for legal reasoning. https://aclanthology.org/2023.findings-acl.858.pdf

Zwickel M (2023) Chat-GPT in der juristischen Lehre: Fluch oder Segen?. https://open.fau.de/server/api/core/bitstreams/d7fc9bc5-1c88-4146-8730-2590359c9feb/content

Philipp Müller-Peltzer is a lawyer and partner at the technology law firm Schürmann Rosenthal Dreyer Rechtsanwälte in Berlin, where he leads the AI and Data Regulation practice group. After studying law at Ruprecht-Karls-University Heidelberg and Albert-Ludwigs-University Freiburg, he completed his legal clerkship at the Higher Regional Court of Brandenburg. Philipp specializes in data regulation, IT law, and digital business. He advises clients in the financial and insurance sectors on legally compliant digital business models, data utilization, and AI compliance, with a focus on designing privacy-centric AI systems and advanced analytics applications.

Valentin Tanczik LL.M. (Groningen) is currently doing his legal clerkship at the Higher Regional Court of Berlin. He studied law at Martin-Luther-University Halle-Wittenberg with a semester abroad in Chongqing, China. He then worked at Schürmann Rosenthal Dreyer Rechtsanwälte in Berlin as a research assistant with an interlude at the University of Groningen, Netherlands, from where he obtained an LL.M. in public international law. He possesses extensive experience in the field of modern and digital technologies. In addition to his expertise in AI regulation, his particular focus lies in international public law and the protection of human rights.

Alexander Holz works as a Consultant in the Data Strategy & AI Department at ISiCO GmbH in Berlin. He advises clients on emerging technologies at the intersection of AI, blockchain, and data regulation, leveraging both legal and technical expertise. He studied law with a focus on data protection at European University Viadrina in Frankfurt (Oder), complementing his studies with international experiences, including a semester at CBL law and Business School in Dubai along with an internship at a major law firm, and an Erasmus term at Aberystwyth University in Wales. Before transitioning to the technology sector, he became a Certified Blockchain Expert (Frankfurt School of Finance & Management) and completed a software engineering program at Le Wagon coding school in Berlin specializing as a Full-Stack Developer.

The (Re)making of a Modern Lawyer: An In-House Counsel's Reinvention Journey

Robert Dilworth

Contents

Views are the author's alone as a member of the New York bar; they do not imply endorsement by his employer or any association. Recommendations are not to, and any perceived criticisms are not of, any single person, legal function, law firm, or other parts of our legal community. The author's sole intent is to promote respectful and robust discussion. He is profoundly grateful to reviewers worldwide (many named, referred to, or cited herein) for their comments, suggestions, and resounding encouragement.

R. Dilworth (✉)
New Rochelle, NY, USA
e-mail: r.dilworth@liquid-legal-institute.org

K. Jacob et al. (eds.), *Liquid Legal – Sustaining the Rule of Law*, Law for Professionals, https://doi.org/10.1007/978-3-031-78596-2_14

Abstract

This chapter chronicles an established Wall Street corporate lawyer's journey towards questioning the legal profession's fitness for purpose in the modern age and committing to personal reinvention. Recent advances in Artificial Intelligence, synthetic biology, and other technologies present vast opportunities and implications for society, including legal professionals. The author argues that these provide lawyers an inflection point to examine their relevance and role in a rapidly changing world, and to adopt changes that would enhance their effectiveness in this new society. This would improve respect for the rule of law and its institutions.

The author uses a storytelling motif to trace his path of discovery and renewal, from pandemic-induced reflection to active engagement with legal innovation communities and thought leaders. It offers lessons and recommendations for individual lawyers, in-house counsel, and law firms to adapt to the digital age and better serve clients and society. Key themes include embracing a growth mindset (upgrading one's "human operating system", or hOS), developing digital fluency, fostering interdisciplinary collaboration, and reimagining legal service delivery models.

The author maintains that the legal profession's centuries-old cultural insularity must end with haste, advocating a shift from lawyer-centric to human-centric approaches. The chapter concludes with a call to action for legal professionals to courageously face ambiguity, reject the seductive appeal of the continuity paradigm, master change, and actively shape the future of law. Lawyers can thereby regain their purpose, become more valuable to modern society, and rebuild their tarnished stature in an era of unending accelerated change.

> The mind, stretched by a new idea, never shrinks back to its original dimension.[1]

This chapter is a corporate lawyer's road to Damascus story of how I came to question my and the prevailing legal culture's fitness for purpose in the modern age and then commit to personal reinvention to remain relevant in a perpetually changing world.

Recent advances in Artificial Intelligence (AI), synthetic and digital biology, neuromorphic computing, and other advanced technologies present vast opportunities and implications for society, including legal professionals and other knowledge workers. We live at the cusp of the fastest transformation in human

[1] Attributed variously, in slightly different forms, to polymath Oliver Wendell Holmes Sr, jurist Oliver Wendell Holmes Jr, and writer Ralph Waldo Emerson.

history,[2] elements of which are comparable to the steam engine of the mind and a cognitive industrial revolution.[3]

Whether willing or reluctant, legal professionals are subjects of, and participants in, some of these fundamental changes. Today should be a collective inflexion point for us to consider the significance for us, our clients, and broader civil society. As well as to examine our fitness for purpose in a new age and our role in participating with non-legal disciplines in informing the responses to the critical questions that these developments present. I hope that some of my experiences and the influences that I have found useful will help you navigate this new world and meet these challenges.

I thank the editors and the Liquid Legal Institute for allowing me to share my journey and thoughts about purpose and possibility. Part I is introductory, Part II the journey, Part III some lessons shared with fellow legal professionals, and Part IV a concluding call to action.

1 Life Is But a Prologue[4]

1.1 Courage to Question

I practise law in a global bank's legal department. My specialism is a dynamic area that developed after I started my career decades ago. I am spoilt to have such able, committed colleagues who embody so much that is noble about lawyers and our profession, complemented by ready access to the world's leading external firms for the thorniest questions and judgments. This combination offers a unique vantage point.

I am a late baby-boomer—JFK was not yet US President, the ink was barely dry on the Treaty of Rome, and the Berlin Wall was yet to stain history. Given this vintage, I am steeped in the profession's elitist, exceptionalist cult(ure). I followed a law degree from a solid US public university in the American South with advanced ones on a fellowship from Columbia University and Paris I Panthéon-Sorbonne, then six years of rigorous training at a top-tier Wall Street law firm. Next came the in-house leap to two global financial institutions working in New York and Frankfurt. These opportunities took me far from my roots and offered me a world I had traveled to before only through books and shortwave radio.

The traditional system has worked quite well for me. I enjoy bleeding-edge work, a secure standard of living, and life across three cultures and fluent languages. Given these benefits, I would seem unlikely to question things versus prudently keeping my

---

[2] Bank of America Institute, Transformation – Next Gen Tech: Computing (and sources cited, 07 June 2024).

[3] Hoffman (2024).

[4] S Kierkegaard (1813–1855). "Life can only be understood backwards; but it must be lived forwards."

head down and mouth shut while coasting towards retirement. While immensely grateful, in recent years, I have reviewed my beliefs against the needs of modern society and how I expect society to evolve. Despite the convenience of taking the easy way out, I am unrepentant in questioning the received wisdom and unwavering in my commitment to reaching others with whom my themes may resonate. I cannot do otherwise.

1.2 "Move Bits, Not Atoms": Dematerialisation, Generative AI, and the Next Modern Age

The magical mastery by humans of radio waves, then electrons and photons, has possessed me since childhood. It is as much a foundation of modernity as antibiotics. An early adopter, I was one of the first in my law firm to adopt Wang word processing, then instal a home fax machine, buy a first-generation notebook computer and work from DOS command prompts. In 1989, my seemingly routine underwriter counsel's due diligence assignment in Silicon Valley at Intel resulted in a facility tour and an unexpected one-on-one interview with microprocessor pioneer and Intel co-founder Gordon Moore. This opportunity was catnip for my imagination. I learned to design and build my first PCs, bought a modem, and joined hobbyist and early legal bulletin boards. I then cobbled my first internet access in 1993 through a group of geek hobbyists in Frankfurt—instructing servers in Tasmania and Massachusetts to help me compile code to hack Windows 3.0 into internet capability. My next "innovation"—despite others' scepticism—came in 1995 by convincing the managing partner of a prominent global law firm that we link email systems via a standard protocol and hourly modem calls to reduce the use of human messengers to carry documents between Wall Street and mid-town Manhattan. This innovation compressed our transactional and decision-making time, which had cost and ESG benefits—all exponentially greater imperatives today.

My curiosity, willingness to experiment, and desire to challenge the status quo are only greater today, extending to cross-border metaverse meetings and deep dives into Generative AI (GenAI) using leading commercial and open-source tools on a home-built AI inference machine. My inspiration was, as now, Nicolas Negroponte's mantra in early issues of *Wired* magazine and his book *Being Digital*: "Move bits, not atoms."[5]

So has been the radically transformed course of our daily lives, personal interactions, and commercial activities—a rapid dematerialisation of physical supports. Dematerialisation has enabled an unparalleled democratisation of access to many goods, services, and experiences, often accelerated by an intense, iterative focus on improved processes and customer experience. Today, Earth's eight billion inhabitants carry almost seven billion smartphones in their pockets, each having many times the computing power of the computers that took humans to the moon

[5] Negroponte (1995).

nearly 60 years ago. We manage almost 350 billion interconnected devices—an average of 70 per person (and expected to triple by 2035)—creating, as of 2024, an estimated 183 zettabytes (trillion gigabytes) of data. This rate doubles in volume every 2 to 3 years.[6]

Today, almost 70 years after the first microchip and 30 years after the democratisation of internet access through the World Wide Web, humanity is poised for another fundamental societal leap. Decades of exponentially doubled computational power, decreased storage costs (predicted by Moore's and Kryder's laws, respectively), and compounded network effects (Metcalfe's law) have all converged to enable vast advances in AI. These advances now create processing needs beyond the limits of the maturing Moore's law that enables them.

Recent science has coupled the application of powerful AI capabilities to the most common expression of human intelligence and the lawyer's currency—language, with easier access and regular model improvement through GenAI tools that use conversational interfaces.[7] This tandem amplifies any capability that expresses cognition through language. It gives legal professionals an unprecedented opportunity to leapfrog legacy technologies and apply new paradigms to research, data and knowledge management, document creation, and to revisit the fundamental function of a document.[8] And most importantly, to improve the delivery of legal services and narrow society's gaping access to justice gaps.

These advances embody the intellectual capital of all human endeavour—their *corpora* contain our shared inheritance, past and future. We are parties to history's most significant data annotation exercise[9] and public beta testing program; we must do so intentionally. Singularity is no longer simply the realm of inventor and futurist Ray Kurzweil's imagination.[10] Progress towards singularity (including legal

---

[6]Bank of America Institute, n.2.

[7]As evidence of this power and potential, in early 2023 one of the most current GenAI models (GPT-4) passed the US Uniform Bar Examination, scoring in the top 90th percentile. The previous version passed only within the lowest 10th percentile. See D Katz, M Bommarito, S Gao, P Arredondo, GPT-4 Passes the Bar Exam, (15 Mar. 2023, last revised 3 Apr. 2024). Whatever the limitations of current AI tools at the time you read this chapter, "Assume that this is the worst AI you will ever use ... There is no reason to suspect the abilities of AI systems are going to stop growing anytime soon." Mollick (2024), pp. 61–62.

[8]The paradigm for efficient knowledge capture and transmission ever since humans developed written language 5,000 years ago uses physical supports or the electronic visualisation of them. The new paradigm is a complete dematerialisation of the intelligence embedded within the written content. Modern AI-empowered systems passively analyse and structure the unstructured data at an individual clause or obligation level virtually. With GenAI, we start the drafting or research process from the reservoir of content from vectors derived from many laws, regulations, contracts, memoranda, opinions, and clause variations, not just a clone or copy/paste of existing work. The document (physical or electronic representation) may become just a visualisation and convenient transmission tool or evidentiary snapshot at a given moment.

[9]D M Katz and R Tromans (interview), in *Generative AI + The Law (part 2), Artificial Lawyer* (9 May 2023).

[10]Kurzweil (2000, 2005, 2024). Per Kurzweil, "singularity" is a predicted future state (expected by 2045) whereby accelerated returns from exponential increase in advanced technologies will result in

singularity) is accelerating, promising enormous opportunities but also equally difficult societal questions and priority choices.[11]

Legal professionals are typically privileged in terms of educational and learning opportunities, as well as access to vital societal actors. We have the talent and duty to participate *with other disciplines* in society's critical decisions about responsible, legal, and ethical[12] development, the balance between human capital and machine learning, and the use of AI and other advanced technologies to affirm and uplift humanity.[13] The more closely humans and machines interact, the greater the need for human values, and emotional (EQ) and social (SQ) intelligence in the design, use, and governance of these tools. Within our professional spheres,[14] they also give us the enormous opportunity—if not duty—to revisit legacy thinking about knowledge diffusion and the related role of the traditional professions, including lawyers.[15] Society challenges us more strongly than ever to broaden our role beyond gatekeeper of esoteric learnings and client guardian to one of enablement and human empowerment.

My transformation, which started during the pandemic lockdowns, gives me new tools and perspectives to navigate this new world and rise to its challenges. I share them in the spirit of helping others who are open to broadened horizons.

2 The Journey: Reflection and Transformation

2.1 Pandemic: Making Virtue from Vice

I was no stranger to remote work in March 2020, having at times used full-kit home offices to balance the needs of a rich but complex transatlantic family life. Forced remote work required no pivot; it was as fluid as switching languages. During the early months of the initial Covid wave, I lost both parents, and my wife's

machine intelligence being infinitely more powerful than all human intelligence combined, culminating in the merging of human and machine intelligence.

[11] "Legal singularity" is a data-informed, prediction-based stable and complete legal order in which the law is knowable to a practical certainty for much of human activity. Most types of legal uncertainty would be resolvable in real time and on demand. Proponents argue that achieving legal singularity (and safely) is necessary for the law and legal institutions to adapt to fulfil their social role during the rest of the twenty-first century and beyond. Aidid and Alari (2023; highly recommended). A lively, rich discussion of competing considerations is Deakin and Markou (2020).

[12] See Perlman (2023) and Lozinsky (2023).

[13] Acclaimed treatments, beyond the scope of this chapter, include Suleyman and Bhaskar (2023), Kissinger et al. (2022), and Lee and Qiufan (2021).

[14] As to the impacts on legal careers, AI-informed digitalisation has significant potential to unleash greater human creativity and job satisfaction for many. See Glock and von Alemann (2022), pp. 215–230. See also Tromans (2023).

[15] See Susskind and Susskind (2023). They write that the professions are unprepared, in denial, and can no longer rely solely on selling their time.

gastronomy business closed under the US lockdowns. Reeling from these shocks, when the first flights resumed in early autumn 2020, we flew from New York to Germany for solace and to check up on heart, home, and hearth—30 passengers, our dog Fritz in-cabin, and 13 very attentive cabin crew. A three-week trip became four, then five. As the infection rates again soared in late autumn, European lockdowns became more severe, and with no vaccine yet approved, came the realisation that we were safest in our small semi-rural town. Moreover, given today's VUCA (volatile, uncertain, complex, and ambiguous) world, our forced immobility was the perfect time to complete a home renovation project and advance my naturalisation and work permit process.

2.2 Quest for Purpose; Renewal

Processing these forced life transitions in such a bucolic setting and with no fixed return date bore reflection about adaptability, meaning, and purpose during my remaining work years. The result was an enriching year-long odyssey of discovery, reimagination, and intense productivity.

I knew several prominent lawyers in the derivatives legal world who had fascinating, purposeful post-Wall Street and Magic Circle careers comprised of a portfolio of activities, paid and unpaid. I contacted them, and they generously advised me by video conferencing. One engaging contact led to another. Through them, I met entrepreneurs at the cusp of FinTech and RegTech, smack in my practice field. I soon had a network of rough contemporaries with growth, lifelong learning mindsets. This vastly expanded my sense of possibility.

Further networking led me to the leading German law school just half an hour from me in Hamburg. I discovered two rich programmes at Bucerius Law School—the Center on the Legal Profession and the Center for Legal Technology and Data Science. I promptly enrolled in their Spring 2021 online Legal Tech Essentials programme, which had a global all-star faculty under the academic direction of Dr Daniel Martin Katz in Chicago. Covering all major areas of our transforming profession, describing it as an eye-opening and mind-stretching experience is an understatement—more than 3000 live participants on Zoom across 100 countries.

The law is comparable to society's operating system (OS), coordinating the execution of human activity.[16] Its role and legitimacy are fundamental to societal cohesion and advancement. I had (and maintain) deeply troubling rule-of-law questions after the 2020 US Presidential election and the events of 6 January 2021. Why were foundational truths core to my being not more widely shared—including by some members of our profession and sworn, elected public servants? Two particularly memorable Bucerius sessions that informed my struggle were with Professor Richard Susskind OBE FRSE KC (Hon) and Professor William (Bill)

[16] Santa Fe Institute, *lawOS: Regulations as society's operating system*, 9 Nov. 2016; I Logvinova (podcast interview with Stephen Poor), Pioneers and Pathfinders, 28 Feb. 2024.

Henderson. I devoured Susskind's *Tomorrow's Lawyers: An Invitation to Your Future* and contacted him—Richard kindly responded, and we had several enriching (at least for me) video chats, then a year later, an in-person mentoring meeting. I became addicted to Bill's highly influential online journal, *Legal Evolution*. Then, a Zoom chat with Dan Katz, and after some end-of-programme suggestions that I made to Bucerius, an invitation to an on-campus meeting with the Center for Legal Technology & Data Science. I had found a new European intellectual home.

Along this path, I discovered Mark Cohen and Isabel Parker at the Digital Legal Exchange (DLEx). I read Mark's many trenchant commentaries, attended some private DLEx functions, and arranged to have my department invited to participate. I joined the Society for Computers and Law, the European and Swiss Legal Technology Associations, and an early thought group on AI and the law sponsored by Bucerius and the Universität Hamburg Rechtsfakultät. I next discovered the most open, engaging, interdisciplinary fellowship of doers and shapers of legal's future—the Liquid Legal Institute (LLI) think-tank.

Sensing that I was onto something of consequence, I created an annual personal professional development budget, built an enrichment and travel program around my work commitments, and followed my curiosity wherever it led. I read scores of books, articles, memos, and studies, heard tens of podcasts, and contacted more leading thought leaders to establish connections—friendships today. I attended conferences and met with founders, presidents and CEOs of start-ups and new law companies. Soon came invitations to appear as a conference panellist, as well as to publish articles,[17] book chapters, and be a podcast guest.

2.3 An Innovator's Mind Re-Awakened: My New "hOS"

While I had renewed my home and mind, I had yet to innovate much else. I struggled with imposter syndrome. Still, prominent people years ahead of my path assured me that I had an innovator's mind and was a divergent thinker in a legal world dominated by convergent thought. And I had a mindset of someone 20 years younger and valuable things to contribute to the calling that has given me so much. Moreover, much to my shock, that I somehow grasped things that only a minority of corporate CEOs and even fewer of their GCs had yet learned. Although I was tempted to have my hearing checked, after a life of often feeling surrounded by aliens, I was no longer alone. My journey's unexpected reward was an upgraded "hOS"—my human operating system.

My life, perspective, and career expectations have permanently changed in less than four years. I am confidently past the talk and now walking the walk. I am my department's legal innovation thought leader, resident futurist, and founding Co-Chair of its AI steering committee. An incomparable personal global network

[17] R Dilworth (book review and commentary), "Exceeds Its Ambitious Title; A Consequential Work" (*Legal Business World*, No. 5, 2021).

nourishes my growth. I am active with fellow DLEx and LLI "doers" worldwide in forward-thinking initiatives and have informal affiliations with elite universities and law schools. As I deepen my network and knowledge, opportunities to share, grow, and improve our profession continue.

3 Lessons Learned and Shared: Towards A Modern Mindset and Toolkit

3.1 To All Legal Professionals: Upgrade and Reboot Your hOS[18]

3.1.1 Our Shared Role and Purpose: The Need for Renewal

Many of us were drawn to the law for idealistic reasons of purpose—in service to a goal more significant than ourselves, rooted in respect for the rule of law. In retrospect, we cannot expect civil society's respect for the rule of law if we do not deliver a legal system worthy of respect and adaptable to human needs as society changes. Unlike the case with scientific principles, our standards for measuring legal system legitimacy depend on social acceptance.[19] I now accept as a contributing cause of the US election aftermath and 6 January 2021 that many ordinary citizens regard the legal system as largely inaccessible and incomprehensible to all but the privileged elite that designed, masters, and profits from it. To them, it is corrupt, inaccessible, and irrelevant.[20] This deepens the current trust deficit in society[21] and contributes to the polarised politics and appeal of populist and anti-elitist movements: the rule of law and institutions built over decades and centuries are viewed by too many citizens as tools to perpetuate elitist privilege. This sad phenomenon is not peculiar to the United States. Even in other Western liberal democratic bulwarks, respect for the rule of law and its institutions is menaced. Less than half of the world's population lives under the protection of a "strong" or "robust" rule of law.[22] Of the slight majority who do, small businesses and ordinary

[18] Alternatively, we need 'new suits'. See DeStefano and Dobrauz (2019).

[19] Barton (1999), reproduced in Barton (2009), p. 161.

[20] On this and adjacent themes, see M Cohen, *Democratic Degradation is Law's Ultimate Disruptor* (2022) and *Is The Legal Function Fiddling While The Rule Of Law Is Burning? The Case For An Integrated Response* (2002); J Um, *Hope: the Invincible Summer* (3 July 2022), in *Legal Evolution* and W Henderson, *The end of the 'End of History' era* (31 Jul. 2022) and companion articles cited therein, all in *Legal Evolution*.

[21] Um and Sohn (2024).

[22] The World Justice Project's Rule of Law Index (2023) notes a deepening rule of law "recession" in many countries. The US ranks in 26th position overall out of 142 countries surveyed (and 26th out of 46 high income countries). It placed 38th and 29th in civil and criminal justice, respectively, but only 116th in "access and affordability of civil justice" (down 41 places since 2015).

citizens can rarely afford the cost of today's legal services.[23] To paraphrase Franz Kafka, everyone has their entrance to the law, but it is closed.[24]

From Gutenberg to the Reformation, Enlightenment, Industrial Revolution, and today's post-modernist trends, the progressive democratisation and dematerialisation of knowledge transmission away from authority structures almost always triumphs.[25] Despite this, a quarter of the way into the twenty-first century, much of our profession and major legal systems remain mired in the muck of twentieth-century ways.

> Where your talents and the needs of the world cross, there lies your vocation (Aristotle)

With a wisp of nostalgic regret but now fierce conviction, I accept as reality that the legal profession's centuries-old cultural insularity must end—today. Our culture feels comfortable and informs much of our being and self-perception—it is *lawyer-centric*. It is maladapted to fulfilling our purpose in a *human-centric* world of accelerated disintermediation, disaggregation of services and expertise, the democratisation of access, and relentless focus on collaboration, sharing, and user/customer empowerment.[26] Too many of us unquestioningly apply twentieth-century (at best) paradigms to intractable twenty-first-century problems.

We double down in resistance to change primarily due to our fragile egos and narrow near-term interests, sadly unmoored from meaningful commitment to social cohesion and the common good.[27] We cling to existing talent delivery models because they benefit *us*, versus regularly recalibrating them to the needs of an evolving *world*. For too many legal professionals, "vocation" and "calling" are quaint terms of yesteryear, disconnected from the sense of purpose for which many of us thirst.

Our self-infatuation is a security blanket that impedes professional renewal—I must drop mine and our more cult-like traits and embrace broadened sources of self-identity. As a profession, many of us individually and collectively need to upgrade and reboot our OS. Remaining trapped in a Windows 95 mindset disserves civil society at a time of existential need.

---

[23] Many individuals and small businesses rely on Google as their legal advisor; Rocket Lawyer, Legal Zoom and equivalents in other countries exist for a reason. Due to its complexity and cost, practical access to the law for most people is elusive.

[24] F Kafka, *Before the Law (Vor dem Gesetz)* (parable, 1915) and powerful interpretation in Strathausen et al. (2017), pp. 1–3.

[25] See T Barton, n.19, pp. 143–163, and Barton (2016), p. 1.

[26] See M Cohen, *Humanising the Legal Function: What it Means and Why it Matters,* particularly the discussion of "what law is for" (Forbes, 15 Feb. 2022), also available at https://www.legalmosaic.com/humanizing-the-legal-function-what-it-means-and-why-it-matters and reprinted as *Foreword* in Jacob et al. (2022), pp. v–ix.

[27] See M Cohen, n.20.

3.1.2 "Shift Happens": The End of Entitlement and Exceptionalism

We have no fundamental human right to enjoy our special status, monopoly, and largely self-regulation. Instead, these rights are grounded in a social contract (the 'grand bargain', as Professors Richard Susskind and Daniel Susskind put it) due to the learned professions' historical role in mastering and applying very specialised knowledge.[28] To remain relevant, effective, and faithful to our calling for clients and society, lawyers and their allied professionals must urgently evolve their thinking and methods. It is intellectual folly and the height of hubris to act as if we have a birthright to resist change or somehow possess a 'lawyers only' wonder vaccine against the trends that transform every other aspect of society. Our duty—born of this bargain and our remaining status—is with courage and boldness to reimagine our role and methods for the balance of a century in which the pace of change will vastly dwarf that of the first quarter.[29]

We must merit our legitimacy to remain a largely independent, self-regulated profession. We must regain our purpose and focus on where we think the profession, our clients, and society will be two, five, and ten years from now,[30] then boldly adapt our mindsets, practices, and legal education and training models.[31] We must recognise, call out and replace our legacy-based thinking. As Richard Susskind put it best about such seductive but feeble attempts to sustain the present and near past, we cannot "walk backwards into the future".[32] *Stare decisis* is a foundational substantive law principle of common law systems; conflating and reflexively applying it to inform *practice methods* in *any* modern legal system is but cultural ballast. Even layering on technology to automate yesterday's practice paradigm is 'Innovation 1.0' at best, a defensive, not transformational, mindset. **The best way to predict our future is to accept the inevitability and constancy of disruptive change courageously, then shape and invent tomorrow *today*.**

---

[28] See generally, Susskind and Susskind (2015; updated edition 2022).

[29] Bank of America Institute, n.2.

[30] See R Susskind, *Tomorrow's Lawyers*, 3rd ed. (2023), pp. 187 – 229 and Bosbach (2022), pp. 231–268. The results of Bosbach's survey of German market participants are entirely extendible to legal professionals in multinational corporations based in other developed nations.

[31] For a critique of the current lawyer training and problem-solving model when faced with modern "wicked" problems and a novel Transaction Lawyering Framework, see Trang (2022), pp. 289–316.

[32] Conservative, informed by precedent and partial to incremental change, we believe that the present and near past provide solid insight into the future. This is premised on *continuity*; our age is one of *discontinuity*. See Susskind (2008), p. 22; Susskind (2023), pxix or in 3rd edition, p. 3 (2023); R Susskind and D Susskind, n. 20, pplvi–lx (Kindle edition). Also, "Professor Richard Susskind Discusses Online Courts", *The Digital Edge – Legal Talk Network* (podcast interview with R. Susskind), 18 May 2020.

3.1.3 Move with Agility from "Survive" to "Thrive": Today's Disruption Is Tomorrow's Opportunity

Tomorrow's world is today's; the pandemic years taught us that we have only today. Do you want to survive in it or thrive? 'Survive' implies a pessimistic, backward look; 'thrive' is a hopeful, forward look.

Expected AI advances, if managed correctly in our workplaces, promise to increase the number of "thrivers" and their opportunity to make a more significant impact. "Thrivers" are the knowledge workers who have and are empowered by the workplace conditions and culture to consistently use higher-level cognitive and social-emotional skills to be at their creative and collaborative best.[33]

In a period of rapid and fundamental change for legal professionals, law firm management committees and corporate General Counsels must balance reason, EQ, SQ and other social sensibility in leading their organisations through these transitions'[34] Innovators Valérie Saintot and Anita Lamprecht call us to summon pathos, ethos and logos in this navigation.[35]

To thrive today, we must grow beyond the near-exclusive use of our highly convergent, binary problem-solving style instilled by classical legal education and law firm training and incentives. This laser-like style is critical for sound legal advice and many problems and phases of a solution. But not always for every problem in life and with equal full-beam intensity.[36]

It is often attributed to humanistic psychologist Abraham Malow that "if one only has a hammer, every problem is a nail". As with everyone else addressing the challenges of the society that we took an oath to serve, we must marshal the full range of convergent, divergent, left-brain (logic, analysis, math, data) and right-brain (creativity, experimentation, empathy, discernment, intuition, visual representation[37]) mental approaches to reach and relate to people as and where they are. We have many of these tools in our factory-installed human kit, just dulled and under-used.

> Institutions will try to preserve the problem to which they are the solution.[38]

We must be effective parts of multidisciplinary (meaning non-lawyer participant) teams, learn to listen to clients truly and accept advice from non-lawyers as quickly as we dispense it. We must drop the near-occult pretension that others must adapt to

---

[33] McKinsey & Company, *To defend against disruption, build a thriving* workforce, 8 May 2024.

[34] J Um and E Sohn, n.21.

[35] V Saintot and A Lamprecht (conference presentation and podcast), "Bildung als Schlüssel zur KI-Kompetenz" (Weblaw, June 2023). See also, Saintot (2023), pp. 6–14.

[36] See generally, A Kohlmeier and M Klemola, *The Legal Design Book – Doing Law in the 21st century* (2021) and R. Dilworth (review and commentary), n.17.

[37] On the role of visualisation for improved drafting, legal interpretation, and knowledge sharing in a data-intense world, see Saintot and Di Matteo (2022), pp. 195–214.

[38] C. Shirky, The Collapse of Complex Business Models (blog, 1 Apr 2010); Cognitive Surplus (Penguin, 2010); "Here Comes Clay Shirky" (interview, Publisher's Weekly, 21 Jun 2010).

and appreciate our ways. And that what we do is *always* of such a high craft artisanal mystery that only we can understand it (and must jealously maintain it—for the protection of others, never for our ego satisfaction or rent extraction). Many of our attitudes remind me of renegade priests, even six decades after Vatican II, who still celebrate Mass in Latin, back to the congregants and keeping the laity as supplicants—we are both self-*referential* and self-*reverential*.[39] The law must become more of an enabler than a barrier.

If we accept the challenge, more profound transformation across legal practice in line with clients and the rest of society will bring significant benefits: improved intergenerational knowledge transfer,[40] increased cognitive and social diversity, and enhanced recruitment, retention, creativity and engagement.[41] It would promote better access to legal services and improved outcomes, helping restore our standing as relevant and committed to the service of society.

We should do this in tandem with promoting cultural growth and greater well-being.[42] All legal professionals should consider the psychological and sociological aspects of change at the individual and organisational levels,[43] as well as the deep interconnections to mental health and well-being in our profession. We have *far* above-average health vulnerabilities. Bettering the work experience through augmenting human workflows with technology will improve well-being and *individual* sustainability. However, despite our great intellects, many of us have mindset obstacles to change. We are prone to common cognitive distortions that impair happiness, openness to help, personal and professional growth, and, by extension, the necessary adaptation of our profession.[44] These desperately require reframing.

[39] See n.24, especially the discussion of the power trip in which many indulge due to our control of specialised knowledge (domain knowledge, or *Herrschaftswissen*).

[40] For a compelling diagnosis and prescriptions, see M Cohen, *Learning From Each Other: Fostering Intergenerational Collaboration* (2023), available at https://www.legalmosaic.com/learning-from-each-other-fostering-intergenerational-collaboration and J Furlong, "Building a generationally integrated law firm", 19 Sept 2024 (Substack blog).

[41] The benefits of social and cognitive diversity on teamwork and decision-making are well established. As well as the preventive contributions that cognitively diverse, growth mindset lawyers and compliance professionals bring to corporate decisions. See DeStefano et al. (2023). M DeStefano posits convincingly that law firms' lagging progress in diversity and innovation initiatives are inextricably related: more innovative, growth mindsets with firms would foster a deeper understanding of the causes of, and more creative solutions to address, poor sustained diversity improvement. Moreover, a more diverse composition within law firms would foster cognitive diversity and increased service innovation. See DeStefano (2023), pp. 1209–1248.

[42] For a construct to counter four common cognitive biases in legal professionals, see Saintot and Lulić (2022), pp. 133–155. See also DeStefano (2018), ch.4 ("Lawyers' Crutches: The Source of the Gap in Skills, Behavior and Mindset") and *Leader Upheaval – A Guide to Client-Centricity, Culture Creation, and Collaboration*, ABA Publishing (2024).

[43] See Kotter et al. (2021).

[44] The LLI's Lawyer Well-Being Project is an example of needed steps to raise consciousness and lift taboos (Call to Action; Survey Findings and White Paper: *"The Silent Pandemic" – Well-being and Personal Health of Legal Professionals in Times of Digital Transformation and Social Change*). See also M. Cohen, n.20 above (*Is the Legal Function Fiddling* ...) and sources cited.

3.2 To In-House Counsel

3.2.1 The Analogue Business and Legal Worlds Are Over; the Only Continuity Is Discontinuity

Upskilling, process, and cultural changes are essential to my and many internal lawyers' continued relevance and well-being. They are a prerequisite to any lasting effort to cope with the constant 'do more for less' pressures[45] and preserve any semblance of career satisfaction while faced with a 'just a cost centre' perception.

Our clients' digital transformations proceed apace. The resulting business volume, coupled with vastly greater legal complexity resulting from today's increased social, economic, and political diversity and interconnection,[46] turbo-charge our workloads. Most corporate legal functions (legal) represent well under 0.5% of the company's workforce. Many are on the losing side of an arms race, vastly outgunned by the business and social equivalents of hypersonic weapons. Regardless of how necessary and beneficial, just wringing out cost efficiencies year after year is insufficient. As Jason Barnwell (Microsoft Legal) aptly said: "That's not the tide coming in. The seas are rising."[47] We struggle already not to drown in the flood. As the above trends intensify due to AI-driven business volumes, legal will soon need to sound a tsunami warning.

Twenty-first-century forces increase demand for our work and on ever-compressed time frames. Even in a fantasy world without headcount restraints, the predominant 1:1 lawyering model can never keep up because it lacks scalability. It is intuitively mathematical: legal professionals must harness the same types of forces and tools in response to the accelerated demand for our work as the forces and digitalised tools that fuel the acceleration. More automation or optimisation is insufficient as this uses existing work paradigms more efficiently, while work volumes and complexity increase due to non-linear, self-reinforcing causes.

The pandemic years upped the ante; our modernity (i.e., mentality) gaps have been quickly laid bare as gaping vulnerabilities. Rapid advances in AI, especially GenAI, vastly accelerate these trends and the threat—but also present our most significant opportunity in generations. McKinsey estimates that GenAI across 63 use cases within a few years could add new economic activity equal to or greater than the

---

[45] R Susskind expects these pressures to continue into the next decade of legal service. *Tomorrow's Lawyers*, 3rd edition (2023), p. 13.

[46] By applying complexity science, the law is a complex adaptive system that is always chasing a society of multiple such systems. D Katz, J B Ruhl, and M Bommarito, "Harnessing Legal Complexity", 31 Mar. 2017, available at https://scholarship.kentlaw.iit.edu/fac_schol/1000/ ("Legal systems are locked in perpetual coevolution with their regulatory targets.") See also Katz et al. (2020), available at SSRN: https://ssrn.com/abstract=3602098 or https://doi.org/10.2139/ssrn.3602098 and Katz and Bommarito (2014), p. 337, revised version available at https://papers.ssrn.com/sol3/papers.cfm?abstract_id=2307352. In the financial institutions' context and the urgent need to change practices to cope with the amount of regulatory data and improve its effectiveness, see Datoo (2019).

[47] Barnwell (2021).

UK's GDP—*annually*.[48] This cycle does not consider the impact of the massively more capable AI tools that the newest clustered parallel processors and eventual quantum computing will enable. Nor the innovations that the converged "power couple" of AI and quantum technologies could enable.[49] There is no end in sight. Nor to the corporate world's digital and AI rewiring of itself to meet and profit from these cycles—which then reinforces and perpetuates them *ad infinitum*.[50]

Inaction today harms our clients and us, is an unconscionable disservice to our younger colleagues' future, delays the inevitable reckoning, and makes facing it later much harder. *The post-pandemic inflationary pressures and hyper-focus on business expense control intensify this dilemma. Still, they could also herald a tipping point in C-suites for leaders who are prescient to grasp and courageous to seize the vast potential for significant, long-term transformation.* One innovator and commentator compares our opportunity to "mov[ing] from the abacus to a voice-activated calculator."[51]

3.2.2 Purpose and Corporate Alignment: Towards the 'Department of Possibilities'

To arrest this dystopian cycle, we must first examine how well our purpose aligns with the company's statement of purpose. The company's digital transformation is likely closely tied to its purpose, reflecting elements of stakeholder capitalism in many modern companies. By better integrating with the enterprise's transformation, legal can recalibrate its corporate alignment and mission. However, even if already well-aligned within a corporation having forward-thinking values and a dynamic culture, legal may still have an active or vestigial subculture. Most of us are products of the law firm culture (and no doubt the educational system and culture of exceptionalism). Often, the same cultural weaknesses that affect many law firms in adapting their lawyers' minds and models also infect in-house counsel mindsets. We can benefit directly or with minor adaptation from many of the same diagnoses and recommendations applicable to law firms; thankfully, we have fewer structural impediments to meaningful change.[52]

Legal must broaden the conversation and internal corporate perception of us beyond the 'just a cost centre' and reactive guardian role. We should be defined more by reason than tradition, more by creativity than rote conservatism, and unleash our teams' whole ambition and potential. The goal is to become, and be perceived as, a risk and reputational guardian *plus* a critical business enabler and value creator, the 'Department of Possibilities.' Not as the place where ideas go to die, often strangled by process. This is the only sustainable hope to improve our lot.

---

[48] *The Economic Potential of Generative AI* – The next productivity frontier (whitepaper, McKinsey & Company, June 2023).

[49] See Bank of America Institute, n.2.

[50] See Lamarre et al. (2023).

[51] Logvinova (2023).

[52] For a masterful treatment, see Parker (2021).

3.2.3 Ways to Start

How to achieve this in fine detail is beyond the scope of this chapter—excellent case studies and practical guides abound.[53] But most include these elements:

- **purpose and its measure**: refining legal's purpose, then defining what value and success mean to legal and how they will be measured quantitatively and qualitatively;
- **maintaining mental clarity—key distinctions:**
  - **Law and Technology**—*Law of technology*—most lawyers should be fluent in how the law applies to technology. *The technology of lawyering—all* lawyers must understand and embrace how technology applies to legal practice.
  - **Optimisation and innovation** - *Optimisation* (including automation and process improvement) has great value but narrows our perspective because it usually applies within an existing lawyering paradigm. *Innovation* considers new paradigms and proven techniques from the rest of society; it enables bigger game hunting. Legal exceptionalism is a poison that retards innovation through its visceral rejection of successful, but 'not invented here, not by lawyers' solutions;[54]
- **being data-driven**[55]: Accept that data is society's new oil and the *lingua franca* of the rest of your company; legal is a laggard. Addressing this gap will elevate legal's value in the eyes of management, clients, and fellow risk partners. It will help legal control and expand its value narrative.[56] Do so by (i) harnessing data (enabled by AI) to harvest insights, detect risk, and uncover missed revenue opportunities, (ii) increasing the proportion of structured, quality data created, retained, and analysed, (iii) using AI to make sense and get more life from your legacy data stack(s), (iv) using reliable, relevant data and qualitative measures to inform holistic key performance indicators (KPIs) or other benchmarking metrics and (v) using data as the foundation of scalable, client-centric service delivery models. Being data-informed enables measuring internal and external resource allocations and aligning them against risk indicators to keep a suitable match. More granular data analysis of external counsel staffing and invoices can greatly support diversity goals and hold external firms to account. **The data cycle starts when legal or external counsel is first engaged.** Internally, portals, front doors,

---

[53] Leading approaches, supported by case studies, are critiqued in M DeStefano, BP Tellmann and D Wu, "Don't Let the Digital Tail Wag the Transformation Dog: A Digital Transformation Roadmap for Corporate Counsel" (6 Feb. 2022), University of Miami Legal Studies Research Paper No 4021593, available at SSRN: https://ssrn.com/abstract=4021593 or https://doi.org/10.2139/ssrn.4021593. An excellent *précis* of this article is Gillespie (2022b). See also Tellmann (2017). These authors favour holistically reviewing and optimising the service delivery model and its related processes before jumping to tech solutions because foundational, non-technology changes are critical if the tech changes are to be successful and add full ROI.

[54] Kennedy (2019), ch.s 2-4.

[55] See Mack et al. (2024).

[56] Cohen (2024b).

or other systematised intake methods are essential tools in building a data-informed legal function;

- **client-centricity**: instilling a client and customer centricity at least equal to the company's—this means learning to understand clients as well as we think we already do;
- **deeper problem analysis**: as a corollary, resisting our instinct to 'solution jump' by instead first investing the time to fully understand the problems and possible solutions (following Albert Einstein's advice[57]);
- **horizontal and multidisciplinary thinking**: reducing silos within legal to discover similar problems and share solutions across practice verticals, including through departmental centres of excellence; equally soliciting, recognising and rewarding colleagues not having or needing a law degree for the unique and essential problem-solving perspectives that they bring as part of an integrated team;
- **enterprise leverage**: finding the right balance between legal-specific and the enterprise's technology and methods; learning from other functions that face similar challenges (such as in contracting, document management, knowledge management, and AI-enabled solutions);
- **legal operations**: elevating and professionalising legal ops to become a *strategic ops* function that is equal in stature to that of the practising lawyers;
- **'no-sourcing'**: accepting that not all risks are equal and that some work may not get done within legal, or even at all within the enterprise;
- **moving lawyers up the value chain**: using all available tools to reduce the amount of time spent on repetitive workflow tasks and lower-value (from a risk perspective) activities, thus enabling lawyers to spend more time practising closer to the top of their licences;
- **standardisation and systemisation**: increasing the use of standard terms, clause libraries, and taxonomies, then embedding these in scalable, AI-enabled processes;
- **externalisation**: empowering clients with intranet intake and chat portals, as well as self-service or automated tools that require 1:1 engagement with legal only at defined escalation points;
- **front office revenue enablement**: otherwise compressing time-to-contracting or decision-making (thus speeding revenue generation);
- **peer collaboration**: just as industry associations do for members, working with peer companies, directly or indirectly, to develop shared solutions in areas of common need that are not competitive or confidential;
- **monetisation**: where legal's solution to such a problem is a clear peer leader, monetising it by licensing to others;

[57]Einstein said, "If I had an hour to solve a problem, I'd spend 55 minutes thinking about the problem and 5 minutes thinking about solutions." Moreover, "It's not that I'm so smart, it's just that I stay with problems longer." A short, insightful comparison of design thinking and legal design as tools in this process and discussion of which method to favour based on specific goals is Gillespie (2022a).

- **innovative external counsel pricing**: using creative, data-driven (beyond time spent[58]) techniques, including reverse auctions, to increase the proportion of external work that is priced based on value-added and outcomes (data, including from GenAI, is your friend here);
- **work process optimisation**: disaggregating work elements to the most cost-effective and quality-consistent providers; and
- **scaling the next summit**: otherwise extending the past two decades' progress in the e-discovery, litigation, and investigations worlds to the transactional and advisory worlds to improve risk control and enable more commercial value. Shift the AI focus from *functions* to *capabilities*.

Above all, fearlessly call out and question accepted truths about the 'possible' and 'impossible', including all sacred cows and common cognitive biases endemic to lawyers. Recognise that our most significant limitations are our self-imposed mental frameworks; break psychological barriers to change by reframing outworn beliefs. Build from the agile muscle memory that the pandemic's forced change management created.

3.3 To Individual Legal Professionals: Change Starts with You

Transformation starts from within us and our teams; it is not imposed. Innovation within any organisation occurs and diffuses within a social context.[59] Both start with individuals who dare to think differently and then model the changes they wish to see more generally. Don't sleep just because others slumber; re-frame this as validation and your opportunity.

Here are common ways to start:

- **Climb out of the silo.** Break the cycle of in-house self-navel observation that may have contributed to the current state. The antidote to insularity and groupthink is awareness, followed by engagement outside the corporate and legal department bubble. Do not just complain; do something.
- **Develop your digital mindset and a mental framework for our era.** Attain fluency at a conceptual (not technical) level of core elements of digital society, e.g., data and analytics, human interaction with AI, digital presence, privacy, and

[58] The billable hour did not come down from Mt Sinai with Moses and the Ten Commandments. Among other catalysts in the US, at least, ironically, was the desire by corporate clients for more transparency in invoices and the use of time as a crude proxy for value. See S L Pardau, *Bill, Baby, Bill . . .*, in *Idaho Law Review*, Vol. 50, No. 1 (April 2014). Better measures for value and price discovery exist today.

[59] See E M Rogers, *Diffusion of Innovations* (5th edition, 2003) and Bill Henderson's application of it to legal professionals in *What is the Roger's Diffusion Curve,* in *Legal Evolution*, 8 May 2013, available at https://www.legalevolution.org/2017/05/rogers-diffusion-curve-004.

security.[60] Build your mental framework with the help of thought leaders and fundamental readings.[61]

- **Engage with innovators.** Start within your enterprise (e.g., AI, metaverse, Web 3.0, data, distributed ledger and other corporate digital transformation experts, any internal innovation lab), then with your peers at similar companies. Many external leaders are active on LinkedIn; develop a network and broaden your horizons. This will enrich your mind, and your contacts will encourage and inspire you when dispirited.
- **Develop an adjacent future-based subject matter expertise.** Legal innovators bring their skills to shape the future and not just to explain the past. Do not wait to be asked; be a leader and seize the initiative. Develop fluency and relative expertise in rapidly emerging areas of transformative potential, such as GenAI. Experiment privately on non-company matters and systems until work use is permitted; learn the limitations, risks and mitigants first-hand. Become the go-to resource for your department or practice group; think about the hard questions. You need not master all the legal issues and technical nuances; no one else can either in emerging areas.
- **Adopt an inquiry, beginner's mindset, and exemplify life-long learning.** Devour books, articles, and podcasts. Join and follow online groups or external organisations. As to costs, if your company does not yet support you, do so yourself with a modest annual budget. **Please do not wait to future-proof yourself until everyone else gets it; this enslaves you to legacy thinking.** Assert leadership of your future, then show others. Light a candle in the darkness; *this* is being a change agent.[62]
- **Join industry group initiatives**. Start with groups to which your company or department may already belong, such as the Association of Corporate Counsel, ISDA, ISLA, ICMA, World Commerce and Contracting Association, or bar associations. There may be e-signature, standardisation, taxonomy, clause library, smart(er) contracts, digital assets, computational law/regulation or other projects. Alternatively, choose your continuing legal education events in these or other emerging areas.
- **External memberships.** Mount the case for one or two critical departmental external memberships. Initially, be willing to join interesting organisations at personal expense, e.g., CLOC, LLI or legal tech organisations offering modest-priced individual memberships. Once armed with first-hand experience, (re)-mount your case.

---

[60] See Leonardi and Neeley (2022), Waisberg and Hudek (2021), Siebel (2019).

[61] See Davies (2023), O Mack, H Noorestani, M Onwudiwe, n.56, E Mollick, n.7; J Um and E Sohn (2023); J Um and E Sohn, n.21. The author would gladly share with interested readers a list of other foundational works. Some are within these endnotes.

[62] See n. 60 and 61.

- **Partner with law schools and law firms.** Engage with law school centres on law and technology or centres on the legal professions—perhaps at your *alma mater* or one near you. Identify law firms with which you work that claim to be innovative; meet to test their commitment and credibility. Smoke out the 'tech and AI-washers' and shutter the 'innovation theatre'. From the remainder, find win-win partnership opportunities and deepen the relationships. Favour those with innovation labs, incubators, internal disruptor subsidiaries, consulting practices, and those whose internal economic model incentivises lawyers to use innovative tools and methods for client benefit.
- **Departmental innovation initiatives.** Test the diffusion theory—innovation within any group diffuses in a social context. Join any existing internal innovation initiatives; otherwise, volunteer to start one or organise educational events that will help broaden the cultural mindset. Employ stealth, circulating articles, book and podcast recommendations, and event invitations as needed. Provide a safe space for curious questions by organising a discussion group or holding a regular open-office hour. You will discover (or, in time, convert) like-minded colleagues. Use your understanding of the company and department's hierarchical dynamics and political levers to advance change.
- **Achieve easy wins.** Work with your colleagues, legal ops and technology partners to identify low-hanging opportunities. Achieve and publicise these. Build hope and enthusiasm that improvement is possible.
- **Build internal alliances.** Seek allies; tie this improvement agenda to any corporate or departmental efficiency, operational excellence, or digital transformation agenda. As well as to any well-being, diversity, pro bono, and intergenerational workplace groups and agendas—the mutually reinforcing inter-relationships and positive outcomes here are well documented.[63] Partner with your legal ops colleagues; support them in professionalising their role and elevating appreciation of its strategic importance within your department.
- **Explore the expected legal careers of the near future,[64] the requisite skills, and ways to develop them.[65]** We cannot know the exact timeframe and confines of the future we build daily. As futurist Ray Amara said, "We tend to overestimate the effect of a technology in the short run and underestimate the effect in the long run." AI and other advanced technologies will not likely replace the need for legal professionals in society. **However, they will change our roles. Indeed, legal**

[63] See n.41.

[64] See R Susskind, n.45, ch. 16. The author outlines 15 legal roles of the future.

[65] See Curphey (2022); M DeStefano, *Legal Upheaval . . .*, n.42, especially ch.3., A Kohlmeier and M Klemola, *The Legal Design Book – Doing Law in the 21st century* (2021), pp. 232–251 (I, X and T professional profiles; Delta and Free-Floating models; new roles in law) and pp. 255–259 (from traditional service delivery models to LUX: Legal User Experience) and Cohen (2024a) (also available at https://www.legalmosaic.com/creating-a-gen-ai-era-legal-function-what-it-means-why-it-matters-and-where-to-start).

professionals who can fluently use and work alongside AI and other technologies are likelier to flourish than those who do not.[66]

Above all, keep an open mind and follow your curiosity as it leads. Do not be discouraged by not understanding everything immediately, especially technical jargon. This did not deter you in law school. **The future needs legal professionals who are life-long learners, 'learn-it-alls', not 'know-it-alls'.** Persevere. Re-awaken your sense of wonder and possibility. Time will reward your foresight.

3.4 External Counsel

After over 30 years as an internal counsel for corporate clients of many global law firms with sophisticated financial services practices, I have several observations and recommendations.

- **Review and frame your firm's purpose for the digital age.** It is likely tied to continuity and perpetuity, maintaining the firm's tradition and what you think differentiates your culture from that of competitors. If you are serious about having a mission of service and ensuring perpetuity, you will reframe your purpose for the digital age. Many of your marketing and recruiting pitches tout, with gratitude, how your firm has grown in substantive and geographic scope in tandem with client needs. Put truth to it by aligning your purpose directly with your corporate clients.
  First, in a service business, your interests are derivative of your corporate clients' interests. We are rigorously mandated to maximise value in every choice. Your job, and the best way to secure loyalty, is to help us do so. Second, we now consider stakeholders beyond the equity owners, e.g., employees and their well-being, vendors, customers, community, sustainability, diversity, and other societal concerns.[67] We increasingly apply benchmarks in these areas as panel selection criteria. Up your game.

- **Accept that you also are no longer in an analogue world**. Very few firms have such unique franchises and business models that they can risk not adapting. Factor expects that GenAI will enable new levels of client-centricity and reshape 80% of the corporate legal wallet to varying degrees based on value tranche; even the most elite work will be affected.[68] A refreshed, modernised purpose should

---

[66] Boehmig (2023). See also R Tromans, *The End of Lawyers? Not Yet*, in *Artificial Lawyer* (16 May 2023).

[67] See I Parker, n.52, ch.9. Note to law firms: If the author, as your client's internal lawyer, can buy and read this book (twice) to understand your strengths, weaknesses, challenges, and opportunities, your management team can read it at least once.

[68] J Um and E Sohn, n.21, pp. 12–16.

inform a review of your overall culture, which would then drive a review of the overall structure and your willingness and capacity to evolve with the needs of clients and broader society. Take a microscope to your structural impediments to true innovation and efficiency; consider mitigants. Even within the traditional partnership model, there are many different approaches to drive innovation for the benefit of clients and other stakeholders. Examples and case studies abound.[69]

- **Learn to listen to clients and their needs.** Emphasise the people who pay you at least as much as you obsess about the people whom you pay. Meet with clients, seek candid feedback, use in-depth surveys with senior legal department management, and consider establishing a client advisory body. Refrain from relying solely on transactional feedback since individual relationships on specific matters between self-interested participants only reflect deal flow, not the digital and transformational vision of the client and its legal department.[70]

- **Avoid games.** Innovation is a strategic exercise, not tactical, and not marketing hype. Some corporate clients may already be ahead of you; they increasingly can detect innovation theatre, poseurs, and smoke-out 'AI and tech-washers'. Clients will increasingly choose from amongst your most serious and forward-thinking competitors.
- **Broaden your hiring pool; live up to your role in the talent ecosystem by taking a systemic view.** Discover and favour young graduates who have future-fit training through participation in law and technology programmes or may have followed non-traditional paths before their legal education or joining your firm. Make a concerted effort to include those with academic or applied backgrounds in management, business, computer science, systems analysis, marketing, etc. These associates will likely bring to their lawyering styles the types of diverse thinking that the future demands. This will make your firm more valuable to your corporate clients, enrich your firm culture, and improve its social diversity.[71]
  Leverage your reputation, hiring power, and alumni influence to support the creation or expansion of law school innovation programmes. Do so through conduct and financially through sponsoring joint activities such as conferences, clinics, hackathons, scholarships, and endowed teaching chairs.
  Start reimagining now the traditional apprentice learning system for law firm trainee and associate development. Focus more on skills and getting your younger lawyers up the skill development curve earlier versus on process tasks since

---

[69] I Parker, n.52 ch.7 and J Armour and M Sako, *AI-Enabled Business Models in Legal Services: From Traditional Law Firms to Next-Generation Law Companies?* (16 Dec. 2019), available at SSRN: https://ssrn.com/abstract=3418810 or https://doi.org/10.2139/ssrn.3418810.J Um and E Sohn, n. 21, pp. 12–16.

[70] See "In conversation with Thomas Barothy ", in *Modern Lawyer* (Globe Law and Business, April 2022), p. 5.

[71] See M DeStefano, "Chicken or Egg: Diversity and Innovation in the Corporate Legal Marketplace", n.41, and related text.

AI-enabled and other technologies will reduce the human capital needed for tasks. More experienced lawyers could spend less time supervising and reviewing process tasks and more time on the substantive skill development of their juniors, as well as practising law at higher points on their licenses.[72]

Since your associates are in-house legal's primary talent pipeline, following these common-sense recommendations will eventually improve the entire talent ecosystem. **We need more 21st-century lawyers, not 20th.** (Legal should monitor these efforts when reviewing panels, just as it does for diversity.)

- **Re-align internal motivations.** Incentivise your lawyers to use innovative tools for client benefit, not just increased partnership profits. Partner with key clients to develop win-win service delivery models. **Success in today's world is both digital and collaborative.** Recalibration grounded in this realisation will secure and increase profitability and client satisfaction. Greater transparency will engender trust and institutional loyalty. If predictions of new economic activity in a data-centric, AI-ubiquitous society are even half correct, you will not want for profitable work.
- **Above all, do not squander the present moment. Your actions define you; your clients' eyes are upon you.** GenAI gives you an unprecedented, litmus test, pass/fail opportunity to build deeper client relationships based on lasting value, move beyond automation to discover innovative and differentiating solutions and assist your corporate clients in their priority quest to become more data-driven and informed. You can facilitate the latter by sharing your learnings, providing co-development opportunities or "client labs", and using GenAI for their benefit by deriving and sharing data from your knowledge of them and their business sectors. This includes client-specific data you possess from your work with them.[73] Offer data-based insights to clients to deepen relationships and make them strategic. Where your innovative work with this data has a differentiating value-add, offer licensing or other pricing solutions that recognise the parties' respective contributions equitably.

The modern corporate law firm and in-house role developed in response to prevailing economic conditions and needs in a mature industrial and analogue era. If created de novo today, they'd likely be different and not have some of the cultural debt discussed in this chapter. Be bold in the present moment; view it as an invitation to re-imagine the corporate client–law firm relationship for the coming age in which human capital is no longer the sole input or measure of value. Reframe it as a reciprocal, strategic, integrated supply chain of learnings, data, solutions, opportunities, and mutual wins. Working together, use your collective hiring and buying power to influence legal education, the talent pipeline, tech vendor product and service development, and other essential ecosystem elements to match your shared vision of the future.

---

[72] I Logvinova, n.51.

[73] For a cautionary note as to whether (or when) many law firms will rise to this challenge, see Cohen (2023).

4 Conclusion: Now Is Our Time, Your Time

The most challenging problems of our age do not arise in isolation—instead, they have systemic causes. Practical, durable solutions require multiple lenses and skills from all critical members of society; lawyers included—healthy and purpose-fit.

Current and expected AI, synthetic and digital biology, and other advanced technological developments are a case in point and an opportunity to prove our worth and relevance. The pace exceeds our ability to adapt laws and regulations on an informed, measured, and coordinated basis. Like it or not, we must build these rocket ships as we fly them. As we improvise and iterate our navigation system in flight, society must live in ambiguity and develop private principles, self-governance and best practices. These multidisciplinary efforts are the best test labs for informed legislation and regulation.[74]

4.1 Planck's Principle and Our Profession: Finding Courage to Lose Sight of the Shore

Lawyers have an instrumental role in this process—if they earn it through readiness for the task. In a slower age, physicist Max Planck was paraphrased as saying that science advances one funeral at a time.[75] *The pace and intensity of change in today and tomorrow's world do not give our profession the luxury of waiting for law schools to modernise and produce successive future-fit generations of lawyers to eventually replace retiring, fixed-mindset colleagues and refresh the in-house hiring pipeline.* Self-intervention and renewal are required. Each of us has agency and can assert ownership of our professional development and outlook; each within our workplaces can light that first flame in the stadium, however dark. The diffusion theory assures us that others who sense there must be a better path will join.

Many lawyers are temperamentally conservative, do not like ambiguity, prefer greater clarity, and may find today's hyper-dynamic world disconcerting. **However, denial is no solution.** Keeping our eyes fixed firmly on the rear-view mirror as we speed towards unknown destinations will not end well.[76] The best lawyers learn to master ambiguity and change well—using multiple cognitive tools to see all sides of a matter and the interests of all the stakeholders, then reducing (or, as needed,

---

[74] See I Logvinova, *Responsible generative AI – drawing AI governance principles and enabling a conversation*, in A Davies, n.61 ch.11, pp. 150–153 (suggesting a flexible, principles-based framework in which an optimized and responsible equilibrium may be found based on the specific case of AI development and deployment).

[75] Literally, "Science advances one funeral after another." (Translated from the paraphrase "Ein Begräbnis nach dem anderen bring die Wissenschaft voran.").

[76] See S Kierkegaard (1813–1855). "There are two ways to be fooled. One is to believe what isn't true; the other is to refuse to believe what is true."

introducing) ambiguity to craft constructive outcomes.[77] As novelist André Gide put it in 1925, we cannot discover new lands unless we are comfortable losing sight of the shore.[78]

We possess these tools; we must awaken, sharpen, and use them. And expand our toolset by learning new tools. Clients and broader society desperately need us to update our kit and embrace these challenges boldly and committed through the rediscovery of our individual and collective purpose. The sooner we do both, the more faithful we can be to our service mission, become more valuable to modern society, and regain some of our tarnished stature.

4.2 Change the Wind or Adjust Our Sails?

Rapid, often disruptive, change is a given—we cannot put the genie back in the bottle. Any stasis may be fleeting; there is no end in sight and no finishing line. In Aristotle's words, "We cannot change the wind, but we can set the sails differently." In such a climate, lawyers and allied professionals still have much to offer society in navigating these constant transitions and adapting our institutions. **In a VUCA world, today *should* be our time.**

We live in exciting times, full of challenges and opportunities. Together, we can face them and better meet our societal role with renewed thinking, boldness, and optimism. I invite you—with head, heart, and hands—to join me and other like-minded souls worldwide in our quest to improve today and build tomorrow.

Our only choice—be a change-maker or a change-taker.

References

Aidid A, Alari B (2023) The legal singularity: how artificial intelligence can make law radically better. University of Toronto Press

Barnwell J (2021) Legal evolution is industrial evolution. Legal Evolution

Barton T (1999) Law and science in the enlightenment and beyond. Soc Epistemol (Taylor & Francis), 13:99

Barton T (2009) Preventive law and problem solving. Vandeplas Publishing, p 161

Barton T (2016) Re-designing law and lawyering for the information age. Notre Dame J Law Ethics Public Policy 30:1

Boehmig J (2023) In: Wilkins D, Boehmig J (interview) in "Speaker's corner – assisting knowledge workers. The practice. Harvard Center on the Legal Profession, March – April 2023

Bosbach M (2022) How will people enter the legal job market in ten years' time. In: Jacob K et al (eds) Liquid legal institute: humanization and the law. Springer, pp 231–268

Cohen M (2023) How transformative will generative AI and other tools be for the legal industry?

[77] R Strathausen, *Masters of Ambiguity: How Legal Can Lead the Business*, in *Liquid Legal*, n.24 pp. 9–32.

[78] A Gide, *Les Faux Monnayeurs (The Counterfeiters), 1925*, "One does not discover a new land without being willing to lose sight of, at first and then for a long time, any shore." ("On ne découvre pas de terre nouvelle sans consentir à perdre de vue, d'abord et longtemps, tout rivage.")

Cohen M (2024a) Creating a gen AI-Era legal function – what it means, why it matters and where to start. Forbes, 16 July 2024
Cohen M (2024b) What Is the legal function's true enterprise value? Forbes, 3 Sept 2024
Curphey A (2022) The legal team of the future: law+ skills. London Publishing Partnership
Datoo A (2019) Legal data for banking – business optimisation and regulatory compliance. Wiley
Davies A (ed) (2023) AI and the legal profession: transforming the future of law. Globe Law & Business
Deakin S, Markou C (eds) (2020) Is law computable? Critical perspectives on law and artificial intelligence. Hart Publishing
DeStefano M (2018) Legal upheaval – a guide to creativity, collaboration and innovation in law. ABA Publishing
DeStefano M (2023) Chicken or egg: diversity and innovation in the corporate legal marketplace. Fordham Law Rev 91:1209–1248
DeStefano M, Dobrauz G (eds) (2019) New suits: appetite for disruption in the legal world. Stämpfli Verlag AG, Bern
DeStefano M, Parker I, Vulcano G (2023) The unconscious conscience of digital transformation: the chief compliance officer? Compliance Elliance J 9(3)
Gillespie A (2022a) Design thinking versus legal design: what's the difference? Legal Evolution (1 June 2022)
Gillespie A (2022b) Q. What is digital transformation? A primer for legal professionals. Legal Evolution
Glock P, von Alemann S (2022) The paradigm shift in AI: from human labor to humane creativity. In: Jacob K et al (eds) Liquid legal institute: humanization and the law. Springer, pp 215–230
Hoffman R (2024) (Podcast interview), At the edge. McKinsey & Company (7 June 2024)
Jacob K, Schindler D, Strathausen R, Waltl B (2022) Liquid legal institute: humanization and the law. Springer, pp v–ix
Katz D, Bommarito M (2014) Measuring the complexity of law: the United States code. Artif Intell Law 22:337
Katz D, Coupette C, Beckedorf J, Hartung D (2020) Complex societies and the growth of the law. Sci Rep 10:18737
Kennedy D (2019) Successful innovation outcomes in law, Kindle edn
Kissinger H, Schmidt E, Huttenlocher D (2022) The age of AI and our human future. Little, Brown in US; John Murray in UK
Kotter J, Akhtar V, Gupta G (2021) Change: how organisations achieve hard-to-imagine results in uncertain and volatile times. Wiley
Kurzweil R (2000) The age of spiritual machines: when computers exceed human intelligence. Penguin
Kurzweil R (2005) The singularity is near: when humans transcend biology. Penguin
Kurzweil R (2024) The singularity is nearer: when we merge with AI. Viking
Lamarre E, Smaje K, Zemmel R (2023) Rewired: the McKinsey guide to outcompeting in the age of digital and AI. Wiley
Lee K-F, Qiufan C (2021) AI 2041: ten visions for our future. WH Allen
Leonardi P, Neeley T (2022) The digital mindset: what it really takes to thrive in the age of data, algorithms, and AI. Harvard Business Review Press
Logvinova I (2023) Legal innovation and generative AI: lawyers emerging as 'pilots', content creators, and legal designers. McKinsey & Company
Lozinsky A (2023) Is AI really about trust? Forbes (Australia) (29 May 2023)
Mack O, Noorestani H, Onwudiwe M (eds) (2024) Legal operations in the age of AI and data. Globe Law and Business
Mollick E (2024) Co-intelligence: living and working with AI. Penguin, pp 61–62
Negroponte N (1995) Being digital. Alfred A Knopf

Parker I (2021) Successful digital transformation in law firms – a question of culture. Globe Law and Business
Perlman A (2023) The implications of ChatGPT for legal services and society. The Practice (Harvard Center on the Legal Profession, (March-April 2023)
Saintot V (2023) Mobilizing the power of what could go right to improve legal ecosystems. Legal Bus World 4:6–14
Saintot VM, Di Matteo G (2022) Helping layers to better visualise their knowledge: a formula and four scenarios. In: Jacob K et al (eds) Liquid legal institute: humanization and the law. Springer, pp 195–214
Saintot VM, Lulić F (2022) Transforming legal ecosystems: a conceptual framework derive from our practice. In: Jacob K et al (eds) Liquid legal institute: humanization and the law. Springer, pp 133–155
Siebel T (2019) Digital transformation: survive and thrive in an era of mass extinction, Rosetta Books
Strathausen R, Jacob K, Schindler D (2017) Run legal as a business. In: Liquid legal – transforming legal into a business savvy, information enabled and performance driven industry. Springer, pp 1–3
Suleyman M, Bhaskar M (2023) The coming wave: technology, power, and the twenty-first century's greatest dilemma. Crown
Susskind R (2008) The end of lawyers? Rethinking the nature of legal services. Oxford University Press, p 22
Susskind R (2023) Tomorrow's lawyers – an introduction to your future (3rd ed.). Oxford University Press
Susskind R, Susskind D (2015) The future of the professions – how technology will transform the work of human experts. Oxford University Press
Susskind R, Susskind D (2023) Generative AI will upend the professions. Financial Times, 18 June 2023
Tellmann BP (2017) Building an outstanding legal team. Globe Law and Business
Trang DV (2022) Injecting humanity (back) into talent development. In: Jacob K et al (eds) Liquid legal institute: humanization and the law. Springer, pp 289–316
Tromans R (2023) The end of lawyers? Not yet. Artificial Lawyer (16 May 2023)
Um J, Sohn E (2023) Sense and sensibility, part 1: general counsel have the power to make good sense of Generative AI. Factor whitepaper, September 2023
Um J, Sohn E (2024) Sense and sensibility, part 2: the challenge for general counsel to influence and lead. Factor whitepaper, April 2024, pp 3–5
Waisberg N, Hudek A (2021) AI for lawyers: how artificial intelligence is adding value, amplifying expertise, and transforming careers. Wiley

Robert Dilworth is managing director & associate general counsel at a global financial institution. His substantive legal focus is financial derivatives and instruments that embed them. He is active in the Digital Legal Exchange and the Liquid Legal Institute think-tank. He is a Faculty Advisor to DLEx and an LLI ambassador to North America. Robert invites reader engagement (LinkedIn; robert@dilworth.de).

GPSR Compliance
The European Union's (EU) General Product Safety Regulation (GPSR) is a set of rules that requires consumer products to be safe and our obligations to ensure this.

If you have any concerns about our products, you can contact us on

ProductSafety@springernature.com

In case Publisher is established outside the EU, the EU authorized representative is:

Springer Nature Customer Service Center GmbH
Europaplatz 3
69115 Heidelberg, Germany

www.ingramcontent.com/pod-product-compliance
Lightning Source LLC
Chambersburg PA
CBHW071957030625
27634CB00003B/39
9783031785955